The Letters of Bishop Basil of Caesarea: Instruments of Communion

Fr Silouan Fotineas

SCD Press
2018

The Letters of Bishop Basil of Caesarea: Instruments of Communion
(Early Christian Studies, 19)
© 2018

by Silouan Fotineas

SCD Press
PO Box 1882
Macquarie Centre NSW 2113
Australia
scdpress@scd.edu.au

All rights reserved. No part of this book may be reproduced or transmitted in any form or by any means, electronic or mechanical, including photocopying, recording or by any information and storage system without permission in writing from the publishers.

ISBN-13: 978-1-925730-06-7 (pbk.)
ISBN-13: 978-1-925730-07-4 (e-book)

Layout and design by: Lankshear Design Pty Ltd
Printed and bound by: Ingram Spark

The Letters of Bishop Basil of Caesarea: Instruments of Communion

Fr Silouan Fotineas

SCD Press
2018

Early Christian Studies 19

SCD Press Editorial Board

Professor Diane Speed

Professor James Harrison

Associate Professor Peter Bolt

Additional Series Editors

Professor Pauline Allen (Australian Catholic University)

Professor Wendy Mayer (Australian Lutheran College)

Professor Bronwen Neil (Macquarie University)

Early Christian Studies

1. Jan Harm Barkhuizen, *Proclus Bishop of Constantinople. Homilies on the Life of Christ* (2001).
2. Robert C. Hill, *Theodoret of Cyrus. Commentary on the Song of Songs* (2001).
3. Johan Ferreira, *The Hymn of the Pearl* (2002).
4. Alistair Stewart-Sykes, *The Life of Polycarp. An anonymous vita from third-century Smyrna* (2002).
5. Daniel Van Slyke, *Quodvultdeus of Carthage. The Apocalyptic Theology of a Roman African in Exile* (2003).
6. Bronwen Neil & Pauline Allen, *The Life of Maximus the Confessor. Recension 3* (2003).
7. George Kalantzis, *Theodore of Mopsuestia. Commentary on the Gospel of John* (2004).
8. Rudolf Brändle, *John Chrysostom. Bishop – Reformer – Martyr* (2004).
9. J. Mark Armitage, *A Twofold Solidarity. Leo the Great's Theology of Redemption* (2005).
10. Alistair Stewart-Sykes, *The Apostolic Church Order. The Greek Text with Introduction, Translation and Annotation* (2006).
11. Geoffrey D. Dunn, *Cyprian and the Bishops of Rome: Questions of Papal Primacy in the Early Church* (2007, 2018).
12. Pauline Allen, Majella Franzmann, & Rick Strelan (eds.), *"I Sowed Fruits into Hearts" (Odes Sol. 17:13). Festschrift for Professor Michael Lattke* (2007).
13. David Luckensmeyer & Pauline Allen (eds.), *Studies of Religion and Politics in the Early Christian Centuries* (2010).

14. Oliver Herbel, *Sarapion of Thmuis: Against the Manicheans and Pastoral Letters* (2011).
15. Raymond Laird, *Mindset, Moral Choice and Sin in the Anthropology of John Chrysostom* (2012, 2017).
16. Alexander L. Abecina, *Time and Sacramentality in Gregory of Nyssa's Contra Eunomium* (2013).
17. Johan Ferreira, *Early Chinese Christianity: The Tang Christian Monument and Other Documents* (2014).
18. Wendy Mayer & Ian J. Elmer (eds.), *Men and Women in the Early Christian Centuries* (2014).
19. Silouan Fotineas, *The Letters of Bishop Basil of Caesarea: Instruments of Communion* (2018).
20. Andrey Romanov, *One God as One God and One Lord. The Lordship of Jesus Christ as a Hermeneutical Key to Paul's Christology in 1 Corinthians (with a special focus on 1 Cor 8:6)* (forthcoming, 2019).

Contents

Abstract 1

Acknowledgements 3

Introduction 5

Letters and Letter-writing in the Fourth Century 13

Basil's 365 Letters 20

Basil's Unwritten Letters and
The Function of Letter-carriers 28

Part One: Historical and Theological Context 37

Chapter One: Basil's Context, Education and Vocation . . . 39
  1.1   Arianism: "The Impious Doctrine of Arius" 40
  1.2   Basil's Nicene Personality and Reputation 44
  1.3   Basil's Education 48
  1.4   Basil Embraces Monasticism 54
  1.5   Basil's Domestic Monasticism 61
  1.6   Basil's Reception into the Ordained Ministry 67
        1.6.1 Basil's Ordination to the Episcopacy 70
  1.7   Conclusion 73

Chapter Two: Basil's Theology 76
  2.1   Scripture and Tradition 76
  2.2   Basil's Theological Treatises:
        Against Eunomius and *On the Holy Spirit* 82
        2.2.1 *Against Eunomius* 82
        2.2.2 *On the Holy Spirit* 88

2.3	Basil's Theology of the Trinity: Three Hypostases, One Essence	94
	2.3.1 Eunomianism	95
	2.3.2 Sabellianism	98
	2.3.3 Pneumatomachianism	104
2.4	The Development of Basil's Trinitarian Theology	107
2.5	Basil's Theology of the Holy Spirit: The *Monarchia* and *Homotimia* of God	110
2.6	The Development of Basil's Theology of the Holy Spirit	115
2.7	Conclusion	122

Chapter Three: Basil as a Bishop in the Context of Late Antiquity . . . 124

3.1	The Ministry of the Bishop in Late Antiquity	125
3.2	Basil as Bishop in Fourth-Century Cappadocia	146
3.3	Basil as Father of the Poor	156
3.4	Basil's *Basiliad*	165
3.5	Basil's *Basiliad* as a Paradigm for Social Change	171
3.6	Conclusion	178

Part Two: Basil's Letters . . . 181

Chapter Four: Church as Communion in the Letters of Basil . . . 183

4.1	Basil's Use of Letters: Instruments of Communion	184
4.2	Basil's Letters to Athanasius: An Example of Κοινωνία	189
4.3	The Term Κοινωνία and its Use in the Letters	201
4.4	Metaphors for Κοινωνία in Basil's Letters	214
4.5	The Witness of Κοινωνία in the Struggles of Basil's Church	219

4.6	The Κοινωνία of the Church and the Κοινωνία of the Trinity	235
4.7	Κοινωνία in the Holy Spirit	240
4.8	Conclusion	245

Chapter Five: The Bishop and the Communion of the Local Church in Basil's Letters ... 247

5.1	The Bishop and the Sacraments	247
	5.1.1 Baptism	247
	5.1.2 Repentance	252
	5.1.3 Eucharist	258
5.2	The Bishop as the Criterion of Communion for the Local Church	269
5.3	The Assistant Bishop in Basil's Church	283
5.4	Conclusion	290

Chapter Six: Basil on Communion at a Universal Level: Inter-episcopal Communion ... 292

6.1	The Synods of the Bishops	292
6.2	One Bishop, One Diocese, One Communion	297
6.3	The Unguarded Communion of Heresy	302
6.4	The Universal Communion of the Bishops	307
6.5	Conclusion	316

Conclusion: Communion in Basil's Letters ... 318

The Characteristics of Communion in Basil Letters ... 327

Bibliography ... 350

Glossary of Terms ... 371

Index ... 377

Abstract

As its title suggests, this book will explore the letters of Bishop Basil of Caesarea as instruments of communion. In particular, it will examine how Basil used his letters as instruments for arriving at, maintaining and expressing communion within a pro-Nicene church. For Basil, the divinity of the Father, Son and Holy Spirit was affirmed best through doxological worship and had ecclesiastical communion as its lasting expression. Basil's letters became the instruments through which he nurtured the fulfilment of his ecclesiological vision of the church as communion. His pastoral and theological message, although often set within an individual and local setting, persistently upheld a social and universal outlook expressed in terms of the church's communion. He insisted that the most fervent relationship with God involves communion with humans as well. Personal being within the church is intrinsically relational and communal. When Christians are united in communion with God through partaking of the Eucharist in any given worshipping community, they are united without division and without confusion with all believers and across all periods of time.

Basil not only addressed and communicated with people from various walks of life but also became a voice for them as well. Whether letters were addressed to clergy, magistrates, civil or military officials, ascetics, youth, widows, friends or congregations, they found their way to being copied and circulated amongst the faithful and proved to be foundational in bringing into communion the churches of the East. Basil regarded maintaining and expressing communion as of the highest importance for the ministry of the bishop. The act of letter-writing between bishops facilitated their "being in communion" within the Nicene church and, when required, served as proof of this communion through establishing a canon of communion. Amongst Nicene bishops, an affirmation of a creed in writing became the guarantor of a bishop's communion and a sign of his collegiality with all other bishops. The collective voice of the bishops on issues of faith, doctrine and morals, was essential not only to safeguard the church's communion but also to enhance its accessibility. As instruments of communion Basil's letters reveal what he understood as the characteristics of ecclesial communion. This book concludes that key characteristics of communion for Basil are that it be eucharistic, in the Spirit and in Christ, Trinitarian, inspired by the New Testament, traditional, nicene, episcopal, ascetical, institutional, identifying with the poor, catholic, accessible and safeguarded, mutually responsible, doing God's will, and beneficial.

Acknowledgements

I would like to acknowledge gratefully my doctoral supervisors, Rev. Prof. Denis Edwards and Prof. Pauline Allen for their encouragement, guidance and inspiration, without which the publication of this book would not be possible.

I express appreciation to the Editorial Board of the Early Christian Studies series and in particular to Prof. Diane Speed, Prof. James Harrison, Assoc.Prof. Peter Bolt, Prof. Pauline Allen, Prof. Wendy Mayer, and Prof. Bronwen Neil. Their invaluable assistance and constructive comments enhanced the content and presentation of my manuscript in many ways.

I express appreciation to Mrs Jenny O'Brien from the "Office of Worship" of the "Catholic Archdiocese of Adelaide" for her invaluable assistance when working with French texts.

I thank the dean and staff of Saint Andrew's Greek Orthodox Theological College, Sydney, for their generous hospitality and flexibility each time I was blessed to visit.

Sincere thanks are also due to the parish council and parishioners of the Holy Monastery of Saint Nectarios, Adelaide, for the patience and understanding afforded to me while I was writing my book.

My particular gratitude goes to His Eminence Archbishop Stylianos Harkianakis, Primate of the Greek Orthodox Church in Australia, for showing me what it means to exemplify all that is revered in the life, ministry and teaching of Saint Basil of Caesarea.

The Letters of Bishop Basil of Caesarea: Instruments of Communion

Introduction

The following book explores the letters of Basil of Caesarea which were mostly written during the years of his ordained ministry from 362–379. Specifically, these letters will be studied from the perspective of how they fostered communion within the Christian church, which at the time was experiencing serious division due to theological differences. The aim is to show how Basil, as a monastically inclined bishop, used his letters as instruments for arriving at, maintaining and expressing communion within the church. To this effect the book explores, through Basil's letters, how he saw communion being lived and realised in the life of the church both within its local (diocesan) and universal (ecumenical) manifestation, and in its theological, pastoral and monastic expressions. In doing so, the book will also explore how ecclesial communion in Basil's letters reflects his theology of the Holy Trinity and his understanding of the relationship that exists amongst the three divine persons. A common thread throughout will be the examination of the extent to which Basil regarded maintaining and expressing communion as of the highest importance for the ministry of the bishop.

St. Basil of Caesarea, called "the Great" and "the shining light of the world",[1] was born in 330 at a time when the Christian church

---

1   See Theodoret, *Ep.* 146: ὁ τῆς Καππαδοκῶν, μᾶλλον δὲ τῆς οἰκουμένης φωστήρ (the shining light of the Cappadocians, or rather, of the whole world). Sources Chrétiennes, 111.224. Hereafter SC will refer to the series Sources Chrétiennes (Paris, 1969–2016).

was experiencing theological controversy, namely the Arian conflict.[2] The Arian position brought into dispute the divinity of the second person of the Trinity, the Son, by referring to him as a creature (κτίσμα). Although condemned at the Council of Nicaea in 325, Arianism and other non-Nicene theological positions continued to flourish in the aftermath of the council. A non-Nicene position would subsequently dominate the "imperial church" for the next few decades. Entering the arena of theological controversy during those years were disputes concerning the divinity of the Holy Spirit, which up until then had not really been questioned. It is into this time of theological conflict that Basil was born and eventually would respond by taking a leading role in opposing those advocating non-Nicene faith positions. At the heart of Basil's opposition was the belief that undermining the divinity of the Son and the Holy Spirit within the Godhead carried immense consequences for the communion that exists within the Trinity. In other words, if Father, Son and Holy Spirit are not all divine, then they are not equal, and if they are not equal, then they are not fully in communion.

The imperial support of Arius and later non-Nicene theologies by Constantine the Great and his successors, enabled non-Nicene theologies not only to exist but also to be officially sanctioned. This led to division amongst the Christian churches and thus to a break in communion. In 370 Basil was ordained as the bishop for Caesarea which, along with all of the other dioceses of the Eastern Roman Empire, was troubled by schism. For Basil, raising the ethical profile of the churches within his jurisdiction and aligning himself with pro-Nicene bishops, went hand in hand with combatting non-Nicene confessions and restoring communion within his diocese. Consequently, Basil's letters became

---

2   For a detailed historical account of Basil's life see Rousseau, *Basil of Caesarea*. Philip Rousseau's study contributes immensely to the understanding of one of the most vital periods in the development of Christian doctrine and institutions in the fourth century of the Roman Empire.

important instruments enabling him to achieve these aims. Often in these letters Basil is critical of Christians who were not acting in the best interests of the church. Well aware of his own personal sin, and what he perceived to be the ambitions of his fellow hierarchs, Basil as a bishop was determined to heal the affairs of the Eastern Christian communion from the inside and restore it to its former glory:

> For we must impute to ourselves and to our sins the blame that the domination of the heretics has become so widespread. For almost no part of the world has escaped the conflagration of heresy [...] On behalf of these [the Christians] do you yourself beseech our Lord, and unite all the noble athletes of Christ in prayer on behalf of the churches, in order that, if there is still some time left for the existence of the world, and the universe is not being driven in the opposite direction, God may become reconciled with his churches and lead them back to their ancient peace.³

The letters of Basil remain largely unutilised with respect to their contribution to ecclesiology, and what they say about communion has been largely overlooked. In response to this neglect, this book

---

3   *Ep.* 164.2: Deferrari, II, 425–427. The Greek text below and subsequently, will use Yves Courtonne's new critical edition of Basil's letters published in 1957 along with a French translation. Ἑαυτοῖς γὰρ λογιζόμεθα καὶ ταῖς ἡμετέραις ἁμαρτίαις τὴν αἰτίαν τοῦ ἐπὶ τοσοῦτον χυθῆναι τῶν αἱρετικῶν τὴν δυναστείαν. Σχεδὸν γὰρ οὐδὲν μέρος ἔτι τῆς οἰκουμένης διαπέφευγε τὸν ἐκ τῆς αἱρέσεως ἐμπρησμόν [...] Ὑπὲρ τούτον αὐτός τε δεήθητι τοῦ Κυρίου καὶ πάντας τοὺς γενναίους ἀθλητὰς τοῦ Χριστοῦ εἰς τὴν ὑπὲρ τῆς Ἐκκλησίας προσευχὴν συμπαράλαβε, ἵνα, εἴπερ ἔτι χρόνοι τινὲς ὑπολείπονται τῇ συστάσει τοῦ κόσμου καὶ μὴ πρὸς τὴν ἐναντίαν φορὰν συνελαύνεται πάντα, διαλλαγεὶς ὁ Θεὸς ταῖς ἑαυτοῦ Ἐκκλησίαις ἐπαναγάγῃ αὐτὰς πρὸς τὴν ἀρχαίαν εἰρήνην. Courtonne, II, 99. See also *Ep.* 247: Courtonne, III, 85. Ὁ μὲν γὰρ πεπόνθαμεν διὰ τὰς ἁμαρτίας ἡμῶν πεπόνθαμεν, τὴν δὲ αὐτοῦ βοήθειαν διὰ τὴν περὶ τὰς Ἐκκλησίας ἑαυτοῦ ἀγάπην καὶ εὐσπλαγχνίαν ὁ φιλάνθρωπος ἐπιδείξεται. "For what we have suffered we have suffered because of our sins, but his succour shall the loving God show forth his love and compassion for the churches". Deferrari, III, 479. For other similar expressions see *Epp.* 98.1, 99.1, 136.2, 248, 258.2, 266.2.

will attempt, first, to bring to the surface the contents of these letters and their notion of ecclesial communion and, second, to show how for Basil the very act of letter-writing was itself an instrument of communion.

The primary focus will be the letters of Basil in the original Greek, situated in the context of his life and his Nicene theology, and in particular the 365 letters compiled by the Maurist Benedictines between 1721 and 1730 that are attributed predominately to the bishop of Caesarea. This reading of the text will pay attention to key terms such as: *koinōnia* (communion), *ekklēsia* (church), *henōsis* (union), *leitourgia* (liturgy), *eucharistia* (Eucharist), *agape* (love) and *eirēnē* (peace), all of which can point to realised communion within the life of the church. To date no English translation exists where these key terms are translated consistently and accurately. This study of Basil's letters will reveal the way they seek to restore, maintain and promote communion in the one Christian church.

Philip Rousseau, *Basil of Caesarea*,[4] and Paul Fedwick, *The Church and the Charisma of Leadership in Basil of Caesarea*,[5] are the only substantial books to appear on Basil in English since the publication of W.K. Lowther Clarke, *St Basil the Great: A Study of Monasticism*.[6] Rousseau makes a broader and more integrated use of the Basilian texts to trace the development of Basil's whole life, whereas Fedwick looks more to the pastoral and leadership aspects of Basil's ministry. The concise biographical work of Andrew Radde-Gallwitz, *Basil of Caesarea: A Guide to His life and Doctrine*,[7] is exemplary in getting to understand Basil as a theologian and a thinker, and as someone who sought unity in the teaching and practice of the Christian faith. Benoît Gain, *L'Église de Cappadoce*

---

4   London: University of California, 1994.
5   Eugene OR: Wipf and Stock, 1979.
6   Cambridge: Cambridge University, 1913.
7   Eugene OR: Cascade Books, 2012.

au IVe siècle d'après la correspondance de Basile de Césarée,[8] offers helpful historical and sociological insight. These four authors make good use of Basil's letters and represent a new generation of Basilian scholarship. Other scholarly works that contribute to the discussion include: Anna M. Silvas, *The Asketikon of St. Basil the Great*;[9] Claudia Rapp, *Holy Bishops in Late Antiquity: The Nature of Christian Leadership in an Age of Transition*;[10] Andrea Sterk, *Renouncing the World Yet Leading the Church: The Monk-Bishop in Late Antiquity*;[11] Adam M. Schor, *Theodoret's People: Social Networks and Religious Conflict in Late Roman Syria*;[12] J. Eric Cooper and Michael J. Decker, *Life and Society in Byzantine Cappadocia*;[13] Richard Finn, *Almsgiving in the Later Roman Empire: Christian Promotion and Practice 313–450*;[14] and Susan R. Holman, *The Hungry are Dying: Beggars and Bishops in Roman Cappadocia*.[15] All of these works have contributed in important ways to the study and understanding of the letters of Basil.

This book does not analyse Basil's letters and their transmission through textual criticism, work that is currently being taken up by Anna Silvas.[16] Rather it demonstrates how Basil used his letters as "instruments of communion". Contemporary and past scholars, in their portraits of Basil, have not methodologically engaged with Basil's letters in the same way that they have with his other writings. This has resulted in sufficient deficiencies when coming to understand Basil as a churchman and a theologian. This books aims to respond to these deficiencies and therefore fulfil a unique niche in the scholarship on Basil. The method is to

---

8   Rome: Pontificium institutum Orientale, 1985.
9   New York: Oxford University, 2005.
10 Berkeley: University of California, 2005.
11 Cambridge: Harvard University, 2004.
12 Berkeley: University of California, 2011.
13 New York: Palgrave Macmillan, 2012.
14 Oxford: Oxford University, 2006.
15 Oxford: Oxford University, 2001.
16 See Silvas, "The Letters of Basil of Caesarea and the Role of Letter-Collections", 113–128.

look at the theological, social and political environment of Basil's day and from this to contextualise Basil's use of letters, as instruments of communion, within his episcopal ministry. Exploring Basil's theology will show how his theology informed the exercise of his episcopal leadership and influenced his pastoral care. Basil's commitment to Christian living and social justice will become evident, as will his desire to bring into the Nicene communion all the churches of the Eastern empire that were under the oversight of a non-Nicene bishop. According to Basil, κοινωνία (communion) with God in the church begins sacramentally with each individual believer but there after includes every member of the clergy and laity under the spiritual jurisdiction of a canonical bishop.

Basil's view of a canonical bishop is that of a bishop who confesses a Nicene faith. In Basil's understanding, a Nicene confession of faith by a Nicene bishop automatically brought him into communion with all other bishops who professed that same faith. Also, when this faith was documented in writing, and in particular a letter, it was treated by Basil and his fellow bishops as a validation of a bishop's allegiance to the Nicene communion of churches. The argument will show how Basil used his letters to facilitate communion in the Nicene church, and how Basil's letters reveal what he considered to be the distinct characteristics of communion in the Nicene church.

To begin, this introduction examines the concept of the letter itself, its structure, purpose, delivery, use and function. Basil's 365 letters, as also his unwritten letters (oral messages), will be set within the particular context of letter-writing in the fourth century, and the function of letter-carriers. Beyond these introductory comments, the book will be in two parts, with three chapters each. Part One will present a historical and theological context for Basil's ministry, and in this way become the platform to Part Two, which will explore Basil's letters themselves and how Basil used them to convey and implement his understanding of communion, both locally and universally, within the Christian church.

The opening chapter will introduce the historical and theological context by tracing Basil's life and vocation, suggesting that Basil's education and monastic sensibilities had a lasting influence on his life, which in turn aroused his desire to enter into the ordained ministry. Even before his formal acceptance of Christianity through baptism, Basil quickly established himself as a key proponent of Nicene Christianity. His baptism and then his priestly ordination and episcopal elevation placed him, for the remaining years of his short life, on the front lines in defence of Nicene Christianity.

After Chapter One establishing Basil's place and personality in the life of the local Caesarean church, the second chapter concerns itself with Basil's theology, and highlights the two pillars upon which Basil saw theology founded, namely Scripture and tradition. Basil's foundational theological treatises, *Against Eunomius* and *On the Holy Spirit*, will then be explored in order to understand Basil's Trinitarian theology and its advocacy for the divinity of the Holy Spirit. Here the aim will be to show that Basil's Trinitarian theology is that of a communion of persons, a view that is foundational for his ecclesiology.

Taking a historical and social perspective, the third chapter will examine the role of the bishop in late antiquity with a particular emphasis on the relationship between church and state, as well as on the understanding of authority and structure in the church of Christian antiquity. An exploration of Basil's immediate pastoral environment, his commitment to social justice, his advocacy for the poor, and his renowned *Basiliad* as a paradigm for social change, will highlight the social character of the Christian ethos in his ministry.

Changing emphasis, the fourth chapter will be the start of part two of this work, which engages more directly with Basil's letters. Chapter Four will look at Basil's letters according to their subjects and addressees, but also in terms of how Basil used the medium of the letter itself. With a priority on the notion of "church as communion" as it is found in Basil's letters and as it is conveyed to his correspondents, the usage of the word *koinōnia* and its associated terms in Basil's letters will be examined, and the way in which these words are to inform his ecclesiology.

The practical application of Basil's concept of communion will be studied in Chapter Five, in particular the way it is realised in personal life, but also within a local church/diocesan setting. Basil establishes a link between the individual believer, his or her local church, and all churches that are under the episcopal jurisdiction of a presiding bishop. Basil sees the ministry of the episcopal office as central to establishing and maintaining communion amongst these three interpenetrating circles of ecclesiological co-existence.

Chapter Six will present Basil's views of communion within the church as it appears at a universal level, showing that for Basil communion amongst all bishops is constitutive of their communion with the church, whether in its local or universal manifestation. He sees participation in the Eucharist as the deepest expression of the communion of bishops. Thus, the Basilian corpus of letters exemplifies a practical fleshing-out and in this way a personification, at a local and universal level, of the ecclesial experience of Basil's theology of the church as communion.

Letters and Letter-writing in the Fourth Century

There are as many definitions of what constitutes a letter as there are letter-writers. Often a letter is understood as one side of a dialogue that is written down. A letter implies that one communicates with someone who is absent as if they were present. Cicero (106 BC – 43 BC) describes two types of letters, the private and public letter. This does not mean that public and private concerns were not interwoven in each type of letter, indeed often they were. Other epistolary theorists suggest up to twenty one types (ps–Demetrius) or even up to forty one types (ps–Libanius).[1] The latter classification takes account of flexibility in genre that depends upon the type of communication being disseminated, for example, an instruction, idea, request or a polemical outburst. In theory each letter was meant to be concise and centred upon its own one theme, but in reality this tended to be somewhat of an exception rather than the norm.[2] Basil, for instance, did not hesitate to disregard such theoretical constraints of epistolary genre when he wrote to Philargrius saying: "Send many letters, and make them as long as you can; for shortness is not a virtue in a letter any more than it is in a man".[3] Gregory of Nazianzus arguably presents one of the clearest descriptions of good epistolary style in Christian antiquity.

> Among people who write letters [...] there are some who write at greater length than is fitting and others who are

---

1 Malherbe, *Ancient Epistolary Theorists*, 21, 31, 67.
2 Allen, Neil and Mayer, *Preaching Poverty in Late Antiquity*, 45.
3 *Ep.* 323: Deferrari, IV, 271. Πολλὰς γε οὖν πέμπε τὰς ἐπιστολὰς καὶ μακρὰς ὡς ἔνι μάλιστα· οὐ γὰρ δὴ ἀρετὴ ἐπιστολῆς ἡ βραχύτης, οὐ μᾶλλόν γε ἢ ἀνθρώπου. Courtonne, III, 195.

much too brief [...] What determines the length of letters is the need they aim to meet. One should not write on and on when the subject matter is limited, nor be stingy with words when there is much to say [...] As to clarity, everyone knows that one should avoid prose-like style so far as possible, and rather incline towards conversational. To put it briefly, the best and most beautifully written letter is the one that is persuasive to the uneducated and educated alike, appearing to the former as written on the popular level, and to the latter as above that level, a letter which furthermore is understood at once.[4]

Late antiquity has been described as the setting in which "an apparent explosion of epistolary activity"[5] has taken place, and it is from this period that one witnesses "our most substantial evidence for Greek and Latin letter-writing and collection practices".[6] Correspondents wrote not just to send information or to be didactic, but also had ambitions to create portraits of themselves, their relationships and their networks. In the fourth century, letter-writing incorporated an important function that today is superseded by social media. In other words, the letter was considered to be an effective medium of publicity (biography-encomium) that people had at their disposal.[7] Libanius' comment, "Any letter you get is immediately known to people here" (Ην ἂν ἐπιστολὴν λάβητε, τοῖς ἐνταῦθα εὐθὺς ἔγνωσται), implies the public nature of a letter, some-

---

4   Ep. 51.1, 2, and 4. Malherbe, Ancient Epistolary Theorists, 59. Τῶν γραφόντων ἐπιστολὰς [...] οἱ μὲν μακρότερα γράφουσιν ἤπερ εἰκός, οἱ δὲ καὶ λίαν ἐνδεέστερα [...] καὶ οὔτε μακρότερα γραπτέον, οὗ μὴ πολλὰ τὰ πράγματα, οὔτε μικρολογητέον, ἔνθα πολλά [...] Περὶ δὲ σαφηνείας ἐκεῖνο γνώριμον, ὅτι χρὴ φεύγοντα τὸ λογοειδές, ὅσον ἐνδέχεται, μᾶλλον εἰς τὸ λαλικὸν ἀποκλίνειν· καί, ἵν 'εἴπω συντόμως, αὕτη τῶν ἐπιστολῶν ἀρίστη καὶ κάλλιστα ἔχουσα, ἢ ἂν καὶ τὸν ἰδιώτην πείθῃ καὶ τὸν πεπαιδευμένον, τὸν μέν, ὡς κατὰ τοὺς πολλοὺς οὖσα, τὸν δέ, ὡς ὑπὲρ τοὺς πολλούς, καὶ ἢ αὐτόθεν γνώριμος. Gallay, Les manuscrits des lettres de Saint Grégoire de Nazianze, 66–67.
5   Gillet, "Communication in Late Antiquity", 816.
6   Ebbeler, "Tradition, Innovation, and Epistolary Mores", 271.
7   See Gibson, "On the Nature of Ancient Letter Collections", 73–77.

thing akin to an act of public intimacy.[8] Synesius dismisses the concept of a secret being confided to paper, because for him the very purpose of a letter is not to keep quiet but to proclaim something in the public arena.[9] What in the technical sense appeared as a letter in reality could present itself, through its content, as a homily or treatise. Although the letter might be presented with tones of intimacy and confidentiality, ultimately its intended purpose could well be that of publication. Bishops presumably had expectations that their letters would be read out aloud or reach new audiences through re-copying, which, generally speaking, was not considered a breach of privacy. Libanius' letter to Basil, marked as *Ep.* 338 in Basil's letter-collection, makes mention of Libanius having an audience when he received Basil's letter. Libanius initially read the letter in silence as if to himself. However, his silence was interrupted with complimentary comments that he made about Basil's writing skills, at which those around Libanius wanted the letter read out to themselves. Alypius, Libanius' associate, read the letter to those present and moreover went on to show it to others before reluctantly returning it back to Libanius.[10]

This example, together with Synesius' comment noted above, does not necessarily imply that there was no place for a private letter between two associates. It was commonly left up to the recipient's discretion as to whether the letter addressed to them was for the private or public domain. If they so choose, the recipients could reserve a letter so that it was only read by themselves or a close circle of friends. The cross-over from the intimacy of a letter to that of a treatise appeared to take place with relative ease for the authors of Christian antiquity. For Basil, some of his letters are only a few lines long, whereas others, such as his canonical letters,[11] surpass ten pages and are presented as outright treatises. The larger body of

---

8   *Ep.* 16.1: Norman, I, 401.
9   See *Ep.* 137 to Herculian: Roques, II, 277.
10 See *Ep.* 338: Courtonne, III, 205–206.
11 See *Epp.* 188, 199, 217.

letters almost always contain a warm personal salutation but on the whole are intended to be truly public documents. Basil's canonical letters addressed to bishop Amphilochius are also intended for other clerics or interested parties use, since they contain the church's authoritative teaching on the regulation of penance.

Within the empire of late antiquity, the letter was perhaps the only way people were kept informed about events, and the way that constituents of one province were made aware of the affairs of another province. If the letter was of interest to others, the addressee would pass on the letter to his or her acquaintances who in turn would do the same, resulting in the letter eventually becoming public property through its wide circulation. Such activity was encouraged especially when letters were posted in some public space. Many of Basil's letters, notably those which he frequently addressed to a church or province, were intended to be public documents for the benefit of all the faithful.

Letters could also be used negatively in ways that promote harm and division. Basil complained of such happenings: "I too, having heard that many letters are being circulated against me, branding and denouncing and accusing".[12] Basil says that his enemies "have deafened all men's ears with letters of invective"[13] that they had composed against him, and that these letters have subsequently "been received by trustworthy persons" (ὑπὸ προσώπων ἀξιοπίστων προκατασχεθῆναι).[14]

As a medium of publicity, Athanasius, Basil, Gregory and others used letters in support of their theological causes despite the imminent threat of persecution from non-Nicene emperors. Some letters were sent to churches that were struggling to survive amongst non-

---

12 *Ep.* 226.1: Deferrari, III, 329. Κἀγὼ ἀκούσας ὅτι πάλαι κατ' ἐμοῦ περιφέρονται ἐπιστολαὶ στίζουσαι ἡμᾶς καὶ στηλιτεύουσαι καὶ κατηγοροῦσαι. Courtonne, III, 24.
13 *Ep.* 223.3: Deferrari, III, 301. Ταῖς στηλιτευτικαῖς ἐπιστολαῖς [...] πᾶσαν περικτυπήσαντες ἀκοήν. Courtonne, III, 13.
14 *Ep.* 224.1: Deferrari, III, 315. Courtonne, III, 18.

Nicenes, while others were sent to console and sustain congregations that had their clergy forcefully removed or exiled. Still others were sent to encourage exiled bishops who were on the brink of despair. These letters brought comfort and encouragement to the addressee. To the persecuted they reinvigorated a sense of hope in their trials and instilled in them the perseverance to continue. Whether such letters were addressed to friends or congregations, they were eventually copied and circulated amongst the faithful and proved instrumental in uniting the Nicene Christians of the East.

The needs of the time demanded that Basil use the full extent of his ability as an educated man. Fundamentally Basil perceived that Christianity was at risk, and that if the non-Nicenes were not defeated, Christianity would dwindle away into being a legend. Many now looked to Basil for a response; his contemporaries, colleagues and disciples all turned to him for guidance. In exercising his leadership as a shepherd of the church, Basil relied just as much on the written word as he did on the oral. This dual method employed by Basil for promulgating and defending Christianity was vivid in the recollections of Gregory of Nazianzus:

> Those who engaged in hand-to-hand conflicts he overthrew at close range by word of mouth. Those who engaged at a distance he struck with arrows of ink, no less significant than the characters in the tables of the law, legislating not for one small Jewish nation, concerning meat and drink, temporal sacrifices, and purifications of the flesh, but for every nation and every portion of the earth, concerning the true doctrine from which comes our salvation.[15]

---

15 *Oration* 43.43: McCauley, 64. Τοὺς μὲν καὶ εἰς χεῖρας ἰόντας ἀγχεμάχοις ὅπλοις τοῖς ἀπὸ γλώσσης καταστρεφόμενος, τοὺς δὲ πόρρωθεν βάλλων τοξεύματα τοῖς ἐκ μέλανος, οὐδὲν ἀτιμοτέρου τῶν ἐν ταῖς πλαξὶ χαραγμάτων, οὐδὲ ἑνὶ τῆς Ἰουδαίας ἔθνει, καὶ μικρῷ τούτῳ, νομοθετοῦντος περὶ βρωμάτων καὶ πομάτων καὶ προσκαίρων θυσιῶν καὶ σαρκὸς καθαρσίων, ἀλλὰ παντὶ γένει καὶ μέρει τῆς οἰκουμένης περὶ τοῦ λόγου τῆς ἀληθείας, ἐξ οὗ καὶ τὸ σώζεσθαι περιγίνεται. SC 384. 216-218.

After their physical separation Gregory was able to know about Basil from his letters. Colloquially put, Gregory was able to see "where Basil was coming from". Through letter-writing Basil became acquainted with people with whom otherwise he would have never had any communication. Where Basil could not be in person he sent his letters instead, which according to Fedwick had the same effect as "face-to-face meetings".[16] In a consolatory letter to the "church of Neocaesarea", Basil wrote: "But since many causes prevented my being with you in person, the only recourse left to me was to share your present troubles by letter (διὰ τοῦ γράμματος κοινωνεῖν ὑμῖν)".[17] To bishop Theodotus, Basil explained: "For this is the means of conversation for those who are so widely separated in person, I mean correspondence by letter".[18] For Basil, distance and time no longer became an obstacle to communication as they were overcome through the action of the written word.[19] Writing to two of his former students he asserted:

> Now not even separation in body is hindrance, since he who made us in the fullness of his wisdom and kindness did not limit thought by the body, nor power of speech by the tongue, but gave greater power even from the standpoint of time to those who are able to benefit others, so that they are able to hand on their instruction not alone to those who are a long distance away, but also to very remote later generations. And experience confirms this statement of ours, since those who were born many years ago still teach the youth, their learning being preserved in

---

16 Fedwick, *The Church and the Charisma of Leadership*, 122.
17 *Ep.* 28.1: Deferrari, I, 161. Ἐπεὶ δὲ τὴν σωματικὴν συνάφειαν πολλὰ τὰ διακωλύοντα, λειπόμενον ἦν διὰ τοῦ γράμματος κοινωνεῖν ὑμῖν τῶν παρόντων. Courtonne, I, 66.
18 *Ep.* 185: Deferrari, II, 475. Οὗτος γάρ ἐστιν ὁ τρόπος τῆς ὁμιλίας τοῖς τοσοῦτον διεζευγμένοις τῷ σώματι, ὁ δι᾽ ἐπιστολῶν. Courtonne, II, 119.
19 See *Ep.* 91. In the opening lines of his letter to Bishop Valerian, Basil, as elsewhere, makes this important point. Ὅς γε τοσοῦτον διεστὼς τῷ σώματι συνῆψας ἡμῖν σεαυτὸν διὰ γράμματος. Courtonne, I, 197. "For you, though so far separated in body, have united yourself to us by letter". Deferrari, II, 129.

writing; and we, although so separated from you in body, are always united with you in thought, and converse easily with you, since teaching is not hindered by land or by sea, if you have any concern at all for your souls.[20]

20 *Ep.* 294: Deferrari, IV, 205. Οὐκοῦν οὐδὲ σώματος κωλύει χωρισμός, τοῦ δημιουργήσαντος ἡμᾶς δι ' ὑπερβολὴν σοφίας καὶ φιλανθρωπίας μὴ συμπεριορίσαντος τοῖς σώμασι τὴν διάνοιαν μήτε μὴν τῇ γλώττῃ τῶν λόγων τὴν δύναμιν, δόντος δέ τι πλεῖον καὶ ἀπὸ τοῦ χρόνου τοῖς ὠφελεῖν δυναμένοις, ὡς μὴ μόνον τοῖς μακρὰν διεστηκόσιν, ἀλλὰ δὴ καὶ τοῖς λίαν ὀψιγόνοις παραπέμπειν δύνασθαι τὴν διδασκαλίαν. Καὶ τοῦτον ἡμῖν ἡ πεῖρα πιστοῦται τὸν λόγον, ἐπείπερ οἵ τε πολλοῖς πρότερον ἔτεσι γενόμενοι διδάσκουσι τοὺς νέους σωζομένης ἐν γράμμασι τῆς διδασκαλίας, ἡμεῖς τε κεχωρισμένοι τοσοῦτον τοῖς σώμασι τῇ διανοίᾳ σύνεσμεν ἀεὶ καὶ προσομιλοῦμεν ῥᾳδίως τῆς διδασκαλίας οὔτε ὑπὸ γῆς οὔτε ὑπὸ θαλάσσης κωλυομένης, εἴ τις ἔστιν ὑμῖν τῶν ἰδίων ψυχῶν φροντίς. Courtonne, III, 169. For other remarks on the written word see *Epp.* 135, 219.1, 297.

Basil's 365 Letters

The first edition of Basil's letters appeared as a small publication in 1499 by Aldine Press. After more than two centuries of revised editions in which editors progressively attended to the critical analysis of highly complex manuscript sources, a new edition of all Basil's works came to fruition. The name of this new edition was *S.P.N. Basilii Opera Omnia* and it was put together by the Maurists Doms Julien Garnier, Prudent Maran and François Faverolles.[1] In this edition, the correspondence of Basil forms a collection of 365 letters,[2] making them one of the largest corpora of letters in the Greek language from late antiquity.[3] It is possible that disciples, admirers or family members had prepared Basil's letters for publication, as was the case for many other letter collections containing encomiastic threads similar to those found in the collection of Basil's letters. Also, Basil's comparatively short life and his challenging ministry may have acted as a catalyst towards the preservation of his letters, especially in view of their "didactic function".[4]

Between 1721 and 1730 the Benedictines compiled Basil's letter collections into three tomes consisting of Greek text and Latin translation with a putative chronological order. The first tome contains Letters 1–46 and consists of the letters written before Basil's ordination to the episcopate (c. 357–370). The second tome contains Letters 47–291 and consists of the letters that Basil wrote during his episcopacy (c. 370–379). The third tome con-

---

1 Silvas, "The Letters of Basil of Caesarea".
2 The numbers assigned to the letters by the Benedictines are today the accepted mode of reference.
3 Silvas, "The Letters of Basil of Caesarea".
4 Gibson, "On the Nature of Ancient Letter Collections", 77.

tains Letters 292–365 and consists of letters which cannot be assigned to any general period, as well as those that are commonly accepted as being doubtful and spurious.[5] This systematic arrangement of Basil's letters is not that of the order contained in the early manuscript traditions but is attributed to the later intervention of copy-editors who used a chronological framework so as to preserve biographical and historiographical information. It is a feature of modern letter collections to assimilate their ordering to a biographical or historical narration. Ancient letter collections, on the other hand, tended to be arranged either by addressee, or theme, or by some other convention rather than a strict chronology.[6] Since the Maurist edition there have been significant advancements in methodologies and in the investigation of the transmission of Basil's letters. There is imminent anticipation that a new critical edition of Basil's works, the new *Basilii Caesariensis Opera*, will be embarked upon soon.[7]

At the start of the twentieth century a comprehensive critical study of the transmission of the Basilian letters was carried out by Abbé Marius Bessières (d. 1918). In his research Bessières worked from twenty-seven manuscripts, eighteen or nineteen more manuscripts than those collated by the Benedictines. Bessières concludes that the most primitive witness to the transmission of Basil's letters is one in which the letters are aggregated in a disor-

---

5 For comments on the authenticity of this section of letters see Rousseau, *Basil of Caesarea*, 57, n. 130; Deferrari, I, xiii–xv.
6 Gibson, "On the Nature of Ancient Letter Collections", 57–64, 70–71.
7 At the forefront of the project is Anna Silvas, who is awaiting news of further funding. The project is at the proposal stage whilst endorsed by a team of scholars and tentatively approved by Brill. Silvas comments: "A new series of critical editions, beginning with this first projected volume of Basil's letters, will collate a wider range of select manuscripts than has been used before, and attend more closely to the pattern of early collections and aggregation in the shaping of the entire corpus of letters. Should this project come to pass, it promises to become the underpinnings of a renewed analysis of the political, religious, social and cultural history of the Eastern Later Roman Empire that the life and literary legacy of the great Basil uniquely afford". Silvas, "The Letters of Basil of Caesarea".

derly way.⁸ In 1944 Anders Cavallin's *Studien zu den Briefen des hl. Basilius* was amongst the first to address the question of the authenticity of Basil's letters. His study revealed that Basil was in fact not the author of several letters, especially *Ep.* 38 with its important theological treatise on the distinction between essence and *hypostasis*. Cavallin assigns *Ep.* 38 to Basil's younger brother, Gregory of Nyssa.⁹ In 1953 the Swedish scholar Rudberg published his *Etudes sur la tradition manuscrite de saint Basile* where he identified another nine accredited codices and brought the tally of Basilian manuscripts to a total of thirty-five.¹⁰ In 1957 Yves Courtonne published his critical edition of Basil's letters and provided a French translation.¹¹ Courtonne made use of almost all the manuscripts recommended by the earlier twentieth century scholars, and, like the Benedictines, he maintained the chronological ordering of the letters but did not attend to questions of authenticity. The Greek Basilian text used in both the body and the footnotes of the present work comes from Yves Courtonne's edition. The English translation is from Roy Deferrari,¹² except when Deferrari's Greek differs from Courtonne's, in which case the author makes his own translation.

In 1993 Paul Jonathan Fedwick's extensive *Bibliotheca Basiliana Vniveralis* instigated a change in the order of Basil's letters. Moving away from the difficulties associated with a chronological order and the establishing of convincing dates, Fedwick implements instead what he calls a "batch-style method" which consists of grouping together letters that are addressed to the same recipients. He explains:

---

8   Silvas, "The Letters of Basil of Caesarea".
9   Cavallin, *Studien zu den Briefen des hl. Basilius*, 71–81. Since this discovery by Cavallin, most scholars have reassigned Basil's *Ep.* 38 to the authorship of his brother Gregory of Nyssa.
10 Rudberg, *Etudes sur la tradition*, 1953.
11 Les Belles Lettres, 1957–1966.
12 Basil, *The Letters in Four Volumes*.

> Any of my numbers, e.g. in the correspondence with Eusebius of Samosata, reflect which letter is placed before another letter. In other words, my numbers, despite not being exactly the numbers of any given manuscript, reflect precisely which letters are placed before or after other letters.[13]

By having the letters arranged alphabetically under the names of recipients, Fedwick, while being loyal to the manuscript traditions in terms of ordering, creates space for future amendments to occur easily in Basil's letter collections. Even in modern times letters continue to be discovered and are added to the corpus of existing letter collections.[14]

It is important to note the significant gaps in the extant materials of letter collections in general. In spite of these collections being one of the most familiar genres of ancient literature, only remnants of each of these collections survive. With the letters of Severus of Antioch (d. 538), for example, there is evidence that only about fifteen percent of them have been preserved. Similar things can be said about Cyril of Alexandria, Augustine and Firmus of Caesarea, as well as all other letter-writers of late antiquity in general. Epiphanius of Pavia and Caesarius of Arles, despite serving lengthy episcopates, have little or no letters attributed to their names.[15]

Benoît Gain suggests that Basil did not personally keep copies of his letters and that any surviving letters of his are a result of recipients preserving his letters. In his view, the letters that have survived would be only a small proportion of Basil's letters since many were either lost in transit or disappeared into private archives.[16] Remarkably only one letter survives between Basil and his brother Gregory of Nyssa (*Ep.* 58). Basil's *Ep.* 14 makes reference to his brother Gregory wanting to meet up with him, sug-

---

13 Fedwick, *Basil of Caesarea: Christian, Humanist, Ascetic*, 673.
14 See Chadwick, "New letters of St. Augustine", 425–452.
15 Allen, "Rationales for Episcopal Letter-Collections", 18–34.
16 Gain, *L'Église de Cappadoce*, 268.

gesting that exchanges of letters between the two brothers did take place. Even so, apart from *Ep.* 58, there are no other manuscripts in existence which show correspondence between Basil and his younger brother Gregory. Neither are there any surviving manuscripts of correspondence between Basil and his brother Peter[17] or his sister Macrina, both of whom Basil would visit at the family monastic estate at Annisa in Pontus.[18] Only one letter of Basil's survives that is addressed to a soldier (*Ep.* 106), an oddity indeed given that the Roman army occupied such a dominant role in Roman society in terms of staff and resources, and therefore was considered the most important component of the organised Roman state. Army commanders were directly involved in forming and executing imperial policy, as well as in arranging the composition of the imperial house.[19] It was not uncommon for bishops to forge direct links with soldiers where they would request favours such as the promise of security. The letters that do survive from authors of late antiquity, although they are incomplete, do give indicators of the mindset, attitudes and intentions of their authors, particularly when viewed as a whole within their collections.

It is worth noting that having access to further surviving letters may well enhance one's understanding in more than a complementary way. It is possible that the discovery of new letters could substantially change one's perceptions of authors and their times. In Basil's surviving correspondence, for example, no letter is dedicated to almsgiving, even though he is clearly committed to social justice and the welfare of the poor in his other writings. There are

---

17 Peter later on in 381 became the bishop of Sebasteia.
18 Rousseau makes the suggestion that Basil's *Ep.* 46 could have possibly been addressed to one of Basil's sisters. Rousseau, *Basil of Caesarea*, 9, n. 23.
19 By 393, during Theodosius' office, the reins of power within the empire were placed in the hands of experienced military generals. See Mitchell, *A History of the Later Roman Empire*, 81–86.

only two letters, *Epp.* 42[20] and 150,[21] where Basil gives two different sets of instructions on how donations should be made to the poor. The former, written when Basil was of a younger age, speaks about giving directly to the poor, whereas the latter, written when Basil was a churchman himself, directs charity to take place through the church administration. If *Ep.* 150 was not in existence, this very practical teaching of Basil would be unknown. Between *Ep.* 42 and *Ep.* 150 there appears to be a possible development of Basil's understanding and practice, but there are no letters in existence that were written in between these epistles that could serve as a base to trace this development.

Being the administrator that he was, and contrary to Gain's opinion mentioned above, it is highly likely that Basil would have made provisions to have an archival copy of his letters kept in his chancery in Caesarea. This is plausible especially in the case of those letters that dealt with controversial dogmatic and political issues, as well as those which were addressed to government officials. These copies would have served as security against the misuse of the original by those hostile to Basil's theology and to his ministry, a hostility that Basil anticipated would continue well after his death. Basil's *Ep.* 223,[22] for example, addressed to his former friend and mentor Eustathius of Sebasteia, was written to protest against what Basil saw as Eustathius' covert non-Nicene allegiances. The significance of this letter on a macro-ecclesial level, together with its public orientation, made it too important for Basil not to keep a reserve copy. The same can be said about Basil's surviving letter to Ambrose of Milan (*Ep.* 197), his letters to Athanasius of Alexandria, to the bishops of the West, to various bishops of Syria, to the church of Nicopolis, and the series of letters that Basil sent to his disciple Amphilochius of Iconium.

20   See *Ep.* 42.3: Courtonne, I, 104.
21   See *Ep.* 150: Courtonne, II, 74.
22   Basil's *Ep.* 223 is his most autobiographical letter. This in itself would be enough of a reason for him to keep a copy.

On some occasions, such as when Basil wrote to officials and persons of rank, the addressees are listed by their function, for example: to a governor/to the governor (*Epp.* 84, 85, 86), to the tax-collector (*Ep.* 88), to monks harassed by Arians (*Ep.* 257), to a widow (*Epp.* 283, 296, 297), to a prison superintendent (*Ep.* 286), to the count of the [imperial] private estates (*Ep.* 303), to a superior (*Ep.* 311) and to a notary (*Ep.* 333). Most of these letters exist towards the end of Basil's letter collections, whether Basil was aware of this at the time is hard to find out. Even if Basil chose not to keep a copy, it is possible, as noted above,[23] that his recipients may have kept a copy for their own records. Eusebius of Samosata, in his capacity as a mentor and guide to Basil, was the recipient of at least nineteen letters from him. These letters contain confidential themes concerning the personal challenges that Basil faced as a bishop when dealing with church life.[24] As they were not intended for the public sphere, it is likely that Eusebius would have kept these personally addressed letters close to himself.

There are reasons why letter-collections might survive as they do. Some letters may have been accidently lost, and others may have been purposely destroyed because of their doctrinal themes. The letters of Theodoret of Cyrrhus (d. c. 458) and Severus of Antioch, for example, were destroyed for not conforming to anti-Chalcedonian sentiments.[25] The reasons for the final shape of each letter collection often remain obscure. Ascertaining the motives and accidents behind these collections remains a demanding area of research. The reader is at the mercy of compilers and transmitters of letter-collectors, and assessments are made from the remnants that they have preserved. Fedwick's chronology, for example, ascribes only four letters to the period of Basil's priest-

---

23   See Gain, *L'Église de Cappadoce*, 268.
24   Basil's *Ep.* 27 is the only letter that is addressed to Eusebius that predates Basil's entry into the episcopacy.
25   See Allen, "Rationales for Episcopal Letter-Collections", 8–11.

hood, two of which he still queries.²⁶ The question needs to be asked: Why such a shortage? Rousseau hypothesises that this absence of letters during Basil's priesthood can be attributed to Basil's subordinate clerical rank, that is, the fact the he was a priest as opposed to a bishop.²⁷ Perhaps as a priest Basil needed to be careful in writing his letters so that these were not misconstrued as coming officially from the church and therefore representing the authoritative view of the church as a whole.²⁸ After all, at least in Basil's understanding, it was the bishop who was considered to be the *voice* of the church.²⁹

---

26 Fedwick, *The Church and the Charisma of Leadership*, 11.
27 Rousseau, *Basil of Caesarea*, 134–135.
28 Gregory of Nazianzus says that his friend Basil appropriated his time in the priesthood in a way that best prepared him for the episcopacy. Until such a time he would remain obedient to ecclesiastical law and discipline, whilst maturing in his faith: Τάξει καὶ νόμῳ πνευματικῆς ἀναβάσεως τῆς τιμῆς ἀξιώσασα [...] Αὐτὸς δὲ ᾔδει νόμους εὐπειθείας καὶ πνευματικῆς τάξεως. SC 384. 184, 198. "He received the honour according to the law and order of spiritual advancement... He himself recognised the laws of obedience and the spiritual order". *Oration* 43.25, 33: McCauley, 50, 55–56.
29 See *Ep.* 28.2.

Basil's Unwritten Letters and The Function of Letter-carriers

Although letters became Basil's dominant form of communication, it becomes evident in his letters that letter-writing itself was not always his preferred choice of communication. Despite the benefits of letters noted above, for Basil the ultimate and "greatest of all goods" (μέγιστον τῶν ἀγαθῶν) was chance encounter (συντυχία).[1] When writing to Melitius, the bishop of Antioch, Basil closes his letter with a plea to being worthy of such an encounter.

> If, in answer to your prayers, we should be thought worthy, while still on earth, to meet you face to face, and from your living speech itself receive helpful instruction, or provision for the journey of both this life and the next, this we should have accounted the greatest of all goods, and should have set it down as an intimation of God's special favour to ourselves.[2]

In his letter to the Alexandrians, Basil in the strongest possible terms asserts his preferred mode of communication:

> Now if it had been possible for me to be with you in person, I should have preferred nothing to such meeting with you, that I might see the athletes of Christ, and embrace you, and to share in your prayers and in your spiritual acts

---

1 See *Ep.* 141.2: Deferrari, II, 343. Courtonne, II, 64.
2 *Ep.* 57: Deferrari, I, 355–357. Εἰ δὲ καταξιωθείημεν ταῖς σαῖς προσευχαῖς, ἕως ἐσμὲν ἐπὶ γῆς, καὶ τῆς κατ᾽ ὀφθαλμοὺς συντυχίας καὶ παρ᾽ αὐτῆς τῆς ζώσης φωνῆς λαβεῖν ὠφέλιμα διδάγματα, ἢ ἐφόδια πρός τε τὸν ἐνεστῶτα αἰῶνα καὶ τὸν μέλλοντα, τοῦτο ἂν μέγιστον τῶν ἀγαθῶν ἐκρίναμεν καὶ προοίμιον τῆς παρὰ Θεοῦ εὐμενείας ἑαυτοῖς ἐτιθέμεθα. Courtonne, I, 144.

of grace (κοινωνῆσαι τῶν προσευχῶν καὶ τῶν πνευματικῶν ἐν ὑμῖν χαρισμάτων).[3]

The dynamism of communication through face-to-face contact with his recipient allowed Basil to deal better with complex and delicate issues. For example, "in reply to the criticisms of the censorious" which got to the ears of the provincial governor Elias, Basil maintains: "this we must pass over in silence at this time as being not only too long for the compass of this letter, but also unsafe (οὐκ ἀσφαλῆ) to be trusted to soulless (ἀψύχοις) written characters".[4] "Living words" (ἔμψυχοι λόγοι), claims Basil, could more readily be trusted, since unlike "written words" (τοῖς γεγγραμμένοις) they were not "open to attack and subject to calumny" (εὐεπιχείρητον καὶ πρὸς συκοφαντίαν εὐάλωτον).[5] There were things that Basil needed to "advise in person" (δι᾽ ἑαυτῶν παραινέσωμεν) and that were "not fitting" (οὐκ ἐνεχώρει) to be conveyed "by letter" (διὰ τῆς ἐπιστολῆς).[6] Certain complex situations or crises were "impossible to learn by report, since no words could be found" to describe "clearly" the situation at hand.[7] By his own admission Basil was able to use "the spoken word much more persuasively than any importunity in writing would be able to effect".[8] According to Fedwick, this is because "writing lacks the warmth

3   *Ep.* 139.3: Deferrari, II, 331. Εἰ μὲν οὖν ἦν δυνατὸν αὐτῷ μοι παραγενέσθαι, οὐδὲν ἂν προετίμησα τῆς συντυχίας ὑμῶν, ὥστε καὶ ἰδεῖν τοὺς ἀθλητὰς τοῦ Χριστοῦ καὶ περιπτύξασθαι καὶ κοινωνῆσαι τῶν προσευχῶν καὶ τῶν πνευματικῶν ἐν ὑμῖν χαρισμάτων. Courtonne, II, 59.
4   *Ep.* 94: Deferrari, II, 153. Περιφροντικότι ἡμῶν τῆς ὑπολήψεις, ἀποκρίνασθαι ἀναγκαῖον νῦν ἀποσιωπῆσαι, ὡς καὶ μακρότερα τοῦ μέτρου τῆς ἐπιστολῆς καὶ ἄλλως οὐκ ἀσφαλῆ γράμμασιν ἀψύχοις καταπιστεύεσθαι. Courtonne, I, 206. See *Ep.* 9.3.
5   *Ep.* 212.2: Deferrari, III, 219. Courtonne, II, 199.
6   *Ep.* 227: Deferrari, III, 349. Courtonne, III, 32.
7   *Ep.* 243: Deferrari, III, 437. Ἀκοαῖς ἀδύνατον παραδέξασθαι τῷ μηδένα λόγον εὑρίσκεσθαι ἐναργῶς παριστῶντα. Courtonne, III, 69.
8   *Ep.* 289: Deferrari, IV, 183. Πολλῷ ἀξιοπιστότερον κεχρημένος τῷ λόγῳ ὅσον ἂν δυνηθείη δυσωπῆσαι τὰ γράμματα. Courtonne, III, 159. See *Epp.* 2, 112.1, 156.2.

and immediacy which characterise so well live human relations".⁹ Elsewhere Basil would tell his reader at the end of his letter that, "countless other matters have been passed over in silence" (μυρίων ἑτέρων ἀποσιωπηθέντων).¹⁰ Included in these "other matters" were of course details about doctrinal matters of faith. As Basil would apologetically explain: "We shall postpone a fuller explanation until we shall have a meeting face to face, which will enable us to resolve objections, and to furnish fuller testimony from the Scriptures, and to confirm every sound article of faith".¹¹

It was not enough, then, for Basil's letter-carriers simply to drop off his letters to their addressed recipients. Schor explains with regard to Theodoret of Cyrrhus:

> Beyond carrying letters, they served as an extra verbal channel, a responsive audience, an observant eye, and a helping hand. Symbolically they became extensions of the bishops themselves.¹²

In addition to simply delivering Basil's letters, his letter-carriers were often asked to "relate everything more accurately" (ἀκριβέστερον πάντα [...] διηγήσεται)¹³ and with greater "detail" (καθ' ἕκαστον ἀπαγγεῖλαι)¹⁴ so as to complement and if need be clarify his written message. The letter-carrier was considered by Basil as being worthy of trust and respect and could be referred to as "our most beloved son" (τὸν ποθεινότατον υἱὸν ἡμῶν).¹⁵ Sometimes the letter-carriers were even called upon to fill in the blanks of his letter's contents: "Whatever has escaped the account contained

---

9   Fedwick, *The Church and the Charisma of Leadership*, 170.
10 *Ep.* 244.9: Deferrari, III, 471. Courtonne, III, 83.
11 *Ep.* 159.2: Deferrari, II, 399. Τὴν δὲ τελειοτέραν διδασκαλίαν εἰς τὴν κατ' ὀφθαλμοὺς συντυχίαν ὑπερθησόμεθα, δι' ἧς καὶ τὰ ἀντικείμενα ἐπιλύσασθαι, καὶ πλατυτέρας τὰς ἐκ τῶν Γραφῶν παρασχέσθαι μαρτυρίας, καὶ πάντα τύπον τὸν ὑγιῆ τῆς πίστεως βεβαιώσασθαι δυνατόν. Courtonne, II, 87.
12 Schor, *Theodoret's People*, 36.
13 *Ep.* 79.2: Deferrari, II, 121. Courtonne, I, 194.
14 *Ep.* 57: Deferrari, I, 357. Courtonne, I, 145.
15 *Ep.* 265.1: Deferrari, IV, 107. Courtonne, III, 128.

in our letter" writes Basil, "they [the letter-carriers] may inform you of themselves".[16] Bishops such as Basil deliberately recruited letter-carriers who could perform an important verbal and social role upon arriving at their destination. This is why, together with a written report, there was also an oral report on the topic at hand, which may have included elements of negotiation and advocacy.[17] Oral reports were considered to be more secure when conveying confidential information, especially when letters were treated as public documents.[18] Because of this, the written word needed to be protected as much as possible, and in particular, as Rousseau mentions, "against seepage from speculative rumination or the hurried formulae of argument".[19] In some instances, difficult situations, rather than being committed to writing, were left for the letter-carrier to explain. In these situations it is possible that the essence of the correspondence was in the verbal message itself rather than the written piece. The deacon Sabinus was expected to relate "by word of mouth whatever is not contained"[20] in Basil's letter, as was Petrus who was specifically sought out and chosen for this task.[21] Similarly deacon Elpidius was described by Basil in his letter as the one "who both conveys the letter and is able of himself to relate to you whatever has escaped the account contained in the letter".[22]

16 *Ep.* 263.5: Deferrari, IV, 101. Ὅσα καὶ τὴν ἐκ τοῦ γράμματος διδασκαλίαν παρέλαθε, ταῦτα παρ᾽ ἑαυτῶν ἀναδιδάξαντες. Courtonne, III, 126.
17 Allen, "Prolegomena to a Study of the Letter-Bearer", 487.
18 See *Ep.* 77 addressed to Therasius a governor of Cappadocia: Πολλὰ δὲ ἔχων εἰπεῖν καὶ περὶ πολλῶν, εἰς τὴν συντυχίαν ὑπερεθέμην, οὐκ ἀσφαλὲς εἶναι ἡγούμενος ἐπιστολαῖς τὰ τοιαῦτα καταπιστεύειν. Courtonne, I, 179. "Though I have much to say on various topics, I have put them off until our meeting, not judging it safe to entrust such matters to letters". Deferrari, II, 85.
19 Rousseau, *Basil of Caesarea*, 119.
20 *Ep.* 92.1: Deferrari, II, 135. Δυνήσεται ὑμῖν καὶ ὅσα τὴν ἐπιστολὴν διαφεύγει παρ᾽ ἑαυτοῦ διηγήσασθαι. Courtonne, I, 199.
21 See *Ep.* 203.4.
22 *Ep.* 265.1: Deferrari, IV, 107. Ὁμοῦ μὲν τὴν ἐπιστολὴν διακομίζοντα, ὁμοῦ δὲ καὶ τὰ παρ᾽ ἑαυτοῦ δυνάμενον ἀναγγεῖλαι ὑμῖν ὅσα τὴν ἐκ τοῦ γράμματος διαπέφευγε διδασκαλίαν. Courtonne, III, 128.

It could also be that the oral components were simply shortcuts taken on behalf of the letter-writer. In this case the letter-carrier was given just some key words from the letter-writer and these became a sufficient lead into an encounter. At any rate the passing of non-written information was not without its dangers. The information received on the other end could be misinterpreted or be considered insufficient and therefore become counter-productive to the correspondence itself. A safer and more persuasive form of communication involved an oral component that could be supported by written documentation.

A final responsibility for letter-carriers was that of waiting around until a reply was forthcoming, bearing in mind that this could take several days. Basil describes the duties of one of his most reliable and frequently used letter-carriers, Dorotheus, who was asked to deliver a letter addressed to multiple participants (bishops) who resided throughout all Italy and Gaul:

> By the grace of God, we have despatched one instead of many, our most pious and beloved brother Dorotheus, fellow presbyter, who is able with his own narrative to supply whatever has escaped our letter, since he has followed all events keenly and has been from the beginning a zealous supporter of the orthodox faith. After receiving him in peace, quickly send him back to us, bearing good tidings to us.[23]

Judging from what there is to know about Basil's letter-carriers, one can see a tendency for this role to be carried out predominately from within the ranks of the clergy. Basil's letter-carriers were mainly deacons who perhaps considered these types of errands for

---

23 *Ep.* 243.5: Deferrari, III, 449. Τῇ τοῦ Θεοῦ χάριτι ἕνα ἀπεστείλαμεν ἀντὶ πολλῶν, τὸν εὐλαβέστατον καὶ ἀγαπητὸν ἡμῶν ἀδελφῶν Δωρόθεον τὸν συμπρεσβύτερον· ὅς καὶ ὅσα διαπέφευγεν ἡμῶν τὰ γράμματα τῇ παρ' ἑαυτοῦ διηγήσει δυνατός ἐστιν ἀναπληρῶσαι, παρακολουθηκὼς πᾶσι μετὰ ἀκριβείας καὶ ζηλωτὴς ὑπάρχων τῆς ὀρθῆς πίστεως. Ὃν προσδεξάμενοι ἐν εἰρήνῃ διὰ ταχέων ἀποπέμψασθε ἀγαθὰ ἡμῖν εὐαγγέλια φέροντα. Courtonne, III, 73.

their bishop as part and parcel of their ordained ministry. There seems to be no blanket rule that limited the role of the letter-carrier to the clergy of the lower orders. Basil's *Ep.* 143, for example, is delivered by one of his assistant bishops. Furthermore, research has shown that there have been lay individuals, male and female, Christian and non-Christian and even strangers, entrusted with the responsibility of letter-carrying and other associated activities such as conveying messages or even gifts on behalf of bishops.[24]

The correspondent might choose not to receive the correspondence if it did not come from a reliable source, since there was not much to differentiate these letters from forgeries. The more a person was prone to writing letters, the more letter-carriers and the wider variety of letter-carriers a person had. By preference, a letter-carrier would have been a familiar and trusted person to the letter-writer, perhaps someone the writer was mentoring. In their absence though, nearly anybody could be asked to deliver a letter if they happened to be around and available at the right time. Basil on one occasion called upon the revenue-collector of the office of prefects to deliver a letter while he was travelling on the *cursus publicus*.[25]

Letter-carrying was not always smooth sailing, and sometimes the letter-carriers were not even acknowledged by their recipients. Augustine states that he did not see the carrier of his letter, nor could he recall his name.[26] At other times they were mistreated or yelled at, depending on how their recipients received their respective letters and whether these contained difficult messages. Libanius told one of the recipients of his letters: "It is right and proper for you, if you are pleased with this letter, to show your

---

24 See Allen, "Prolegomena to a Study of the Letter-Bearer", 481–491; Gain, *L'Église de Cappadoce*, 24, 92.
25 See *Ep.* 215: Courtonne, II, 206.
26 See *Ep.* 149.1.2; NBA 22, 456–459.

gratitude to the bearer and, if you are annoyed, to punish him".[27] Worst of all, some letter-carriers did not even make it to their destination because they died *en route*, as was the case with Basil's deacon Theophrastus who became ill and died unexpectedly.[28]

By way of concluding this section on letters and their carriers, it is important to note that there is, as yet, no detailed study on the place and role of letters and letter-carriers in late antiquity.[29] At most one can find information from the studies of letter-collections that are connected to individual writers such as Basil of Caesarea. From reviewing existing letter collections, it becomes evident that letter-writing activity was highly developed during Basil's era, suggesting that it was no longer limited to those who could afford a private postal service. Basil's ministry was largely dependent on his ability to write letters and receive replies. Although he acknowledged that letters were second place to direct contact and communication, this was not to say that they did not have the potential to substitute sufficiently for direct contact and communication.

The above introduction has shed light on letters and letter-writing from a fourth century perspective, irrespective of whether these letters were used as vehicles of communication or as mediums of publicity. This was done so as to contextualise Basil's 365 letters, many of which were dependent on, or at least complemented by, his unwritten letters (oral messages). At the same time, it was important to authenticate Basil's letters from those written by others, such as his brother Gregory of Nyssa, and even to separate spurious letters from being attributed to Basil's authorship. Nearly all complete presentations of Basil's letters do not readily make this distinction between Basilian and non Basilian letters.

---

27 *Ep.* 40.18: Norman, I, 495. Δίκαιον δέ, εἴτε ἡσθείσης τοῖς γράμμασι, τῷ φέροντι τὴν χάριν ἔχειν, εἴτε δηχθείσης, παρὰ τοῦ φέροντος τὴν δίκην λαβεῖν. Norman, I, 495.
28 *Ep.* 95: Courtonne, I, 207–208.
29 Allen, "Prolegomena to a Study of the Letter-Bearer", 483.

Nevertheless, the 365 letters of Basil that do survive are still only a fraction of the letters that he actually wrote. Furthermore, his letter-carriers also had information to convey that was not put down in print. Part Two of this book will occupy itself in greater detail with Basil's use of letters. For now it is enough to get a contextual historical insight into Basil's Letters. The chapter that immediately follows this introduction will build upon any historical context mentioned thus far by looking into Basil's own upbringing and education, his monastic leanings, and the theological environment of his day. It will be shown that Basil's formal education, his zeal for monasticism, and his Nicene personality, all shaped his decision to enter into the ordained ministry. It is only when Basil becomes a bishop of a pro-Nicene church that his letters do indeed become "instruments of communion".

Part One: Historical and Theological Context

Chapter One:
Basil's Context, Education and Vocation

Anthony Meredith draws the following succinct conclusion about Basil's life: "In his whole life and policy Basil represents the best type of ecclesiastic".[1] This book explores this ecclesial leadership of Basil through his letters, specifically Basil's 365 letters in which one will find the pastoral prolongation of his actions and the tangible extension of his very presence: "he who presents this letter of ours stands to me in place of a son".[2] The introduction of this book, in attempting to locate Basil's letters within fourth century letter-writing in general, is a precursor to what will follow in this chapter where Basil's life and context, education and vocation, will be examined.

This chapter traces Basil's life as it was shaped by his education, monastic outlook and zeal for Nicene orthodoxy. It will become apparent that the core ethos that Basil associated with monasticism was in practice the living out of the Gospel commandments found in Scripture, and that Basil's Nicene position was invariably connected to his understanding of salvation. Non-Nicene sentiments receive no sympathy from Basil, even if they purport to honour the sovereignty of one God, the Father. Throughout his priesthood and episcopal ministry Basil consistently opposed every non-Nicene expression of faith, which he identified as a threat to the communion of the church. By turning to Arianism as a starting point for this chapter, a context will be established that locates the responsibilities that Basil sets before himself. For him it was important not only to make the problems he encountered his own, but also to

1 Meredith, *The Cappadocians*, 35.
2 *Ep.* 280: Deferrari, IV, 167. Ὁ τοίνυν τὴν ἐπιστολὴν ταύτην ἡμῶν ἐπιδιδοὺς ἐν υἱοῦ μοι τάξει καθέστηκεν. Courtonne, III, 152–153.

respond to them through his vocation as a bishop of the church.

The afflictions of the world were indeed challenging for Basil and he certainly did not shy away from lamenting over them. Translating these afflictions into a church setting, Basil cries: "The churches exhibit a condition almost like that of my [deteriorating] body, for no ground of good hope comes into view, and their affairs are constantly drifting towards the worse".[3] However, it is Basil's response to these afflictions that proved to be the catalyst to his episcopal success. Basil's letters seek to show how obstacles of division can be overcome and permanently reconciled in the embrace of the church's communion.

1.1 Arianism: "The Impious Doctrine of Arius"[4]

The birth of Basil in 330 came at a time of extreme theological tension in the church. Approximately ten years earlier in 319, Bishop Alexander of Alexandria (c. 244–337) had come into conflict with one of his priests named Arius (c. 250–336), who had begun to question the eternal status of the Word of God. Arius' primary claim was that the Son had a beginning and was neither eternal nor part of the essence of God; for him the mere fact that the Son was said to be begotten meant that the Son was created, and thus there was a "time" when the Son was not.[5] He reasoned

---

3   *Ep.* 30: Deferrari, I, 175–177. Αἱ δὲ Ἐκκλσίαι σχεδόν τι παραπλησίως τῷ σώματί μου διάκεινται, ἀγαθῆς μὲν ἐλπίδος οὐδεμιᾶς ὑποφαινομένης, ἀεὶ δὲ πρὸς τὸ χεῖρον τῶν πραγμάτων ὑπορρεόντων. Courtonne, I, 72.
4   *Ep.* 263.3: Deferrari, IV, 95. Τὸ δυσσεβὲς δόγμα τοῦ Ἀρείου. Courtonne, III, 123.
5   According to the letters that Alexander of Alexandria sent to Alexander of Constantinople and Emperor Eusebius of Nicodemia, Arius taught: Οὐκ ἀεὶ ἦν ὁ τοῦ Θεοῦ Λόγος, ἀλλ᾽ ἐξ οὐκ ὄντων γέγονεν [...] 'Διὸ καὶ ἦν ποτὲ, ὅτε οὐκ ἦν'· Κτίσμα γάρ ἐστι καὶ ποίημα ὁ Υἱός. SC 477. 66. "The Word of God was not from eternity but was made out of nothing... wherefore there was a time when he did not exist, inasmuch as the Son is a creature and a work". Socrates Scholasticus, *Church History* 1.6.9: Hartranft, *A Select Library of Nicene and Post-Nicene Fathers of the Christian Church*, 2nd Series, vol. 2, 4. Hereafter NPNF will refer to the series Nicene and Post-Nicene Fathers. See the anathema against Arius and his followers at the end of "The Profession of Faith of the 318 Fathers" in Tanner, *Decrees of the Ecumenical Councils*, 5.

that if the Son was considered to be uncreated and eternal, then the Son would also be unbegotten like the Father. With this understanding the Son would be a second Father and ultimately a second principle cause. From the beginning, the thrust of Arius' argument lay in establishing the primacy and therefore superiority of the Father to the Son, with the created Son being the product of the will of the creator Father. Bishop Alexander refused to accept Arius' position, arguing that the Son, although begotten, is not created. He maintained that what divine begetting is cannot be known, and that divine begetting certainly does not mean creating. Alexander asserted that there was no "prior" moment where Christ can be contemplated as only human, since by his nature Christ is always regarded as the Son of God. Moreover Alexander affirmed that the Son of God is proper (ἴδιος) to the Father, implying that the Son and the Father are co-eternally one.[6]

The controversy in Alexandria between Bishop Alexander and Arius soon spread and eventually affected the whole church, becoming what Rowan Williams described as "the most dramatic internal struggle the Christian church had so far experienced".[7] The division between Alexander and Arius became so intense that the wider church became involved and the majority of bishops of Egypt and Libya had Arius condemned.[8] In 325, in an attempt to restore doctrinal harmony within the church and unity within his empire, Constantine called for a council to take place in Nicaea and it was convened in the audience-hall of the imperial palace.[9]

---

6 Behr, *The Nicene Faith*, 126–127.
7 Williams, *Arius*, 1.
8 See Davidson, *A Public Faith*, 31.
9 See Eusebius, *Life of Constantine* 2.72. Barnes argues that Constantine did not preside over the Council of Nicaea and refutes modern scholars who make this conclusion. Instead he quotes Eusebius about Constantine's presence at presumably the Council of Arles in 314 where Constantine's involvement was simply one where he sat "in the middle just like one of the many" (καθῆστό τε καὶ μέσος, ὡσεὶ καὶ τῶν πολλῶν εἷς). Eusebius, *Life of Constantine* 1.44. Patrologia Graeca, 960A. Hereafter PG will refer to the series Patrologia Graeca (Paris, 1857–1866). Barnes, "Emperor and Bishops", 57.

Alexander attended the council with his deacon and future successor Athanasius. A year before the council in 324, Constantine had written to both Alexander and Arius encouraging them to embrace a unified position.[10] Amongst Constantine's concerns in his letters was the fact that any theological division threatened the unity of his empire. He rebuked Alexander and Arius for entangling themselves in theological affairs that were beyond human understanding. In the end, out of public and political concern, Constantine thought he had no choice but to intervene, especially as new disputes in Antioch between Arian supporters and those opposed were increasingly disturbing the peace of the state.[11]

In his letters Basil describes Arius as being "the author of those wicked blasphemies against the only begotten".[12] Although Nicaea succeeded in bringing about the rejection of the teaching of Arius, it failed to bring peace to the church or to the state for that matter. In fact, the conflict worsened; its formal defeat was short-lived since a non-Nicene position was found within the secure confines of the imperial court which inevitably controlled world order.[13]

---

10 See Eusebius, *Life of Constantine* 2.64–2.72.
11 See Eusebius, *Life of Constantine* 2.69.
12 *Ep.* 263.3: Deferrari, IV, 95. Τὰς πονηρὰς κατὰ τοῦ Μονογενοῦς συνθεὶς βλασφημίας. Courtonne, III, 123.
13 It is incorrect to say that the non-Nicene position supported by the empire was that held by Arius. Arianism had many nuances in the fourth century and could hardly point solely to the definitive teaching of Arius. Commenting on the era Williams notes: "There was no single 'Arian' agenda, no tradition of loyalty to a single authoritative teacher. Theologians who criticised the Creed of Nicaea had very diverse attitudes to Arius himself, and part of the continuing difficulty of identifying the main line of Arius' theology arises from this fact". Williams, *Arius*, 247. Gwynn in his reflections of Arius and the theological postulations attributed to his name asserts: "There is considerable doubt that even Arius himself really taught all of the elements that comprise this definition" (i.e. Arianism). Gwynn, "*Hoi peri Eusebion*", 55. For many non-Nicene theologians, the Nicene Creed or Nicene theology had no significance in their theological formulations. For this reason, this book avoids labelling non-Nicene thinkers as Arian or anti-Nicene. Accordingly, realising that the theological reality of these thinkers was far more complex, it simply refers to them as non-Nicene. See Ayres, *Nicaea and its Legacy*, 85–110; Gwynn, *The Eusebians*; Williams, *Arius*, 2; Barnes, "The Career of Athanasius", 392; Behr, *The Nicene Faith*, 132–134.

The abuse of imperial power, Basil recalls, resulted in "persecutions of presbyters and teachers, and all such things as men might do who make use of the power of government in accordance with their will".[14] The empire could make use of false accusations and lies against anyone that threatened its role as a guarantor of cosmic order and as a custodian of every aspect of its subject's lives.[15] Despite the difficulties of such a state of affairs, Basil felt he had no choice but to work within this context and try to influence change. He said his strategy consisted of keeping "his mind on God" which through God's grace "keeps it moving onward, gazing steadily upon the future" (τὴν διάνοιαν Θεῷ συμπορευομένην καὶ τὸ μέλλον ἀποσκοποῦσαν).[16]

> Just as workers in smithies, whose ears are struck with a din, become inured to the noise, so we by the frequency of strange reports have at length become accustomed to keep our heart unmoved and undismayed at unexpected events. Therefore, the charges that have from old been fabricated by the Arians against the church, although many and great and noised throughout the whole world, can nevertheless be endured by us because they come from open enemies and foes of the word of truth.[17]

With imperial endorsement, supporters of Nicene Christianity were exiled, including Popes Julius (337–352) and Liberius of Rome (352–366). Essentially each of these men were punished

---

14　*Ep.* 248: Deferrari, III, 481. Διωγμοὺς πρεσβυτέρων καὶ διδασκάλων, τὰ ἄλλα ὅσα ἂν ποιήσειαν ἄνθρωποι τῇ ἐκ τῆς ἀρχῆς δυναστείᾳ πρὸς τὸ ἑαυτῶν βούλημα κεχρημένη. Courtonne, III, 86.
15　Mitchell, *A History of the Later Roman Empire*, 155–156.
16　*Ep.* 293: Deferrari, IV, 201. Courtonne, III, 167.
17　*Ep.* 266.1: Deferrari, IV, 121. Ὃς γὰρ οἱ ἐν τοῖς χαλκείοις τὰς ἀκοὰς κατακτυπούμενοι ἐν μελέτῃ εἰσὶ τῶν ψόφων, οὕτως ἡμεῖς τῇ πυκνότητι τῶν ἀτόπων ἀγγελιῶν εἰθίσθημεν λοιπὸν ἀτάραχον ἔχειν καὶ ἀπτόητον τὴν καρδίαν πρὸς τὰ παράλογα. Τὰ μὲν οὖν παρὰ τῶν Ἀρειανῶν ἔκπαλαι κατὰ τῆς Ἐκκλησίας σκευωρούμενα, εἰ καὶ πολλὰ καὶ μεγάλα καὶ κατὰ πᾶσαν διαβεβοημένα τὴν οἰκουμένην, ἀλλ᾽ ἡμῖν ἐστι διὰ τὸ παρὰ φανερῶν ἐχθρῶν καὶ πολεμίων τοῦ λόγου τῆς ἀληθείας γίνεσθαι. Courtonne, III, 133–134.

for adhering to the Nicene position which affirmed Christ to be "of one essence" or consubstantial with the Father and therefore truly God. Their opposition to emperors and bishops who sympathised with a non-Nicene faith position ("bishops of the empire" or "state bishops"), far from being political was considered to be a fundamental expression of their ecclesial experience. In their view, any subordinationism with respect to the person of Christ was seen as undermining salvation in Christ. For them, it is the fact that Christ is truly God that makes salvation possible for "if the Son were a creature, man would have remained no more than mortal, not being joined to God" (εἰ ὁ υἱός, ἔμενεν ὁ ἄνθρωπος οὐδὲν ἧττον θνητὸς, μὴ συναπτόμενος τῷ θεῷ).[18] They saw holiness as existentially aligned with the faith of the church articulated at Nicaea and, for such upholders of Nicaea, it was this existential significance that mattered most of all.

1.2 Basil's Nicene Personality and Reputation

In the attempts to overthrow the decrees of Nicaea by non-Nicene emperors and their delegates, defenders of Nicaea received scathing critiques. It was into such a whirlwind of tensions that Basil was born.[19] To ancient Christian historians of the likes of Rufinus, Socrates, Sozomen and Theodoret, Basil's unyielding dedication to the faith of the church articulated at Nicaea made him not only a success story but also a prototype for a bishop whose way of life was patterned on saintliness. The ancient historians' view of Basil, like that of other champions of Nicene orthodoxy, facilitated a legacy of admiration that has been preserved by Christian believers down to the present day. Rousseau sees Basil as valuing prayer and the eremitic way of life, but also makes the point that this type of life lived

18 Athanasius, *Four Discourses Against the Arians*, 21.69.98. PG 25. 293A.
19 The imperial capital itself, Constantinople, had only one remaining Nicene church, this being the small church of the Resurrection that would later be served by the Nicene patriarch of Constantinople, St. Gregory the Theologian. See Sozomen, *Church History* 7.5.

for God was not opposed to public life ("the world") but rather led Basil towards it. He understands from Basil's letters that "a life of piety [...] was bound to involve one in 'the afflictions of the world.'"[20] Basil was exceptional to a certain extent *politically* in that he held his episcopal post (without any exiles)[21] during some of the most turbulent years of the Christian empire. In the context this may have been an unlikely outcome, but, as will be made evident below, it was no accident. The same could not be said for Basil's pro-Nicene counterparts who also served in the Orient under Emperor Valens (364–378), and whose Nicene (*homoiousian/ homoousian*) proclivities forced many of them to go into exile.[22] Greogry of Nyssa and Eusebius of Samosata, for example, were

20 Rousseau, *Basil of Caesarea*, 92. See *Ep.* 18: Οὔτε μὴν τοῖς εὐσεβῶς ζῆν ἑλομένοις ἡ κατὰ τὸν ἐνεστῶτα κόσμον θλίψις ἀμελέτητος [...] Ἐλπίδες γάρ, πάντα τὸν τῶν ἀνθρώπων βίον συνέχουσαι καὶ συγκροτοῦσαι, τὴν ἐφ ἑκάστῳ τούτων παραμυθοῦνται δυσκολίαν. Courtonne, I, 48. "To those who have chosen to live the life of piety the afflictions of this world are not unforeseen... For hopes, which hold and weld together man's entire life, give consolation for the hardships". Deferrari, I, 119.
21 Radde-Gallwitz attributes this "success" of Basil to his "force of character" which he explains was viewed "less as theologically persuasive and more as politically immobile". He applauds Basil as being a personality that was "most intellectually gifted and well connected", which thus allowed him to uphold Nicene Christianity in a non-Nicene world. Radde-Gallwitz, *Basil of Caesarea*, 4, 138. Rousseau on the other hand draws the following conclusion after his study on almost every aspect of Basil's life: "I have ended up thinking that he was probably rather odd, and not entirely successful". Rousseau speaks about "obvious fractures" in Basil's ministry, especially in regard to "his attempt to define and display the social diplomacy proper to his task as a bishop". He does concede, however, that these "tensions [...] helped him to create, nevertheless, a moral theory and a religious anthropology that were most exalted in their finest expressions". Rousseau, *Basil of Caesarea*, xiii, 151, 189. In a similar way to Rousseau, Fedwick comments that Basil "not infrequently showed a certain lack of practical judgement [...] indications of this can be seen in his choice of friends". However, "these shortcomings in no way should diminish Basil's greatness which remains indisputable". Fedwick, *The Church and the Charisma of Leadership*, 132. Hans von Campenhausen on the role of Basil as a church politician writes: "He found his work as an ecclesiastical politician so difficult because he was not only wiser and more farseeing but also more profound and more honest than most of his colleagues". Campenhausen, *The Fathers of the Greek Church*, 97.
22 Some of the many bishops exiled by Valens were: Meletius of Antioch, Eusebius of Samosata, Pelagius of Laodicaea, Barses of Edessa and Abraham of Batna. Fedwick, *The Church and the Charisma of Leadership*, 103.

both driven out of their sees as a result of their pro-Nicene persuasions. Basil, on the contrary, remained in his diocese from where he could be fully committed to his people, despite the fact that according to Radde-Gallwitz "for the final five years of his life, his network must have seemed in shambles".[23] Basil managed to stay in Caesarea while maintaining a consistent theological stance on the one hand, and on the other hand, not being wedded (or confined) to any one single theological formula.[24]

At the interface of imperialism and non-Nicenism, Basil carefully espoused and promulgated a Nicene theology that asserted the divinity of the Holy Spirit and its[25] equal membership in the consubstantial Trinity.[26] In his letters he would proclaim that he "never held erroneous opinions about God".[27] Should Basil have been alive after his 49th birthday, he would have been the beneficiary of an imperial change, not only to the throne of the empire but also to its theological persuasions. Within the year of Basil's death in 379,[28] Theodosius I (379–395) became emperor with pro-Nicene inclinations and subsequent legislation. In 381 non-Nicene doctrines were outlawed and all subjects, *cunctos populos*,

---

23 Radde-Gallwitz, *Basil of Caesarea*, 133.
24 Hanson emphatically insists on this point when he maintains: "There never has been a single formula adopted by the majority of Christians designed to express the doctrine of the Trinity, and the Cappadocians never imagined that there could be one". Hanson, *The Search for the Christian Doctrine of God*, 677.
25 The pronoun used for the Holy Spirit in this book will regularly be "it" even though Deferrari in his translations uses he/him. In Basil's letters, as also in the New Testament, the noun πνεῦμα is in the neuter gender. The neuter gender used for the Holy Spirit does not take away from the doctrinal truth that the Holy Spirit is a person of the Holy Trinity. Deferrari's he/him translations have this in mind.
26 See *Epp.* 51.2, 81, 159.1, 226.3, 244.5, 258.2.
27 *Ep.* 223.3: Deferrari, III, 299. Οὐδέποτε πεπλανημένας ἔσχον τὰς περὶ Θεοῦ ὑπολήψεις. Courtonne, III, 12.
28 It was on January 1, 379 in which Gregory of Nyssa delivered his *Encomium on His Brother* that became identified with the date of Basil's death. In his *Encomium* Gregory makes no mention of this date as being the actual day of the death of Basil. There is considerable movement amongst scholars suggesting that Basil's death was around September 378. See Radde-Gallwitz, *Basil of Caesarea*, 141. Rousseau presents the claim that Basil may have died as early as September 377. Rousseau, *Basil of Caesarea*, 360–363.

of the empire were ordered to align themselves with the Nicene faith of Pope Damasus of Rome (366–384).[29] Peace and tranquillity were solidified within the empire through the convocation of the Council of Constantinople in 381 which ended for the final time the ascendancy of non-Nicene doctrines. At the Ecumenical Council of Constantinople, the decrees of Nicaea were reaffirmed and the divinity of the Holy Spirit proclaimed. Basil, of course, did not live to see this council but his work, primarily as a bishop of the church, contributed to its success in bringing an end to the division in the church and to establishing communion.

In his lifetime Basil's theological reflections were shaped by his commitment to the communion of the church. Specifically his theological footprint was manifested in his deepening of the theology of the Holy Spirit, that is to say, clarifying the Spirit's role and identity in the Holy Trinity.[30] Assisting and supporting him were his great friend Gregory of Nazianzus (c. 329–389) and to a lesser extent his brother Gregory of Nyssa (c. 335–394). All three theologians were part of a larger network of fourth-century theologians determined to establish the theological doctrine of the divinity of the Holy Spirit, and of the Spirit's consubstantiality with the Father and the Son. Admittedly only a few theologians insisted on the Spirit's consubstantiality; it was not a widespread principle and was not included in the Creed. In the East, these theologians were represented through the likes of Athanasius and Didymus the Blind (c. 313–398), and in the West, by Hilary (c. 315–367), Ambrose (c. 339–397), and Augustine (354–430). All these theologians espoused theological statements of faith concerning the divinity of the Holy Spirit that paved the way for the doctrinal definition of the Nicene-Constantinopolitan Creed of 381.

Basil's theological expression throughout his life evolved as did his rapport with all his constituents. Chapter Two will trace

---

29 Mitchell, *A History of the Later Roman Empire*, 247–248.
30 See Chapter Two.

how Basil's theology evolved from a *homoiousian* (of like/similar essence) to a neo-Nicene *homoousian* (of same essence) expression. Here one will see that Basil moved from preferring *prosōpon* to *hypostasis* to describe what is three in God. On account of these modifications, Basil explains:

> I did not change from one opinion to another with the maturity of reason, but I perfected the principles handed down to me [...] For just as the seed, in developing, becomes larger instead of small, but is the same in itself, not changing in kind but being perfected in development, so I consider that also in me the same doctrine has been developed through progress, and what now is mine has not taken the place of what existed in the beginning [...] Through progress a certain amplification is witnessed in what we say, which is not a change from worse to better, but is a completing of that which was lacking, according to the increment of our knowledge.[31]

1.3 Basil's Education

Pre-dating Basil's education and, therefore, regarded as the foundation of his studies, was his immersion in the Scriptures which for Basil and his siblings began at infancy νηπίους ὄντας[32] through the influence of his devout Christian family. Basil's "conception of God" (ἔννοιαν περὶ Θεοῦ) was instilled in him at "childhood" (ἐκ παίδος) from his "blessed mother and grandmother Macrina" (μακαρίας

---

31   *Ep.* 223.3,5: Deferrari, III, 299, 305. Οὐ γὰρ ἄλλα ἐξ ἄλλων μετέλαβον ἐν τῇ τοῦ λόγου συμπληρώσει, ἀλλὰ τὰς παραδοθείσας μοι παρ᾽ αὐτῶν ἀρχὰς ἐτελείωσα. Ὥσπερ γὰρ τὸ αὐξανόμενον μεῖζον μὲν ἀπὸ μικροῦ γίνεται, ταὐτὸ δέ ἐστιν ἑαυτῷ, οὐ κατὰ γένος μεταβαλλόμενον, ἀλλὰ κατ᾽ αὔξησιν τελειούμενον· οὕτω λογίζομαι ἐμοὶ τὸν αὐτὸν λόγον διὰ τῆς προκοπῆς ηὐξῆσθαι [...] Ἐκ προκοπῆς τινα αὔξησιν ἐπιθεωρεῖσθαι τοῖς λεγομένοις, ὅπερ οὐχὶ μεταβολή ἐστιν ἐκ τοῦ χείρονος πρὸς τὸ βέλτιον, ἀλλὰ συμπλήρωσις τοῦ λείποντος κατὰ τὴν προσθήκην τῆς γνώσεως. Courtonne, III, 12-13,14-15.
32   *Ep.* 204.6: Courtonne, II, 178.

μητρὸς [...] καὶ τῆς μάμμης Μακρίνης).³³ Prior to embarking upon an ecclesiastical career, Basil completed what was regarded as the best education available in his day. Beginning with his elementary training in Neocaesarea, which took place through his father, Basil senior,³⁴ himself a distinguished rhetorician and "teacher of virtue" (παιδευτὴν ἀρετῆς),³⁵ Basil received the combination of a classical curriculum and Christian piety. Upon the death of Basil senior in 345, Basil proceeded to attend schools in Caesarea and the Eastern Mediterranean for "middle" studies (junior high school). This included a one year stint in Constantinople where, amongst others, he studied under the famous pagan orator Libanius. From 349–356 Basil lived in Athens where he was enrolled in advanced studies at the great centres of learning in Athens. Among Basil's teachers in Athens were Himerius "one of the most elusive writers of the fourth century"³⁶ and Prohaeresius, a Christian, both of whom epitomised the intellectual life of his age.

The privilege of being born into an aristocratic Christian family and to a father who was an eminent teacher of rhetoric, made Athens the obvious destiny for Basil, which according to Lee had the reputation of being "the centre of the ancient inheritance of literature, philosophy and culture".³⁷ As Deferrari puts it, Athens was "the pattern of excellence to a world that elected to see in Atticism the cultural ideal".³⁸

33 *Ep.* 223.3: Deferrari, III, 299. Courtonne, III, 12. See *Ep.* 236.1. Basil, *On the Judgement of God*, 1: Θεοῦ τοῦ ἀγαθοῦ καὶ φιλανθρωπίᾳ ἐν χάριτι τοῦ Κυρίου ἡμῶν Ἰησοῦ Χριστοῦ κατ᾽ ἐνέργειαν τοῦ ἁγίου Πνεύματος, τῆς μὲν κατὰ παράδοσιν τῶν ἔξωθεν πλάνης ῥυσθεὶς, ἄνωθεν δὲ καὶ ἐξ ἀρχῆς ὑπὸ Χριστιανοῖς γονεῦσιν ἀνατροφεὶς, παρ᾽ αὐτοῖς μὲν ἀπὸ βρέφους καὶ τὰ ἱερὰ γράμματα ἔμαθον, ἄγοντά με πρὸς ἐπίγνωσιν τῆς ἀληθείας. PG 31. 653A. "The good God, in his kindness and love for humanity in the grace of our Lord Jesus Christ and through the operation of the Holy Spirit, preserved me from the delusion of pagan tradition, for I was raised by Christian parents from the very first. From the womb I learned from them the sacred writings, which brought me to a knowledge of the truth". *Saint Basil the Great: On Christian Ethics*, Van Sickle, 39.
34 See Gregory of Nazianzus, *Oration* 43.5–8.
35 Gregory of Nazianzus, *Oration* 43.12. SC 384. 140.
36 Barnes, "Himerius and the Fourth Century", 207.
37 Lee, "Why Didn't St. Basil Write in New Testament Greek?", 12.
38 Deferrari, I, xviii.

The varied distractions of university life did not hinder Basil's dedication to his studies and, going by the witness of his contemporaries, he excelled in all subjects: grammar, poetry, history, rhetoric, dialectics, metaphysics, astronomy, geometry.[39] His admiration for classical authors and their language can be seen in his writings where he quotes from writers including Homer, Hesiod, Theognis, Plato, Aristotle and Solon. Throughout Basil's writings, such classical authors and many others are either cited or alluded to with noticeable frequency.[40] Basil had mastered the use of a high level literary Attic Greek which allowed him to employ all the devices, subtleties of language and rhetoric available to any competent writer.[41] A concise summary of Basil's learning is commemorated on St. Basil's feast day of January 1, where the liturgical service book entitled the *Minaion* says of Basil: "In classical learning he surpassed not only his contemporaries but even the ancients; for passing through every kind of training, he acquired mastery in each".[42]

It was in Athens while undergoing "every kind of training" that Basil met his very close friend and study partner Gregory, the son of a bishop who came from Nazianzus, a small village neighbouring Caesarea. Together they forged a relationship that was to shape the rest of their lives and which in the words of McGuckin was "one of the most longstanding, famous and stormy friendships in Christian history".[43] According to Gregory, in their pursuit of "philosophy" (φιλοσοφίαν εἶναι τὸ σπουδαζόμενον)[44] they only had one aim in life: "to be and to be called Christians" (χριστιανοὺς καὶ εἶναι καὶ ὀνομάζεσθαι).[45] Upon the completion of his studies in 356, much to

---

39   See Gregory of Nazianzus, *Oration* 43.23.
40   See *Epp.* 249-291.
41   Cameron, "Poetry and Literature Culture in Late Antiquity", 327-354.
42   Ἐν δὲ λόγοις οὐ μόνον τοὺς καθ᾽ αὑτόν, ἀλλὰ καὶ τοὺς παλαιοὺς ὑπερέβαλε· διὰ γὰρ πάσης ἐλθὼν ἰδέας παιδεύσεως, ἐν ἑκάστῃ τὸ κράτος ἐκτήσατο. Μηναῖον τοῦ Ἰανουαρίου (Ἐν Ἀθήναις: Ἀποστολικὴ Διακονία, 1991), 24.
43   McGuckin, *St. Gregory of Nazianzus*, 54.
44   Gregory of Nazianzus, *Oration* 43.19. SC 385. 162.
45   Gregory of Nazianzus, *Oration* 43.21. SC 385. 168.

the disappointment of Gregory,[46] Basil left Athens "scorning everything there" (ὑπεριδὼν τῶν ἐκεῖ)[47] and went on a pilgrimage with his then spiritual mentor and family associate[48] Eustathius of Sebasteia. Guided by Eustathius from whom he had hoped to have received "a guidance to the introduction to the teachings of religion" (χειραγωγίαν πρὸς τὴν εἰσαγωγὴν τῶν δογμάτων τῆς εὐσεβείας),[49] since at that time Basil had considered Eustathius to have "taken to himself the experience of all mankind" (τὸν πάντων ὁμοῦ τὴν πεῖραν ἀναδεξάμενον), they visited monastic settlements in Alexandria and all Egypt, Palestine, Syria and Mesopotamia with the view of meeting ascetics and "to have learned their minds" (νόον γνῶναι).[50]

In addition to the edification derived from visiting places of prayer, the impressionable Basil was perhaps being led by Eustathius to think about the possibilities of a response to non-Nicene theo-

---

46 See Gregory of Nazianzus, *Oration* 43.24.
47 *Ep.* 1: Deferrari, I, 3. Courtonne, I, 3. See *Epp.* 223.2, 271.
48 *Ep.* 223.5 makes a point of highlighting how familiar Eustathius was to Basil and his family. Ποσάκις ἡμᾶς ἐπισκέψω ἐπὶ τῆς μονῆς τῆς ἐπὶ τῷ Ἴριδι ποταμῷ [...] τὸν αὐτόν μοι τοῦ βίου σκοπὸν διανύων; Courtonne, III, 14. "How often did you visit us in the monastery on the river Iris... achieving the same purpose in life as myself?" Deferrari, III, 303. In Deferrari's older text edition the following clarification is made: Πόσας δὲ ἡμέρας ἐπὶ τῆς ἀντιπέραν κώμης, παρὰ τῇ μητρί μου, ἔνθα ὡς φίλοι μετ' ἀλλήλων διάγοντες. "And how many days did we spend in the village opposite, at my mother's, living there as a friend with a friend". Deferrari, III, 303. Courtonne omits this point and the sentences following it from his revised edition. There does not appear to be any manuscript evidence that supports Deferrari's reading.
49 *Ep.* 223.2: Deferrari, III, 293. Courtonne, III, 10.
50 *Ep.* 74.1: Deferrari, II, 69. Courtonne, I, 172. See *Ep.* 204.6: Ἐπεὶ δὲ καὶ αὐτοὶ τὴν τοῦ φρονεῖν δύναμιν ἀπελάβομεν τοῦ λόγου ἡμῖν διὰ τῆς ἡλικίας συμπληρωθέντος, πολλὴν ἐπελθόντος γῆν τε καὶ θάλασσαν, εἴ τινας εὕρομεν τῷ παραδοθέντι κανόνι τῆς εὐσεβείας στοιχοῦντας, τούτους καὶ πατέρας ἐπεγραψάμεθα καὶ ὁδηγοὺς τῶν ψυχῶν ἡμῶν εἰς τὴν πρὸς Θεὸν πορείαν ἐποιησάμεθα. Courtonne, II, 178. "And when we ourselves received the power of thinking, after reason had been developed in us by age, having travelled over many a land and sea, whomever we found walking according to the traditional rule of piety, these we both listed and regarded as guides of our souls in the journey to God". Deferrari, III, 169. For Basil's contact with Eustathius and the ascetics under him see *Ep.* 223.5.

logical attitudes.⁵¹ The message brought home to Basil was that the church was in a state of theological mayhem as a result of individualism, disorder and impiety in its ministerial functioning. In Clarke's words there was "great dissension and strife taking place among churchmen, each man deserting the teaching of our Lord Jesus Christ and arbitrarily claiming the right or arguments and definitions of his own, wishing to rule over against the Lord rather than to be ruled by him".⁵² In spite of the turmoils affecting the church (and possibly to counteract them), from the fourth century onwards monasteries were appearing in different parts of the Christian world. There were many of them and, although often initially remote and hidden, they quickly became known and popular.

Upon the completion of his expedition with Eustathius, Basil returned to his native province of Caesarea where, according to Gregory of Nazianzus, he was received "as a second founder and guardian of the city" (ὥς τινα δεύτερον οἰκιστήν τε καὶ πολιοῦχον).⁵³ The enthusiasm for monasticism that Basil experienced during his brief pilgrimage to hermitages was momentarily replaced by his prospect of a teaching chair in rhetoric. Much to the delight of his late father, Basil senior, whose legacy he seemed to be pursuing, Basil was now heading in an entirely different direction, that of academia and specifically pagan academia, a career which according to Rousseau was considered to be "at the highest levels of the Eastern empire".⁵⁴ Similarly Radde-Gallwitz explains it as a path that was destined to lead Basil "to eminence and honour in society" given that Basil was establishing himself as a distinguished professor and quite possibly as a candidate for imperial administration.⁵⁵ Through holding a "chair in rhetoric", Basil's responsibil-

---

51 Anna Silvas is correct in describing this aspect of Basil's relationship with Eustathius as being one in which Basil "was calculatedly initiated into disturbing currents in the life of the church at large". Silvas, *The Asketikon of St. Basil the Great*, 71.
52 Clarke, *St. Basil the Great*, 78.
53 Gregory of Nazianus, *Oration* 43.25. SC 384. 182.
54 Rousseau, *Basil of Caesarea*, 61.
55 Radde-Gallwitz, *Basil of Caesarea*, 23.

ities included propagating pagan literature and learning all within the standard of the classical literature of the time, a considerable amount of which, according to Cameron, was either directly or indirectly concerned with pagan gods and mythology.[56] However, within two years the dreams of Basil senior were cut short as Basil's older sister, Macrina (324-379), intervened and successfully dissuaded him from what was fast becoming a brilliant secular career. "She took him in hand" (Λαβοῦσα τοίνυν αὐτὸν) narrates Gregory of Nyssa "and drew him with such speed towards the goal of philosophy" (τάχει κἀκεῖνον πρὸς τὸν τῆς φιλοσοφίας σκοπὸν ἐπεσπάσατο).[57] Macrina saw that what Basil preserved and safeguarded in Athens in terms of his Christian faith, he risked losing through the flattery and glory of his chair in

---

56 Cameron, *The Later Roman Empire AD 284-430*, 153.
57 Gregory of Nyssa, *Life of Macrina*, 8.3: Silvas, *Macrina the Younger*, 117. SC 178. 162. Macrina's powerful influence on her brother has led to her being labelled with the title of true founder of what is sometimes called "Basilian" monasticism. Highlighting this is Saint Gregory of Nyssa's account of how his brother's conversion took place: Ὠικονομήσατο, ἐπάνεισιν ἐν τούτῳ τῶν παιδευτηρίων πολλῷ χρόνῳ προασκηθεὶς τοῖς λόγοις ὁ πολὺς Βασίλειος ὁ ἀδελφὸς τῆς προειρημένης. Λαβοῦσα τοίνυν αὐτὸν ὑπερφυῶς ἐπηρμένον τῷ περὶ τοὺς λόγους φρονήματι καὶ πάντα περιφρονοῦντα τὰ ἀξιώματα καὶ ὑπὲρ τοὺς ἐν τῇ δυναστείᾳ λαμπροὺς ἐπηρμένον τῷ ὄγκῳ, τοσούτῳ τάχει κἀκεῖνον πρὸς τὸν τῆς φιλοσοφίας σκοπὸν ἐπεσπάσατο, ὥστε ἀποστάντα τῆς κοσμικῆς περιφανείας καὶ ὑπεριδόντα τοῦ διὰ τῶν λόγων θαυμάζεσθαι πρὸς τὸν ἐργατικὸν τοῦτον καὶ αὐτόχειρα βίον αὐτομολῆσαι, διὰ τῆς τελείας ἀκτημοσύνης ἀνεμπόδιστον ἑαυτῷ τὸν εἰς ἀρετὴν βίον παρασκευάζοντα. Gregory of Nyssa, *Life of Macrina*, 6: SC 178. 160-162. "The eminent Basil, brother of whom we speak, returned from the schools where he had been undergoing long training in eloquence. He was at the time excessively puffed up with the thought of his own eloquence and was disdainful of local dignities, since in his own inflated opinion he surpassed all the leading luminaries. She, however, took him in hand and drew him with such speed towards the goal of philosophy that he withdrew from the worldly show and despised the applause to be gained through eloquence, and went over of his own accord to the life where one toils even with one's own hands, thus providing for himself through perfect renunciation a life that would lead without impediment to virtue". Gregory of Nyssa, *Life of Macrina*, 8.1-4: Silvas, *Macrina the Younger*, 117. Silvas makes the point that what Macrina was proposing for Basil was not anything new or requiring an essential conversion as inferred in Gregory of Nyssa's writings, but rather a "recalling [...] to the piety of their childhood upbringing and to the intention he had formed even in Athens to seek a life of 'philosophy'." Silvas, *The Asketikon of St. Basil the Great*, 70. See Sterk, *Renouncing the World Yet Leading the Church*, 36.

Caesarea. Gregory of Nyssa had similar views to Macrina about his brother and depicts Basil as "excessively puffed up with the thought of his own eloquence and disdainful of local dignities" (ὑπερφυῶς ἐπηρμένον τῷ περὶ τοὺς λόγους φρονήματι καὶ πάντα περιφρονοῦντα τὰ ἀξιώματα), considering himself better than "all the leading luminaries" (λαμπροὺς ἐπηρμένον τῷ ὄγκῳ).[58] Perhaps Macrina perceived in Basil a complacent catechumen who seemed just too comfortable (spiritually unchallenged/uncultivated) by floating around in the environs of an advanced secular curriculum. The concept of the Christian aristocrat and professional man did have a place in society, including the world-view of the church, but one senses that for Macrina, her mother Emelia and late brother Naucratius, this was considered second place to a life of monasticism and ascetic discipline. In the end it was Basil's own resolve to "shun those who praised and admired"[59] him, to be baptised and to dedicate his life to God. As will be shown below, the fact that Basil left behind the world of pagan learning and what he considered as all its temptations of conceit, did not necessarily mean that Basil forgot what he had learned. Through his education and its acquaintances, Basil was being prepared for the challenging career that awaited him. His transition from an Athenian scholar to a Christian ascetic actively involved in church ministry was not straightforward but something that evolved in an unpredictable way.

1.4 Basil Embraces Monasticism

By the summer of 358 Basil resolved to embrace a life of asceticism. The two years he had spent travelling with Eustathius of Sebasteia visiting the monasteries of the East had given him firsthand expe-

---

58 Gregory of Nyssa, *Life of Macrina*, 8.1–3: Silvas, *Macrina the* Younger, 117.
59 *Ep.* 210.2: Deferrari, III, 199. Τοὺς ἐπαινοῦντάς [...] και θαυμάζοντας ἀποφεύγων. Courtonne, II, 191.

rience of what a life of asceticism entailed.⁶⁰ After an initial refusal, joining Basil in his pursuit for monastic life was his study partner from Athens and long-time friend Gregory of Nazianzus.⁶¹ Before long, Basil saw his family estate at Annisa⁶² near the river Iris in

60 See *Ep.* 223.2: Καὶ δὴ πολλοὺς μὲν εὗρον κατὰ τὴν Ἀλεξάνδρειαν, πολλοὺς δὲ κατὰ τὴν λοιπὴν Αἴγυπτον καὶ ἐπὶ τῆς Παλαιστίνης ἑτέρους και τῆς κοίλης Συρίας καὶ τῆς Μεσοποταμίας· ὧν ἐθαύμαζον δὲ τὸ καρτερικὸν ἐν πόνοις, ἐξεπλάγην τὴν ἐν προσευχαῖς εὐτονίαν ὅπως τε ὕπνου κατεκράτουν ὑπ᾽ οὐδεμιᾶς φυσικῆς ἀνάγκης κατακαμπτόμενοι, ὑψηλὸν ἀεὶ καὶ ἀδούλωτον τῆς ψυχῆς τὸ φρόνημα διασώζοντες ἐν λιμῷ καὶ δίψει, ἐν ψύχει καὶ γυμνότητι, μὴ ἐπιστρεφόμενοι πρὸς τὸ σῶμα, μηδὲ καταδεχόμενοι αὐτῷ προσαναλῶσαί τινα φροντίδα, ἀλλ᾽ ὡς ἐν ἀλλοτρίᾳ τῇ σαρκὶ διάγοντες ἔργῳ ἐν οὐρανῷ. Ἐκεῖνα θαυμάσας καὶ μακαρίσας τῶν ἀνδρῶν τὴν ζωήν, ὅτι ἔργῳ δεικνύουσι τὴν νέκρωσιν τοῦ Ἰησοῦ ἐν τῷ σώματι περιφέροντες, ηὐχόμην καὶ αὐτός, καθόσον ἐμοὶ ἐφικτόν, ζηλωτὴς εἶναι τῶν ἀνδρῶν ἐκείνων. Courtonne, III, 10-11. "Indeed I found many men in Alexandria, and many throughout the rest of Egypt, and others in Palestine, and in Coele-Syria and Mesopotamia, at whose continence in living I marvelled, and I marvelled at their steadfastness in sufferings, I was amazed at their vigour in prayers, at how they gained the mastery over sleep, being bowed down by no necessity of nature, ever preserving exalted and unshackled the purpose of their soul, in hunger and thirst, in cold and nakedness, not concerning themselves with the body, nor deigning to waste a thought upon it, but as if passing their lives in alien flesh, they showed in deed what it is to sojourn here below, and what to have citizenship in heaven. Having marvelled at all this and deemed the lives of these men blessed, because by deed they show that they bear about in their body the mortification of Jesus, I prayed that I myself also, in so far as was attainable by me, might be an emulator of these men". Deferrari, III, 293-295.
61 Basil wrote *Epp.* 14 and 2 (in that order) from Annisa as a culmination of his efforts to get Gregory to join him. At Annisa they both studied the works of Origen. See Behr, *The Nicene Faith*, 263.
62 Basil's *Ep.* 14.2 written to Gregory of Nazianzus gives a description of the physical environment of Annisa which resembles more a pleasant country abode than the forbidding wilderness of the desert familiar to Egyptian monasticism. Annisa was considered to be located one day's journey west of Neocaesarea in Pontus. Silvas notes that Annisa "is located 8 km west of the junction of the Iris and the Lycus. This means that Annisa had ready access to Neocaesarea since it lay on the Via Pontica, the major artery of communication across northern Anatolia. This road forded the Iris just north of its junction with the Lycus, at or near by the city of Magnopolis... The Via Pontica went past the front gate of the villa, if not through the estate". Silvas, *The Asketikon of St. Basil the Great*, 43-45. A useful summary about the location of Annisa is also found in Rousseau, *Basil of Caesarea*, 62, n. 7: "Annisa is now Sonusa or Ulukoy, near the confluence of the Yesil Irmak (the Iris) and the Kelkit Cayi (the Lycus); and that the Ibora is now the Iveronu. While Basil's own ascetic retreat (vividly described in *Ep.* 14) was clearly situated in a steep, wooded valley, of which many run down in this district towards the coast, Annisa was close also to fertile plateau country to the south, attractive and profitable to any aspiring landowner".

Pontus, gradually transform into a monastic community. Basil's sister Macrina began this transformation and, after persuading her mother Emelia, they both formalised their existing decision to lead an ascetic life. Macrina together with Emelia subsequently established a monastic community for men and women that advocated for a Christian ascetic life.[63] Peter Brown comments: "From her retreat in Pontus, ten days' journey from Caesarea, Macrina presided over the disintegration of a civic dynasty".[64] Macrina was highly regarded as a model ascetic who attracted numerous followers, and she had a continued influence on the ascetic principles of her brother. The spiritual refurbishment of Annisa began in the 350s but was not completed until some ten years later, implying that what started as a slow change gained momentum as time progressed. At all times Basil considered God to be the dispenser of these affairs: "For surely he administers our affairs better than we should if the choice were ours".[65] At Annisa, men and women lived in separate sections and only came together for prayer just as they did in the monastic communities that Basil visited during his travels. Cooper and Decker provide a useful summary of what life was like at Annisa.

> Men and women worshipped in the same church but took meals and worked separately; women remained on one side of the river and men on the other, and strangers would lodge with their respective sex. Men and women each had their own leader: Lampadion was in charge of the women and Peter, the younger brother of Basil and Macrina, headed the male group, while Macrina oversaw all. Some features that later became firmly entrenched in cenobitic monasticism were practised at Annisa: the singing of psalms, recitation of Scripture, extension of hospi-

---

63 See Basil, *Epp.* 204.6, 210.1, 223.3.
64 Brown, *The Body and Society*, 278.
65 *Ep.* 1: Deferrari, I, 7. Ἄμεινον γάρ που πάντως ἢ ὡς ἂν ἡμεῖς προϊδοίμεθα διοικεῖ τὰ ἡμέτερα. Courtonne, I, 5.

tality, ministry to the needy, and productive work were the core of the ascetic ideal there.[66]

Anna Silvas describes Basil's spiritual influence over Annisa as follows:

> A threefold remedy crystallised in Basil's mind: obedience to the Lord and his teachings, a passionate commitment to the church and its apostolic tradition, and the necessity of each Christian's engagement in the moral and spiritual endeavour required by baptism; in brief: Scripture, church, and piety, not one sustainable without the other.[67]

Without a doubt Basil came to see this "threefold remedy" as the best way of life, a conviction which he solidly defended:

> What then is more blessed than to imitate on earth the anthems of angels' choirs; to hasten to prayer at the very break of day, and to worship our Creator with hymns and songs; then, when the sun shines brightly and we turn to our tasks, prayer attending us wherever we go, to season our labours with sacred song as food and salt? For that state of soul in which there is joy and no sorrow is a boon bestowed by the consolation of hymns.[68]

In his description of his monastic community at Annisa, Basil was proud to say:

> We boast of having a body of men and women whose conversation is in heaven, who have crucified their flesh with its affections and desires, who do not concern themselves

---

[66] Cooper and Decker, *Life and Society in Byzantine Cappadocia*, 109–110. See Gregory of Nyssa, *Life of Macrina*, 6; Silvas, *The Asketikon of St. Basil the Great*, 20–21.
[67] Silvas, *The Asketikon of St. Basil the Great*, 91.
[68] *Ep.* 2.2: Deferrari, I, 13. Τί οὖν μακαριώτερον τοῦ τὴν ἀγγέλων χορείαν ἐν γῇ μιμεῖσθαι· εὐθὺς μὲν ἀρχομένης ἡμέρας εἰς εὐχὰς ὁρμῶντα ὕμνοις καὶ ᾠδαῖς γεραίρειν τὸν κτίσαντα, εἶτα ἡλίου καθαρῶς λάμψαντος ἐπ᾽ ἔργα τρεπόμενον, πανταχοῦ αὐτῷ τῆς εὐχῆς συμπαρούσης, καὶ τῶν ὕμνων ὥσπερ ἅλατι παρατύειν τὰς ἐργασίας; Τὸ γὰρ ἱλαρὸν καὶ ἄλυπον τῆς ψυχῆς κατάστημα αἱ τῶν ὕμνων παρηγορίαι χαρίζονται. Courtonne, I, 7–8.

with food and clothing, but, being undistracted and in constant attendance upon the Lord, remain night and day in prayer. Their mouths do not proclaim the works of men, but they sing hymns to our God unceasingly, while they work with their hands that they may have something to share with those who have need.[69]

As with the monastic assembly under Macrina's spiritual oversight at Annisa, so also in Basil's later established monastic communities, did men, women and children come together as separate houses into one community for prayer, worship and the practice of Christian ethics.[70] Basil's *Ep.* 173 is addressed to the canoness Theodora who lived in a religious community that was composed of both men and women. Basil's letters present ascetics as a distinct group within the Christian community, separate from that of the clergy and laity, although with not "necessarily a high degree of organisation".[71] Basil favoured the cenobitic form of life above that of the eremitical, which was even less structured and mostly exercised by the advanced and experienced.

A key feature of Basil's institutionalised monasticism, as exemplified throughout his *Rules (Asketikon)*,[72] was its engagement with

---

69 *Ep.* 207.2: Deferrari, III, 185-187. Ἡμεῖς εὐχόμεθα καὶ ἀνδρῶν καὶ γυναικῶν συντάγματα ἔχειν, ὧν τὸ πολίτευμά ἐστιν ἐν οὐρανοῖς, τῶν τὴν σάρκα σταυρωσάντων σὺν τοῖς παθήμασι καὶ τοῖς ἐπιθυμίαις, οἳ οὐ μεριμνῶσι περὶ βρωμάτων καὶ ἐνδυμάτων, ἀλλ᾽ ἀπερίσπαστοι ὄντες καὶ εὐπάρεδροι τῷ Κυρίῳ νυκτὸς καὶ ἡμέρας προσμένουσι ταῖς δεήσεσιν. Ὦν τὸ στόμα οὐ λαλεῖ τὰ ἔργα τῶν ἀνθρώπων, ἀλλὰ ψάλλουσιν ὕμνους τῷ Θεῷ ἡμῶν διηνεκῶς, ἐργαζόμενοι ταῖς ἑαυτῶν χερσίν, ἵνα ἔχωσι μεταδιδόναι τοῖς χρείαν ἔχουσι. Courtonne, II, 185-186. Other references to "the order of virgins" (τὸ τάγμα τῶν παρθένων) and "the order of monks" (τῷ τάγματι τῶν μοναζόντων) are in *Ep.* 199.18, 19: Deferrari, III, 106-107, 110-111. Courtonne, II, 155, 157.
70 Silvas, *The Asketikon of St. Basil the Great*, 322-333.
71 Rousseau, *Basil of Caesarea*, 198. See for example *Epp.* 52, 116, 117, 199.18, 200, 284.
72 In principle this work is more of a general question-and-answer format betraying a gradual development of monasticism and not a dissertation that contains rules for a confined group of enthusiasts. See Radde-Gallwitz, *Basil of Caesarea*, 35-40; Silvas, *The Asketikon of St. Basil the Great*, 28-30, 102-29, 187; Rousseau, *Basil of Caesarea*, 191-196, 216-217, 354-359; Fedwick, *The Church and the Charisma of Leadership*, 17-18, 161-165.

the local community. When someone strayed and fell into sin, for example, their reconciliation was not only directed towards God but also towards the community. Living amongst others, Basil argued, was necessary so as to practise charity, remain humble and avoid complacency. He believed that the correction and discipline of others ensured that one was not blind to one's own faults and so led to a progress in prayer and repentance. Under Basil's oversight, ascetic retreats were not only regarded as centres of common worship but were also places of ministry, with monks and nuns leading the way in religious service, social morality and the distribution of alms. Here they fulfilled an inherent need to act, especially on behalf of others. Basil's *Longer Rules*, in particular, advocates for cenobitic monasticism while being critical of the eremitic forms of monasticism. In Question Three of his *Rules* he observes that "the human being is a tame and communal animal, and is neither solitary nor savage", and that "nothing is so proper to our nature as to share our lives with each other, and to need each other, and to love our own kind".[73] In Basil's view, the spiritual benefits arising from community life were more easily accessible: "the presence of others" in this sense "was a necessary condition for the exercise of virtue".[74]

Basil retreated to the solitude of Pontus where he busily engaged himself in the organisation of ascetical communities, "giving them a structure and ethos that remained normative for Eastern monasticism ever since".[75] Consequently, it has been said that within such a setting Basil became the "founder of cenobitic monasticism"[76] and by extension "the father of canonical cenobitic monasticism in the universal church".[77] In Basil's understanding,

---

73 Saint Basil the Great: *On the Human Condition*, Harrison, 117. Ἥμερον καὶ κοινωνικὸν ζῶον ὁ ἄνθρωπος, καὶ οὐχὶ μοναστικόν, οὐδὲ ἄγριον. Οὐδὲν γὰρ οὕτως ἴδιον τῆς φύσεως ἡμῶν, ὡς τὸ κοινωνεῖν ἀλλήλοις, καὶ χρῄζειν ἀλλήλων, καὶ ἀγαπᾶν τὸ ὁμόφυλον. PG 31. 917A.
74 Rousseau, *Basil of Caesarea*, 207.
75 Behr, *The Nicene Faith*, 266. See Rousseau, *Basil of Caesarea*, 354-359.
76 Phan, *Grace and the Human Condition*, 153.
77 Silvas, "The emergence of Basil's social doctrine: a chronological enquiry", 133.

the corporate way of Christian life (κοινὸς βίος – common life) had definitely prevailed over the individual way[78] and was modelled on the apostolic community of Jerusalem, since this was considered to be in accordance with Christ's polity (τῆς ὁδοῦ τῆς κατὰ Χριστὸν πολιτείας).[79] In a letter to the monks under his care in Pontus, Basil exhorts them to: "accept the community life in imitation of the apostolic manner of living".[80] Basil's concern was that Christian enthusiasts who were independent, living in isolation and only answerable to themselves, were susceptible to error and therefore were to be discouraged. He readily admits: "We are easily victims to preferment and cannot easily lay aside some degree of pride in ourselves. In guard against these things I think that I have need also of a great and experienced teacher".[81] For this reason Basil wants his monks living communally and under an attested spiritual guide, "for great is our desire both to see you brought together (συνηγμένους), and to hear concerning you that you do not favour the life that lacks witnesses, but rather that you all consent to be both guardians of each other's diligence and witnesses of each other's success".[82] Basil never tired of emphasising that Christian life in its fullness demanded the ability to be in communion with God and one's neighbours.

---

78 See Basil, *Homily on the Words: Be Attentive to Yourself*. Πρόσελθε τῇ συγκλήτῳ τῶν μοναχῶν. (Join yourself to the gathering of the monks.) PG 31. 205A.
79 *Ep*. 150.1: Deferrari, II, 361. Courtonne, II, 71. See Fedwick, *The Church and the Charisma of Leadership*, 14, 20, 22, 24.
80 *Ep*. 295: Deferrari, IV, 207. Τὴν ἐπὶ τὸ αὐτὸ καταδέξασθαι εἰς μίμημα τῆς ἀποστολικῆς πολιτείας. Courtonne, III, 169–170.
81 *Ep*. 150.1: Deferrari, II, 363. Ἡττήμεθα δὲ καὶ τιμῆς καὶ τὸ ἐφ᾽ ἑαυτοῖς τι φρονεῖν οὐ ῥᾳδίως ἀποτιθέμεθα. Πρὸς ταῦτα μεγάλου μοι δεῖν καὶ ἐμπείρου λογίζομαι διδασκάλου. Courtonne, II, 72.
82 *Ep*. 295: Deferrari, IV, 209. Πολλὴ γὰρ ἡ ἐπιθυμία καὶ ἰδεῖν ὑμᾶς συνηγμένους καὶ ἀκοῦσαι περὶ ὑμῶν ὅτι οὐχὶ τὸν ἀμάρτυρον ἀγαπᾶτε βίον, ἀλλὰ μᾶλλον καταδέχεσθε πάντες καὶ φύλακες τῆς ἀλλήλων ἀκριβείας εἶναι καὶ μάρτυρες τῶν κατορθουμένων. Courtonne, III, 170.

1.5 Basil's Domestic Monasticism

Although the monastics' well-ordered way of life and communal living distinguished them from their fellow Christians and society at large, Basil considered the ascetic ideal to be applicable to all Christians and not just the prerogative of the monks. After all, "there is only one way leading to the Lord, and all who travel toward him are companions of one another and travel according to one agreement as to life (κατὰ μίαν συνθήκην τοῦ βίου πορεύεσθαι)".[83] It was part and parcel of the Christians' "heavenly vocation" (ἐπουρανίου κλήσεως) which behoved them "to conduct" (πολιτεύεσθαι) themselves "worthily of the Gospel of Christ (ἀξίως τοῦ Εὐαγγελίου τοῦ Χριστοῦ)".[84] Likewise Basil believed that "he who approaches God ought to embrace poverty in all things [...] He should not be desirous of money, nor treasure up unnecessary things to no avail".[85] All the baptised were urged by Basil to dedicate their possessions for the edification of the church, so that, through the local bishop, that which was necessary could be distributed to the poor and needy. In imitation of Christ and illuminated by the Holy Spirit, all Christians were called to show obedience to the commandments of God. The instructions that Basil gave to Gregory of Nazianzus in *Ep.* 2, to encourage him towards monastic life, generally sound no different to what one would hear preached in a congregation.[86]

83 *Ep.* 150.2: Deferrari, II, 365. Μίαν εἶναι ὁδὸν τὴν πρὸς τὸν Κύριον ἄγουσαν, καὶ πάντες τοὺς πρὸς αὐτὸν πορευομένους συνοδεύειν ἀλλήλοις, καὶ κατὰ μίαν συνθήκην τοῦ βίου πορεύεσθαι. Courtonne, II, 73.
84 *Ep.* 22.1: Deferrari, I, 131. Courtonne, I, 52–53.
85 *Ep.* 22.3: Deferrari, I, 141. Ὅτι δεῖ τὸν προσερχόμενον Θεῷ ἀκτημοσύνῃ ἀσπάζεσθαι κατὰ πάντα [...] Ὅτι οὐ δεῖ φιλάργυρον εἶναι οὐδὲ θησαυρίζειν εἰς ἀνωφελῆ ἃ μὴ δεῖ. Courtonne, I, 57.
86 See Basil, *Homily on Humility*, 3, 7: Τοῦτο ὕψος ἀνθρώπου, τοῦτο δόξα καὶ μεγαλειότης, ἀληθῶς γνῶναι τὸ μέγα, καὶ τούτῳ προσφύεσθαι, καὶ δόξαν τὴν παρὰ τοῦ Κυρίου τῆς δόξης ἐπιζητεῖν [...] Τοῖς γὰρ ἐπιτηδεύμασιν ὁμοιοῦται ψυχή, καὶ πρὸς ἃ πράττει, τυποῦται, καὶ πρὸς ταῦτα σχηματίζεται. PG 31. 529C, 537B. "This is what truly exalts a person; this is what truly confers glory and majesty: to know in truth what is great and to cling to it, and to seek the glory which comes from the Lord of glory. [...] For the soul grows like what it pursues, and is molded and shaped according to what it does". Saint Basil the Great: *On Christian Doctrine and Practice*, Delcogliano, 112, 117.

Basil's advice to Gregory on prayer, the reading of Scripture and simplicity of life, is equally applicable to those in monastic life as it is to those in family life. From the cenobitic life associated with Basilian monasticism, arose a "domestic ascetic movement" or "family asceticism", which was simply regarded by Basil as Christian life "derived from the divinely inspired Scriptures" (ὡς ἔμαθον ἐξ αὐτῆς τῆς θεοπνεύστου Γραφῆς)[87] and, as Fedwick argues, "marked by the best humanism of the time".[88]

The pursuit of a life of Christian piety was intended to be the norm for all Christians and not merely for the isolated elite. Basil writes:

> From among us the people (ὁ λαός) rise early at night to go to the house of prayer, and in labour and affliction and continuous tears confessing God, finally rise from their prayers and enter upon the singing of psalms [...] All in common (πάντες κοινῇ) [...] each one forming his own expressions of repentance.[89]

It was Basil's conviction that an ascetic lifestyle was applicable to all Christians in all *sectors* of society, and that any necessary withdrawal from the "world" was more spiritual than physical.[90] In this sense, for Basil, there was no sharp distinction in principle between "monastic" and "ordinary" Christianity, since both appealed to an ethical commitment and not merely an institutional one. To Basil and his peers, asceticism was simply viewed as an authentic form of Christianity, what Radde-Gallwitz describes as "the logical outcome of baptism".[91] The household asceticism practised in

---

87   *Ep.* 22.1: Deferrari, I, 129. Courtonne, I, 52.
88   Fedwick, *The Church and the Charisma of Leadership*, xvii.
89   *Ep.* 207.3: Deferrari, III, 187–189. Ἐκ νυκτὸς γὰρ ὀρθρίζει παρ' ἡμῖν ὁ λαὸς ἐπὶ τὸν οἶκον τῆς προσευχῆς, καὶ ἐν πόνῳ καὶ ἐν θλίψει καὶ συνοχῇ δακρύων ἐξομολογούμενοι τῷ Θεῷ, τελευταῖον ἐξαναστάντες τῶν προσευχῶν εἰς ψαλμῳδίαν καθίστανται [...] Πάντες κοινῇ [...] ἴδια ἑαυτῶν ἕκαστος τὰ ῥήματα τῆς μετανοίας ποιούμενοι. Courtonne, II, 186.
90   See *Epp.* 2.2, 18, 116, 117, 232.2, 299.
91   Radde-Gallwitz, *Basil of Caesarea*, 38.

Basil's own family was popular in Asia Minor and Syria, and Basil wanted other families to live by the same rule of life. From such families were to come the most refined possessors of the Christian faith: the martyrs and confessors. In his appeal to the presbyters of Nicopolis, Basil indicates that this witness of family piety was indeed realistic and furthermore widespread: "You are children of confessors, and children of martyrs, who strove unto blood against sin. Let each of you employ his own kindred (οἰκείοις) as examples for constancy in behalf of the true faith".[92]

In response to coercively non-Nicene imperial policies, the Christian family household was called upon to take an explicitly spiritual orientation where obedience to the scriptural word informed the practice of daily life. Basil's *Ep.* 363 to Apollinarius of Laodicea gives the reader an indication of the fervour in which Basil embraced the Scriptures, especially in times of anguish and confusion for the church: "And now the love of the knowledge of those divine sayings lays hold of my soul more than ever".[93]

---

92 *Ep.* 240.2: Deferrari, III, 423–425. Τέκνα ὁμολογητῶν καὶ τέκνα μαρτύρων ἐστὲ τῶν μέχρις αἵματος ἀντικαταστάντων πρὸς τὴν ἁμαρτίαν. Τοῖς οἰκείοις ἕκαστος χρησάσθω ὑποδείγμασι πρὸς τὴν ὑπὲρ τῆς εὐσεβείας ἔνστασιν. Courtonne, III, 63. Every year on the 7th of September Basil honoured the memory of St. Eupsychius, a married layman who was martyred in Caesarea during Julian's reign for participating in the destruction of a pagan temple dedicated to the goddess Fortuna. See Sozomen, *Church History* 5.11; Rousseau, Basil of Caesarea, 182, n. 220. Today this same feast day is celebrated in both the East and the West on the 9th of April, whereas the 7th of September is dedicated to an older Eupsychius, also from Caesarea, who was martyred during the reign of Emperor Hadrian (c. 117–138). Basil, as will be shown in Chapter Six, used the feast day of the newer St. Eupsychius as the occasion to hold his annual synod at Caesarea and thereby strengthen, inspire and encourage his clergy through having them participate in the liturgical celebrations honouring the memory of St. Eupsychius. See also *Epp.* 100, 142, 176, 252, 282.

93 *Ep.* 363: Deferrari, IV, 343–345. Καὶ νῦν δὴ πλέον ὁ ἔρως τῆς γνώσεως θείων λογίων ἅπτεται τῆς ψυχῆς μου. Courtonne, III, 224. *Epp.* 361–364 have been questioned as to their authenticity of being included in the corpus of Basil's letters and therefore have been the subject of much discussion. Both the theology and ideas expressed in these letters are consistent with all other Basilian writings. George L. Prestige makes strong arguments to show that there is no reason to doubt the authenticity of these letters. See Prestige, *St. Basil the Great and Apollinaris of Laodicea*.

Rousseau attests that for Basil:

> The appeal to Scripture was characteristic. It provided the only context within which the question at hand could acquire any urgency. One could not prompt religious sentiment, or safeguard religious values, simply by scoring logical points.[94]

To his correspondent, the young bishop Amphilochius of Iconium, Basil counsels: "read the Scriptures carefully and there you will find the solution of your question".[95] Perhaps Basil was exhorting Amphilochius to attend to a more focused reading of the specific passage of Scripture that he had inquired Basil about. The Benedictine scholar, Jean Gribomont, remarks on the importance of Basil's own attentiveness to the Scriptures and its application to all members within the church, but above all, to the ascetics and the bishops. Referring to Basil, he notes that the "saint devoted years to coming to know the scriptural standard in all its details, with the words of Jesus as the norm". With Basil's solid grounding in the Scriptures, Gribomont concludes that that he employed the precepts of the Gospels selectively and with the precision necessary to guide his listeners: "Before speaking, his enlightened gaze has picked out whichever Gospel precepts are applicable and to which he must lead his hearers".[96]

Prayer, fasting and manual work, as inspired by Scripture, became the order of the day for those under Basil's pastoral duty of care. Here it was not only certain members of the family (typically women) living an ascetical life but rather all family members pursued a commitment to living a Christian life of piety. Devout families attended to philanthropy, not merely as a social or civil responsibility, but rather in imitation of Christ. The reading of

---

94 Rousseau, *Basil of Caesarea*, 107.
95 *Ep.* 188.16: Deferrari, III, 47. Πρόσεχε οὖν ἀκριβῶς τῇ Γραφῇ καὶ αὐτόθεν εὑρήσεις τὴν λύσιν τοῦ ζητήματος. Courtonne, II, 131.
96 Gribomont, "Christ and the Primitive Monastic Ideal", 109.

Scriptures and temperance in life-style, became a cathartic process that allowed families to see more clearly their relationship with God and their responsibility before people.[97] In this vein, the New Testament with the rest of the Scriptures (Old Testament) became the basis of faith and moral guidance that Basil exhorted for all Christians.

> A most important path to the discovery of duty is also the study of the divinely-inspired Scriptures. For in them are not only found the precepts of conduct, but also the lives of saintly men, recorded and handed down to us, lie before us like living images of God's government (οἷον εἰκόνες τινὲς ἔμψυχοι τῆς κατὰ Θεὸν πολιτείας) for our imitation of their good works. And so in whatever respect each one perceives himself deficient, if he devote himself to such imitation, he will discover there, as in the shop of a public physician, the specific remedy for his infirmity. [...] And in general, just as painters in working from models constantly gaze at the exemplar and thus strive to transfer the expression of the original to their artistry, so too he who is anxious to make himself perfect in all the kinds of virtue must gaze upon the lives of the saints as upon statues, so to speak, that move and act, and must make their excellence his own by imitation.[98]

---

97 For an informative account of the domestic ascetic movement occupying fourth century Christianity in the East and West see Silvas, *The Asketikon of St. Basil the Great*, 75–83.

98 *Ep.* 2.3: Deferrari, I, 15-17. Μεγίστη δέ ὁδὸς πρὸς τὴν τοῦ καθήκοντος εὕρεσιν ἡ μελέτη τῶν θεοπνεύστων Γραφῶν. Ἐν ταύταις γὰρ καὶ αἱ τῶν πράξεων ὑποθῆκαι εὑρίσκονται, καὶ οἱ βίοι τῶν μακαρίων ἀνδρῶν ἀνάγραπτοι παραδεδομένοι, οἷον εἰκόνες τινὲς ἔμψυχοι τῆς κατὰ Θεὸν πολιτείας, τῷ μιμήματι τῶν ἀγαθῶν ἔργων πρόκεινται. Καὶ τοίνυν περὶ ὅπερ ἂν ἕκαστος ἐνδεῶς ἔχοντας ἑαυτοῦ αἰσθάνηται, ἐκείνῳ προσδιατρίβων, οἷον ἀπό τινος κοινοῦ ἰατρείου, τὸ πρόσφορον εὑρίσκει τῷ ἀρρωστήματι φάρμακον [...] Καὶ πανταχοῦ, ὥσπερ οἱ ζωγράφοι, ὅταν ἀπὸ εἰκόνα γράφουσι, πυκνὰ πρὸς τὸ ἑαυτῶν σπουδάζουσι μεταθεῖναι φιλοτέχνημα, οὕτω δεῖ καὶ τὸν ἐσπουδακότα ἑαυτὸν πᾶσι τοῖς μέρεσι τῆς ἀρετῆς ἀπεργάσασθαι τέλειον, οἱονεὶ πρὸς ἀγάλματά τινα κινούμενα καὶ ἔμπρακτα, τοὺς βίους τῶν ἁγίων ἀποβλέπειν καὶ τὸ ἐκείνων ἀγαθὸν οἰκεῖον ποιεῖσθαι διὰ μιμήσεως. Courtonne, I, 8–9.

The ascetical movement of the fourth century sought to create a new kind of society faithful to the Gospel *kerygma* that anticipated as closely as possible the mode of existence expected at the second *parousia* of Christ. It became increasingly apparent that the Christian ascetic vision of human existence was central to Basil's theology. Its models were nothing short of the heavenly hosts of angels united in love, service to God and the glorification of God's name. It aspired to resemble the life of paradise before the fall, where humans lived as their creator intended.[99] In this state of being, deprivation was unheard of; instead all were immersed in plenitude through being filled with the glory of God. Like the first Christian community in Jerusalem,[100] Basil had in mind a sense of community where all the faithful participated in a common life of prayer and worship, and where all things were held for the common good.

> For thus each one will receive both the perfect reward given on his own account and that given on account of his brother's progress; which reward it is fitting that you should supply to one another by both word and deed and through constant intercourse and encouragement.[101]

True to Basil's purpose, ascetic life was lived out within the parameters of a well-ordered comprehensive community life. Private ownership was foreign within such an environment; if anything was to be owned it was one's personal sins.

Basil's understanding of the ascetic life did not lead him to withdrawal from ecclesiastical affairs but rather obliged him to use his talents for the benefit of the church as a whole. The solitude sought by Basil was more from secular life than from human company:

---

99 See Brown, "The Notion of Virginity in the Early Church", 427–433.
100 See Acts 2:44.
101 *Ep.* 295: Deferrari, IV, 209. Οὕτω γὰρ ἕκαστος καὶ τὸν ἐφ᾽ ἑαυτῷ μισθὸν τέλειον ἀπολήψεται καὶ τὸν ἐπὶ τῇ τοῦ ἀδελφοῦ προκοπῇ, ὃν καὶ λόγῳ καὶ ἔργῳ παρέχεσθαι ἡμᾶς ἀλλήλοις προσήκει ἐκ τῆς συνεχοῦς ὁμιλίας καὶ παρακλήσεως. Courtonne, III, 170.

There is but one escape from all this – separation from the world altogether. But withdrawal from the world does not mean bodily removal from it, but the severance of the soul from sympathy with the body [...] and it also means the readiness to receive into one's heart the impressions engendered there by divine instruction.[102]

Only by becoming strangers to the world and free from earthly attachments, Basil argued, could Christians acquire the kingdom of heaven.[103] Basil's aim was to search for a community, a brotherhood, within which to explore, develop, and defend fundamental elements of religious life. Moreover, as mentioned above, the ideals that Basil defended were suited to all Christians and not just limited to segregated communities of monastics. On account of this, Basil's ascetic life was combined not only with a growing sense towards a pastoral vocation, but also with a growing interest in the religious conflicts that lay at the heart of church affairs at that time. Feeling called towards a public role in the church, Basil wanted to create a renewal from the *inside* which would therefore remain longstanding. It may well have been that this is what was behind Basil eventually getting ordained.

1.6 Basil's Reception into the Ordained Ministry

Basil entered into the minor orders of the ordained ministry as a reader through the hands of Bishop Dianius of Caesarea in 356, shortly after his baptism. In the year of Dianius' death in 362, Basil was ordained a priest by Dianius' successor Eusebius, and initially accepted this role with "unhesitating commitment".[104] Parish

---

102 *Ep.* 2.2: Deferrari, I, 11. Τούτων δὲ φυγὴ μία, ὁ χωρισμὸς ἀπὸ τοῦ κόσμου παντός. Κόσμου δὲ ἀναχώρησις οὐ τὸ ἔξω αὐτοῦ γενέσθαι σωματικῶς, ἀλλὰ τῆς πρὸς τὸ σῶμα συμπαθείας τὴν ψυχὴν ἀπορρῆξαι [...] ἕτοιμον ὑποδέξασθαι τῇ καρδίᾳ τὰς ἐκ τῆς θείας διδασκαλίας ἐγγινομένας τυπώσεις. Courtonne, I, 6-7.
103 See *Epp.* 2, 45.
104 Rousseau, *Basil of Caesarea*, 151.

ministry in Caesarea, however, was short-lived, since within a few months of his ordination Basil was back at his Annisa ascetic retreat in Pontus.[105] Basil could not find the community life he so desired and cherished during the opening months of his priesthood in Caesarea, and the responsibilities of priesthood together with the essential discipline of asceticism seemed irreconcilable, to the point where Basil left it all and hastily made his way back to the comforts of his former environs. It was obvious that Basil and Eusebius could not get along, perhaps because Basil may have thought that he could be a better bishop than Eusebius or, that Eusebius found Basil's piety, advanced education and resulting popularity threatening. Indeed there is insufficient evidence to really know the precise reasons for the tensions between Basil and his bishop Eusebius.[106] In the end, it was upon the advice of his friend, Gregory of Nazianzus, that Basil withdrew to his fatherland of Pontus where he remained poised as its itinerant ascetic leader.[107]

Until the time of his episcopal election, Basil sought constant refuge in his monastic retreat at Annisa, from where he masterminded the teaching and reform needed to foster the growth and development of monastic communities within both the regions of Pontus and abroad (Cappadocia). It is true to say that Basil was also "clearly at work defining the kind of church over which he would eventually preside".[108] Once Basil entered the episcopacy eight years later, the demands placed on him as the bishop of Caesarea made it difficult for him to stay away from his diocese for prolonged periods of time. His vigilance towards the spiritual needs of his own diocese, coupled with the preservation of Nicene

---

105 See Gregory of Nazianzus, *Oration* 43.29. Rousseau explains Basil's move back to Pontus occurred as a result of "an argument" he had "with the new bishop of Caesarea, Eusebius". Rousseau, *Basil of Caesarea*, 67.
106 See Radde-Gallwitz, *Basil of Caesarea*, 64.
107 See Gregory of Nazianzus, *Epp.* 8, 19.
108 Rousseau, *Basil of Caesarea*, 232.

faith against the influence of non-Nicene persuasions, brought him into the very midst of public affairs and responsibilities. In short, he sensed that the world needed him.

With Julian's (361–363) accession to the imperial throne for twenty months after the death of Constantius in November 361, and Julian's commitment to bring about a revival of paganism, the Christian church was looking at ways of adopting a different kind of structure and governance that would make its wellbeing less dependent on the state.[109] In an effort to restore the appeal and significance of traditional religion, imperial policies were put in place that were designed to reverse the favours granted to Christians by Julian's predecessors, Constantine and Constantius. Such a move, argues Brown, was not so much a pagan "reaction" to Christianity as it was an expression of the changing sensibility of paganism itself in view of a rising Christian church.[110] Nevertheless, under Julian, Christian clergy no longer had tax exemptions or were the beneficiaries of land holdings and grain distributions, but rather were required to fulfil their fiscal and civil obligations to their cities.[111] Sozomen's *Ecclesiastical History* makes reference to Julian confiscating all "the possessions and money belonging to the churches of Caesarea and its countryside"[112] as well as conscripting clergy into the army. One of Julian's most publicised measures saw him forbid Christians from serving as rhetoricians and teachers within the cities of the empire, a measure that

---

109 Fedwick makes mention of a "project of church reform on the pattern of the pre-Constantinian model or, better yet, of the apostolic community of Jerusalem". Fedwick, *The Church and the Charisma of Leadership*, 14.
110 Brown, *Society and the Holy in Later Antiquity*, 94–98. Julian's relief for the poor was modelled on Christian activities, he also organised pagan clergy along the same administrative framework as their Christian counterparts. See Brown, *Poverty and Leadership in the Later Roman Empire*, 1–3. For Basilian references to paganism in the Cappadocian countryside during Julian's reign see Trombley, *Hellenic Religion and Christianisation c. 370–529*.
111 Mitchell, *A History of the Later Roman Empire*, 245 –246, 269. See Fedwick, *The Church and the Charisma of Leadership*, 13.
112 Sozomen, *Church History* 5.4.4. Πάντα δὲ τὰ κτήματα καὶ τὰ χρήματα τῶν ἐν Καισαρείᾳ καὶ ὑπὸ τοὺς αὐτῆς ὅρους ἐκκλησιῶν. SC 495. 108.

Cameron describes as curbing the potential conversion of pagan students to Christianity by their Christian teachers.[113]

The attempt to replace the Christianity that began with the imperial mission of Constantine with the old divine order was also strategic to Julian's military advances and successes into the territories of the Persian Empire. Julian's untimely death[114] at thirty two years of age in 363, and his replacement by Jovian, had no effect on changing the new prevailing attitude of the state towards the church. At the forefront of the church's aim for self-reliance was the strengthening of its internal unity as expressed through the consensus and collegiality of its bishops (τὴν πίστιν συμφωνίας,[115] τῆς πίστεως κοινωνίᾳ,[116] ὁμοδόξους κοινωνίαν καὶ ἕνωσιν).[117] Basil's ordination to the episcopacy rested on his hope to bring about collegiality amongst his brother bishops in the East through their acceptance of a Nicene faith (ἐκ τῆς κατὰ τὴν πίστιν κοινωνίας),[118] which he regarded as foundational to fulfilling the church's mission for communion.

1.6.1 Basil's Ordination to the Episcopacy

After completing *Against Eunomius*, and upon the death of Eusebius of Caesarea, Basil was elevated to the rank of a bishop in 370,[119] and he was to remain the uninterrupted bishop of the see

---

113 Cameron, *The Later Roman Empire*, 94.
114 According to Mitchell, "Julian paid with his life when he recklessly plunged into a minor rear-guard engagement without putting on his body armour". Mitchell, *A History of the Later Roman Empire*, 55. Admittedly Julian embarked on one of the most determined incursions of a Roman army into Persian territory. See Brown, *Society and the Holy in Later Antiquity*, 83–102.
115 *Ep.* 191: Courtonne, II, 144.
116 *Ep.* 154: Courtonne, II, 78.
117 *Ep.* 82: Courtonne, I, 185.
118 *Ep.* 133: Courtonne, II, 47.
119 Gregory of Nazianzus' *Oration* 43.37 makes allusions to Basil making advances to procure his own election on the vacant episcopal throne of Caesarea. Caesarea in the early 370s was hardly a see that would entice one who had self-ambition. Basil's disinterest in an ecclesiastical career and his willingness to act for the edification of the church through enforcing the mandates of Nicaea make Gregory's references seem untenable. See Gregory of Nazianus, *Oration* 43, SC 384.

of Caesarea for the last nine years of his life. Establishing a reputation for himself as respected guide, humanitarian and sought-out teacher in Caesarea made Basil's episcopal elevation seem obvious, despite his struggling with increasingly poor health. All these factors, claims Finn, more or less created the environment for Basil to utilise "the mantle of episcopal authority at least a year before his election as bishop".[120] From the ministry of his priesthood years any unbiased observer could see that Basil was "the chief pastor of Caesarea"[121] and that he was esteemed as the most likely to bring about change in the interest of orthodoxy, and to bring about "the old order of things" (τῆς παλαιᾶς καταστάσεως) through a return to the "ancient glory of orthodoxy" (τὸ ἀρχαῖον καύχημα τῆς ὀρθοδοξίας).[122] Specifically, the catholic church's acceptance of the doctrinal tenets affirmed by the Council of Nicaea in 325 and subsequently elaborated and confirmed (posthumously for Basil) in the Council of Constantinople in 381. In a broader sense, any theological formulation that leant towards Nicaea was sufficient to be considered as Nicene/neo-Nicene and thus orthodox.

Basil's role as the defender and promulgator of the Nicene cause pitted him not only against the non-Nicenes and their imperial champion, Emperor Valens, but also against those Basil called the Pneumatomachi ("fighters of the Spirit") who denied the deity of the Holy Spirit.[123] The presence of schism and disorder certainly brought great discouragement to Basil, but never to the point where he was overcome by despair. Irrespective of his current circumstances, Basil was always on the lookout for the improvement and growth of his ministry. From his letters it is not difficult to see that Basil's ministry was founded on a real presence of hope and a confidence that change will come. His hope and confidence were placed in nothing else than the presence of God in the life of the church:

---

120 Finn, *Almsgiving in the Later Roman Empire*, 226.
121 Rousseau, *Basil of Caesarea*, 16.
122 *Ep.* 92.3: Deferrari, II, 141, 143. Courtonne, I, 201, 203.
123 Pneumatomachianism will be discussed to a greater extent in Chapter Two.

> When I behold evil faring well [...] I am filled with discouragement. But when contrariwise I consider the great hand of God, and that he knows how to restore those who are broken and to deal lovingly with the just, and to crush the haughty, and to take the powerful down from their seats, I change again and become more buoyant in my hopes.[124]

Under Basil's guidance, Cappadocia was spiritually united and in communion with the Christians of Egypt, Syria and the West through their common Nicene faith. Anyone who was seen as not upholding the Nicene faith was considered anathematised by the church.

> As for such who say, "there was a time when he [the Son] was not", and "before he was begotten he was not", or that "he came into existence from what was not", or who profess that the Son of God is of a different person or substance, or that he changes, or is variable, such as these the catholic and apostolic church anathematises.[125]

From his position as the bishop of Caesarea, Basil was able to get a clearer sense of the world around him and its problems. This allowed him to detect interests that were antagonistic towards his own, as well as to associate with different ecclesiastical sees and groups of supporters.

Already from the opening years of Basil's episcopacy one can get an insight as to how ardent he was to lead his diocese along Nicene lines. This was evident in 372 with the visitation of

---

124 *Ep.* 266: Deferrari, III, 477. Ὅταν ἴδω καὶ τὸ κακὸν εὐοδούμενον [...] ἀθυμίας πληροῦμαι. Ὅταν δὲ πάλιν τὴν μεγάλην χεῖρα τοῦ Θεοῦ ἐννοήσω καὶ ὅτι οἶδεν ἀνορθοῦν τοὺς κατερραγμένους καὶ ἀγαπᾶν δικαίους, συντρίβειν δὲ ὑπερηφάνους καὶ καθαιρεῖν ἀπὸ θρόνων δυνάστας, πάλιν μεταβαλὼν κουφότερος γίνομαι ταῖς ἐλπίσι. Courtonne, III, 84-85.
125 *Ep.* 125.2: Deferrari, II, 265-267. Τοὺς δὲ λέγοντας· ἦν ποτε ὅτε οὐκ ἦν καὶ πρὶν γεννηθῆναι οὐκ ἦν, καὶ ὅτι ἐξ οὐκ ὄντων ἐγένετο ἢ ἐξ ἑτέρας ὑποστάσεως ἢ οὐσίας φάσκοντας εἶναι ἢ τρεπτὸν ἢ ἀλλοιωτὸν τὸν Υἱὸν τοῦ Θεοῦ, τοὺς τοιούτους ἀναθεματίζει ἡ καθολικὴ καὶ ἀποστολικὴ Ἐκκλησία. Courtonne, II, 32-33.

Emperor Valens and his entourage to Cappadocia, where Basil was determined to celebrate Epiphany on January 6 with the congregation of Caesarea. As recorded in Gregory of Nazianzus' encomiastic eulogy for his esteemed friend Basil, not even the liturgical celebrations could stop an apparent duel from unfolding between Emperor Valens and Basil. It is said that Valens, with fear and trembling, would attempt to bring his gifts to the altar as he was surrounded by an onslaught of the boisterous chanting of psalms. Basil, the mastermind behind the choral offensive according to the appraisal of Gregory, did not shy away from demonstrating his superiority by remaining unperturbed like "a statue affixed to God and the altar" (ἐστηλωμένον, ἵν' οὕτως [...] Θεῷ καὶ τῷ βήματι).[126] With such recollections, explains Gregory, commenced the beginning of Basil's "war with worldly authorities" (κοσμικὸς πόλεμος)[127] over non-Nicenism.

1.7 Conclusion

During Basil's episcopacy, opposing imperial authority brought on severe consequences that in some cases led to much suffering and even death. This chapter has shown that Basil's life of religious conversion and monastic zeal was put to the test in an environment where theological controversy was fomented by ecclesiastical intrigues as witnessed through personal agendas. Challenges to Basil were mounted not simply by those diametrically opposed to him with non-Nicene persuasions, but also by some of his most

---

126 Gregory of Nazianzus, *Oration* 43.52. SC 384. 234.
127 Gregory of Nazianzus, *Oration* 43.58. SC 384. 248.

personal friends like Eustathius, as will be seen in Chapter Four,[128] and generally by those opposed to his style of ecclesiastical administration, his asceticism, and "his notion of what 'church' should mean".[129] Broken, damaged and repaired friendships which caused Basil "much sorrow" (πολλὴν λύπην)[130] served as a context for many parts of his dialogue with others. The seemingly unevenly yoked worlds of philosophical reflection, theological controversy, and pastoral responsibility needed each other if Basil was to successfully explore, develop, and defend fundamental principles of Christian life.

From the above, it has been shown that Basil's ecclesiastical career was spurred on by an imperially endorsed non-Nicene theological faith position which he perceived to be a serious threat to the communion of the church. Basil's privileged upbringing gave him access to an elite education in which he excelled in all subject matters. It was only natural for him, and therefore expected of him, to follow in his Father's academic footsteps, which for a short while Basil did when he occupied a teaching chair in rhetoric. Within two years, however, Basil's love for monasticism took over any ambitions he may have had for what was quickly promising to be a successful academic career. For Basil, monasticism had a place in all areas of society and not just in monasteries. He advocated

---

128 During Basil's earlier monastic years in Pontus at his family estate in Annisa (c. 356) Eustathius of Sebasteia was his mentor. Rousseau describes Eustathius as a bishop who wanted "to make the church as much a force for social change as for cultic enthusiasm, and who certainly wished to inject into Christian experience a degree of moral seriousness that would affect public life as well as personal development". Rousseau, *Basil of Caesarea*, 75. It was because of Eustathius' influence that Basil became further preoccupied with social morality. Basil valued his friendship with Eustathius and others so long as he sensed that the honour due to God had prior claim. His disenchantment with Eustathius was triggered by Eustathius' Trinitarian theology, and in particular his attitude to the Holy Spirit, whose divinity he seemed to oppose. In return Basil was accused by Eustathius of being an exponent of the Sabellian tradition. See Hildebrand, *The Trinitarian Theology*, 19–20.
129 Rousseau, *Basil of Caesarea*, 241.
130 *Ep.* 263.3: Deferrari, IV, 93. Courtonne, III, 123.

for a monasticism that was inclusive of all types of family households, and that was simply part and parcel of domestic life. A shared life with shared resources had the intended purpose of increasing communion with God through increasing communion with one another. Importantly, Basil's monastic outlook, and also his pro-Nicene faith position, were motivated by his allegiance to Scripture and tradition, and undoubtedly to his understanding of salvation. His ordination to the episcopacy placed him in the best position to share the Nicene faith position and the ideals of monasticism as effectively and as widely as possible.

Chapter Two:
Basil's Theology

After having looked at some of the key historical events and influences that shaped Basil's life, and subsequently determined his ecclesiastical career, the following chapter will trace the development of Basil's theology, its purpose, its expression in his theological works, and its distinct contribution. Basil's theology was a lived-out theology that was centred upon communion with God and proclaimed in doxological worship. This chapter commences by looking at the two pillars upon which Basil founded his theology, namely Scripture and tradition. Basil moved freely in a theological world where he sought to set forth theological concepts that he saw as expressions of transcendent truth. Moreover, Basil saw this transcendent truth as becoming a tangible reality that is applicable to life inasmuch as he was concerned with communicating God's activities in the world and not his ineffable essence. This chapter explores Basil's Trinitarian theology, with a particular emphasis on his proclamation of the divinity of the Holy Spirit. Arguably Basil advocated a relationship with God that is Trinitarian, that is communal, and that is expressed in its greatest possible way when it is proclaimed doxologically.

2.1 Scripture and Tradition

Basil, together with many other church personalities of his era, believed that right belief on the subject of God the Trinity had a direct impact on one's salvation. A correct judgment on the Trinitarian issue, for Basil, affected one's definition of what it is to be a human, as well as one's understanding of human destiny and of the moral path by which it was to be fulfilled. The basis of

Basil's theological teachings is founded upon the dual authority of Scripture and tradition (παράδοσις), especially when the latter had to do with the lives of holy men and women of the past. Specifically for Basil, Scripture is not juxtaposed to tradition, like equal measures of weight on a balanced scale, but rather Scripture is constitutive of tradition. On the other hand, as fundamental as Scripture is to tradition's existence, it is certainly not exhaustive of tradition. Tradition rather is the culmination of the written and the unwritten (ἄγραφα)[1] sources of witness, a heritage handed on from one person to another. Most important for Basil was the body of knowledge (tradition) that he regarded as belonging to the whole church.

Basil uses Greek *paideia* to explore biblical truth;[2] hence philosophy, ethics, grammar, rhetoric and all forms of Greek literature are eclectically employed to inform his exegesis of Scripture. Basil considered the classics as serving an organic role in a Christian's formation. It became obvious to him that there was "some affinity (οἰκειότης) between the two bodies of teachings",[3] namely between "the biblical message and the classical voice".[4] This combination of Greek learning (cultural formation) and biblical Christianity was successful because of Basil's discernment in appropriating Greek terms, and because he was able to "baptise" them, much like his predecessors, and give them a Christian theo-

---

1 See *Epp.* 70, 204. Ἄγραφα can also be a reference to un-scriptural writings as opposed to simply everything "unwritten". Herein lies evidence of oral traditions that were perhaps written down and not included in the written testimony of the Scriptures. Modes of worship were certainly central components of the unwritten tradition of the church. See Radde-Gallwitz, *Basil of Caesarea*, 118-119; Fedwick, *The Church and the Charisma of Leadership*, 73.
2 Hildebrand, *The Trinitarian Theology*, 12-14.
3 Ἔστι τις οἰκειότης πρὸς ἀλλήλους τοῖς λόγοις. *To Young Men* 3.1: Deferrari, IV, 385.
4 Rousseau, *Basil of Caesarea*, 59.

logical nuance.⁵ Basil's originality lay in his ability to present the biblical worldview by appropriating new terms from the philosophical language and categories of his time, terms that were "recycled within the fabric of a Christian building".⁶ He thus contextualised scriptural mandates in the pre-existing norms of Graeco-Roman society. In doing so, Basil Christianised existing moral language and "independently" drew "conclusions to what [...] [had] been taught" (παράδοσις).⁷ For Basil, it was not only possible but even necessary to combine Greek and Christian thought artfully in the expression of transcendent truth. Outside this transformation of culture within a Christian society, knowledge had no standing:

> Do you not see the teachings of the nations, this empty philosophy, how subtle and farfetched they are concerning the inventions of their teachings, both in the rational speculations and in the moral injunctions, and in certain natural sciences and the other so-called esoteric teachings? How all things have been scattered and rendered useless,

---

5   It is a known fact to any researcher of the early church that church Fathers before and after Basil were able to employ innovatively Greek terms and concepts in order to express accurately Christian doctrine. For antecedents to Basil see Young, "Classical genres in Christian guise; Christian genres in classical guise", 251–258. As a contrast to this, there are other Christian apologists, such as Tatian and Theophilus, who were rather scathing in their remarks as to the usefulness of Greek philosophy. Hermas, for example, produced a work entitled "Abuse of the Pagan Philosophers", clearly a statement indicative of his attitude towards pagan learning. See Padelford, "Essays on the Study and Use of Poetry by Plutarch and Basil the Great", 33–43.
6   Rousseau, *Basil of Caesarea*, 56.
7   *Ep.* 188: Deferrari, III, 7. Ὧν ἐδιδάχθημεν [...] ἐπιλογίσασθαι. Courtonne, II, 121. Rousseau concisely summarises what Basil was trying to achieve in his synthesising approach to the use of Scripture and tradition. "Basil wished, therefore, to control both the redevelopment of ancient material and the insights and responses that naturally followed upon the reading of such material. In one sense, Christians had to content themselves with the formulae they inherited. In another sense, they could bring experience to bear upon the texts. What they were not permitted to do was express them afresh in their own words – although, with caution and privacy, they could produce the occasional ad hoc statement of their own (which no one else was bound to regard as further παράδοσις)". Rousseau, *Basil of Caesarea*, 122.

and the truths of the Gospel alone now hold place in the world?[8]

Exegesis and homily became Basil's sphere of influence and served as his polemical artillery. In his vocabulary, Basil, while trying to combat controversy, was also interested in drawing clearer lines between orthodoxy and heresy. Even though Basil insisted that Christianity had its own rules for public declamation, this did not stop him from shaping his writings with traditional skills.[9] In this vein, the methodologies of pagan tradition are applied by Basil in a Christian context only when they have good to offer and are profitable for moral life. Classical rhetoric therefore, is used by Basil in Christian ways. In this context Finn explains that "Christian discourse" seeks "to incorporate and reinterpret its classical counterpart in pursuit of its own ends". The success of this requires a "confident reworking of classical culture in the service of the Gospel".[10] Consequently, far from discarding the pagan classics as without value, Basil maintained:

> We should, then, partake of pagan literature (λόγοι) exactly in the manner of bees: for they do not approach all the flowers equally, nor do they try to carry off the whole of those on which they land, but taking as much of them as is suitable for their work, they bid the rest goodbye; so we, if we are wise, receiving from them (i.e. pagan literature)

---

8 Basil, *Homily on Psalm 32*, 7: Saint Basil: *Exegetical Homilies*, Way, 240. Οὐχ ὁρᾷς τὰ τῶν ἐθνῶν δόγματα, τὴν ματαίαν ταύτην φιλοσοφίαν, ὅπως λεπτοὶ καὶ περιττοὶ περὶ τὰς εὑρήσεις τῶν δογμάτων εἰσὶν ἔν τε λογικοῖς θεωρήμασι καὶ ἠθικαῖς διατάξεσι, καὶ φυσιολογίαις τισὶ καὶ δόγμασιν ἄλλοις τοῖς ἐποπτικοῖς λεγομένοις; Πῶς διεσκέδασται πάντα, καὶ ἠχρείωται, μόνη δὲ ἐμπολιτεύεται νῦν τῷ κόσμῳ ἡ ἀλήθεια τοῦ Εὐαγγελίου; PG 31. 341A.

9 See Basil, *A Homily on the Martyr Gordius*, 2: Οὐκ οἶδεν οὖν ἐγκωμίων τὸν θεῖον διδασκαλεῖον. PG 31. 492B. "Teaching pertaining to God knows nothing of encomium". In some cases, in order to impress his more literary friends, Basil would make superficial reminiscences to classical writings. In *To Young Men* alone, quotations and reflections can be found from Homer, Hesiod, Theognis, Plato, Aristotle and Solon.

10 Finn, *Almsgiving in the Later Roman Empire*, 221, 238.

as much is suitable (οἰκεῖον) to us and related (συγγενές) to the truth, will go past the remainder."

The above simile, among other things, allowed for the mechanics of rhetorical method to be transformed and henceforth serve as a defence in orthodox apologetics. In the final analysis, however, it was Basil's attachment to the testimony of Scripture (γραφικῶν ἀποδείξεων)[12] that always asserted itself, especially since the goal of Basil's work was to explain biblical revelation. Rousseau notes, "Priority [by Basil] was to be given, therefore, to faith and Scripture; but once that priority was conceded, all other sources of knowledge could be harnessed".[13] The testimony of Scripture was considered by Basil to be a sufficient (and thus complete) moral authority for all Christians without distinction. Its binding authority was provided by the Holy Spirit which, through its illumination, made tangible the Gospel commandments. To a religious woman living on her own, Basil writes: "If you possess the consolation of the divine Scriptures, you will need neither us nor anyone else to help you see your duty, for sufficient (αὐτάρκη) is the counsel and guidance to what is expedient which you receive from the Holy Spirit".[14]

According to Rousseau, Basil's thoughts and expressions, prior

---

11 *To Young Men* 4.8. Translated by Lee, "Why Didn't St. Basil Write in New Testament Greek?" 15. Κατὰ πᾶσαν δὴ οὖν τῶν μελιττῶν τὴν εἰκόνα τῶν λόγων ἡμῖν μεθεκτέον· ἐκεῖναι τε γὰρ οὔτε ἅπασι τοῖς ἄνθεσι παραπλησίως ἐπέρχονται, οὔτε μὴν οἷς ἐπιπτῶσιν ὅλα φέρειν ἐπιχειροῦσιν, ἀλλ᾿ ὅσον αὐτῶν ἐπιτήδειον πρὸς τὴν ἐργασίαν λαβοῦσαι, τὸ λοιπὸν χαίρειν ἀφῆκαν· ἡμεῖς τε, ἢν σωφρονῶμεν, ὅσον οἰκεῖον ἡμῖν καὶ συγγενὲς τῇ ἀληθείᾳ παρ᾿ αὐτῶν κομισάμενοι, ὑπερβησόμεθα τὸ λειπόμενον. Wilson, *Saint Basil on the Value of Greek Literature*, 48. The full title of this famous work is: Πρὸς τοὺς νέους, ὅπως ἂν ἐξ Ἑλληνικῶν ὠφέλοιντο λόγων, "To young men, on how they might benefit from Greek literature".
12 See *Ep.* 243.4: Courtonne, III, 124.
13 Rousseau, *Basil of Caesarea*, 323.
14 *Ep.* 285: Deferrari, IV, 173. Ἔχουσα δὲ τὴν ἐκ τῶν θείων Γραφῶν παράκλησιν, οὔτε ἡμῶν ἄλλου τινὸς δεηθήσῃ πρὸς τὸ τὰ δέοντα συνορᾶν, αὐτάρκη τὴν ἐκ τοῦ Ἁγίου Πνεύματος ἔχουσα συμβουλίαν καὶ ὁδηγίαν πρὸς τὸ συμφέρον. Courtonne, III, 155.

to taking their final form, were first "modified by an older and deeper loyalty to the values and techniques of Scripture".[15] Basil considered Scripture essential to an understanding of God and as occupying a central place in the life of the church. As will be shown below, in his defence of the co-substantiality of the Holy Trinity, Basil made sure that he used a theological language that reflected his understanding of the biblical view of a distinction of each of the three divine persons (as *hypostases*) and at the same time their inseparable unity of essence. In his commentary on Scripture, Basil offers what Hildebrand calls a "spiritual"[16] interpretation (exegesis), which combines both allegorical and historical interpretations as the kerygmatic need arises. Admittedly, in discussing Basil's theology of the Scriptures, Hildebrand fails to bring out the balance between Basil's view of inspiration and his understanding of the finiteness of language. For Basil, human finite language will always fall short of the reality that it is trying to describe. He sees the conventional use of theological language as operating with word-signs/conceptualisations (κατ' ἐπίνοια)[17] and therefore never capturing the reality with absolute adequacy. In a detailed study on Basil's "Anti-Eunomian Theory of Names", DelCogliano points out that Basil employs conceptualisations so as to "name aspects of God from a human point of view". Thus Basil's conceptualisations, according to DelCogliano, seek to "describe God in relation to human beings".[18] In this way, Basil sees words as having the distinct (and therefore limited) purpose of expressing the *how* of God's existence and never the *what*. His ultimate aim consists in responding to the pastoral needs of the faithful which involves, amongst his other pastoral endeavours, presenting the truth of the

---

15 Rousseau, *Basil of Caesarea*, 93.
16 Hildebrand, *The Trinitarian Theology*, 129.
17 See *Against Eunomius*, 1.7. SC 299. 190; Radde-Gallwitz, *Basil of Caesarea*, 76; Behr, *The Nicene Faith*, 282–290.
18 Delcogliano, *Basil of Caesarea's Anti-Eunomian Theory of Names*, 171. Delcogliano's work surveys Basil's and Eunomius' respective epistemologies and their understanding of how names apply to God.

Gospel in a language that is both familiar and accessible to his listeners. From biblical texts, Basil not only identifies their moral precepts but also offers instruction on how these can be lived out with rigor and exactitude.

2.2 Basil's Theological Treatises: *Against Eunomius* and On the Holy Spirit

2.2.1 *Against Eunomius*

It is a startling indicator of the lack of material on Basil in Western scholarship, except for some recent treatments of his theology,[19] that it is only since 2011 that there is an English translation of *Against Eunomius*.[20] Basil wrote his first major theological work, *Against Eunomius*, or in full "Refutation of the Apologetic of the Impious Eunomius" (Ἀνατρεπτικὸς τοῦ ἀπολογητικοῦ τοῦ δυσσεβοῦς Εὐνομίου), in the early 360s as a response to Eunomius' *Apology*.[21] *Against Eunomius* was written from Basil's ascetic retreat in Annisa at the instigation of his spiritual mentor, Eustathius, and more than likely for Eustathius' own use.[22] Basil makes some attempt to understand Eunomius before refuting him through exposing Eunomius' defence as deficient. Immersed in Scripture, *Against Eunomius* aims to ascertain the principle of communion in the church while also addressing the parameters in which theological inquiry can be conducted in the life of the church. In his letter to the Athenian sophist Leontius, Basil modestly refers to

---

19 One may cite as examples: Fedwick, *Basil of Caesarea: Christian, Humanist, Ascetic*; Fedwick, *The Church and the Charisma of Leadership*; Rousseau, *Basil of Caesarea*; Behr, *The Nicene Faith*; Hildebrand, *The Trinitarian Theology*; Andrew Radde-Gallwitz, *Basil of Caesarea, Gregory of Nyssa and the Transformation of Divine Simplicity* (New York: Oxford University, 2009); and Radde-Gallwitz, *Basil of Caesarea*.
20 Basil of Caesarea, *Against Eunomius*, trans. Mark Delcogliano and Andrew Radde-Gallwitz, The Fathers of the Church (Washington, DC: Catholic University of America, 2011).
21 Radde-Gallwitz, *Basil of Caesarea*, 50.
22 See Rousseau, *Basil of Caesarea*, 102.

his three-volumed work as "scanty" (εὑρετικόν) and "child's play" (παιδιὰν χρή).²³ Clearly Basil was understating its effectiveness. Eunomius (d. c. 393)²⁴ was the disciple of the non-Nicene Aetius, who held the position that the Son was essentially "unlike" (ἀνόμοιος) the Father.²⁵ Eunomius claimed that the essence of the Father was "unbegotten" and therefore ontologically superior to the "begotten" essence of the Son. In January 360 there was a council held in Constantinople to address this issue and it was here that Eunomius delivered his *Apology*. Leaving his monastic retreat in Pontus, Basil, still just a reader of the church, attended with his bishop, Dianius. Together in attendance they observed at first hand the storms created by the theological controversies surrounding Christ and his relationship to God the Father. At the time Nicene support in the East was at an all-time low. The Council of Constantinople did little to dissuade the non-Nicene sympathisers, moreover, the council was considered as a victory for them. Eunomius was elevated to the bishopric where he acquired the historic metropolitan see of Cyzicus. Obedient to imperial decree, Dianius subscribed to the creed promulgated at the Council of Constantinople in 359. Basil, disappointed at Dianius' acceptance of the creed of Constantinople, and as an act of protest towards his revered bishop, returned to his ascetic

---

23 See *Ep.* 20: Deferrari, I, 125. Courtonne, I, 51.
24 For a concise biographical note on Eunomius' life see Behr, *The Nicene Faith*, 268-270. For a detailed account see Vaggione, *Eunomius of Cyzicus and the Nicene Revolution*.
25 See Arius who asserted: Ξένος τοῦ Υἱοῦ κατ 'οὐσίαν ὁ Πατὴρ, ὅτι ἄναρχος ὑπάρχει. Thalia, On the Councils of Ariminum and Seleucia, 15. PG 26. 708A. "The Father is other than the Son in essence [κατ' οὐσίαν] because he is without beginning". Ayres, Nicaea and its Legacy, 55. Aetius was the first to take up the teachings of Arius as legitimate, maintaining that the Son was unlike (ἀνόμοιος) the Father, see *Ep.* 223.5. From his Christological doctrinal persuasions his followers took on the name Anomoeans.

retreat.[26] Here it is fitting to quote St. Jerome who wrote of the period: "The whole world groaned and was astonished to find itself Arian" (*ingemuit totus orbis, et Arianum se esse miratus est*).[27] In due time Basil made a similar observation when he found himself forced to be "excommunicated from all the churches in the world" (πάσαις ταῖς κατὰ τὴν οἰκουμένην Ἐκκλησίαις [...] ἐκκηρύκτους ἡμᾶς ποιῆσαι).[28] Of course what Basil really meant was that "almost (πᾶσαν σχεδόν) the whole East [...] (by East I mean everything from Illyricum[29] to Egypt), is being shaken by a mighty storm and flood, since the heresy sown long ago by Arius".[30]

In the three books of *Against Eunomius*, Basil formulated a theological vision that became the foundation of his Trinitarian theology. Basil explains how the *one* God is related to his only begotten Son, Jesus Christ, and to the Holy Spirit, which in the Old Testament is seen as being the "breath" of God.[31] As his first major work on Trinitarian theology, *Against Eunomius* became the vehicle through which Basil educated himself firsthand with

---

26 In Basil's view Dianius naively accepted (as a result of imperial pressure) non-Nicene synodal decrees. His *Ep.* 51.2 makes it clear that Dianius in his simplicity essentially held Nicene sentiments. Even so, it was only at the final moments before Dianius' death that Basil returned to Caesarea to be reconciled with him. See Silvas, *The Asketikon of St. Basil the Great*, 96–97.
27 PL 23. 181C. Jerome, *The Dialogue Against the Luciferians* 19: Fremantle, NPNF, vol. 6, 329.
28 *Ep.* 226.2: Deferrari, III, 335. Courtonne, III, 26.
29 An Eastern prefecture of Diocletian and his successors, consisting today of parts of Albania and Croatia as well as Bosnia and Herzegovina.
30 *Ep.* 70: Deferrari, II, 40. Ἡ Ἀνατολὴ πᾶσαν σχεδόν [...] (λέγω δὲ Ἀνατολὴν τὰ ἀπὸ τοῦ Ἰλλυρικοῦ μέχρις Αἰγύπτου) μεγάλῳ χειμῶνι καὶ κλύδωνι κατασείεται, τῆς πάλαι μὲν σπαρείσης αἱρέσεως ὑπὸ τοῦ ἐχθροῦ τῆς ἀληθείας Ἀρείου. Courtonne, I, 165. See *Ep.* 92.2: Ἀπὸ τῶν ὅρων τοῦ Ἰλλυρικοῦ μέχρι Θηβαΐδος τὸ τῆς αἱρέσεως κακὸν ἐπινέμεται. Ἧς τὰ πονηρὰ σπέρματα πρότερον μὲν ὁ δυσώνυμος Ἄρειος κατεβάλετο· ῥιζωθέντα δὲ διὰ βάθους ὑπὸ πολλῶν τῶν ἐν μέσῳ φιλοπόνως τὴν ἀσέβειαν γεωργησάντων, νῦν τοὺς φθοροποιοὺς καρποὺς ἐξεβλάστησεν. Courtonne, I, 200. "The curse of this heresy is spreading out from the borders of Illyricum to the Thebaid; its baneful seeds were formerly scattered by the infamous Arius, and, taking deep root through the efforts of many who have cultivated them assiduously in the meantime, they have now produced their death-dealing fruits". Deferrari, II, 137.
31 See *Against Eunomius*, 2.20–22. SC 305. 80–92.

the intricacies of the "dogmatic disputes of his day"[32] and, in particular, those that had to do with the Father-Son relationship. In *Against Eunomius* Basil articulates a distinction between the common essence of the Father and the Son, and their distinct individuated properties (ἰδιότητες), which he also calls "distinguishing marks" (ἰδιώματα). By drawing on an analogy with human names like "Peter" and "Paul", Basil aims to show that although as humans they share a common essence, yet their proper names do not articulate this common essence. Instead these names communicate the individual's (Peter's or Paul's) distinctive features, which include elements of their individual unique character and not properties of their common human nature which is shared with other human beings.[33] When it comes to the Father and the Son, fatherhood and sonship for Basil simply constitute their "distinguishing marks".[34] The distinction is one at the level of cause (αἰτία) and point of origin (ἀρχή) and not at the level of essence. Basil insists: "The originator of things is one, he creates through the Son and he perfects through the Spirit".[35] One of the most extensive accounts of the distinction between οὐσία and ἰδιότητες is found in *Against Eunomius*: "This is the character of individuated properties, to reveal in the identity (ταυτότητι) of essence the otherness (ἑτερότητα)".[36] Otherness in the divine *hypostases*' distinctive features (ἰδιότητες), argues Basil, upholds the common essence and inseparable communion that exits between the Father and the Son (and the Holy Spirit), and therefore does not undermine or threaten their equality.

What alarmed Eunomius' opponents was his claim to know God as God knows himself, and the further claim that this knowl-

---

32 See Radde-Gallwitz, *Basil of Caesarea*, 66.
33 See *Against Eunomius*, 2.4. SC 305. 18–22.
34 See *Against Eunomius*, 2.28. SC 305. 120.
35 On the Holy Spirit, 16:38: Anderson, 62. Ἀρχὴ γὰρ τῶν ὄντων μία, δι᾽ Υἱοῦ δημιουργοῦσα, καὶ τελειοῦσα ἐν Πνεύματι. SC 17. 378.
36 *Against Eunomius*, 2.28. Αὕτη γὰρ τῶν ἰδιωμάτων ἡ φύσις, ἐν τῇ τῆς οὐσίας ταυτότητι δεικνύναι τὴν ἑτερότητα. SC 305. 120.

edge of God is revealed in Christ's teachings.³⁷ For Eunomius, true knowledge of God could not be discursive, but in order to be real needed to be immediate. Words for Eunomius, far from being unable to explain the incomprehensible, could in actual fact "provide a picture entirely faithful to reality".³⁸ Based on this logic Eunomius claimed that God the Father is "unbegotten essence" (αὐτὸς ἔστιν οὐσία ἀγέννητος)³⁹ who is communicated and revealed through this unbegotten essence. The problem that Basil found here is that knowledge of God is reduced "to one significance, the contemplation of the very substance of God" (ἐπὶ ἓν σημαινόμενον τὴν γνῶσιν ἕλκουσι, τὴν θεωρίαν αὐτῆς τοῦ Θεοῦ τῆς οὐσίας).⁴⁰ In one of his homilies Basil argued that "begotteness" and "unbegotteness" are distinct intelligible properties of divine personhood, and they lead respectively to the ideas of Father and Son.⁴¹ According to Basil, a "begetting worthy of God" is "without passion, without division, without separation and without time".⁴² Behr notes: "The Son's 'begetting', therefore, refers not so much to a discrete divine act as to the particular relationship in which the Son stands to the Father, one of derivation and identity of being".⁴³ By their uniqueness then, "begotteness" and "unbegotteness" make a distinction

---

37   Radde-Gallwitz, *Basil of Caesarea*, 52.
38   Rousseau, *Basil of Caesarea*, 109.
39   Vaggione, *Eunomius: The Extant Works*, 40–41. See SC 299. 194; Behr, *The Nicene Faith*, 271–276.
40   *Ep.* 235.3: Deferrari, III, 383–385. Courtonne, III, 46.
41   See Basil, *Homily Against Sabellians, Arius and Anomoians*, 4: Ὅταν δὲ εἴπω μίαν οὐσίαν, μὴ δύο ἐξ ἑνὸς μερισθέντα νόει, ἀλλ' ἐκ τῆς ἀρχῆς τοῦ Πατρὸς τὸν Υἱὸν ὑποστάντα, οὐ Πατέρα καὶ Υἱὸν ἐκ μιᾶς οὐσίας ὑπερκειμένης. Οὐ γὰρ ἀδελφὰ λέγομεν, ἀλλὰ Πατέρα καὶ Υἱὸν ὁμολογοῦμεν. PG 31. 605B. "But when I say 'one substance', do not think that two are separated off from one, but that the Son has come to subsist from the Father, his principle. The Father and Son do not come from one substance that transcends them both. For we do not call them brothers, but confess Father and Son". Saint Basil the Great: *On Christian Doctrine and Practice*, Delcogliano, 295.
42   *Against Eunomius*, 2.16. Νοεῖν μὲν ἀξίαν τοῦ Θεοῦ γέννησιν ἀπαθῆ, ἀμέριστον, ἀδιαίρετον, ἄχρονον. SC 305. 64.
43   Behr, *The Nicene Faith*, 309.

in that which is common but without disrupting the consubstantiality of the essence. For Basil, even though "it is the first concern of the mind to recognise our God" (προηγούμενόν ἐστι τῷ νῷ τὸν Θεὸν ἡμῶν ἐπιγινώσκειν),[44] God's essence will always transcend humanity's understanding; a person will never be able to know exactly and definitely what or who God is. Basil classifies knowledge of God's essence as "the perception of his incomprehensibility" (ἡ αἴσθησις αὐτοῦ τῆς ἀκαταληψίας).[45] In Basil's reasoning, all one can do is recognise God "in such a way as the infinitely great can be known by the very small" (οὕτως ὡς δυνατὸν γνωρίζεσθαι τὸν ἀπειρομεγέθη ὑπὸ τοῦ μικροτάτου),[46] since to know God in his essence would be equivalent to becoming God by nature. To overcome this impasse caused by the unknowable essence of God, Basil argues that God is known by his activities (ἐνεργειῶν), by means of one reflecting (κατ᾽ ἐπίνοια) on his presence in the world: "For it is by perceiving his wisdom and power and goodness and all his invisible qualities as shown in the creation of the universe that we come to a recognition of him".[47] Thus, according to Basil: "From his activities we know our God, but his substance itself we do not profess to approach. For his activities descend to us, but his substance remains inaccessible".[48] Fundamental to Basil is the premise that one can know God only from his revelation. This knowledge, he claims, is communicated through the prism of God's external activities in the world and not through his unapproachable and ineffable essence.

---

44 *Ep.* 233.2: Deferrari, III, 369. Courtonne, III, 40.
45 *Ep.* 234.2: Deferrari, III, 375. Courtonne, III, 43.
46 *Ep.* 233.2: Deferrari, III, 369. Courtonne, III, 40.
47 *Ep.* 235.1: Deferrari, III, 379. Σοφὸν γὰρ καὶ δυνατὸν καὶ ἀγαθὸν καὶ πάντα αὐτοῦ τὰ ἀόρατα ἀπὸ τῆς τοῦ κόσμου κτίσεως νοοῦντες ἐπιγινώσκομεν. Courtonne, III, 44.
48 *Ep.* 234.1: Deferrari, III, 373. Ἡμεῖς δὲ ἐκ μὲν τῶν ἐνεργειῶν γνωρίζειν λέγομεν τὸν Θεὸν ἡμῶν, τῇ δὲ οὐσίᾳ αὐτῇ προσεγγίζειν οὐχ ὑπισχνούμεθα. Αἱ μὲν γὰρ ἐνέργεια αὐτοῦ πρὸς ἡμᾶς καταβαίνουσιν, ἡ δὲ οὐσία αὐτοῦ μένει ἀπρόσιτος. Courtonne, III, 42. See *Against Eunomius*, 1.12.

2.2.2 On the Holy Spirit

Basil's treatise *On the Holy Spirit*, written approximately between 373 and 376, was spurred on by complaints that people made about the varieties which he introduced into the doxologies of liturgical worship. For Basil's opponents, confusion arose in that he sometimes ascribed glory to the Father *with* (μετά) the Son and *with* (σύν) the Holy Spirit,[49] and sometimes to the Father, *through* (διά) the Son and *in* (ἐν) the Holy Spirit. Specifically Basil defended his use of the formula "*with* (σύν) the Spirit". Here he advocated a theology of communion and defended the equal worship, glory and honour of the persons of the Trinity: "But *with* (σύν) is an especially useful word because it testifies to eternal communion and unceasing cooperation [...] *With* reveals the communion among the persons more explicitly".[50] In Basil's mindset, communion is a question of being united with the very person of God the Father, through the Son and in the Holy Spirit. As Zizioulas puts it, since God "exists" on account of a person, the person (*hypostasis*) of the Father, and not on account of his substance (essence), it follows that at a deeper level communion is a union *with* the personhood of God the Father, who is inseparably and coeternally united in freedom and love *with* the Son and *with* the Holy Spirit.[51]

It was from the use of prepositions that Pneumatomachians (Spirit-fighters) were accustomed to argue against the divinity of the Holy Spirit. They appealed to ancient philosophy, most notably Aristotelian, for an understanding of prepositions and relationships. According to Basil, what they failed to realise was that Scripture never adopted such rigidity in its use of prepositions. In their arguments the Pneumatomachians alleged that prepositions such as "by", "by means of", "through", "of", "according to" and "in" all indi-

---

49 See *On the Holy Spirit*, 1.3, 7.16, 25.58.
50 *On the Holy Spirit*, 25.59: Anderson, 91. Ἐξαίρετον ἔχει τῆς ἀϊδίου κοινωνίας καὶ ἀπαύστου συναφείας τὸ μαρτύριον [...] ἡ δὲ σὺν πρόθεσις τὴν κοινωνίαν πως συνενδείκνυται. SC 17. 460.
51 Zizioulas, *Communion and Otherness*, 121.

cate the creator, instrument or product of something. For example, a bench is made *by* a carpenter, *by means of/through* an axe, *according to* a particular style *for* a customer *in* their house. In their doxological glorification of the Holy Trinity, the Pneumatomachians preferred to use "in" the Spirit, because to them "in" implied space and therefore justified their reasoning that since the Holy Spirit is contained in space, it must be a creature.

Basil has no hesitation in admitting that he uses these prepositions but goes to great lengths to show that they do not necessarily imply such a restriction in meaning. In response to his opponents' attack on his doxologies as being unscriptural, Basil says that there are no laws governing the use of prepositions in the Bible, and no restriction of prepositions to the Father alone, to the Son alone, or to the Holy Spirit alone. Besides this, he argues it is appropriate to think of words as unscriptural not so much when they are not found literally in Scripture but rather when they contradict the meaning of Scripture.[52] For Basil, the preposition applied to any of the divine persons of the Trinity varies according to the relation of the divine persons towards the believer. Thus, he says that when the believer contemplates the dignity of the Son, he or she will ascribe him glory *with* the Father. When the believer reflects upon the blessings that he or she has received from the Son, the believer acknowledges that this grace is brought to him or herself *in* him and *through* him. In this context, all such prepositions for Basil describe not the essence of the divine persons but the economy of their operations.[53]

In many ways *On the Holy Spirit* is a treatise on prepositions since Basil spends much time defending his use of prepositions in doxological worship while highlighting the flexible use of prepositions in Scripture.[54] Basil reasoned that since Christ commissioned

---

52 Hildebrand, *The Trinitarian Theology*, 147. See Fedwick, *The Church and the Charisma of Leadership*, 84–85. See also n. 1.
53 Smith, *St. Basil and the Doctrine of the Holy Spirit*, 95–105.
54 Basil's work *On the Holy Spirit* has an A B A structure. Approximately the first and last thirds of his work are dedicated to prepositions. Beginning at Chapter Nine Basil's treatise *On the Holy Spirit* forms the centre (and thus the central) part of his work.

his apostles to make "disciples of all nations" by "baptising them in the name of the Father and of the Son and of the Holy Spirit",[55] it followed that worship should be professed in the same way: *lex orandi, lex credendi*. Basil believed that only when one was "right" about doctrine could one pay the proper homage to God. Belief and worship were so inextricably bound together for Basil that neither took precedence over the other:

> For, as we have received it from the Lord, so do we baptise; as we baptise, so do we believe; as we believe, so do we pronounce the doxology, neither separating the Holy Spirit from the Father and Son, nor placing him before the Father, nor saying that the Spirit is older than the Son.[56]

Similarly in his letter to a certain "Eupaterius and his daughter", Basil mentions:

> Since, then, baptism has been given to us by our Saviour in the name of the Father and of the Son and of the Holy Spirit, we offer the confession of our faith in accordance with our baptism, and in accordance with our faith we also recite the doxology, glorifying the Holy Spirit along with the Father and the Son, because we are convinced that he is not foreign to the divine nature.[57]

---

55 Matt. 28:19. Πορευθέντες οὖν μαθητεύσατε πάντα τὰ ἔθνη, βαπτίζοντες αὐτοὺς εἰς τὸ ὄνομα τοῦ Πατρὸς καὶ τοῦ Υἱοῦ καὶ τοῦ Ἁγίου Πνεύματος.
56 *Ep.* 251.4: Deferrari, IV, 17. Ὡς γὰρ παρελάβομεν ἀπὸ τοῦ Κυρίου, οὕτω βαπτιζόμεθα· οὕτω πιστεύομεν ὡς βαπτιζόμεθα· ὡς πιστεύομεν, οὕτω καὶ δοξολογοῦμεν· οὔτε χωρίζοντες Πατρὸς καὶ Υἱοῦ τὸ Ἅγιον Πνεῦμα, οὔτε προτεθέντες Πατρὸς ἢ πρεσβύτερον εἶναι τοῦ Υἱοῦ τὸ Πνεῦμα λέγοντες. Courtonne, III, 92. See *Ep.* 91. Ὥστε σύμφωνον τῷ σωτηρίῳ βαπτίσματι τὴν δοξολογίαν ἀποπληροῦσαι τῇ μακαρίᾳ Τριάδι. Courtonne, I, 198. "So that the doxology in harmony with saving baptism may be duly rendered to the blessed Trinity". Deferrari, II, 131; *On the Holy Spirit*, 12.28, 27.68.
57 *Ep.* 159.2: Deferrari, II, 395-397. Ἐπειδὴ οὖν βάπτισμα ἡμῖν δέδοται παρὰ τοῦ Σωτῆρος εἰς ὄνομα Πατρὸς καὶ Υἱοῦ καὶ Ἁγίου Πνεύματος, ἀκόλουθον τῷ βαπτίσματι τὴν ὁμολογίαν τῆς πίστεως παρεχόμεθα, ἀκόλουθον δὲ καὶ τὴν δοξολογίαν τῇ πίστει, συνδοξάζοντες Πατρὶ καὶ Υἱῷ τὸ Ἅγιον Πνεῦμα τῷ πεπεῖσθαι μὴ ἀλλότριον εἶναι τῆς θείας φύσεως. Courtonne, II, 86.

Furthermore elsewhere Basil states:

> He who puts the Holy Spirit before the Son, or declares him to be older than the Father, sets himself in opposition to God's commandment, and is a stranger to the sound faith, since he does not preserve the traditional form of the doxology, but invents for himself a new-fangled expression for the satisfaction of men.[58]

In his writings Basil makes the subtle point that it is only in doxological worship that a person can begin to approach and convey the mystery of the church's experience of God. As a vehicle for expressing theological truths, prayers that glorify God (doxology) will always supersede semantics. Where human words and expressions fall short when confronted with the transcendence of God, doxological praise, Basil suggests, can provide some understanding. What remains paramount for Basil is that the best way to confess theology is to do so with a doxological outlook.

Basil wrote *On the Holy Spirit* at a time of theological and ecclesiastical maturity in his life. This was a period when he had grown confident in what he wanted to say about God, as well as in being a bishop and in living a Christian life.[59] His ultimate aim was to bring doctrinal and ecclesiological peace and unity to Christians especially living in Western Asia Minor.[60] "To bring back into union (ἕνωσιν) the churches that have been severed from one another at sundry times and in diverse manners".[61] In this regard, *On the Holy*

---

58 *Ep.* 52.4: Deferrari, I, 335. Ὁ δὲ προτιθεὶς Υἱοῦ ἢ πρεσβύτερον λέγων Πατρός, οὗτος ἀνθίσταται μὲν τῇ τοῦ Θεοῦ διαταγῇ, ἀλλότριος δὲ τῆς ὑγιαινούσης πίστεως, μὴ ὂν παρέλαβε τρόπον δοξολογίας φυλάττων, ἀλλ ' ἑαυτῷ καινοφωνίαν εἰς ἀρέσκειαν ἀνθρώπων ἐπινοῶν. Courtonne, I, 136.
59 Philip Rousseau correctly reflects this when he writes: "[The writing of *On the Holy Spirit*] marked a moment of new assurance, of self-definition, of choice in Basil's life [...] Friendship had been lost or modified, opportunities rejected or forgotten. Challenges had been faced – not just those of the Arians but [...] by those opposed to his style of episcopacy, his asceticism, his notion of what 'church' should mean". Rousseau, *Basil of Caesarea*, 241.
60 Evidence of this concern is reflected in *Epp.* 113 and 114.
61 *Ep.* 114: Deferrari, II, 225. Τὸ ἐπαναγαγεῖν πρὸς ἕνωσιν τὰς Ἐκκλησίας τὰς πολυμερῶς καὶ πολυτρόπως ἀπ ' ἀλλήλων διατμηθείσας. Courtonne, II, 18.

Spirit was aimed at the Eunomians and the Macedonians. Like the Eunomians discussed above, the Macedonians denied the divinity of the Holy Spirit and saw it as subordinate to the Son.

In the opening lines of Chapter Ten of *On the Holy Spirit*, Basil sets the tone for which the rest of his narrative will follow. His proof of the deity of the Holy Spirit lies in the fact that all of the operations and relations which are peculiarly divine are ascribed to it. In *On the Holy Spirit* Basil clings to the theological vision he outlined in *Against Eunomius*. This is because in *Against Eunomius* Basil saw that arguments against his opponents were sufficiently rehearsed. There was little to do in *On the Holy Spirit* but repeat, albeit in more specific ways, positions already worked out. The theological arguments that Basil laid out in *Against Eunomius* become the coherent centre of his Trinitarian thought. Moreover Rousseau notes that "those ideas acquired greatest precision".[62] In *On the Holy Spirit* Basil extends the biblical image of the Father and Son used in *Against Eunomius* to include the Holy Spirit.

Basil addresses *On the Holy Spirit* to his disciple, bishop Amphilochius of Iconium. Amphilochius is worried about the turmoil plaguing his diocese of Iconium as a result of new teachings against the divinity of the Holy Spirit. The prevailing divisions are not unique to the diocese of Iconium but by this time are widespread within the Eastern empire. From the outset it is evident that Basil's letter to Amphilochius also served as an apology to his opponents who undermined the divinity of the Holy Spirit. Specifically Basil's purpose was to bring back to a pro-Nicene theology, in the easiest possible way, members of the faithful who had veered away from it. For Basil, "those who do not call the Holy Spirit a creature (κτίσμα)" may be "received in communion".[63] Actions of this nature were deemed necessary in that they aimed to, as Meredith states,

---

62 Rousseau, *Basil of Caesarea*, 116.
63 *Ep.* 113: Deferrari, II, 223. Τοὺς μὴ λέγοντας κτίσμα τὸ Πνεῦμα τὸ Ἅγιον δέχεσθαι εἰς κοινωνίαν. Courtonne, II, 17. See *Epp.* 113, 114, 140.

"preserve the fragile peace of the church".[64] This helps explain why nowhere in Basil's treatise does he say that "the Holy Spirit is God"[65] but rather leaves it to his readers and, in particular, to his opponents to draw this conclusion.[66] Consequently, throughout his writings, Basil preferred to ascribe the adjective "divine" (θεῖος) to the Spirit rather than to call the Holy Spirit God (Θεόν) explicitly.

Considered as "one of the classic treatments of the subject",[67] *On the Holy Spirit* presents the Holy Spirit as being of equal dignity with the Father and the Son. Previous correspondence with Amphilochius had always featured the topic of the Holy Spirit prominently, since Basil viewed the Holy Spirit as central to the ministry of priesthood. By nature of the sacrament of ordination, Basil considered the priest to be a vehicle of divine grace through his "union with the Spirit" (συνεργείᾳ τοῦ πνεύματος),[68] so that the priest had the ability to impart this grace to others and especially to those entrusted to his care. It took Basil approximately three years to complete his work which he wrote from the see of his diocese in Caesarea. In the young bishop Amphilochius, still in his thirties, Basil saw that the fulfilment of his own vision of ecclesiology could be realised.[69]

---

64 Meredith, *The Cappadocians*, 33. See *Ep.* 71.
65 See *On the Holy Spirit*, Anderson, 10.
66 The so-called "discretion of Saint Basil". Gregory of Nazianzus in his oration at Basil's funeral (see *Oration* 43.69) argued that Basil solemnly swore that his theology was that of the consubstantiality and co-honour of the Father, Son and Holy Spirit. See Gregory of Nazianzus, *Ep.* 58 (PG 37. 113C–116B).
67 Radde-Gallwitz, *Basil of Caesarea*, 80.
68 *Ep.* 227: Deferrari, III, 345. Courtonne, III, 30. Deferrari's Greek text incorrectly uses συνηθείᾳ instead of συνεργείᾳ.
69 Basil invited Amphilochius to scrutinise closely the message of God's word, πειρᾶσθαι τὸν ἐν ἑκάστῃ λέξει καὶ ἐν ἑκάστῃ συλλαβῇ κεκρυμμένον νοῦν ἐξιχνεύειν. *On the Holy Spirit* 1.2. SC 17. 252. "To search out the hidden meaning in this phrase or that syllable". Anderson, 16. For background information on Amphilochius see Rousseau, *Basil of Caesarea*, 258–263; Geerard, *Clavis Patrum Graecorum*. Volumen II, 230–242.

2.3 Basil's Theology of the Trinity: Three Hypostases, One Essence

To Basil, an orthodox "confession" (ὁμολογία) regarding the three persons "of the divine and saving Trinity" (τῆς θείας καὶ σωτηρίου Τριάδος)[70] was essential to being accepted into the communion of the church. Basil made it clear that without a correct confession of the Trinity, communion cannot be granted. Speaking on behalf of the church, Basil defended what he regarded as the church's immutable teaching on the Trinity. He admonished: "We [...] [do not] tolerate the separation and severance of any member from the divine and blessed Trinity, nor do we receive [into communion] those who are ready to reckon any member as a part of creation".[71]

The Trinitarian baptismal formula from Matthew's Gospel sanctioning baptism to be conducted "in the name of the Father and of the Son and of the Holy Spirit"[72] became for Basil an indispensable criterion for establishing communion within the church. Without these specific names of the Godhead being mentioned, baptism was considered void: "Those have not been baptised", declares Basil, are those "who have been baptised in the names which have not been handed down to us".[73] Basil makes this same point vividly in a letter to the educated people of Neocaesarea:

> You must not judge by this that only one name has been handed down to us. For just as one who says "Paul and Silvanus and Timothy", has said three names but joined them to each other by the syllable "and", so he who says the name of the Father and of the Son and of the Holy Spirit, though he has said three, he has joined them by the conjunction, showing that a distinct signification underlines

---

70 Ep. 90.2: Deferrari, II, 127. Courtonne, I, 196.
71 Ep. 159.2: Deferrari, II, 399. Οὔτε αὐτοὶ τῆς θείας καὶ μακαρίας Τριάδος χωρίσαι καὶ διατεμεῖν ἀνεχόμεθα, οὔτε τοὺς εὐκόλως τῇ κτίσει συναριθμοῦντας ἀποδεχόμεθα. Courtonne, II, 87.
72 Matt. 28:19. Εἰς τὸ ὄνομα τοῦ Πατρὸς καὶ τοῦ Υἱοῦ καὶ τοῦ Ἁγίου Πνεύματος.
73 Ep. 188.1: Deferrari, III, 15. Οὐ γὰρ ἐβαπτίσθησαν οἱ εἰς τὰ μὴ παραδεδομένα ἡμῖν βαπτισθέντες. Courtonne, II, 122.

each name, because names are significant of things. [...] For unless the mind becomes free from confusions as to the proper ties of each, it is impossible for it to render doxology to the Father and to the Son and to the Holy Spirit.[74]

Basil's Trinitarian theology was developed in response to challenges imposed by three schools of thought that undermined the tri-hypostatic divine nature of the Trinity. These schools of thoughts were known as Eunomianism, Sabellianism and Pneumatomachianism. Eunomius together with his followers, as noted above, were characterised as Anomeans and took an extreme form of Arianism that denied the divinity of the Son. Sabellius (d. c. 250) was thought of as refusing to accept in the Trinitarian God three distinct persons. Instead he was considered as maintaining that God was essentially an impersonal monad who at any given time took on one of three appearances: that of the Father, or the Son, or the Holy Spirit. The Pneumatomachians were united in their denial of the divinity of the Holy Spirit in that they claimed that the Spirit of God was simply another creature, similar to an angel, that was created to serve God. Following below is a more detailed analysis of, and Basil's response to, Eunomianism, Sabellianism and Pneumatomachianism.

2.3.1 Eunomianism

Eunomianism was seen as a renewed and more sophisticated argument that appealed to a non-Nicene faith position. By way of Aristotelian dialectic, the Eunomians asserted that the "begotten"

---

74 *Ep.* 210.4: Deferrari, III, 205-207. Οὐ παρὰ τοῦτο χρὴ νομίζειν ἓν ἡμῖν ὄνομα παραδεδόσθαι. Ὡς γὰρ ὁ εἰπὼν Παῦλος καὶ Σιλουανὸς καὶ Τιμόθεος τρία μὲν εἶπεν ὀνόματα, συνέδησε δὲ αὐτὰ ἀλλήλοις διὰ τῆς συλλαβῆς· οὕτως ὁ εἰπὼν «ὄνομα Πατρὸς καὶ Υἱοῦ καὶ Ἁγίου Πνεύματος», τρία εἰπὼν συνέπλεξεν αὐτὰ τῷ συνδέσμῳ ἑκάστῳ ὀνόματα ἴδιον ὑποβεβλῆσθαι τὸ σημαινόμενον ἐκδιδάσκων, διότι πραγμάτων ἐστὶ σημαντικὰ τὰ ὀνόματα [...] Ἀμήχανον γάρ, μὴ ἐν τοῖς ἑκάστου ἰδιώμασι τὴν διάνοιαν γενομένην ἀσύγχυτον, δυνηθῆναι Πατρὶ καὶ Υἱῷ καὶ Ἁγίῳ Πνεύματι τὴν δοξολογίαν ἀποπληρῶσαι. Courtonne, II, 193-194.

Son is totally *unlike* the "unbegotten" (ἀγέννητος) essence of the Father. If the Son is begotten as the Son of the Father, they argued, then he cannot be God from God. Along these lines the logical outcome is that the Son is derived from the deity as a begotten being and therefore as a creature of God the Father. The Eunomians concluded that since the Son is "begotten" as Nicaea affirms, he falls outside the being or essence of God who is "unbegotten".

Basil argued against the Eunomians by using the same Aristotelian categories that they employed in their arguments. He maintained that words would always be inferior to thoughts since they inadvertently created limits to human language that detracted from reality. Unbegotteness, according to Basil, is an aspect of the conception (ἐπίνοια) of God and not an absolute definition of his divine being.[75] In his own words, "'unbegotten' is indicative of what does not belong to God [...] Therefore, whoever holds that this term is indicative of the substance itself is a liar".[76] To refute Eunomianism, a sharp distinction needed to be made between essence and person in God. Basil achieved this through establishing a distinction between the natures and the individuated realities of the divine persons. This enabled him to assert that the Father and the Son are indeed the same in essence, but distinct at another level, thus preserving a certain order among the persons:

> For the divinity is one and we can clearly see the unity as being according to the principle of the essence. Which means that the differentiation lies in the number, and in

---

[75] See Radde-Gallwitz, *Basil of Caesarea, Gregory of Nyssa and the Transformation of Divine Simplicity*, 98–104; Hildebrand, *The Trinitarian Theology*, 41–45.

[76] *Against Eunomius*, 1.10: Delcogliano and Radde-Gallwitz, 106. Τό γε μὴν 'ἀγέννητον' τῶν μὴ προσόντων ἐστὶ σημαντικόν [...] ὥστε ψευδὴς ὁ τιθέμενος τῆς οὐσίας εἶναι τὴν φωνὴν ταύτην δηλωτικήν. SC 299. 206–208. In summary, Basil is simply saying: "The essence of God is unbegotten, but unbegotteness is not his essence". *Against Eunomius*, 1.11. Τὴν μὲν οὐσίαν τοῦ Θεοῦ ἀγέννητον εἶναι καὶ αὐτὸς ἂν φαίην· οὐ μὴν τὸ ἀγέννητον τὴν οὐσίαν. SC 299. 208. See *Against Eunomius*, 1.15.

the properties that characterise each one; while in the principle of divinity we see unity.[77]

In Basil's understanding, when God is called Father or "unbegotten", this is a reference to his personhood and not his essence (what God is).[78] Basil argues that "unbegotteness" concerns how God is, that is, by what means God has his existence. As unknown, nothing at all can be said about the essence of God which is known only by the Son and the Holy Spirit. All descriptions such as one, undivided, absolutely simple and uncompounded, point to God's total unknowability and not his essence.[79] According to Basil, all properties (ἰδιώματα) that speak about the *hypostases* of God refer to his personhood, thus unbegotteness is said for the Father, begotteness is said for the Son and procession is said for the Holy Spirit. Distinguishing the hypostatic properties are their incommunicable nature and their absolute uniqueness, whereas the one divine essence is communicated amongst the three divine persons of the Holy Trinity.

Although the hypostatic properties are not communicated, the notion of person is inconceivable outside a relation (σχέσις). Being is simultaneously relational and hypostatic. An ontology based on this conception of personhood sees the unity of the persons of the Trinity emerging from relationships and not from their one common essence. Logically and ontologically none of the three persons can be conceived without reference to the other two.

---

77 *Against Eunomius*, 1.19. Κατὰ τοῦτο γὰρ καὶ θεότης μία· δηλονότι κατὰ τὸν τῆς οὐσίας λόγον τῆς ἑνότητος νοουμένης, ὥστε ἀριθμῷ μὲν τὴν διαφορὰν ὑπάρχειν καὶ ταῖς ἰδιότησι ταῖς χαρακτηριζούσαις ἑκάτερον· ἐν δὲ τῷ λόγῳ τῆς θεότητος, τὴν ἑνότητα θεωρεῖσθαι. SC 299. 242.
78 Behr, *The Nicene Faith*, 129.
79 Hildebrand summarises accordingly the unknowability of the essence of God as follows: "God's *ousia* so far transcends the human mind that any human knowledge of it is necessarily fragmentary". For Hildebrand, knowledge of God will always be limited because of the transcendence of God's being. He states that Basil's "doctrine of concepts" is used not only in response to the limitations of the human mind, but also to highlight God's transcendence. Hildebrand, *The Trinitarian Theology*, 52.

The existence of God will always manifest itself as an event of inseparable communion where the "one" *hypostasis* of the Father eternally requires "the other two" in order to exist. The Father is the Father because he eternally begets the Son and eternally sends forth the Holy Spirit.[80] From Basil's image of the Holy Trinity, otherness is the *sine qua non* of unity. Each of the persons of the Holy Trinity is so unique and thus "other" that their hypostatic or personal properties are totally incommunicable from one person to the other. In Basil's understanding, the unbreakable communion that exists between the three "different" modes of existence (τρόπος ὑπάρξεως) within the Holy Trinity is not subject to division or confusion. For Basil, God is one and three simultaneously as opposed to being first one and then three. The *hypostasis* of the Father, Son and Holy Spirit is both particular and relational. Father, Son and Holy Spirit are all names indicating relationship. Hence no divine person can be different unless the divine person is related.

2.3.2 Sabellianism

It is Basil of Caesarea who develops the fundamental distinction between the persons (*hypostases*) and the essence (οὐσίαν) of the Triune God. As has just been seen above, he shows that the divine persons are entirely unique and thus distinct as to "who" they are,[81] yet absolutely identical in "what" they are, namely truly divine. Initially Basil was among the "*homoiousians*" (ὅμοιος κατ᾽ οὐσίαν) who saw themselves as upholding the basic sense of Nicaea. Admittedly any fourth century theologian could profess the Son to be "like the Father", including Arius, Eusebius of Caesarea, Athanasius, Apollinarius, Eustathius of Sebasteia,

---

80 Zizioulas, "The Doctrine of the Holy Trinity", 47-48.
81 See *Ep.* 210.5. Χρὴ ἕκαστον πρόσωπον ἐν ὑποστάσει ἀληθινῇ ὑπάρχον ὁμολογεῖν. Courtonne, II, 196. "It is necessary to confess that each Person subsists in a true hypostasis". Deferrari, III, 211. In his text translation, Deferrari translates ὑποστάσει as personality which is incorrect. For this reason Deferrari's translation has been adapted to show hypostasis instead. See *Ep.* 125.1.

and of course Basil himself. While all made this profession, they attributed to it very different meanings. For St. Athanasius, a staunch supporter of Nicaea in 325, and in line with classical Greek and Roman antiquity, *hypostasis* did not differ from *ousia* in that both terms were used interchangeably to indicate "being" or "existence".[82] Basil changed this by dissociating *hypostasis* from *ousia*, and instead identified *hypostasis* with the concept of *prosōpon* (person). He did this in order to avoid any leanings towards Sabellianism which saw the three persons of the Holy Trinity as simply three masks on the being of God.[83] As Basil put it: "If anyone says that the Father and Son and Holy Spirit are the same, and assumes one thing under many names, and one person expressed by three terms, such a one we class in the party of the Jews".[84] For Basil, a differentiation needed to occur between *hypostasis* and *ousia* so that it could serve as a protection against the teachings of Sabellius. Without this differentiation, Basil feared that "those who say that substance (οὐσίαν) and persons (ὑπόστασιν) are the same are forced to confess different persons (πρόσωπα) only, and in hesitating to speak of three persons (τρεῖς ὑποστάσεις) they find that they fail to avoid the evil of Sabellius".[85]

In the Sabellian view, Father, Son and Holy Spirit are three ways or modes in which humanity perceives God. Sabellianism denied the eternal distinction among the three persons of the Holy Trinity in order to avoid any perceived identification with

---

82 The Synod of Confessors in 362 held under the patronage of Athanasius went so far as to admit that there were different usages for the terms *ousia* and *hypostasis*.
83 Zizioulas, *The Doctrine of the Holy Trinity*, 47.
84 *Ep.* 226.4: Deferrari, III, 341. Εἴ τις τὸν αὐτὸν Πατέρα λέγει καὶ Υἱὸν καὶ Ἅγιον Πνεῦμα, καὶ ἓν πρᾶγμα πολυώνυμον ὑποτιθέμενος καὶ μίαν ὑπόστασιν ὑπὸ τριῶν προσηγοριῶν ἐκφωνουμένην, τὸν τοιοῦτον ἡμεῖς ἐν τῇ μερίδι τῶν Ἰουδαίων τάσσομεν. Courtonne, III, 28.
85 *Ep.* 236.6: Deferrari, III, 403. Οἱ δὲ ταὐτὸν λέγοντες οὐσίαν καὶ ὑπόστασιν ἀναγκάζονται πρόσωπα μόνον ὁμολογεῖν διάφορα, καὶ ἐν τῷ περιίστασθαι λέγειν τρεῖς ὑποστάσεις εὑρίσκονται μὴ φεύγοντες τὸ τοῦ Σαβελλίου κακόν. Courtonne, III, 54.

pagan polytheism. As such, its proponents claimed that Father, Son and Holy Spirit were not full persons in an ontological sense but "roles" assumed by the one God. Basil presents Sabellius as saying "the same God, though one in substance, is transformed on every occasion according to necessary circumstances, and is spoken now as Father, and now as Son, and now as Holy Spirit".[86] For Sabellius and his followers, the Scriptures portrayed these various roles of God according to the needs of the time. In the Old Testament, the abstract and impersonal divine being of God appeared as the Father; in the New Testament and up until Pentecost, God appeared as a Son; and after Pentecost, God's mode of being changed to that of the Holy Spirit.

At the time of Basil's letter-writing, fourth-century opponents of Marcellus of Ancyra accused him of adhering to the Sabellian conception of God and used "Sabellius" as a cipher for his views.[87] In a letter to Athanasius of Alexandria about Marcellus' rejection of the real existence of the incarnate God as the Son of God and the second person of the Trinity, Basil wrote:

> He [Marcellus] gives it as his opinion that the only begotten was called "the Word", that he made his appearance in time of need and in due season, but returned again whence he came, and that neither before his coming did he exist nor after his return does he still subsist.[88]

A confession of three *prosōpa* (persons) was not enough of a defence against Sabellianism. In his polemic against Sabellianism,

---

86   *Ep.* 210.5: Deferrari, III, 211. Τὸν αὐτὸν Θεόν, ἕνα τῷ ὑποκειμένῳ ὄντα πρὸς τὰς ἑκάστοτε παραπιπτούσας χρείας μεταμορφούμενον, νῦν μὲν ὡς Πατέρα, νῦν δὲ ὡς Υἱόν, νῦν δὲ ὡς Πνεῦμα Ἅγιον διαλέγεσθαι. Courtonne, II, 196. See *Ep.* 265.2.
87   For further reading on the teachings of Marcellus of Ancyra see Lienhard, *Contra Marcellum: Marcellus of Ancyra and Fourth Century Theology.*
88   *Ep.* 69.2: Deferrari, II, 45. Ὃς Λόγον μὲν εἰρῆσαι τὸν Μονογενῆ δίδωσι, κατὰ χρείαν καὶ ἐπὶ καιροῦ προελθόντα, πάλιν δὲ εἰς τὸν ὅθεν ἐξῆλθεν ἐπαναστρέψαντα, οὔτε πρὸς τῆς ἐξόδου εἶναι οὔτε μετὰ τὴν ἐπάνοδον ὑφεστάναι. Courtonne, I, 163.

Basil found it necessary to distinguish *hypostasis* and *ousia*. He aimed for an unconfused understanding of divine plurality and divine unity amongst the persons of the Trinity. This is why *hypostasis* came to designate what is three in God, and *ousia* what was common in God. Furthermore, in his letters Basil describes the relationship of *ousia* and *hypostasis* as being akin to that between the general (κοινόν) and the particular (ἴδιον).[89]

> Substance and person have the distinction that the general has with reference to the particular [...] For this reason we confess one substance for the Godhead, so as not to hand down variously the definition of its existence, but we confess a person that is particular, in order that our conception of Father and Son and Holy Spirit may be for us unconfused and plain. For unless we think of characteristics that are sharply defined in the case of each, as for example paternity and sonship and holiness, but from the general notion of being confess God, it is impossible to hand down a sound definition of faith. Therefore, we must add the particular to the general and thus confess the faith.[90]

In Basil's understanding, the particular was not secondary to the general in being or nature, but was equal and free in an absolute sense. The proper conception of the Father, Son and Holy Spirit occurs by "adding" the general with the particular. In this way the *ousia* is never alone in the sense of being without a *hypostasis* or being without a mode of existence (τρόπος ὑπάρξεως). Thus the

---

89 See Behr, *The Nicene Faith*, 297–298.
90 *Ep.* 236.6: Deferrari, III, 401–403. Οὐσία δὲ καὶ ὑπόστασις ταύτην ἔχει τὴν διαφορὰν ἣν ἔχει τὸ κοινὸν πρὸς τὸ καθ᾽ ἕκαστον [...] Διὰ τοῦτο οὐσίαν μὲν μίαν ἐπὶ τῆς θεότητος ὁμολογοῦμεν, ὥστε τὸν τοῦ εἶναι λόγον μὴ διαφόρως ἀποδιδόναι· ὑπόστασιν δὲ ἰδιάζουσαν, ἵν᾽ ἀσύγχυτος ἡμῖν καὶ τετρανωμένη ἡ περὶ Πατρὸς καὶ Υἱοῦ καὶ Ἁγίου Πνεύματος ἔννοια ἐνυπάρχῃ. Μὴ γὰρ νοούντων ἡμῶν τοὺς ἀφωρισμένους περὶ ἕκαστον χαρακτῆρας, οἷον πατρότητα καὶ υἱότητα καὶ ἁγιασμόν, ἀλλ᾽ ἐκ τῆς κοινῆς ἐννοίας τοῦ εἶναι ὁμολογούντων Θεόν, ἀμήχανον ὑγιῶς τὸν λόγον τῆς πίστεως ἀποδίδοσθαι. Χρὴ οὖν τῷ κοινῷ τὸ ἰδιάζον προστιθέντας, οὕτω τὴν πίστιν ὁμολογεῖν. Courtonne, III, 53. See *Ep.* 214.4.

Father is the divine *ousia* plus unbegotteness, the Son is divine *ousia* plus begotteness, and the Holy Spirit is divine *ousia* plus procession. Specifically Basil uses ὅμοιος κατ' οὐσίαν ἀπαραλλάκτως (like in essence without variation) to describe the relationship of the Father and the Son:

> I accept the phrase "like in substance", provided the qualification "invariably" (ἀπαραλλάκτως) is added to it, on the ground that it comes to the same thing as "identity of substance" (ταὐτὸν τῷ ὁμοουσίῳ), according, be it understood, to the sound conception of the term. It was with precisely this thought in mind that the Fathers of Nicaea consistently added "of the same substance" when they addressed the only begotten as "Light from Light", true God from true God", and so forth.[91]

According to Basil, the Father as mysteriously united to the Son, generates the being of the Son. It is the Son's eternal existence as generated that qualifies his mode of being as distinct from the Father's.[92] For Basil, ὅμοιος κατ' οὐσίαν ἀπαραλλάκτως came to be synonymous with ὁμοούσιος (of one essence/of the same essence): "when both the cause and that which has its origin from that cause are of the same nature, then they are called 'alike in substance' (ὁμοούσια λέγεται)".[93] On the effectiveness of the term ὁμοούσιος, Basil explains:

---

91 *Ep.* 9.3: Deferrari, I, 97. Ἐγὼ δὲ [...] τὸ ὅμοιν κατ 'οὐσίαν, εἰ μὲν προσκείμενον ἔχει τὸ ἀπαραλλάκτως, δέχομαι τὴν φωνὴν ὡς εἰς ταὐτὸν τῷ ὁμοουσίῳ φέρουσαν, κατὰ τὴν ὑγιᾶ δηλονότι τοῦ ὁμοουσίου διάνοιαν. Ὅπερ καὶ τοὺς ἐν Νικαίᾳ νοήσαντας, Φῶς ἐκ Φωτὸς καὶ Θεὸν ἀληθινὸν ἐκ Θεοῦ ἀληθινοῦ καὶ τὰ τοιαῦτα τὸν Μονογενῆ προσειπόντας, ἐπαγαγεῖν ἀκολούθως τὸ ὁμοούσιον. Courtonne, I, 36. See *Ep.* 361: Ὅμοιον δὲ κατ 'οὐσίαν ἀκριβῶς καὶ ἀπαραλλάκτως ὀρθῶς [...] λέγεσθαι. Courtonne, III, 221. "Like in substance entirely without difference could be said correctly". Deferrari, IV, 335. See *Against Eunomius*, 1.19.
92 Ayres, *Nicaea and its Legacy*, 188–191.
93 *Ep.* 52.2: Deferrari, I, 333. Ὅταν καὶ τὸ αἴτιον καὶ τὸ ἐκ τοῦ αἰτίου τὴν ὕπαρξιν ἔχον τῆς αὐτῆς ὑπάρχῃ φύσεως, ὁμοούσια λέγεται. Courtonne, I, 135.

This term [*homoousios*] also sets aright the error of Sabellius; for it does away with the identity of person (*hypostasis*), and introduces a perfect notion of the persons of the Godhead. For nothing is itself of like substance with itself, but one thing is of like substance with another thing; consequently, the term is a good one, and consistent with piety, differentiating as it does the individuality of the persons, and at the same time setting forth the invariability of their nature.[94]

Admittedly *homoousios* is unacceptable when it implies the existence of two ultimate causes (αἰτίαι) or origins (ἀρχαί), as also when it implies that the Father and the Son have no distinction. Thus, for Basil, the "Father generates the being of the Son in such a way that there is a mysterious unity between them, and yet the Son's existence as generated qualifies his existence as in some manner distinct from the Father's".[95] During the mid-360s Basil seems to have abandoned ὅμοιος language, and thereafter his letters written in the 370s increasingly use *homoousios*. In spite of this, however, and in order to avoid provoking his opponents, Basil was hesitant to use *homoousios* for the Holy Spirit. In *On the Holy Spirit*, for example, Basil was "notoriously reticent"[96] in using *homoousios* as a reference to the Holy Spirit. He acted pastorally in this way so as to accommodate the sensibilities of those wavering in the faith. These were mainly people who were ready to espouse non-Nicene language if the divinity of the Holy Spirit was expressed to them

---

94 *Ep.* 52.3: Deferrari, I, 333. Αὕτη δὲ ἡ φωνὴ καὶ τὸ τοῦ Σαβελλίου κακὸν ἐπανορθοῦνται· ἀναιρεῖ γὰρ τὴν ταυτότητα τῆς ὑποστάσεως καὶ εἰσάγει τελείαν τῶν προσώπων τὴν ἔννοιαν· οὐ γὰρ αὐτὸ τί ἐστιν ἑαυτῷ ὁμοούσιον, ἀλλ' ἕτερον ἑτέρῳ· ὥστε καλῶς ἔχει καὶ εὐσεβῶς, τῶν τε ὑποστάσεων τὴν ἰδιότητα διορίζουσα καὶ τῆς φύσεως τὸ ἀπαράλλακτον παριστῶσα. Courtonne, I, 135–136.
95 Ayres, *Nicaea and its Legacy*, 190–191.
96 Ayres, *Nicaea and its Legacy*, 211.

in terms outside the standard testimony of Scripture.⁹⁷ For the time being it was enough for Basil's opponents to conclude from his writings that the Holy Spirit is indeed divine. Hence Basil uses repeated statements where he claims one way or the other that the "Holy Spirit partakes of the fullness of divinity" (τῆς κατὰ τὴν φύσιν κοινωνίας)⁹⁸ and, because of this, "he [the Holy Spirit] completes the all praised and blessed Trinity" (συμπληροῦν τὴν πολυύμνητον καὶ μακαρίαν Τριάδα).⁹⁹ In a letter to "Eupaterius and his Daughter" on the Nicene faith and its teaching on the Holy Spirit, Basil emphasises this same very important point:

> He [the Holy Spirit] is holy by nature, as the Father is holy by nature, and the Son is holy by nature; and neither do we, for ourselves, tolerate the separation and severance of any member from the divine and blessed Trinity, nor do we receive those who are ready to reckon any member as a part of creation.¹⁰⁰

2.3.3 Pneumatomachianism

A number of Basil's works, including the aforementioned, are directed against Pneumatomachians¹⁰¹ ("Spirit-fighters"), that is, those who deny the divinity of the Holy Spirit and its consub-

---

97 Anderson captures this sense well when he writes: "This is not rhetorical hair-splitting; rather, it reveals a great pastoral wisdom: present all the evidence so that confession of the Spirit's divinity is the only possible orthodox choice, but avoid, at a time when unspiritual men yearn to multiply controversies, the use of an unprecedented statement". *On the Holy Spirit*, Anderson, 10. See n. 66.
98 *On the Holy Spirit*, 18.46: Anderson, 73. SC 17. 408.
99 *On the Holy Spirit*, 18.45: Anderson, 72. SC 17. 408.
100 *Ep.* 159.2: Deferrari, II, 397–399. Ὁ τοίνυν φύσει ἅγιον, ὡς φύσει ἅγιος ὁ Πατὴρ καὶ φύσει ἅγιος ὁ Υἱός, οὔτε αὐτοὶ τῆς θείας καὶ μακαρίας Τριάδος χωρίσαι καὶ διατεμεῖν ἀνεχόμεθα, οὔτε τοὺς εὐκόλως τῇ κτίσει συναριθμοῦντας ἀποδεχόμεθα. Courtonne, II, 87. In several letters Basil is clear about his doctrine pertaining to the divinity of the Holy Spirit, see *Epp.* 105, 159.2, 226.2, 250.4, especially *Ep.* 236.6: "Πιστεύω καὶ εἰς τὸ θεῖον Πνεῦμα τὸ Ἅγιον". Courtonne, III, 54. "I believe also in the divine Holy Spirit". Deferrari, III, 403.
101 For a detailed analysis and response to the Pneumatomachian controversy see Haykin, *The Spirit of God: The Exegesis of 1 and 2 Corinthians in the Pneumatomachian Controversy of the Fourth Century*.

stantiality with the Father and the Son.[102] The Pneumatomachians first emerged in the 360s in Constantinople, and were commonly referred to as "Macedonians" after their founder Macedonius (d. 360s), a semi-Arian bishop. The Pneumatomachians proclaimed that the Holy Spirit was created, just as Arius and others had done in their theological positions against the divinity of the Son. Consequently, Basil carries over to the Holy Spirit arguments that were used in support of the Son's *homoousian* status.

For Basil, there is a community of essence (τὸ κοινὸν τῆς οὐσίας)[103] between the Father, the Son and the Holy Spirit, although what that essence is remains unknown. One's "sense" or "concept" (ἔννοια) of God can only be gathered by God's activity (ἐνέργεια) towards him or herself. In Basil's understanding, since there is only one divine nature, so also is there only one divine ἐνέργεια. A common activity demonstrates a common essence. By 370 Basil had formulated the proposition that the activities of God all come from the Father, are worked in the Son, and are completed in the Holy Spirit.[104] Basil's *On the Holy Spirit* dramatically likens the Holy Spirit's closeness to the Father and the Son, to the closeness of a person's spirit to the self:

> The greatest proof that the Spirit is one with the Father and Son is that he is said to have the same relationship to God as the spirit within us has to us: "for what person knows a man's thought except the spirit of the man which is in him? So also no one comprehends the thoughts of God except the Spirit of God (1 Cor. 2:11)".[105]

---

102 Hanson, *The Search for the Christian Doctrine of God*, 678.
103 See *Against Eunomius*, 1.19: τὸ κοινὸν τῆς οὐσίας (the community of essence). SC 299. 240–242.
104 Ayres, *Nicaea and its Legacy*, 196.
105 *On the Holy Spirit*, 16.40: Anderson, 67. Τὸ δὲ μέγιστον τεκμήριον τῆς πρὸς Πατέρα καὶ Υἱὸν τοῦ Πνεύματος συναφείας, ὅτι οὕτως ἔχειν λέγεται πρὸς Θεόν, ὡς πρὸς ἕκαστον ἔχει τὸ πνεῦμα τὸ ἐν ἡμῖν. Τίς γὰρ οἶδε, φησίν, ἀνθρώπων τὰ τοῦ ἀνθρώπου, εἰ μὴ τὸ πνεῦμα τὸ ἐν αὐτῷ; Οὕτω καὶ τὰ τοῦ Θεοῦ οὐδεὶς ἔγνωκεν, εἰ μὴ τὸ Πνεῦμα τὸ ἐκ τοῦ Θεοῦ. SC 17. 390.

In Basil's pneumatology, the sanctifying work of the Holy Spirit is directly related to the work of God in his economic dealings with people.[106] In other words, through the "assistance" (βοηθείᾳ) of the Holy Spirit, one is equipped "to know truth and recognise God" (τὴν ἀλήθειαν γνωρίσει καὶ Θεὸν ἐπιγνώσεται).[107] The Holy Spirit is intrinsic to God's divine activity since it is used as an instrument of sanctification that conveys God's love. According to Basil, from the activities of God comes "knowledge, and from knowledge comes worship. Therefore, we believe in him whom we understand, and we worship him in whom we believe".[108]

Basil considered it of immense importance to see the place of the Holy Spirit in the Trinity as distinct and not simply as another Son, "because he proceeds from the mouth of the Father and is not begotten like the Son".[109] Crucial to this understanding is the distinction between the generation of the Son and the "procession" (ἐκπόρευσης) of the Holy Spirit, as implied in John 15:26. Inseparably united to the Father and the Son, the Holy Spirit completes and brings to fruition what the Father accomplishes through the Son.[110] In the final analysis, Basil argues for the need of a special θεωρία (contemplation) to grasp the nature of the Holy Spirit. Thus the Holy Spirit enables the pure in heart to see God, and it is God who grants the gift of this purity. For Basil, an account of the character of true Christian θεωρία provides a context within which he can begin to articulate how one learns to speak appropriately of the divine being. Furthermore, he creates a polemic tool for describing ways in which non-Nicene exegesis and theology fail.

---

106 See *Ep.* 214.4; *Against Eunomius*, 3.2.
107 *Ep.* 233.2: Deferrari, III, 371. Courtonne, III, 41.
108 *Ep.* 234.3: Deferrari, III, 377. Οὐκοῦν ἀπὸ μὲν τῶν ἐνεργειῶν ἡ γνῶσις, ἀπὸ δὲ τῆς γνώσεως ἡ προσκύνησις [...] Ὥστε πιστεύομεν μὲν τῷ γνωσθέντι, προσκυνοῦμεν δὲ τῷ πιστευθέντι. Courtonne, III, 43–44.
109 See *On the Holy Spirit*, 18.46: Anderson, 73. Ὡς ἐκ τοῦ Θεοῦ προελθόν· οὐ γεννητῶς ὡς ὁ Υἱός, ἀλλ᾽ ὡς ὁ Πνεῦμα στόματος αὐτοῦ. SC 17. 408.
110 Hanson, *The Search for the Christian Doctrine of God*, 689.

2.4 The Development of Basil's Trinitarian Theology

If one could put names to the most significant figures forging pro-Nicene doctrines of the Trinity, Athanasius and the Cappadocians would stand out the most. In particular, one finds in their later works some of the key principles whose implications are worked over during the period between 360 and 380. With these names a pro-Nicene theological "culture" is established where distinct pro-Nicene traditions are identified. Admittedly, personalities such as Eusebius of Caesarea, Epiphanius, Didymus and Marius Victorinus can be added to the aforementioned figures, however their contributions towards systematic theology are greatly understudied or even omitted in some circles of contemporary scholarship.

In their endeavours to understand Nicene theology, Ayres[111] and Hanson[112] look at a whole range of literature and topics, and in this way they do not limit their research to only technical Trinitarian treatises. A key feature of Ayres' historical narrative is his parallel treatment of Greek, Latin and Syriac speakers. Ayres is of the understanding that the Fathers of the fourth century shared a common set of fundamental strategies in their Trinitarian theologies. With Hanson, writers are treated individually and not as heresiarchs such as "Arian" or "Apollinarian". For him, all "controversy" is nothing other than a vigorous search for a Christian doctrine of God. As Hanson sees it, inherent in the formulation of Christian doctrine is a process of "trial and error", which leads to a "discovery" and therefore brings about much needed "genuine change".[113]

As has been shown above, over time Basil's theology evolved from a *homoiousian* (of like essence) to a neo-Nicene *homoousian*

---

111 *Nicaea and its Legacy*, 187–221.
112 Hanson, *The Search for the Christian Doctrine of God*, 181–207.
113 Hanson, *The Search for the Christian Doctrine of God*, 872–875.

(of same essence) position.[114] Of the many architects of the pro-Nicene cause, it is Basil of Caesarea who most clearly develops the distinction between the persons and the essence of the Triune God. He says: "For it must be clearly understood that as one who does not acknowledge the community of essence falls into polytheism, so he who does not grant the individuality of the persons is carried off into Judaism".[115] Anyone holding non-Nicene convictions faced anathematisation and was considered by Basil as proclaiming a faith "utterly foreign to Christianity" (Χριστιανισμοῦ μὲν παντελῶς ἀλλοτρίαν),[116] and in some cases labelled as approaching "the error of the Greeks" (ἐγγὺς εἶναι τῆς Ἑλληνικῆς τιθέμεθα πλάνης).[117]

Basil establishes a clear terminological distinction between *ousia* (essence) and *hypostasis*, which previously were sometimes used as synonyms. Here there appears to be the first fruits of what later became known as the classical Cappadocian formula that shaped all theological language referring to the Trinity: "one divine

---

114 Lewis Ayres (*Nicaea and its Legacy*) and Richard P.C. Hanson (*Search for the Christian Doctrine of God*) successfully give an account of what was called "pro-Nicene" Trinitarian theology in the second half of the fourth century. All of the significant protagonists and participants of this period are considered and their thoughts are presented. Both authors are pragmatic in their approach and despite the historical complexities surrounding the later part of the fourth century, they are able to ascertain and reflect upon the various fourth-century attempts at creed making. The ascendancy and decline of various creeds and the hierarchs embracing them depended as often as not on the intrigues of political power and the oscillating beliefs of various emperors. In any case, once freed from the usurpations of political power, most creed making attempts, especially after the 360s, identified with Nicaea. For perhaps the most extensive study of Basil's theology in print see Drecoll, *Die Entwicklung der Trinitätslehre des Basilius von Cäsarea: Sein Weg vom Homöusianer zum Neonizäner*.
115 *Ep*. 210.5: Deferrari, III, 211. Εὖ γὰρ εἰδέναι χρὴ ὅτι ὥσπερ ὁ τὸ κοινὸν τῆς οὐσίας μὴ ὁμολογῶν εἰς πολυθεΐαν ἐκπίπτει, οὕτως ὁ τὸ ἰδιάζον τῶν ὑποστάσεων μὴ διδοὺς εἰς τὸν Ἰουδαϊσμὸν ὑποφέρεται. Courtonne, II, 195.
116 *Ep*. 263.5: Deferrari, IV, 101. Courtonne, III, 125.
117 *Ep*. 226.4: Deferrari, III, 341. Courtonne, III, 28.

essence in three *hypostases*".[118] Hildebrand divides the development of Basil's Trinitarian theology into four distinct stages, each of which is defined by the theological term that Basil preferred. These distinct stages of linguistic development took shape between the years 359–379 and are approximately divided in the following way:

> the *homoiousian* years, c. 360–365;
>
> the movement from *homoiousios* to *homoousios*, c. 365–372;
>
> the use of *prosōpa* for what is three in God, c. 372; and
>
> the emergence of *hypostasis*, c. 375–379, for the same purpose of expressing that which is three in God.[119]

Initially Basil evolves from preferring *homoiousios* to *homoousios* to describe the relation between the Father and Son. With reference to the deliberations of Nicaea, Basil summarises: "their view was that whatever the Father is in substance this should be understood of the Son also".[120] This allows Basil to proclaim: "the Son is confessed to be consubstantial (*homoousios*) with the Father, and to be of the same nature as the one who begot him".[121] From this under-

---

118 Of course, this doctrine itself cannot be wholly credited to the Cappadocians, but it was they who offered the first stage of precision to the terminology that others had already employed. As Hanson argues, the Cappadocians "were together decisively influential in bringing about the final form of the doctrine of the Trinity and thereby resolving the conflict about the Christian doctrine of God which had vexed the church for fifty years before their day". Hanson, *The Search for the Christian Doctrine of God*, 676. In Basil's writings "three hypostases" is first used in *Against Eunomius* 3.3. By 376 it became his preferred language for naming the three persons of the Trinity. See *Epp.* 210, 236, 258. Radde-Gallwitz describes Basil as "the architect of the pro-Nicene confession of three hypostases and one substance". Radde-Gallwitz, *Basil of Caesarea*, 134.
119 Hildebrand, *The Trinitarian Theology*, 77–92.
120 *Ep.* 226.3: Deferrari, III, 337. Οὐ γὰρ τοῦτο ἐνόησεν ἡ ἁγία ἐκείνη καὶ θεοφιλὴς σύνοδος, ἀλλ᾽ ὡς, ὅπερ ἐστὶ κατὰ τὴν οὐσίαν ὁ Πατήρ, τοῦτο ὀφείλοντος νοεῖσθαι καὶ τοῦ Υἱοῦ. Courtonne, III, 26–27.
121 *Ep.* 159.1: Deferrari, II, 395. Ὁμοούσιος ὁμολογεῖται ὁ Υἱὸς τῷ Πατρὶ καὶ τῆς αὐτῆς ὑπάρχων φύσεως ἧς ὁ γεννήσας. Courtonne, II, 86.

standing Basil refines his terminology and moves from preferring *prosōpon* to *hypostasis* to describing what is three in God. Basil's subsequent use of the term *hypostasis* involves a moving from a preoccupation with the relation between the Father and the Son to a full focus on the theology of the Holy Spirit. It is Basil's attachment to the notion of "image" of the Son, and then to the presentation of the Spirit as the light in which the image becomes visible, that the dynamism of Basil's Trinity is manifested. This provides the basis for a detailed analysis of the intra-Trinitarian relations of the Son and Holy Spirit to the Father. For Basil, the Father, Son and Holy Spirit exist in an uninterrupted, unbroken and continuous communion.

2.5 Basil's Theology of the Holy Spirit: The Monarchia and Homotimia of God

If there is one scriptural idea that forms the cornerstone of Basil's theology of the Holy Spirit, Hildebrand argues that this is found in 1 Cor. 12:3: "No one can say 'Jesus is Lord' except in the Holy Spirit" (Οὐδεὶς δύναται εἰπεῖν, Κύριος Ἰησοῦς, εἰ μὴ ἐν πνεύματι ἁγίῳ).[122] Just as in the sacrament of Baptism, the Son is the mediator without whom one cannot have access to the Father, so too the Holy Spirit is the mediator without whom one cannot have access to the Son. For Basil, without the Holy Spirit, one cannot have divine knowledge of the Father through the Son. Only the Holy Spirit can make known the glory of Christ. In this sense the Holy Spirit is the light by which one sees the image of the Son. The Holy Spirit himself is not looked at but rather the Holy Spirit is "he" in whom and by whom one sees; his illuminating work is done *in himself*. This Spirit of knowledge, says Basil, "gives those who love the vision of truth the power which enables them to see

---

122 Hildebrand, *The Trinitarian Theology*, 173–187.

the image, and this power is himself".[123]

According to Basil, it is from the third person of the Holy Trinity, the Holy Spirit, that the event of communion is realised. In each person's relation to Christ, the Holy Spirit is not simply an assistance to the individual in reaching Christ, but the *in*, in which he or she participates in Christ. This explains why Baptism was seen from the beginning to be taking place "*in* the Spirit" and "*into* Christ".[124] According to Basil, Father, Son and Holy Spirit each have a distinctive role in creation: the Father commands, the Son creates, and the Holy Spirit sanctifies. What is true of creation is also true of Christian life. Through the distinct roles of the Trinity, a person comes to know the Father through his image, the Son, by his or her union with the Holy Spirit. As the sanctifier, teacher and revealer of mysteries, Basil sees the Holy Spirit as dwelling in Christians and as facilitating their salvation.

Nearly all doctrinal disagreements on the Holy Spirit arise from trying to understand the relationship of the Holy Spirit with the second person of the Holy Trinity, the Son. If it is true that the Holy Spirit is manifested in the Son, does this mean that it receives its existence through and from him? Also, if the Holy Spirit is manifested through the Son, not only temporally by also eternally, can procession *from* still be attributed to the Father alone? The correct understanding, as Basil would have it, is to see the procession of the Holy Spirit *from* the Father and *through* the Son as an expression of the personal relationship that exists between the Father and the Son.

In his later works Basil consistently presents the Father as the

---

123 On the Holy Spirit, 18.47: Anderson, 74. Τὴν ἐποπτικὴν τῆς εἰκόνος δύναμιν ἐν ἑαυτῷ παρεχόμενον τοῖς ἀληθείας φιλοθεάμοσιν. SC 17. 412.
124 See On the Holy Spirit, 10.24: Εἰ γὰρ ὁ μὲν Κύριος σαφῶς ἐν τῇ παραδόσει τοῦ σωτηρίου βαπτίσματος προσέταξε τοῖς μαθηταῖς βαπτίζειν πάντα τὰ ἔθνη «εἰς ὄνομα Πατρὸς καὶ Υἱοῦ καὶ ἁγίου Πνεύματος». SC 17. 332. "When the Lord established the baptism of salvation, did he not clearly command his disciples to baptise 'in the name of the Father, and of the Son, and of the Holy Spirit?' He did not disdain his fellowship with the Holy Spirit". Anderson, 45.

source of the Trinitarian persons and of the essence that the three share. Staniloae summarises this well when he says that in the relations of the Trinitarian Godhead "only the uncaused Person: the Father"[125] is the eternal cause of the Son and the Holy Spirit. According to Basil, the Holy Spirit belongs to the Father in as much as it has its existence from within him, while in reference to the Son, the Holy Spirit comes forth through him from the Father and shares a unity of being and glory with him. Through the generation of the Son and the procession of the Holy Spirit, God's perfection is eternally realised. The distinction between the generation of the Son and the procession of the Holy Spirit is apparent only at the level of cause (αἰτία) and point of origin (ἀρχή), and not at the level of essence. In his *Homily on Faith*, Basil states that along with being the source of the Godhead, the Father is also the source of created existence in general. From this homily it becomes evident that the *hypostasis* of the Father is presented as "the principle of all, the cause of being for whatever exists, the root of the living. From him proceeded the source of life, the wisdom, the power and the indistinguishable image of the invisible God".[126]

With primacy belonging to the Father, as *primal cause* of the Son's generation and the Holy Spirit's procession, a distinct ordering and differentiation is seen within the persons of the Trinity.

125 Staniloae, *Theology and the Church*, 22.
126 Homily on Faith, 2: Delcogliano, 235-236. Πατήρ· ἡ πάντων ἀρχή, ἡ αἰτία τοῦ εἶναι τοῖς οὖσιν, ἡ ῥίζα τῶν ζώντων. Ὅθεν προῆλθε ἡ πηγὴ τῆς ζωῆς, ἡ σοφία, ἡ δύναμις, ἡ εἰκὼν ἡ ἀπαράλλακτος τοῦ ἀοράτου Θεοῦ. PG 31. 465D. Elsewhere in On the Holy Spirit Basil wrote: Ἐν δὲ τῇ τούτων κτίσει ἐννόησόν μοι τὴν προκαταρκτικὴν αἰτίαν τῶν γινομένων, τὸν Πατέρα· τὴν δημιουργικήν, τὸν Υἱόν· τὴν τελειωτικήν, τὸ Πνεῦμα· ὥστε βουλήματι μὲν τοῦ Πατρὸς τὰ λειτουργικὰ πνεύματα ὑπάρχειν, ἐνεργείᾳ δὲ τοῦ Υἱοῦ εἰς τὸ εἶναι παράγεσθαι, παρουσίᾳ δὲ τοῦ Πνεύματος τελειοῦσθαι. Τελείωσις δὲ ἀγγέλων, ἁγιασμός, καὶ ἐν τούτῳ διαμονή. On the Holy Spirit, 16.38. SC 17. 376-378. "When you consider creation I advise you to first think of him who is the first cause of everything that exists: namely, the Father, and then of the Son, who is the creator, and then the Holy Spirit, the perfector. So the ministering spirits exist by the will of the Father, are brought into being by the work of the Son, and are perfected by the presence of the Spirit, since angels are perfected by perseverance in holiness". Anderson, 62.

While the Holy Spirit is third in order (τῇ τάξει), Basil maintains that the Holy Spirit is not third in order of essence, but equal just like the Son. The laws of arithmetic[127] do not apply to the simple and transcendent God, and therefore it is illogical, says Basil, to assume that the Holy Spirit is third in nature based on it occupying third place in the baptism formula:[128] "When the Lord taught us the doctrine of the Father, Son, and Holy Spirit, he did not make arithmetic a part of this gift! He did not say, 'In the first, the second, and third', or 'In one, two, and three.'"[129] Hence it is possible for Basil to speak of an order among the divine persons without depreciating or subordinating any of the *hypostases*. From this understanding Basil maintains that the Holy Spirit is accorded equal worship and honour with the Father and the Son, and so is numbered with them.[130] Thus the three persons, in the sense that they are divine, are called upon to be worshipped and glorified together. In espousing the equality of honour amongst the three persons of the Trinity, Basil implicitly proclaims their identity in essence.

It was most important for Basil that the one ἀρχή in the Trinity came to be understood ontologically as referring to the person of the Father and not the one essence. What causes God to be, proclaims Basil, is the person of the Father. Behr concludes that, for

127 See *On the Holy Spirit*, 18.44: Οὐχὶ ἀπαιδεύτῳ ἀριθμήσει πρὸς πολυθεΐας ἔννοιαν ἐκφερόμεθα. SC 17. 404. "We will not let a stupid arithmetic lead us astray to the idea of many gods". Anderson, 72.
128 The author of Basil's *Ep.* 8 categorically excludes any numbering when talking about God. For example in *Ep.* 8.2 one reads: Πρὸς δὲ τοὺς ἐπηρεάζοντας ἡμῖν τὸ τρίθεον ἐκεῖνο λεγέσθω ὅτιπερ ἡμεῖς ἕνα Θεόν, οὐ τῷ ἀριθμῷ ἀλλὰ τῇ φύσει, ὁμολογοῦμεν. Courtonne, I, 24. "In reply to those who slander us as being Tritheists, let it be said that we confess one God not in number but in nature". Deferrari, I, 53. Certain scholars argue that *Ep.* 8 should be attributed to Evagrius of Pontus. See Bousset, *Apophthegmata*, 335–336.
129 *On the Holy Spirit*, 18.44: Anderson, 71. Πατέρα καὶ Υἱὸν καὶ ἅγιον Πνεῦμα παραδιδοὺς ὁ Κύριος, οὐ μετὰ τοῦ ἀριθμοῦ συνεξέδωκεν. Οὐ γὰρ εἶπεν ὅτι εἰς πρῶτον καὶ δεύτερον καὶ τρίτον· οὐδὲ εἰς ἓν καὶ δύο καὶ τρία. SC 17. 402.
130 See *On the Holy Spirit*, 10.25: Ὁ μὲν Κύριος ὡς ἀναγκαῖον καὶ σωτήριον δόγμα τὴν μετὰ Πατρὸς σύνταξιν τοῦ ἁγίου Πνεύματος παραδέδωκε. SC 17. 334. "The Lord has delivered to us a necessary and saving dogma: the Holy Spirit is to be ranked with the Father". Anderson, 46.

Basil, the divine essence is not a shared genus to which all three *hypostases* belong, but rather that the Father is to be seen as the cause of the Trinity.[131] Thus the ontological ἀρχή in the Trinity is the Father,[132] who is in this sense the one God.[133] Everything in God, *ad extra* and *ad intra*, begins with the "good pleasure" (εὐδοκία) of the Father[134] who has given the "beginning of being" (ἀρχὴ τοῦ εἶναι)[135] to the other persons. In this vein, Fatherhood is not the name (essence) *of* God but a name *about* God, arising out of the essence of God.[136] *Monarchia* locates the unity of the Trinity in the Father, who is subsequently the sole eternal source of the Son and the Holy Spirit.[137]

Basil insists on the equality of the *hypostases* while at the same time expressing their unity: "The way to divine knowledge ascends from one Spirit through the one Son to the one Father. Likewise natural goodness, inherent holiness and royal dignity reach from

---

131 See Behr, *The Nicene Faith*, vol. 2, 307–308.
132 Gregory of Nazianzus adopted this teaching of Basil in his own theological exposition regarding the causality of the Father. See *Theological Orations* 27–31. For a comprehensive summary see McGuckin, *St. Gregory of Nazianzus*, 229–310.
133 See *Ep.* 203.3. Εἷς ἡμῶν Κύριος, μία πίστις, ἐλπὶς ἡ αὐτή. Courtonne, II, 170. "Our Lord is one, our faith one, our hope the same". Deferrari, II, 149
134 See *On the Holy Spirit*, 16.38. SC 17. 376.
135 See *Against Eunomius* 2.22. SC 305. 88–92.
136 See *Against Eunomius* 1.5.
137 See *Against Eunomius* 1.14–15. By making the Father the only cause of divine existence, Basil, together with the rest of the Cappadocians, sought to bring out God's freedom in ontology. Zizioulas expresses this well when he says: "The one ontological *arche* in the immanent and economic Trinity is the Father, who as the willing one is the initiator of divine freedom". Zizioulas, *Communion and Otherness*, 121. In this way God's oneness is safeguarded by the *monarchia* of the Father and not so much by the unity of substance as claimed by St. Augustine and others. Traditionally, Western theologians describe this view as overly subordinationist and hierarchical, and instead propose that personhood should be seen as an expression of the interactivity among the three persons which in turn eliminates any need to search for a single cause. For Zizioulas personhood is ultimately located in God the Father since it is the Father that "causes" the Son's and the Spirit's existence.

the Father through the only begotten Son to the Spirit".[138] In this way the *monarchia* is not lost in the confession of the *hypostases*: "Thus we do not lose the true doctrine of one God by confessing the person"[139] says Basil, since "the Trinity is one God" (εἷς Θεὸς ἡ Τριάς).[140] Linguistically Basil uses *monarchia*[141] and *homotimos* as part of his effort to persuade his opponents that since the Holy Spirit is equal in honour with the Father and Son, in that he is divine, he must be ranked with God. To deny the Holy Spirit's divinity is to question the deity of the Father and the Son. Basil, as witnessed above, uses *monarchia* ("monarchy" or "single cause") in his Trinitarian vocabulary and applies *homotimos* ("same in honour") to the Holy Spirit. The point Basil is making here is: "that which had been alienated by its nature could not have shared in the same honours".[142]

2.6 The Development of Basil's Theology of the Holy Spirit

In 325 the Council of Nicaea had condemned all teachings that spoke against the divinity of Christ. Fifty years later however, other teachings arose that undermined the divinity of the Holy Spirit. Developments in theology made it clear to Basil that his old essay written ten years prior, *Against Eunomius*, was not sufficiently equipped to address new challenges. The central problem

---

138 *On the Holy Spirit*, 18.47: Anderson, 74-75. Ἡ τοίνυν ὁδὸς τῆς θεογνωσίας ἐστὶν ἀπὸ ἑνὸς Πνεύματος, διὰ τοῦ ἑνὸς Υἱοῦ, ἐπὶ τὸν ἕνα Πατέρα. Καὶ ἀναπάλιν, ἡ φυσικὴ ἀγαθότητης, καὶ ὁ κατὰ φύσιν ἁγιασμός, καὶ τὸ βασιλικὸν ἀξίωμα, ἐκ Πατρός, διὰ τοῦ Μονογενοῦς, ἐπὶ τὸ Πνεῦμα διήκει. SC 17. 412.
139 *On the Holy Spirit*, 18.47: Anderson, 75. Οὕτω καὶ αἱ ὑποστάσεις ὁμολογοῦνται, καὶ τὸ εὐσεβὲς δόγμα τῆς μοναρχίας οὐ διαπίπτει. SC 17. 412.
140 *Ep.* 129.1: Deferrari, II, 285. Courtonne, II, 40.
141 "Monarchia" is only used twice in all of Basil's works, and both these instances are found in On the Holy Spirit in a context in which Basil is arguing against the Macedonians' denial of the Holy Spirit's divinity. The unity of the Godhead can only be maintained by acknowledging the Father to be the sole ἀρχή or πηγὴ θεότητος, who from all eternity has communicated his own Godhead to his co-eternal and consubstantial Son and Spirit.
142 *Ep.* 159.2: Deferrari, II, 397. Οὐ γὰρ τῶν αὐτῶν μετέσχε τιμῶν τὸ ἀπεξενωμένον κατὰ τὴν φύσιν. Courtonne, II, 86-87.

now was the dignity of the Holy Spirit and the Spirit's equality in nature and activity with the Father and the Son. Questions once asked about the divinity of the second person of the Trinity, the Son, were now asked of the third person of the Trinity, the Holy Spirit. Ending the Nicene Creed of 325 with a brief statement "I believe in the Holy Spirit"[143] was not enough to make clear that the Holy Spirit was divine and thus of one essence (ὁμοούσιον) with Father and the Son.

For Basil's opponents, the Holy Spirit was regarded as an administering spirit similar to that of an angelic order.[144] They argued that to see the Holy Spirit in any other light, namely as divine, risked elevating all other instruments used in the economy of God's plan of salvation to the status of a divine being. The logical conclusion to this analysis was considered to be an obscure form of pantheism. Initially Basil refused to be drawn into a detailed discussion on this particular theological issue, and in his defence characteristically said: "We can add nothing to the Creed of Nicaea, not even the slightest thing, except the glorification of the Holy Spirit".[145] Behind this statement, however, was an affirmation about the nature of the creed-writing itself, since creeds were

---

143 Καὶ εἰς τὸ ἅγιον πνεῦμα. Ραφτάνη, Πηδάλιον, 122.
144 See *On the Holy Spirit*, 9.23: Anderson, 44.
145 *Ep.* 258.2: Deferrari, IV, 41. Οὐδὲν δυνάμεθα τῇ κατὰ Νίκαιαν πίστει προστιθέναι ἡμεῖς, οὐδὲ τὸ βραχύτατον, πλὴν τῆς εἰς τὸ Πνεῦμα τὸ Ἅγιον δοξολογίας. Courtonne, III, 101–102. Sometimes the best of Basil's reaction to the taunts and threats of his opponents was silence: Ἦ τάχα οὗτος ἦν «ὁ καιρὸς τοῦ σιγᾶν», κατὰ τὸν σοφὸν Σολομῶντα. Τί γὰρ ὄφελος τῷ ὄντι κεκραγέναι πρὸς ἄνεμον, οὕτω βιαίας ζάλης κατεχούσης τὸν βίον, ὑφ᾽ ἧς πᾶσα μὲν διάνοια τῶν τὸν λόγον κατηχουμένων, οἷον ὀφθαλμὸς κονιορτοῦ τινος, τῆς ἐκ τῶν παραλογισμῶν ἀπάτης ἀναπλησθεῖσα συγκέχυται· πᾶσα δὲ ἀκοὴ βαρυτάτοις καὶ ἀήθεσι ψόφοις κατακτυπεῖται· δονεῖται δὲ πάντα καὶ ἐν κινδύνῳ ἐστὶ τοῦ πτώματος. *On the Holy Spirit*, 29.75. SC 17. 252. "But perhaps this is a time for silence, as wise Solomon wrote in Ecclesiastes. When life is tossed about by so violent a storm that minds of everyone instructed in the word have been thrown into confusion and filled with the deceit of false reasoning, like an eye blinded by sand, when everyone is stunned by strange and terrible noises, when all the world is shaken and everything tottering to its fall, what use is it to cry to the wind?" Anderson, 113.

considered to be definitive, theologically consistent, irrevocable and therefore not open to change. In one of his letters Basil says: "If we must compose different creeds at different times and change them with the occasion, false is the declaration of him who said: 'One Lord, one faith, one baptism' (Eph. 4:5)".[146] Basil considered it a mark of his adversaries "to employ the words of the creed, like physicians, according to occasion, adapting it to their existing condition now in one way now in another".[147] If changes to the Creed of Nicaea are to be permitted, these, Basil says, can only be in the form of additions that are primarily "being made for clarification" (προστεθῆναι εἰς τράνωσιν).[148] In this way Basil was arguing that changes could in theory be made to the Nicene Creed so long as "no one of the statements" made at Nicaea (μηδεμίαν τῶν ἐκεῖ λέξεων)[149] was denied:

> Let us then seek nothing more, but merely propose the Creed of Nicaea to the brethren who wish to join us; and if they agree to this, let us demand also that the Holy Spirit shall not be called a creature, and that those who do call him shall not be communicants with them. [...] For I am convinced [...] even if there should be need of some addition being made for clarification, the Lord who works all things together unto good to such as love him will concede this.[150]

---

146 *Ep.* 226.3: Deferrari, III, 337. Εἰ γὰρ ἄλλοτε ἄλλας πίστεις δεῖ συγγράφειν καὶ μετὰ τῶν καιρῶν ἀλλοιοῦσθαι, ψευδὴς ἡ ἀπόφασις τοῦ εἰπόντος· Εἷς Κύριος, μία πίστις, ἓν βάπτισμα. Courtonne, III, 27.
147 *Ep.* 226.3: Deferrari, III, 337. Τοῖς ῥήμασι τῆς πίστεως, ὡς ἰατροί, κέχρηνται κατὰ καιρόν, ἄλλοτε ἄλλως πρὸς τὰ ὑποκείμενα πάθη μεθαρμοζόμενοι. Courtonne, III, 27.
148 *Ep.* 113: Deferrari, II, 225. Courtonne, II, 17.
149 *Ep.* 114: Deferrari, II, 227. Courtonne, II, 18.
150 *Ep.* 113: Deferrari, II, 225. Μηδὲν τοίνυν πλέον ἐπιζητῶμεν, ἀλλὰ προτεινώμεθα τοῖς βουλομένοις ἡμῖν συνάπτεσθαι ἀδελφοῖς τὴν ἐν Νικαίᾳ πίστιν, κἂν ἐκείνῃ συνθῶνται, ἐπερωτῶμεν καὶ τὸ μὴ δεῖν λέγεσθαι κτίσμα τὸ Πνεῦμα τὸ Ἅγιον μηδὲ κοινωνικοὺς αὐτῶν εἶναι τοὺς λέγοντας [...] Πέπεισμαι γὰρ ὅτι [...] καὶ εἴ τι δέοι πλέον προστεθῆναι εἰς τράνωσιν, δώσει ὁ Κύριος ὁ πάντα συνεργῶν εἰς ἀγαθὸν τοῖς ἀγαπῶσιν αὐτόν. Courtonne, II, 17.

Basil understood the Nicene position, from the very beginning of its application, to be an expression of the longstanding biblical and early patristic faith. He appealed to it always within the context of a wider tradition that included "the teachings of the Fathers" (τὰ τῶν Πατέρων δόγματα) and "the apostolic traditions" (ἀποστολικαὶ παραδόσεις).[151] With this in mind, he never tired in his insistence that "the creed of the Fathers who assembled at Nicaea has been honoured by us" (ἡ τῶν ἐν Νικαίᾳ συνελθόντων Πατέρων πίστις [...] προτετίμηται [ἡμῖν]).[152] In his letter to the "church of Antioch", he affirms:

> As to creed, we accept no newer creed written for us by others, nor do we ourselves make bold to give out the product of our own intelligence, lest we make the words of our religion the words of man; but rather that which we have been taught by the holy Fathers do we make known to those who question us. We have, then, enfranchised in our church from the time of the Fathers the creed which was written by the holy Fathers convened at Nicaea.[153]

Elsewhere, Basil proclaims: "Let us also pronounce with boldness that good dogma of the Fathers, which overwhelms the accursed heresy of Arius, and builds the churches on the sound doctrine, wherein the Son is confessed to be consubstantial (ὁμοούσιος) with the Father, and the Holy Spirit is numbered with them in like hon-

---

151 *Ep.* 90.2: Deferrari, II, 125. Courtonne, I, 195.
152 *Ep.* 159.1: Deferrari, II, 395. Courtonne, II, 86.
153 *Ep.* 140.2: Deferrari, II, 335–337. Πίστιν δὲ ἡμεῖς οὔτε παρ ἄλλων γραφομένην ἡμῖν νεωτέραν παραδεχόμεθα οὔτε αὐτοὶ τὰ τῆς ἡμετέρας διανοίας γεννήματα παραδιδόναι τολμῶμεν, ἵνα μὴ ἀνθρώπινα ποιήσωμεν τὰ τῆς εὐσεβείας ῥήματα, ἀλλ' ἅπερ παρὰ τῶν ἁγίων Πατέρων δεδιδάγμεθα ταῦτα τοῖς ἐρωτῶσιν ἡμᾶς διαγγέλομεν. Ἔτσι τοίνυν ἐκ πατέρων ἐμπολιτευομένη τῇ Ἐκκλησίᾳ ἡμῶν ἡ γραφεῖσα παρὰ τῶν ἁγίων Πατέρων πίστις τῶν κατὰ τὴν Νίκαιαν συνελθόντων ἡμῖν. Courtonne, II, 61.

our (ὁμοτίμως) and so adored (συλλατρεύεται)".[154]

Basil, in his defence on the silence of the Nicene Fathers about the divinity of the Holy Spirit, argues:

> But since the doctrine of the Holy Spirit had not yet been defined, for no Pneumatomachians had as yet arisen at that time, they [the Nicene Fathers] were silent about the need of anathematising those who say that the Holy Spirit is a created and servile nature. For nothing at all in the divine and blessed Trinity is created.[155]

Basil holds the view that at the time of the composition of the Creed of Nicaea, the divinity of the Holy Spirit, although not expressly stated, was a belief contained within the conscience of the Christian faithful. It was always "unassailably inherent in the souls of the faithful" (ἀνεπιβούλευτον ἐνυπάρχειν ταῖς τῶν πιστευόντων ψυχαῖς).[156] Basil explains: "Our fathers [from Nicaea and other councils] mentioned this topic incidentally, since the question regarding him [the Holy Spirit] had not yet been raised at that time".[157] Put simply, there was not much written concerning the Holy Spirit "because there was no dispute about it", hence it "has remained unexplained" (διὰ τὸ ἀναντίρρητον, ἀδιάρθωτον καταλείφθη).[158] For Basil and his Christian contemporaries, a belief of the Christian church becomes an expressly stated creed only

---

154 *Ep.* 90.2: Deferrari, II, 127. Λαλείσθω καὶ παρ᾽ ὑμῖν μετὰ παρρησίας τὸ ἀγαθὸν ἐκεῖνο κήρυγμα τῶν Πατέρων, τὸ καταστρέφον μὲν τὴν δυσώνυμον αἵρεσιν τὴν Ἀρείου, οἰκοδομοῦν δὲ τὰς Ἐκκλησίας ἐν τῇ ὑγιαινούσῃ διδασκαλίᾳ ἐν ᾗ ὁ Υἱὸς ὁμοούσιος τῷ Πατρὶ ὁμολογεῖταί καὶ τὸ Πνεῦμα τὸ Ἅγιον ὁμοτίμως συναριθμεῖταί τε καὶ συλλατρεύεται. Courtonne, I, 196. See *Ep.* 159.2.
155 *Ep.* 140.2: Deferrari, II, 337–339. Ἐπειδὴ δὲ ἀδιόριστός ἐστιν ὁ περὶ τοῦ Ἁγίου Πνεύματος λόγος, οὔπω τότε τῶν πνευματομάχων ἀναφανέντων, τὸ χρῆναι ἀναθεματίζεσθαι τοὺς λέγοντας τῆς κτιστῆς εἶναι καὶ δουλικῆς φύσεως τὸ Πνεῦμα τὸ Ἅγιον ἐσίγησαν. Οὐδὲ γὰρ ὅλως τῆς θείας καὶ μακαρίας Τριάδος κτιστόν. Courtonne, II, 62.
156 *Ep.* 125.3: Deferrari, II, 267. Courtonne, II, 33.
157 *Ep.* 258.2: Deferrari, IV, 41. Τὸ ἐν παραδρομῇ τοὺς Πατέρας ἡμῶν τούτου τοῦ μέρους ἐπιμνησθῆναι· οὔπω τοῦ κατ᾽ αὐτὸ ζητήματος τότε κεκινημένου. Courtonne, III, 102. See *Ep.* 125.3.
158 *Ep.* 159.2: Deferrari, II, 395. Courtonne, II, 86.

when its efficacy is challenged or undermined. Basil explicitly declares: "The doctrine of the Holy Spirit was laid down cursorily, not being considered as necessary of elaboration, because at that time this question had not yet been agitated, but the sense of it was unassailably inherent in the souls of the faithful".¹⁵⁹ In Basil's understanding, in the past the theological understanding of the Holy Spirit had not been challenged, and so had not warranted a new doctrinal formulation that would safeguard its status. In his own context, however, Basil felt the need had arisen to take a more definitive stance on the divinity of the Holy Spirit and therefore "anathematise those who call the Holy Spirit a creature (κτίσμα) [...] [and] deprive him of his divine (θείας) and blessed nature".¹⁶⁰ Consequently, Basil states that one must not "have communion with those who so speak of" (μὴ μέντοι μηδὲ τοῖς λέγουσι κοινωνεῖν)¹⁶¹ the Holy Spirit as a creature. In the context of Pneumatomachianism, he was ready to declare that:

> Any innovation (καινοτομία) in the position of the Holy Spirit involves the abolition of his very existence, and is equivalent to a denial of the whole faith. It is therefore in like manner impious either to degrade him to the position of a creature, or to raise him above either Son or Father in either time or position.¹⁶²

Basil, in one of his letters publicly declared: "We pity those who call the Spirit a creature, because they fall into the unpardonable

---

159 *Ep.* 125.3: Deferrari, II, 267. Ὁ δὲ περὶ τοῦ Πνεύματος λόγος ἐν παραδρομῇ κεῖται οὐδεμιᾶς ἐξεργασίας ἀξιωθεὶς διὰ τὸ μηδέπω τότε τοῦτο κεκινῆσαι τὸ ζήτημα, ἀλλ᾽ ἀνεπιβούλευτον ἐνυπάρχειν ταῖς τῶν πιστευόντων ψυχαῖς. Courtonne, II, 33.
160 *Ep.* 125.3: Deferrari, II, 267. Ἀναθεματίζειν τοὺς λέγοντας κτίσμα τὸ Πνεῦμα τὸ Ἅγιον [...] ἀλλ᾽ ἀποξενοῦντας αὐτὸ τῆς θείας καὶ μακαρίας φύσεως. Courtonne, II, 33.
161 *Ep.* 114: Deferrari, II, 229. Courtonne, II, 19.
162 *Ep.* 52.4: Deferrari, I, 337. Ἡ περὶ τὴν τάξιν καινοτομία αὐτῆς τῆς ὑπάρξεως ἀθέτησιν ἔχει καὶ ὅλης τῆς πίστεώς ἐστιν ἄρνησις. Ὁμοίως οὖν ἐστιν ἀσεβὲς καὶ ἐπὶ τὴν κτίσιν καταγαγεῖν καὶ ὑπερτιθέναι αὐτὸ Υἱοῦ ἢ Πατρός, ἢ κατὰ τὸν χρόνον, ἢ κατὰ τὴν τάξιν. Courtonne, II, 33.

error of blasphemy against him by the use of such language".[163] To profess the faith in such a way was considered by Basil to be no different from cutting oneself off from the communion of the church. This is why in his letter to the priests at Tarsus he states that only "those who do not call the Holy Spirit a creature should be received in communion" (τοὺς μὴ λέγοντας κτίσμα τὸ Πνεῦμα τὸ Ἅγιον δέχεσθαι εἰς κοινωνίαν).[164] Generally speaking, for Basil, all "innovations in regard to the faith" (περὶ τὴν πίστιν καινοτομουμένων) and all things spoken of that were "contrary to sound teaching" (ὑπεναντίως τῇ ὑγιαινούσῃ διδασκαλίᾳ), were outlawed.[165] Basil considered his teaching on the Holy Spirit to be in line with tradition since it was an inherent element of the received deposit (παρακαταθήκη) of faith, and relevant, in that it ascribed glory to all three persons of the Trinity.[166] Basil argues that what he is advocating has credibility since it was transmitted by men of holiness: "There is the custom observed among us, which we can cite in defence of our position, a custom having the force of the law, because our ordinances have been handed down to us by holy men".[167] To the accusation, then, of being an innovator, and in response to the "common talk" that appears to be branding Basil and his supporters with "the charge of heterodoxy" (οἱ νῦν ἡμᾶς διαθρυλήσαντες ἐπὶ κακοδοξίᾳ),[168] Basil responds:

> We confess what indeed we have received, that with Father and Son is placed the Paraclete, and is not numbered among the creatures [...] For this reason never do we sep-

---

163 *Ep.* 159.2: Deferrari, II, 397. Τοὺς δὲ κτίσμα λέγοντας τὸ Πνεῦμα τὸ Ἅγιον ἐλεοῦμεν ὡς εἰς τὸ ἀσυγχώρητον πτῶμα τῆς εἰς αὐτὸ βλασφημίας, διὰ τῆς τοιαύτης φωνῆς, καταπίπτοντας. Courtonne, II, 87.
164 *Ep.* 113: Deferrari, II, 223. Courtonne, II, 17.
165 *Ep.* 126: Deferrari, II, 273. Courtonne, II, 35.
166 See *Ep.* 105: Deferrari, II, 200. Courtonne, II, 6.
167 *Ep.* 160.2: Deferrari, II, 401. Τὸ παρ' ἡμῖν ἔθος, ὃ ἔχομεν προβάλλειν νόμου δύναμιν ἔχον διὰ τὸ ὑφ' ἁγίων ἀνδρῶν τοὺς θεσμοὺς ἡμῖν παραδοθῆναι. Courtonne, II, 88.
168 *Ep.* 223.3: Deferrari, III, 301. Courtonne, III, 13.

arate the Paraclete from his union with the Father and the Son [...] Therefore, neither do we ourselves invent names, but we call the Holy Spirit also Paraclete, nor do we suffer ourselves to refuse the glory which is due him. These teachings are ours in all truth.[169]

It was only two years after Basil's death in 381 that the Nicene Creed was amended at the Council of Constantinople. "I believe in the Holy Spirit" was expanded to "And in the Holy Spirit, the Lord, the giver of Life, who proceeds from the Father, who together with the Father and the Son is worshipped and glorified".[170] Although Radde-Gallwitz thinks otherwise,[171] it seems very plausible that the path to the Council of Constantinople was influenced by Basil of Caesarea. Perhaps this explains why Gregory of Nazianzus was grateful to his precious friend Basil for the final victory of neo-Nicene theology in the Eastern empire, calling him "a light for the whole world" (τῇ οἰκουμένῃ πάσῃ πυρσεύουσα).[172]

2.7 Conclusion

Throughout Basil's theological writings he takes on all those who refuse to honour the Holy Spirit with the Father and the Son. Basil's overall concern was to defend intelligently his beliefs against all viewpoints undermining Nicene theology and, in particular, the divinity of the Holy Spirit. At his disposal he had the Scriptures

---

169 *Ep.* 226: Deferrari, III, 339. Ἡμεῖς γὰρ ὁμολογοῦμεν ὃ καὶ παρελάβομεν, μετὰ Πατρὸς καὶ Υἱοῦ τετάχθαι τὸν Παράκλητον, οὐ μετὰ τῆς κτίσεως ἀριθμεῖσθαι [...] Διὰ τοῦτο οὐδέποτε τῆς πρὸς Πατέρα καὶ Υἱὸν συναφείας τὸν Παράκλητον ἀποσπῶμεν [...] Οὔτε οὖν ὀνόματα παρ' ἑαυτῶν ἐπινοοῦμεν, ἀλλὰ Πνεῦμα Ἅγιον καὶ Παράκλητον ὀνομάζομεν, οὔτε τὴν ὀφειλομένην αὐτῷ δόξαν ἀθετεῖν καταδεχόμεθα. Ταῦτά ἐστι τὰ ἡμέτερα μετὰ πάσης ἀληθείας. Courtonne, III, 27.
170 *The Divine Liturgy of Our Father among the Saints John Chrysostom*, Lee, 29. Καὶ εἰς τὸ πνεῦμα τὸ ἅγιον, τὸ κύριον καὶ ζωοποιόν, τὸ ἐκ τοῦ πατρὸς ἐκπορευόμενον, τὸ σὺν πατρὶ καὶ υἱῷ συμπροσκυνούμενον καὶ συνδοξαζόμενον. Text in Hahn, *Bibliothek der Symbole und Glaubensregeln der Alten Kirche*, 162.
171 Radde-Gallwitz, *Basil of Caesarea*, 79.
172 Gregory of Nazianzus, *Oration* 43.25. SC 384. 184.

and his philosophical learning which he employed extensively to accomplish his aims. While it is true that Basil's technical terminology was flexible and never acquired the status of a definition, what matters is how he understood Greek words from a biblical frame of reference. Irrespective of the development of his thoughts or his change of vocabulary, Basil's theology continued to remain coherent. Despite the clear difference between the "early" and "late" Basil, the theological vision proposed in *Against Eunomius* always remained "the basis of his Trinitarian thought".[173]

From this chapter, Basil's basic theological argument has three parts: (1) that unbegotteness does not express the essence of God; (2) that the Father, Son and Holy Spirit, although different as *hypostases*, are same in essence; and (3) that the divine generation of the Son or the procession of the Holy Spirit are not influenced by time and materiality. Forming a coherent order, these three arguments are logically connected in that the first prepares for the second, which in turn is strengthened by the third. Here Basil first shows that God's essence is not unbegotteness before he demonstrates that the begotten *hypostasis*, and by implication the proceeded *hypostasis*, are the same in essence to the unbegotten *hypostasis*. Once the sameness of the Father, the Son and the Holy Spirit is established, Basil moves on to explain what accounts for their distinction: namely, divine unbegotteness, divine generation and divine procession. Basil's concept of *monarchia* locates the Father as the eternal source of the Son and the Holy Spirit, who therefore guarantees the unity and *homotomia* of the Trinity. The glorification of the Trinity promulgated by Basil was a proclamation of his theology of communion, which for him was best realised in worship.

---

173 Hildebrand, *The Trinitarian Theology*, 22.

Chapter Three:
Basil as a Bishop in the Context of Late Antiquity

It was not enough for Basil to keep his Trinitarian Theology with its distinct emphasis on the divinity of the Holy Spirit for himself. These theological positions analytically explored in the previous chapter would have their greatest outreach once he became a bishop of the church. For Basil, the church's identity, mission and ministry was intimately connected to and founded upon these confessed theological truths, without which the church's communion could not be actualised. Being a bishop allowed Basil to fight in the greatest possible way for theological and social change. He advocated for a Nicene Christianity that went hand in hand with moral uprightness and that consequently was also social in character. The episcopacy gave him a voice and therefore presented him with what was perhaps the only means possible through which he could inspire doctrinal orthodoxy and spiritual edification. This chapter examines the role of the bishop within the context of the later years of Basil's life. An emphasis will be placed on Basil's ministry years, particularly the period of the reign of Emperor Valens (364–378), the non-Nicene sympathiser who did all that he could to make Basil change from his Nicene position and adopt the religious policy of the imperial regime. At the same time, Basil's Caesarea will be viewed from the vantage point of its administrative/theological demographics, its pastoral outreach and the philosophical framework underpinning its functionality. It will be shown that Basil's care for the poor was a defining feature of his episcopal ministry, which found expression in his commitment to social justice. Finally, it will be pointed out that the underlying current of Basil's activities was his monastic outlook, which entailed a life of shared resources, as well as reciprocal care and charity, all of which facilitated and nurtured communion in the church.

3.1 The Ministry of the Bishop in Late Antiquity

For Christians living in the first two decades of the fourth century, their primary concern was their very survival. They were up against a Roman government that was trying systematically to destroy the Christian church in support of the polymorphous paganism of the ancient classical world. In this context, it was only natural for the theological controversies that came to the fore with Arius in 319 at worst to go unnoticed, or, at best, to catch many by surprise. Conflict was not limited to those from outside the church (government policy) but now also came from within (through theological disputes). The imperial toleration of Christianity through the Edict of Milan in 313, which removed the label of *religio illicita* from Christianity, was still too weak to put an end to persecutions altogether.

By 324, under Emperor Constantine, Christianity had become the dominant and state-sanctioned religion of the Roman Empire. This provided for the restoration of Christian property and also accommodated compensation from the state for any confiscations it had executed on Christian possessions. Mitchell notes that no new pagan temples were founded, and that the many major centres of pagan worship that remained, gradually either fell into disrepair or were replaced by churches.[1] Consequently, while becoming the "dominant social force in the Roman world",[2] the church had to redefine its position and no longer consider itself as being in opposition to the state. With the new imperial status quo, the church had everything at its disposal to cooperate with the

---

1 Mitchell, *A History of the Later Roman Empire*, 335.
2 Holman, *The Hungry are Dying*, vii.

state and work within the existing social order.³ Due to an absence in the clarification of the roles between church and state, Brown argues that it was not necessarily smooth sailing for the church in that the new imperial regime, through its efforts to maintain public good, brought frequent challenges to the ministry of the clergy.⁴ Even so, with Constantine as emperor, the church and its constituents were included within the wider institutions of the empire, which created a significant precedent for positive future relations between church and state.

Accordingly, under Constantine's regime, clerics were excluded from civic liturgies and the paying of taxes, bishops could act as arbitrators in legal disputes, and celibacy/virginity was no longer considered as a punishable crime for a childless couple.⁵ As detailed in Eusebius of Caesarea's ten-volume *Church History*, Christianity was identified with the good of the empire, and Christian clergy were alleviated of fiscal demands and curial responsibilities. According to Eusebius, under Constantine the clergy are: "completely free to serve their own law [Christianity] at all times. In thus rendering wholehearted service to the Deity, it is evident that they will be making an immense contribution to the welfare of the community".⁶ Amongst the greatest surprises, as will be shown below, was the sanctioning of church construction so as to propagate the worship of the God of the Christians. Seemingly there had been a definitive end to persecution.

While the state toleration of Christianity gave birth to its increase in numbers, it also tried to forge a marriage with Christianity which introduced secular values into the Christian church. Arnold Jones explains:

---

3   Rapp, *Holy Bishops in Late Antiquity*, 7.
4   Brown, *Poverty and Leadership in the Later Roman Empire*, 31–33.
5   Corcoran, *The Empire of the Tetrarchs*, 320. Barnes, *Constantine and Eusebius*, 50.
6   Eusebius, *Church History* 10.7.2: Williamson, 327. Ἄνευ τινὸς ἐνοχλήσεως τῷ ἰδίῳ νόμῳ ἐξυπηρετῶνται, ὥνπερ μεγίστην περὶ τὸ θεῖον λατρείαν ποιουμένων πλεῖστον ὅσον τοῖς κοινοῖς πράγμασι συνοίσειν δοκεῖ. SC 55. 112–113.

With Constantine's conversion the situation was completely changed. Wealth poured in on the church, and the middle classes began to press into holy orders. It was no longer a social disadvantage and a slight risk to be a Christian. Converts could not only feel secure, but might hope to gain material advantages from their conversion. As a result, the number of Christians grew, especially among the middle and upper classes.[7]

New opportunities for public officers and careers amongst the Christian faithful brought with them new challenges unforeseen by the stakeholders of the church's leadership. Power, prestige, glory and wealth, which were once foreign to Christianity, were within Christianity's range, especially now that Christianity was becoming very much a part of the public profile of the Roman Empire. This is in particular true within the hierarchical governance of the Christian church which, under Constantine, saw the beginning of a dramatic transformation in the status of the bishop. In the past, in 257, Emperor Valerian had decreed the death penalty for all members of the clergy and especially the bishops. Seventy years later, these very same occupations became positions of distinction and privilege. The social prestige of the bishop only increased with the passing of time.[8] Bishops of large cities, such as Rome, Alexandria and Antioch, considered themselves to be amongst the higher echelons of the church's hierarchy and were

---

[7] Jones, *The Later Roman Empire*, 96. See Fedwick, *The Church and the Charisma of Leadership*, 18, n. 91.
[8] On the raising status of the episcopate and its significance see Drake, *Constantine and the Bishops*, 309-352; Rapp, "The Elite Status of Bishops in Late Antiquity in the Ecclesiastical, Spiritual and Social Context", 379-399.

treated as such.⁹ This led to the more formal ranking of clerical offices and their corresponding episcopal sees.

With the patronage of the empire, ecclesiastical governance now operated within the sphere of influence of imperial authority, and depending on its integrity (or lack thereof) would either resist opportunities of expediency or create opportunities of expediencies for the sake of personal gain. The late antiquity historian Theodoret, in attempting to make sense of the exiles enacted during the reign of the first Christian emperor, Constantine, explains: "It ought not to excite astonishment that Constantine was so far deceived as to send many great men into exile: for he believed the assertions of bishops of high fame and reputation, who skilfully concealed their malice".¹⁰ For Theodoret, the church hierarchy was responsible for informing the imperial policy that constituted the governance of the church. Church conflicts interplayed with imperial politics which in turn often heavily influenced the outcome of these conflicts. Through political intrigues, every action was justified by an imperial state that had as a set agenda the overturning of the Council of Nicaea and its decrees. Indeed the non-Nicene position, with its subordination of the Son of God to the level of creature, could be seen to lend itself to the

---

9　The episcopacy of Antioch was so desired by bishops for its connection to the New Testament as well as its prerogatives over regional jurisdiction that during the fourth century it was contested by up to four rival bishops each representing different factions. It was often referred to as Great Antioch (Ἀντιόχεια τὴ Μεγάλη). The episcopacy of Alexandria included all of Egypt in its jurisdiction and was renowned for its immense wealth. The see of Constantinople acquired a "seniority of honour" by the second Ecumenical Council in 381 and was ranked "second only to the bishop of Rome" due to it being the see of the imperial capital. Not surprisingly its eminence was further enshrined with the epithet "New Rome". The bishop of the see of Rome was seen as the successor of the Apostle Peter.

10　Theodoret, *Church History* 1.33.1: Jackson, NPNF, vol. 3, 64. Θαυμαζέτω δὲ μηδεὶς εἰ τηλικούτους ἄνδρας ἐξαπατηθεὶς ἐξωστράκισεν. Ἀρχιερεῦσι γὰρ κρύπτουσι μὲν τὴν πονηρίαν, τὴν δὲ ἄλλην ἔχουσι περιφάνειαν, ἐξαπατῶσιν ἐπίστευσεν. SC 501. 322–324. When translating Theodoret's *Church History* into English, Jackson's chapter numbers appear to be one or two less than the numbering mentioned in the Greek edition of Sources Chrétiennes.

continued acknowledgment of the Roman ruler cult, albeit now with pseudo-Christian overtones. If Christ the Son and Logos of God the Father is not worshipped as God, then this creates an opening for the emperor, by which, as in former pagan days, the eternity and hence divinity of the emperor is established. Seen in this light, non-Nicenism, even if it added nothing philosophically to the emperors' way of life, at the very least helped him stake a greater claim for prominence and importance within his empire.

During the reign of Constantius (337–361), joint synods were convoked in Ariminum and Nicomedia in 359 that were attended by Eastern and Western bishops respectively. As a side issue to the emperor's agenda to bring all bishops "to be of the same mind" (ὁμοδόξους [...] ποιήσειεν)[11] within the immovable parameters of a non-Nicene expression of faith, the council managed to extol the emperor as "eternal" which among other things implied that the empire's wellbeing depended exclusively on the wellbeing or happiness of its emperor. This orchestrated appraisal of the emperor in consultation with his own men ("bishops of the *oikoumene*") implied that Constantius now had complete authority to control unilaterally the religious affairs of the empire. He was considered to be the chief priest (*pontifex maximus*) of the empire. Acquiring the ruler cult status that hitherto had been applied to pagan emperors, albeit without Olympian attributes and qualities explicitly associated with Jupiter and Hercules, meant that Constantius had the jurisdictional authority to determine the "form" (Nicene or non-Nicene) of Christianity that was to be taken up by his empire. Pagans, Jews and non-conforming ("heretical") Christian sects were treated with disdain and a greater level of intolerance.[12] Rufinus in his *Church History* (c. 402) describes the negative state of affairs of the church at the time in a most lamentable way: "This

---

11 Socrates Scholasticus, *Church History* 2.37.1. SC 493. 162.
12 Non-imperial sanctioned religious observances and practices, like many other aspects of life in late Roman antiquity, often escaped the grasp of the state. See Mitchell, *A History of the Later Roman Empire*, 229–234.

was the time when the face of the church was foul and exceedingly loathsome, for now it was ravaged, not as previously by outsiders, but by its own people".[13]

Up until the 350s disputes and factions were fluctuating in the Roman East, but after 360 those who adhered to a Nicene standard of faith were marginalised. Valens (364–378) actively tried to compel church leaders to compromise and accept a non-Nicene faith position, which led to a deepening of schism and a distraction to Nicene faith. Valens' acceptance of non-Nicene persuasions was politically motivated in that he used the forced adherence of a non-Nicene agenda as a means of exercising control on his constituents. Appropriating the Roman notion of *concordia*, Valens, just like his predecessor Constantine, and to a greater extent Constantius, took an interest in resolving theological disputes only so that he could unite his empire in what he considered to be times of discord. Christianity in its different forms was used by the empire as a universal religion that lent itself to shaping a centralised uniform culture. Since the time of Constantine and his successors, all statements or actions by emperors and their successors were presented in a Christian tone that only got louder with the passing of time as the affairs of church and state became more and more bound to one another.

For the most part, patronage was so fundamental to the imperial regime in late Roman antiquity that it transcended any religious or political ideology. Philosophically it was the fierce pursuit for unity within the empire that mattered most for state officials and not the safeguarding and nurturing of one's salvific experience as realised within the communion of the church, and as having its most lasting expression in a theological formula. The Christian identity became a political force to the extent where Barnes argues

---

13   Rufinus, *Church History* 10.22: Amidon, p. 33. "Ea tempestate facies Ecclesiae foeda et admodum turpis erat; non enim sicut prius ab externis, sed a propriis vastabatur". *Eusebius Werke, Band II*. Die Griechischen Christlichen Schriftsteller der Ersten Drei Jahrhunderte, Schwartz, 988.

that "no emperor could rule securely without the acquiescence of his Christian subjects".[14]

Imperial policy aimed to create a single unified church that could include the largest possible number of the empire's inhabitants. Essential tenets of Christian faith were used as a unifying principle during the later Roman Empire and therefore were enforced. After 368 Valens did not shy away from exiling non-compliant bishops in his efforts to do whatever he could to avoid a schism.[15] Furthermore those Christians whose religious convictions did not toe the line of official imperial policy were made subject to harsh measures. Behind the scenes Basil argued that non-Nicene prelates instigated non-Nicene government policies by making "use of the power of government in accordance with their will"[16] and therefore became the catalyst to their enforcement. Demosthenes, for example, much to Basil's disapproval, used civil fiscal burdens as a form of punishment that he imposed on non-Nicene opponents. It is no wonder that Basil described Demosthenes as one who is "friendly to heretics, and no more friendly to them than he is full of hate towards us".[17] The aim of the non-Nicene hierarchs was to undermine the decrees of the Council of Nicaea with what Basil described as a "long-standing deception" (χρονίας ἀπάτης).[18] With the right amount of pressure applied, especially with the backing of the imperial court, it was hoped that Nicene doctrinal networks would not be able to stand. In his *Church History*, Theodoret remarks: "Such were the murders to which the blasphemy of Arius gave rise. Their mad rage against the

---

14   Barnes, "Christians and Pagans under Constantius", 308.
15   Mitchell, *A History of the Later Roman Empire*, 68.
16   *Ep.* 248: Deferrari, III, 481. Τῇ ἐκ τῆς ἀρχῆς δυναστείᾳ πρὸς τὸ ἑαυτῶν βούλημα κεχρημένοι. Courtonne, III, 86.
17   *Ep.* 237.2: Deferrari, III, 409. Φιλαιρετικὸς καὶ οὐ πλέον ἐκείνους φιλῶν ἢ πρὸς ἡμᾶς ἀπεχθῶς ἔχων. Courtonne, III, 56.
18   *Ep.* 243.4: Deferrari, III, 447. Courtonne, III, 72.

only begotten was matched by cruel deeds against his servants".[19]

St. Jerome (d. 420) was not so forgiving of the emperor's errors as Theodoret. In his view, the emperor should have known better than to be led astray by the theological errors of mischievous hierarchs. In his *Chronicle*, he blames Constantine for all the problems created by non-Nicene prelates: "Constantine, baptised by Eusebius of Nicodemia at the very end of his life, falls into the dogma of Arius, and from that time until now seizures of churches and discord of the whole world have followed (*totius orbis est secuta discordia*)".[20]

The bishop in late antiquity was considered the head (προεστώς) and therefore the very centre of the church community. Excluding parts of North Africa, the Council of Nicaea afforded special status to the metropolitan of every province while assigning a primacy of honour to the primates of Rome, Alexandria and Antioch. As a result of this ruling, from as early as Constantine the local church within an administrative jurisdiction was defined by reference to its bishop. Although a local bishop in theory was part of an established system of loose mutual oversight, in practice he more often than not governed in an autonomous way. Writing towards the end of 324 to Eastern bishops, Constantine turned to them, irrespective of their hierarchical rank, to build and organise the running of churches with expenses paid by imperial funds. In doing so, Finn points out that he was also replicating "the generosity shown by pagan predecessors to pagan temples".[21] The following letter, written c. 330, although personally addressed to one bishop, was sent by Constantine to every place where an ecclesiastical authority resided.

---

19 Theodoret, *Church History* 2.5.4: Jackson, 67. Τοιαύτας μιαιφονίας ἡ Ἀρείου βεβλάστηκε βλασφημία. Τῇ γὰρ κατὰ τοῦ μονογενοῦς λύττῃ συμβαίνει τὰ κατὰ τῶν ἐκείνου θεραπόντων τολμήματα. SC 501. 346.
20 St. Jerome, *Chronicle*, book II: Baghos, "Apology for Athanasius", 70. "Constantinus extremo vitae suae tempore, ab Eusebio Nicomediensi episcopo baptizatus, in Arrianum dogma declinat; a quo usque in praesens tempus ecclesiarum rapinae et totius orbis est secula discordia". PL 27. 679–680.
21 Finn, *Almsgiving in the Later Roman Empire*, 13.

Where therefore you yourself are in charge of churches, or know other bishops and presbyters or deacons to be locally in charge of them, remind them to attend to the church buildings, whether by restoring or enlarging the existing ones, or where necessary build new. You yourself and the others through you shall ask for the necessary supplies from the governors and the office of the prefect, for these have been directed to cooperate wholeheartedly with what your holiness proposes.[22]

To the bishop was entrusted the spiritual and material well-being of his subjects, which Basil saw as involving a lifetime committed to devotion and service. Along with this, according to Basil, came the responsibility of maintaining the "communion of the good" (τῆς τοῦ ἀγαθοῦ κοινωνίας),[23] that is to say, the eucharistic communion of the churches under the bishop's spiritual oversight. If necessity dictated, Basil argued that the bishop was called upon to exclude from the Christian community unworthy members, "not receiving [them] into [eucharistic] communion until they cease from the sin".[24] The life-time appointment of a bishop within his episcopal see meant that he was not subject to changes that were brought about by appointed aristocrats entering and exiting any given eparchy. Likewise Canon Fifteen of Nicaea prescribed that a bishop was not allowed to transfer to another see (e.g. a vacant see with greater affluence) upon his own accord, nor could a bishop apply for occasional retirement and subsequent return. In the words of Van Dam, bishops knew all too well that they had to

22 Eusebius, *Life of Constantine* 2.46: Cameron and Hall, 111. Ὅσων τοίνυν ἢ αὐτὸς προΐστασαι ἐκκλησιῶν, ἢ ἄλλους τοὺς κατὰ τόπον προϊσταμένους ἐπισκόπους, πρεσβυτέρους τε ἢ διακόνους οἶσθα, ὑπόμνησον σπουδάζειν περὶ τὰ ἔργα τῶν ἐκκλησιῶν, καὶ ἢ ἐπανορθοῦσα τὰ ὄντα, ἢ εἰς μείζονα αὔξειν, ἢ ἔνθα ἂν χρεία ἀπαιτῇ, καινὰ ποιεῖν. Αἰτήσεις δὲ καὶ αὐτός, καὶ διὰ σοῦ οἱ λοιποὶ τὰ ἀναγκαῖα παρά τε τῶν ἡγεμόνων, καὶ τῆς ἐπαρχικῆς τάξεως. Τούτοις γὰρ ἐπεστάλη, πάσῃ προθυμίᾳ ἐξυπηρετήσασθαι τοῖς ὑπὸ τῆς σῆς ὁσιότητος λεγομένοις. PG 20. 1024A-B.
23 *Ep.* 199.24: Deferrari, III, 127. Courtonne, II, 159.
24 *Ep.* 199.18: Deferrari, III, 109. Οὐ πρότερον παραδεξάμενοι εἰς κοινωνίαν πρὶν ἢ παύσασθαι τῆς ἁμαρτίας. Courtonne, II, 156.

"remain faithful to their sees for life. A see was a bishop's wife"[25] and, unless extreme circumstances required it, they could not meddle into the affairs of another ecclesiastical jurisdiction. Such a life-time tenure of a bishop's office made upward promotion by lesser orders of the clergy very stringent and extremely rare, with a large pool of possible candidates to choose from.

The patronage of bishops by the imperial court changed the way the ministry of the episcopacy functioned in unprecedented ways. Christians were being accommodated and integrated into the social and political landscape of the empire. For the bishops this meant that they became a new ruling group of leading citizens (albeit still in the making), in principle distinct from the Roman *curia*, although this line between the two groups sometimes became blurred. Ideally the bishops were not there to replace the *curia* and its functions, nor were they there to be amalgamated into its role, but they were to work in parallel with those who dominated leadership in civil matters.[26] Seen as community leaders, bishops could utilise their influence to stimulate action amongst leaders and their people for the common good. Finn notes, for example, that "their words had their place in facilitating, increasing, shaping, and interpreting the flow of alms from the rich to very poor".[27]

Imperial subsidies were granted to the Christian church commensurate to its demographics in a locality and as evidenced by its number of clergy as well as its people in need. In time, government subsidies became institutionalised which in turn enhanced the financial standing of the churches and their bishops. While Basil experienced the start of this in the fourth century, later centuries saw the church's financial position multiply substantially to the point where, in the words of Cameron, it developed "into a pow-

---

25 Van Dam, "Bishops and Society", 353.
26 See Rapp, *Holy Bishops in Late Antiquity*, 279-289.
27 Finn, *Almsgiving in the Later Roman Empire*, 175.

erful and wealthy institution".[28] Basil was part of a new era where the church for the first time ever had its own real estate and, furthermore, received supplementary revenue through regular contributions, government subsidies, imperial donations and, significantly from 321, through the legalisation of pious bequests.[29] Individual episcopal sees became substantial land owners, with bishops taking on the duty of managing estates.[30]

Amongst other things, bishops had the complete responsibility of using the income from their sees for the needs of their diocese which involved providing charity to the needy, the upkeep of churches, and the creation of permanent church infrastructure through various building projects.[31] As the unconditional protector of the poor and disenfranchised, the bishop had to represent and respond to the needs of a large discernible group within a city's population.[32] His reputation as a moral authority was instrumental in securing further funds which, together with all other charitable monies, he distributed through his priests and deacons.[33]

To assist the organisational running of a diocese, ecclesiastical

---

28 Cameron, *The Later Roman Empire*, 77. See Brown, *Poverty and Leadership in the Later Roman Empire*, 54.
29 Van Dam comments: "Constantine was very generous to various churches. At Rome he endowed the churches with estates located throughout the empire that produced over 400 pounds of gold annually in rents, and he brightened their interiors with silverware, gold chandeliers and porphyry columns. Some private benefactors, including bishops themselves, were almost as beautiful". Van Dam, *Bishops and Society*, 359. See Jones, *The Later Roman Empire*, 894–910; Finn, *Almsgiving in the Later Roman Empire*, 36.
30 See Lizzi, "Vir Venerabilis: The Bishop, Fiscal Privileges and Status Definition in Late Antiquity", 125–144.
31 Finn loosely describes the bishops as having a "considerable theoretical freedom of manoeuvre in what was spent". The needs of a diocese were at the mercy of a bishop's esteemed priorities. Building projects, for example, often ran into the income available for almsgiving. Finn, *Almsgiving in the Later Roman Empire*, 59.
32 See Brown, *Power and Persuasion in Late Antiquity*, 71–118; Rapp, *Holy Bishops in Late Antiquity*, 260–273.
33 See *Ep.* 150; *Apostolic Constitutions*, 8.47.41. The total income at the discretional disposal of the bishop surpassed the income of some of the most prominent professionals and statesmen within the empire.

jurisdictions were patterned on existing imperial jurisdictions, which nevertheless changed over time. Van Dam states that by the early fourth century, the empire had over one hundred provinces that were each administered by a provincial governor who in turn was supported by a substantial staff of lawyers and other advisors.[34] Along with ensuring that a city met its tax obligation to the empire, provincial governors held executive powers over public buildings and services, and administered proceedings for local courts of justice.[35] In practice this model was a replica of the supreme authority of the emperor and his chief ministers who operated within a framework of strict procedures and protocols.[36] Ecclesiastical dioceses corresponded to the civil provinces and sub-provinces with the bishop of the capital city of each province becoming the metropolitan bishop, his civil counterpart being the governor. The title of Basil's *Ep.* 252 "To the Bishops of the diocese of Pontus" (Ἐπισκόποις τῆς Ποντικῆς διοικήσεως)[37] is an example of how an ecclesiastical jurisdiction is commensurate with a civil division and unit of government.

Whereas in the past bishops had been loosely connected through letters and occasional visits, now they had a more extensive organisation. Their social and spiritual duties were endorsed by law. Through the metropolitan bishop, provincial councils could be convened more regularly, which allowed disputes to be resolved between bishops, or between a bishop and his clergy or his congregation. Leading up to the Nicene council in 325 and until it was revoked by Julian, Emperor Constantine granted Christian bishops free access to public conveyance so that in their travels they could more readily attend to synodical gatherings.[38]

---

34 Van Dam, *Bishops and Society*, 350.
35 Jones, *The Later Roman Empire*, 732-763.
36 Mitchell, *A History of the Later Roman Empire*, 173-180.
37 Courtonne, III, 93.
38 See Eusebius, *Life of Constantine* 3.6; Theodoret, *Church History* 1.6; Silvas, *The Asketikon of St. Basil the Great*, 41-42.

Through attending synods and councils at a local and regional level, bishops received, articulated and safeguarded orthodox theology and dealt with matters of church governance.

Now almost every city in the empire had a bishop, with the more prominent cities serving as metropolitan sees. Where there were no cities, it was not uncommon to find villages having their own assistant bishop, as well as to see large areas of landed estates under the supervision of rural bishops (χωροεπίσκοποι).[39] The presence of theological controversies within the empire brought about the consecration of rival bishops in any given city, which meant that some cities could have as much as two or even three bishops. From her own research, Rapp estimates that all together there were up to two thousand bishops in the later Roman Empire, not including renegade bishops.[40] To help solve controversies over doctrine and the establishment of parallel bishoprics, councils of bishops were convened which were heavily assisted by the empire and which were modelled on imperial administration.

In past centuries, Christian bishops and their congregations had been marginalised within a centralised system of Roman polity. In Basil's era they were being augmented and even called upon by emperors to serve as judges and envoys. By 355, bishops had become key players in the arena of the empire. They represented as much as six million believers by this date, or upwards of 10 percent of the empire's population.[41] With an ever-increasing role in the public life of the later Roman Empire, bishops were no longer seen only as doctrinal partisans by government forces, but were esteemed as valuable social leaders in a local setting, "the *ombudsman* of an entire local community",[42] who had the capacity to run

---

39 See Chapter Five.
40 Rapp, *Holy Bishops in Late Antiquity*, 173.
41 Drake, *Constantine and the Bishops*, 73. Similar figures are found in Keith Hopkins, "Christian Number and its Implications". *Journal of Early Christian Studies*, vol. 6, no. 2 (1998): 192. See Finn, *Almsgiving in the Later Roman Empire*, 6–7.
42 Brown, *The Rise of Western Christendom*, 78.

law courts and organise festivals. Schor lists bishops as "teachers, liturgical leaders, pastoral caregivers, legal arbitrators, charity distributors, community organisers and voices of appeal".[43] The bishop's role in practical matters was analogous to that of the *patronus* or public benefactor whose access to steady financial resources, influence through social networking, and persuasion through rhetoric, assisted him in his activities. Individual beneficiaries of Basil's patronage included a defamed priest, a falsely accused man, offenders in need of mediation, and slaves who had offended or enraged their masters.[44]

In Basil's context all these activities took place without losing sight of the fact that the bishop was primarily a shepherd of his flock. This identity could easily be forgotten through financial administration, building works and other concerns that in reality only indirectly contributed to the spiritual nourishment of a bishop's congregation. Scholars such as Chadwick[45] and Rousseau[46] present the bishop's ministry as an integrative combination of the spiritual and the secular, a natural movement from theory to practice. A bishop's actions were very much an extension of his beliefs; his social interactions were founded upon theological principles and were considered inalienable to his prayer life. Likewise Sterk, in her detailed studies on Cappadocia and late antiquity, traces the interconnection between the role of the monk and that of the bishop.[47] The trend among these and other English-speaking scholars like Brown[48] is not to compartmentalise the bishopric of late antiquity as an isolated social or political phenomenon; rather the bishopric is viewed as a construct of secular and religious ele-

---

43 Schor, *Theodoret's People*, 199. Arnold Jones makes reference to church officials doubling up as traders, artisans and small landowners. See Jones, *The Later Roman Empire*, 906-909.
44 See *Epp.* 72, 73, 177, 178, 273-275, 307.
45 Chadwick, "Bishops and Monks", 45-61.
46 Rousseau, "The Spiritual Authority of the 'Monk-Bishop'", 380-419.
47 Sterk, *Renouncing the World Yet Leading the Church*.
48 Brown, *Poverty and Leadership in the Later Roman Empire*.

ments that ultimately complement each other. For this reason Rapp concludes that the former pronounced dichotomy of charisma versus institution, that once characterised the role of the bishop in scholarship, is no longer given serious consideration.[49]

The office of the bishop in late antiquity experienced a period of growth and change as necessity dictated and as circumstances permitted. As Christianity grew in numbers, so also the office grew in importance, thereby immensely amplifying the public role of the bishop.[50] As cities were becoming increasingly Christianised, so bishops increasingly became spokesmen for their cities and took up a leadership role in civic life. The protection that bishops afforded people translated into a loyal following. Once upon a time the bishops were limited to the outskirts of a province where the state regime gave them no choice but to operate incognito; now, through state incentives, they had new churches and shrines constructed for them and in areas that were also known to all. Easter and Christmas festivals, together with their street processions led by the bishop, were very much part of a fixture of the civil calendar.[51] The bishop in theory could be trusted and therefore not pose a threat to the emperor through political ambition or intrigues. The bishops were able to establish monasteries, orphanages, charitable institutions for the poor and oppressed, and even make inroads into civic amenities. In the words of Cooper and Decker, they became the "spiritual and public focal point of the church".[52]

---

49 Rapp, *Holy Bishops in Late Antiquity*, 16.
50 For a good introduction into the growing public role of a bishop in late antiquity see Jones, *The Later Roman Empire*, 724–763.
51 With the passage of time, the Apostles, local martyrs and former bishops were also commemorated. Pagan festivals were not removed all together as Eusebius' *The History of the Church* would like its readers to believe. There are many historical sources which suggest that non-Christian festivals and rituals continued to be celebrated throughout the empire. See Bowersock, *Hellenism in Late Antiquity*; Mitchell, *A History of the Later Roman Empire*, 229–234; Cameron, *The Later Roman Empire*, 57–58. For pagan cultural practices and attitudes in late antiquity see MacMullen, *Christianity and Paganism in the Fourth to Eighth Centuries*.
52 Cooper and Decker, *Life and Society in Byzantine Cappadocia*, 140.

It is these initiatives that set bishops apart from other aristocratic patrons of the period and which contributed to Christianity being attractive to prospective converts where they were enabled, as Cameron says, to move "in the upper echelons of society".[53] The emperor at times had more faith in the bishops of the church than in his very own senators (traditionally the highest Roman rank) and military commanders. According to Van Dam, the bishops were now powerbrokers in their cities: "As local patrons they [the bishops] represented their cities and individual citizens before imperial magistrates".[54] Rapp heralds them as being the most powerful figures in late antiquity who were capable of challenging or usurping civil authority.[55] Constantine and subsequent Christian emperors allowed bishops to mediate formal court proceedings and hear all types of cases involving civil conflict. Civil magistrates were expected to enforce a bishop's decision, which naturally had Christian overtones rather than the strict application of the Roman code of law.[56] In such situations Basil insisted that charity prevailed and that all decisions of justice were measured against Christian teachings: "For what the stripes of the court do not accomplish, this we have often known the fearful judgments of the Lord to effect".[57] In this regard Basil consciously aimed to spare the guilty party too heavy a punishment.

In response to acts of servitude towards the State, hierarchs were now able to turn to the civil leadership of their constituents and ask

---

53 Cameron, *The Later Roman Empire*, 73.
54 Van Dam, *Bishops and Society*, 344.
55 Rapp, *Holy Bishops in Late Antiquity*, 3–7.
56 See Gregory of Nazianzus *Ep.* 78.6: Οἱ μὲν ἄμετροι, καὶ πικροὶ, καὶ μέχρις αἵματος προϊόντες· ἡμῖν δὲ χρηστοὶ καὶ φιλάνθρωποι, καὶ μὴ συγχωροῦντές τι τῷ θυμῷ χρῆσθαι κατὰ τῶν ἀδικούντων. PG 25. 148C. "[Roman laws] are excessive, harsh and susceptible to blood penalties, while our laws are kind and generous, and they do not permit any use of anger against wrongdoers". Van Dam, Becoming a Christian, 71.
57 *Ep.* 286: Deferrari, IV, 177. Ἃ γὰρ αἱ τῶν δικαστηρίων πληγαὶ οὐκ ἐργάζονται, ταῦτα ἔγνωμεν πολλάκις τὰ φοβερὰ κρίματα τοῦ Κυρίου κατορθοῦντα. Courtonne, III, 157.

for assistance. Basil did not hesitate to argue that it was the absolute duty of civil authorities and their fiscal officers to complete what the bishops lacked. In a letter addressed to the magistrates of Nicopolis, Basil asserted: "What was in the power of the most God-beloved bishops has been completed, but what remains now looks to you [the magistrates]".[58] The prefect's accountant was asked by Basil to equip his assistant bishop "with whatever he requests" (πάντα αὐτῷ παρέξῃ τὰ ἐπιζητούμενα), namely financial assistance for Basil's poor houses (πτωχοτροφεῖα).[59] Acting as a spokesman in petitions to the imperial authorities, Basil's six letters to the prefect Modestus[60] contained appeals for tax exemption[61] for the clergy and requests for clemency[62] on behalf of the faithful living in dire straits. Monks too, in *Epp.* 284 and 285, also benefited from Basil's patronage, for he had to make a special plea for their tax exemption since they were not considered to be part of the clergy. Regarding monks, Basil's written request asked taxation officials:

> To relieve from taxation those who have long ago withdrawn from the world, and have mortified their bodies so that neither with money nor with bodily service can they contribute anything useful to the public welfare. For if they are living according to their profession, they have neither money nor bodies, having spent the one for the general needs of the poor and having consumed the other in fasting and prayer.[63]

All these new entitlements from the imperial state were of great benefit to Basil in his ministry and certainly removed any legal

---

58 *Ep.* 230: Deferrari, III, 357. Ὁ μὲν ἦν ἐπὶ τοῖς θεοφιλεστάτοις ἐπισκόποις πεπλήρωται· τὸ δὲ λειπόμενον ἤδη πρὸς ὑμᾶς βλέπει. Courtonne, III, 35.
59 *Ep.* 143: Deferrari, II, 347. Courtonne, II, 65.
60 *Epp.* 104, 110, 111, 279, 280, 281.
61 See *Ep.* 104: Deferrari, II, 197.
62 See *Ep.* 281
63 *Ep.* 284: Deferrari, IV, 173-175. Τοὺς πάλαι ἀποταξαμένους τῷ βίῳ, νεκρώσαντας δὲ ἑαυτῶν τὸ σῶμα, ὡς μήτε ἀπὸ χρημάτων μήτε ἀπὸ τῆς σωματικῆς ὑπηρεσίας δύνασθαί τι παρέχειν τοῖς δημοσίοις χρήσιμον, ἀφιέναι τῶν συντελειῶν. Καὶ γάρ, εἴπερ εἰσὶ κατὰ τὸ ἐπάγγελμα ζῶντες, οὔτε χρήματα ἔχουσιν οὔτε σώματα, τὰ μὲν εἰς τὴν τῶν δεομένων κοινωνίαν ἀποκτησάμενοι, τὰ δὲ ἐν νηστείαις καὶ προσευχαῖς κατατρίψαντες. Courtonne, III, 155.

obstacles that would impede his letters from arriving at their destination. From the tone of Basil's letters, one can see that irrespective of the "good will" (εὐμενείας)⁶⁴ shown by those in authority, Basil never rested on his laurels. His underlying concern was that the Christian faith was becoming stagnant and all because "privileges" (δωρεᾷ) and "kind favours" (φιλανθρωποτάτης χάριτος)⁶⁵ had done away with persecution at the expense of Christian witness. The clarity of the once polarised positions of the Christian communion was becoming obscured. According to Basil, in their complacency the faithful, who were influenced by the new state regime of late antiquity, were not as forthcoming in professing their allegiance of "either confessing communion with the enemies of faith or denying it".⁶⁶ It is as if Basil was attributing the lower levels of spirituality amongst the faithful to the progressive institutionalisation of the church. From the past, one thing was obvious for him: under persecution the church all the more confessed Christ.

Ambition, competition and access to finances introduced elements which made the episcopal office attractive, but which also went against the grain of core tenets of Christian life. In the bishopric certain aspirants saw power and honour as an additional distinction to their careers and not as an opportunity for work and service.⁶⁷ This ran contrary to Basil's own standards, which declared that a bishop ought to be "a servant of God, a workman that needed not to be ashamed, not considering the things that are his own, but those of the many, that they may be saved".⁶⁸ The conceits that once tempted Basil as an educated man upon his graduation from Athens found a different kind of expression in the episcopal

---

64 See *Ep.* 280: Deferrari, IV, 167. Courtonne, III, 152.
65 See *Ep.* 281: Deferrari, IV, 169. Courtonne, III, 153.
66 *Ep.* 128.2: Deferrari, II, 279. Ἡ ὁμολογῶν τὴν κοινωνίαν πρὸς τοὺς ἐχθροὺς τῆς πίστεως ἢ ἀρνούμενος. Courtonne, II, 38.
67 See Rapp, *Holy Bishops in Late Antiquity*, 200-203.
68 *Ep.* 190: Deferrari, III, 71-73. ἤ τις δοῦλος Θεοῦ, ἐργάτης ἀνεπαίσχυντος, μὴ σκοπῶν τὸ ἑαυτοῦ, ἀλλὰ τὸ τῶν πολλῶν, ἵνα σωθῶσιν. Courtonne, II, 38.

office.[69] To the lay person Basil said that this presented itself as "forgetfulness of friends" (λήθη φίλων) and "haughtiness which is engendered by power" (ὑπεροψία ἐκ δυναστείας ἐγγινομένη).[70] To such an observation from a lay person, Basil responded: "If we are filled with the conceit of empty pride and arrogance, then we are fallen into the sin of the devil from which there is no escape".[71] In his defence, however, Basil concluded his response with the affirmation: "Never assume that a man's preoccupation with affairs is a sign of his character of malice".[72] No one was invulnerable to the enticements of the episcopal office or at least unaware of what it could potentially offer, whether rightly or wrongly. The bishopric was part of the competition for social status in Roman society; as such, charges of misappropriation and maladministration were never far away.

There is considerable debate regarding the proportion of Christians and pagans who were high ranking officials in the fourth century and there is uncertainty about the rate at which Roman senators converted to Christianity. Barnes argues that Christians obtained the majority of senior government posts from the time of Constantine and Constantius (c. 335–340), at least 30–40 years earlier than most commonly held views.[73] Certainly by Basil's time there were Roman senators who found in the prestigious vocation of the bishopric opportunities to preserve and enhance their nobility, thereby furthering their aristocratic leanings. If the nobility of senatorial rank entertained acting in this way, it was very impressionable for others in society to follow suit. Simony and nepotism were common in this era, so that once someone got "in" to the

---

69 See Chapter One.
70 *Ep.* 56: Deferrari, I, 353. Courtonne, I, 143.
71 *Ep.* 56: Deferrari, I, 353. Εἴτε φρονήματος κενοῦ καὶ ἀλοζονείας ὑπεπλήσθημεν τυφωθέντες, ἐμπίπτομεν εἰς τὸ ἄφυκτον κρίμα τοῦ διαβόλου. Courtonne, I, 143.
72 *Ep.* 56: Deferrari, I, 353. Μὴ τοίνυν ποτὲ τὰς ἀσχολίας σημεῖον τρόπου καὶ κακοηθείας ποιήσῃ. Courtonne, I, 143.
73 Barnes, "Statistics and the Conversion of the Roman Aristocracy", 135–147.

bishopric this created an opening for others of his kind to follow, culminating in the creation of "ecclesiastical families".[74] Ever since Emperor Constantine extended tax immunity to cover the bishops,[75] episcopal service for some aspirants became more attractive and much to be desired, and was considered to be as honourable as serving in the imperial administration.

Notwithstanding all that has been said, many bishops and the clergy assigned to them were, above all, men of faith that were motivated by a spiritual commitment to serve the church. Any prestige or authority accumulated along the way was to be used for the good of their respective ministry. They could now more readily lend aid to individuals and congregations and take on a greater supportive role for dependents such as widows, their children and beggars. Like most Roman notables, bishops were now better placed to carry out their correspondence with their constituents. They could send out pastoral letters about life-style choices to the monastic communities that they supervised, whereas to congregations they could readily communicate advice on family issues. With some sense of acquired status and respect they could write to officials about taxation subsidies or apply what Liebeschuetz identifies as "continuous moral pressure" and appeal to the charity of wealthy aristocrats for donations.[76] As the church's resources increased so too did Christian philanthropy. Basil used increased access to financial resources and other state sanctioned benefits to create charitable foundations (like houses for the poor), build churches and attend to the needy. Throughout these activities

---

74 Van Dam, *Bishops and Society*, 347. Chapter Five deals with Basil's reaction to nepotism, especially in the way in which suffragan bishops were elected.
75 Julian in his endeavours to revive paganism tried to cancel this privilege of granting tax immunity; whereas subsequent Christian emperors from Jovian to the mid-fifth century at the very least modified or restricted this privilege. Importantly they did not remove it altogether. See Theodoret, *Church History* 1:11.3; 4:4.6; Sterk, *Renouncing the World Yet Leading the Church*, 44; Mitchell, *A History of the Later Roman Empire*, 73–79; 245–246.
76 Liebeschuetz, *Barbarians and Bishops*, 251.

bishops were increasingly being entrusted to carry out secular undertakings that were centred on philanthropy. Gone were the days where all the bishop had to do was to appoint and supervise clerics. Now stemming from the primary task of the bishop, which was centred on the Eucharist and the ministry of the word (preaching), were new and unprecedented undertakings.

The legal recognition of the bishop's ministry by the state brought with it official duties, not least of which included the management of finances and the administration of charitable institutions. In the hands of the church, social responsibilities that once upon a time fell within the jurisdiction of the state organically took on a Christian framework. The financial assistance and other benefits received from the state, such as tax exemptions, were never interpreted by Basil as being a "cost" to the state but rather as benefiting the state. The more the state provided to the church, the greater beneficiary it was of the church's prayer and affection. Financially any monies the church could save through its tax exemptions were saved for the primary purpose of giving to the poor and needy. Basil lauded the prefect Modestos' much anticipated generosity by having reminded "so great a man" (ἄνδρα τοσοῦτον) that because he was able to "stretch forth a helping hand" (χεῖρα ὀρέξαι) to a people "bowed to its knees" (εἰς γόνη [...] κλιθείσῃ), heavenly protection awaited him.[77] In his plea to Modestos, Basil remarked:

> This will not only keep the glory of the good deeds of your great lordship immortal, but it will also increase the number of those who pray for the imperial house, and will confer a great benefit even upon the public revenues, since we give the relief which is derived from our immunity from taxation, not altogether to the clergy, but to those who are

---

77 *Ep.* 104: Deferrari, II, 195. Courtonne, II, 5.

at any time in distress; indeed, this is just what we do when we are free to do so, as anyone who wishes may find out.[78]

Behind every ministry administered by the church was the hope and even anticipation of a Christianised society, that is, that the Christian faith would influence and shape the dominant worldview.

3.2 Basil as Bishop in Fourth-Century Cappadocia

In Basil's case the civil prominence of Caesarea (today Kayseri or south thereof) as the capital of the district of Cappadocia, acknowledged him as a metropolitan bishop. Cappadocia is situated to the east of central Asia Minor in a land-locked mountainous region that rises 8000 feet above sea level and was recognised to be "rich in olives, grapes, grain and livestock".[79] All major roads and trading routes between Constantinople and Syria passed through Cappadocia, many of which intersected at Caesarea and assisted the continuous thoroughfare of "soldiers, traders, vagrants and other travellers".[80] As a metropolitan bishop, Basil had jurisdiction (episcopal oversight) over twelve other bishops in the province of Cappadocia, as well as fifty "rural bishops" (χωροεπίσκοποι)[81] or assistant bishops for presumably the vast imperial estates[82] and ranches in Cappadocia that were generally leased to long-standing

---

78 Ep. 104: Deferrari, II, 197. Ταῦτα καὶ τῇ σῇ μεγαλοφυΐᾳ ἀθάνατον τὴν ἐπὶ τοῖς ἀγαθοῖς δόξαν διαφυλάξει καὶ τῷ βασιλικῷ οἴκῳ πολλοὺς τοὺς ὑπερευχομένους παρεσκευάσει καὶ αὐτοῖς τοῖς δημοσίοις μέγα παρέξει ὄφελος, ἡμῶν οὐ πάντως τοῖς κληρικοῖς, ἀλλὰ τοῖς ἀεὶ καταπονουμένοις τὴν ἀπὸ τῆς ἀτελείας παραμυθίαν παρεξομένων, ὅπερ οὖν καὶ ἐπὶ τῆς ἐλευθερίας ποιοῦμεν, ὡς ἔξεστι γνῶναι τῷ βουλομένῳ. Courtonne, II, 5.
79 Holman, *The Hungry are Dying*, 70.
80 Holman, *The Hungry are Dying*, 70.
81 See *Epp.* 53, 54, 142, 143, 290.
82 "Much of the land dating back to royal property of pre-Roman days". Rousseau, *Basil of Caesarea*, 174, n. 181.

tenants.⁸³ While not exercising ministry over empty landscapes, these rural bishops carried out the function of what today would be classified as a local parish priest. Episcopal oversight over what was primarily rural territory required Basil to make many journeys during his career, including visits to his suffragan bishops but also to assist in affairs beyond the borders of his diocese.⁸⁴ In Armenia, for example, Basil took on the role of a peacemaker as he co-ordinated the appointment of bishops there.⁸⁵ The same would apply with his visits to the provinces of Isauria and Pontus.⁸⁶ In 376 Basil claimed to have travelled to Pisidia "to settle the affairs of the brethren in Isauria with the bishops there".⁸⁷ From his position as a metropolitan bishop, Basil was entrusted with the responsibility to chair and convene provincial episcopal councils, resolve conflicts amongst bishops, or mediate when there was a dispute between a bishop and the members of his flock. Without Basil's consent no new bishops could be appointed for Cappadocia.⁸⁸

Basil's understanding of his episcopal ministry was significantly influenced by what he perceived as the crisis of the church in his day. Emperor Valens, who ruled in the Christian East during most of Basil's ecclesiastical career, was described a century later as one "who persisted in waging war" against "the champions of the

---

83 See Sterk, *Renouncing the World Yet Leading the Church*, 72; Mitchell, *A History of the Later Roman Empire*, 306. For a recent scholarly monograph on the history of Cappadocia, see Cooper and Decker, *Life and Society in Byzantine Cappadocia*. Rousseau notes: "Much of the land around Caesarea belonged to the imperial fisc, which invited frequent contact with officials responsible to the court rather than to local provincial authorities". Rousseau, *Basil of Caesarea*, 134.
84 See *Epp*. 95, 99, 125, 126, 224.2.
85 On Basil's activities and challenges in Armenia see *Ep*. 99.1-3. For a comprehensive commentary on the work of Basil in Armenia see Rousseau, *Basil of Caesarea*, 278-288.
86 See *Ep*. 99 regarding Armenia and *Epp*. 216, 217.1 regarding Isauria and Pontus.
87 *Ep*. 216: Deferrari, III, 239. Ὥστε μετὰ τῶν ἐκεῖ ἐπισκόπων τὰ κατὰ τοὺς ἐν τῇ Ἰσαυρίᾳ ἀδελφοὺς τυπῶσαι. Courtonne, II, 207.
88 See Chapter Five.

Apostolic decrees".[89] Contemporary commentator Radde-Galwitz asserts that Valens "initiated a purge of Nicene bishops from their sees".[90] With non-Nicenism as the stabilising force behind Valens' empire, Basil did not hesitate to communicate with those who came from the ranks of the imperial court and who were considered as figures of wealth and influence. He associated with the powerful not only because he had to live with them, but also, and most importantly, so as to establish alliances and work with them. Without their support and without working "within" the socio-political landscape of his day, he simply could not operate.[91] With the hope of obtaining Christian policies, Basil assures Count Terentius that he will only be too happy to obey an "imperial ordinance" (βασιλικῷ προστάγματι).[92]

Exercising the primary centre of power, the imperial court was made up of twenty-four individuals who indefinitely served as high officers (that is, as prefects, consuls, and chamberlains among others). Together they became the emperor's orbit of power where they implemented his decisions and acted as links to his office. Although at the time of Basil's episcopacy officials from the emperor's court were theologically hostile to Nicaea (excluding the prefect Modestos), Basil wasted no opportunity to ask them for whatever he could, from the waiving or lowering of taxes (*Epp.* 88, 142, 284) to having the provisional boundaries of his diocese redrawn (*Epp.* 74–76). Basil's correspondence at this level was always measured and never permitted even the slightest acknowl-

---

89 Theodoret, *Church History* 5.21.3: Jackson, 146. Πολεμῶν διετέλει τοῖς τῶν ἀποστολικῶν ὑπερμαχοῦσι δογμάτων. SC 530. 424.
90 Radde-Gallwitz, *Basil of Caesarea*, 133.
91 For example one brings to mind Basil's cooperation with Emperor Valens regarding the ecclesiastical affairs affecting Armenia, see Rousseau, *Basil of Caesarea*, 278–288. For a study on episcopal eloquence, influence and its authority in late antiquity see Brown, *Power and Persuasion in Late Antiquity*. Gain attributes Basil's frequent successes in the political sphere to the personal relationships that he established with civil officials. Gain, *L'Église de Cappadoce*, 321.
92 *Ep.* 99.1: Deferrari, I, 214. Courtonne, II, 171.

edgement of a non-Nicene faith. Nevertheless his correspondence, as was standard for bishops of the time, did involve pleading for help and some implicit understanding of an exchange of favours which resulted in promised loyalties.

Basil endeavoured to act within the parameters of his monastic vocation and episcopal responsibility. He was up against an imperial system that often saw private and public interests as being closely interconnected. Basil was no stranger to the temptations surrounding the bishopric by the time of his episcopal ordination in 370. His letters made it very clear that no tenet of the Christian faith should ever be compromised for the sake of public relations with civil authorities. Basil made a point of mentioning that some people "in order to be accepted by those now in power" had acted in ways by which they "renounced communion".[93] Basil's letters give evidence that he thought it possible, especially if necessity dictates, to communicate with those in power without compromising one's beliefs. Studies of the bishoprics of Asia Minor in Basil's era reveal that for bishops to fulfil their ministry effectively, not only did they have to accept the existing social order, but they also had to take into consideration the leading people of their respective cities.[94] The bishop needed to be a stabilising force, and to do this it was imperative to develop relationships with the nobility and to operate in conjunction with them.

In some instances local notables occupied more of a bishop's energy than other members of the laity. Many of these notables served on civic councils where they implemented imperial law and wrote appeals, and the wealthiest amongst them controlled hundreds of estates or even whole villages. Local notables in Basil's day were called upon to use their resources to support a bishop's causes

---

93 *Ep.* 223.7: Deferrari, III, 311. ῎Ινα μηδὲν ἐκ τῆς ὁμολογίας δόξῃ αὐτοῖς ἐμπόδιον ἀπαντᾶν πρὸς τὸ ὑπὸ τῶν νῦν κρατούντων παραδεχθῆναι, ἀπείπαντο τὴν πρὸς ἡμᾶς κοινωνίαν. Courtonne, III, 17.
94 See Whittow, "Ruling the Late Roman and Early Byzantine City", 3–29.

and fund his projects.[95] Some notables were recruited by bishops to serve as clerics, including physicians, orators and lawyers who used their influence to secure tax breaks. In return, the notables benefited from being the recipients of a bishop's advice (life coaching), and from having access to the bishop's vast network of connections. Hunt claims that most bishops in late antiquity came from the municipal elite, the *curiales*, who were the landowning families and who often left their status and land dwellings as an inheritance to their children.[96] Rapp supports this view by further stating that the *curiales* were the largest recruiting ground for all orders of the clergy.[97]

Basil's elevation to the episcopacy was accompanied by the trimming of his episcopal see in Caesarea in early 372. Strictly speaking Cappadocia found itself partitioned into two unequally sized provinces: Cappadocia Prima, with Caesarea remaining as its capital, and Cappadocia Secunda, with Tyana as its new capital city. The smaller part of Cappadocia was left to the diocese of Caesarea and thus to Basil's omophorion, whereas Tyana promptly had Anthimus installed as its presiding hierarch. Except for Caesarea, all the cities of the former province now belonged to Secunda.[98] Scholars such as Fedwick and Baynes[99] attribute this trimming of Caesarea to retaliation on the part of Emperor Valens

---

95 See *Epp.* 142, 143.
96 Hunt, "The Church as a Public Institution", 264. It is true that in the fourth century cities were nominally governed by local landowners who represented local interests. See Mitchell, *A History of the Later Roman Empire*, 9.
97 Rapp, *Holy Bishops in Late Antiquity*, 185.
98 For details on the partitioning of Cappadocia see Arnold H.M. Jones, *The Cities of the Eastern Roman Provinces* (Oxford: Clarendon, 1971), 182–187; Van Dam, "Emperor, Bishops, and Friends in Late Antique Cappadocia", 53–76; Gain, *L'Église de Cappadoce*, 307–309.
99 See Fedwick, *The Church and the Charisma of Leadership*, 13–16. Fedwick's chronology of Basil's life and works rests upon the assumption (albeit implied) that Cappadocia was divided following the confrontation between Valens and Basil. Norman Baynes, not mincing his words, makes it clear that "the emperor Valens will divide the city province of Cappadocia in order to strike a blow at the authority of Saint Basil". Baynes, *Byzantine Studies and other Essays*, 99.

who wanted to settle the score with Basil as a result of their previous confrontation at the liturgical celebration of Epiphany.[100] The timing of the administrative division of Caesarea which quickly followed this event is enough in itself to raise suspicions. Since, as has been mentioned, ecclesiastical boundaries generally followed administrative ones, it was within the means of the non-Nicene sympathiser Valens to exhort his power and diminish the influence of Basil by decreasing the geographical territory under his oversight. Deferrari holds this to be the case and for this reason connects the shrinking of Basil's diocese with Emperor Valens' enmity towards the "orthodox" bishop.[101]

Raymond Van Dam dismisses the charge of imperial retaliation and instead asserts that the diminishment of Basil's diocese was simply an administrative move on behalf of the empire so as to accommodate its collection of fiscal revenue.[102] Sterk in a similar vein maintains that Valens more than likely "acted out of purely secular political motives in keeping with the general policy of dividing excessively large provinces for administrative purposes".[103] Basil's letters themselves indicate no sympathetic overtones that would support Van Dam's or Sterk's understanding. On the contrary, the very few letters that deal with the administrative division of Caesarea emphasise more than anything else the loss that

---

100 See Chapter One.
101 Deferrari, II, 66. As Deferrari understands it, "Valens was ever hostile to Cappadocia. Partly to vent his wrath upon in, and partly to obtain a greater amount of revenue, he had in 370 determined to divide it into two provinces". Deferrari, II, 160, n. 1.
102 "With these changes, then, Valens was trying to improve administrative and thereby fiscal control in Cappadocia". Van Dam, *Bishops and Friends in Late Antique Cappadocia*, 55.
103 Sterk, *Renouncing the World Yet Leading the Church*, 72. Cooper and Decker in their pragmatic explanation as to why Tyana was elevated to a metropolis over the new province of Cappadocia Secunda affirm: "The city's standing really owed to its situation in the midst of the fertile plains of the south and its strategic importance – it was a major stop on the road linking Anatolia with Cilicia on the way to Syria through the Cilician Gates". Cooper and Decker, *Life and Society in Byzantine Cappadocia*, 17. See Gain, *L'Église de Cappadoce*, 309.

now befell Caesarea. Instead of gaining from its administrative division (what Anthony Meredith brands "administrative convenience"),[104] it became apparent, according to Basil, that Caesarea had lost all that she ever had:

> What they have done is about the same as if a man, possessing a horse or an ox, should divide it into two parts, and then consider that he had two animals instead of the one he had. For he [Valens] has not created two [dioceses], he has destroyed the one.[105]

Even without determining the final reasons behind what Basil refers to as "incompetent people" (κακοί) and "inexperience" (ἀπειρίᾳ)[106] leading to the division of his diocese, the resulting situation meant that Basil had fewer areas and thus fewer bishops under his direct pastoral jurisdiction. To his enemies this signified good news as it guaranteed an automatic reduction in Basil's sphere of influence, his supporters' base having shrunk in size as it had in prominence and efficacy.

Having succumbed to the shaving of his diocese, Basil was not content simply to accept its demotion without any attempt to return it to its former prestige. Left as it was, Basil's diocese and Caesarea itself were unrecognisable since many of Caesarea's citizens left and migrated to Tyana, the new capital of Cappadocia Secunda. According to Basil, the new administration imposed on Caesarea was nothing short of total destruction, even though he made every effort to increase the number of sees in his diocese. In his comments to his friend and former fellow student Sophronius, the prefect of Constantinople, Basil complains: "No city destroyed

---

104 Meredith, *The Cappadocians*, 2.
105 *Ep.* 74.2: Deferrari, II, 71. Τί πεποιήκασιν ὥσπερ ἂν ἔι τις ἵππον ἢ βοῦν κεκτημένος, εἶτα δίχα διελών, δύο νομίζοι ἔχειν ἀνθ᾿ ἑνός· οὔτε γὰρ δύο ἐποίησε καὶ τὸν ἕνα διέφθειρεν. Courtonne, I, 174. This letter is Basil's most explicit reaction to Valens' reforms. *Epp.* 75 and 76 contain similar images of dismay and requests for help following the administrative division of Caesarea.
106 *Ep.* 74.1: Deferrari, II, 71. Courtonne, I, 173.

by earthquakes or buried by floods of water has met with such sudden effacement from the earth, as our own, swallowed up by this new administration of our affairs".[107] This sudden transformation imposed on Caesarea immediately prompted Basil to write letters to the most influential acquaintances whom he had at his disposal. He wanted them to "stretch a hand" (χεῖρα ὀρέξαι) to a "city now fallen to her knees" (τῇ πόλει ἡμῶν εἰς γόνυ κλιθείσῃ).[108] His hope was for these civil officials to intervene and overturn the imperial mandates placed on his diocese.

Basil wanted these friends, amongst whom was a future prefect of Rome, to appeal directly to the imperial court (if not to the emperor himself) so as "to give up the notion that they possess two provinces instead of one".[109] Determined, Basil was not going to back off from his request, his challenge to the authorities was clear: "Unless they quickly change (μεταβουλεύσωνται) their policies, they will not have any to whom they may show their benevolence".[110] Three letters, *Epp.* 74, 75 and 76 written from the autumn of 371, outlined Basil's requests and made a point of emphasising that the new administrative changes instituted on Caesarea, rather than improving Caesarea, had instead depleted Caesarea from all its resources. Basil remarked: "All that formerly made our city famous have left us [...] since those in authority have been removed, the whole edifice will collapse".[111] By Basil's estimates only a third of the citizens remained in Caesarea after its partitioning. This

---

107 *Ep.* 76: Deferrari, II, 81-83. Οὐ σεισμοῖς ἐκτριβεῖσα πόλις, οὐχ ὕδασιν ἐπικλυσθεῖσα εἰς ἀπώλειαν ἐχώρησε παντελῆ οὕτως ὡς ἡ ἡμετέρα, τῇ καινῇ ταύτῃ τῶν πραγμάτων οἰκονομίᾳ καταποθεῖσα, εἰς ἀθρόον ἦλθεν ἀφανισμόν. Courtonne, I, 178.
108 *Ep.* 76: Deferrari, II, 83. Courtonne, I, 178-179.
109 *Ep.* 74.2: Deferrari, II, 71. Μήτοι νομίζειν αὐτοὺς δύο κεκτῆσθαι ἀντὶ μιᾶς ἐπαρχίας. Courtonne, I, 174.
110 *Ep.* 74.3: Deferrari, II, 77. Ἐὰν μὴ ταχὺ μεταβουλεύσωνται, οὐδ 'ἔξουσιν εἰς οὕς τὴν φιλανθρωπίαν ἐνδείξονται. Courtonne, I, 176.
111 *Ep.* 74.3: Deferrari, II, 75. Ὅσα πρότεραν ἐποίει τὴν ἡμετέραν ὀνομαστὴν πόλιν ἡμᾶς ἐπιλελοίπασιν [...] Τῶν κρατούντων ὑφαιρεθέντων, ὥσπερ ἐρείσμασι πεσοῦσι συγκατενεχθῆναι τὰ πάντα. Courtonne, I, 175.

remaining third, for Basil, represented those who were "too weak to cope with the necessities of their situation" (τῆς χρείας ἀτονώτεροι ἀπελεγχόμενοι πρὸς αὐτό) and who "despair of life itself" (τὸ ζῆν ἀπειρήκασι).[112]

In the end it was not all bad news for Basil and his requests, even if the decision to partition his diocese was irrevocable. Theodoret records that Emperor Valens gave parcels of land as a donation to the poor and the sick under Basil's care. For Basil, this translated into imperial real estate being granted as gifts to the church of Caesarea for housing, for hospitals and for schools specialising in vocational training, and thereby contributed to the city's regional importance.[113] Consequently, as claimed by Cooper and Decker, Caesarea received "considerable and recurrent investment" with respect to its building works and civil infrastructure in the decades that followed up until the Council of Chalcedon in 451 (where Constantinople assumed the rank of the chief see in the East) and was the highest ranked church in all of Anatolia.[114] The events accompanying the partitioning of the Caesarean diocese were followed by Valens allowing Basil to have a certain amount of autonomy over the churches within his jurisdiction

---

112 Ep. 74.3: Τριῶν τοίνυν μοιρῶν, οἳ μὲν φεύγουσιν αὐταῖς γυναιξὶ καὶ ἑστίαις ἀπαναστάντες· οἳ δὲ ἀπάγονται ὥσπερ αἰχμάλωτοι, οἱ πλεῖστοι τῶν ἐν τῇ πόλει ἄριστοι, ἐλεεινὸν φίλοις θέαμα, ἐχθροῖς δὲ εὐχὴν ἐκπληροῦντες, εἰ δή τις γέγονεν ὅλως τοσοῦτον ἡμῖν ἐπαρασάμενος. Τριτάτη δέ που μοῖρα λέλειπται. Οὗτοι δὲ τήν τε ἀπόλειψιν τῶν συνήθων οὐ φέροντες καὶ ἅμα τῆς χρείας ἀτονώτεροι ἀπελεγχόμενοι πρὸς αὐτὸ τὸ ζῆν ἀπειρήκασι. Courtonne, I, 176. "Of the three sections of our city, some are going into exile, departing with their wives and hearths; some are being led away as captives, the majority of the best citizens, a miserable spectacle to their friends, but thus fulfilling their enemies' prayers, if indeed any enemy that ever lived has called down so terrible a curse on us. About a third part of the citizens is still left here; and these, because they cannot endure the separation from their old acquaintances, and being at the same time too weak to cope with the necessities of their situation, despair of life itself". Deferrari, II, 77.
113 Theodoret, Church History 4.16, 19. See Sterk, Renouncing the World Yet Leading the Church, 72; Radde-Gallwitz, Basil of Caesarea, 4.
114 Cooper and Decker, Life and Society in Byzantine Cappadocia, 16, 141-142, 213.

and thus independence from the supervision of the provisional governor. Valens also granted Basil ecclesiastical jurisdiction over the province of neighbouring Armenia which lay outside Basil's immediate metropolitanate.[115] To date no scholars have effectively been able to explain precisely why Valens granted Basil episcopal oversight in Armenia, a responsibility he had to share with Theodotus, the bishop of Nicopolis.[116] Rousseau states that this move "thrust Basil onto 'the world stage' with vengeance".[117] Basil, by right of "imperial ordinance" (βασιλικῷ προστάγματι),[118] could now "furnish bishops to Armenia" (δοῦναι ἐπισκόπους τῇ Ἀρμενίᾳ)[119] who in allegiance to him would uphold a Nicene position[120] and in this way work "for the best interests of the common organization of the churches"

---

115 Basil makes reference to this order from Valens in *Ep.* 99.1. *Epp.* 102 and 122 show how Basil designated bishops for Armenia Minor.
116 Fedwick, *The Church and the Charisma of Leadership*, 104, glosses over the point with an informative footnote (n. 9) that has no definitive conclusion. Rousseau comments: "The natural association of Caesarea with the Armenian church and Basil's personal connections around Neocaesarea would have made him an attractive envoy". Rousseau, *Basil of Caesarea*, 283. Van Dam suggests that the extra privileges granted to Basil were a sort of compensation granted to him by Valens since he divided his eparchy. See Van Dam, *Bishops and Friends in Late Antique Cappadocia*, 57. Andrew Radde-Gallwitz concludes that Valens "actively supported" Basil. Radde-Gallwitz, *Basil of Caesarea*, 3.
117 Rousseau, *Basil of Caesarea*, 283.
118 *Ep.* 99.1: Deferrari, II, 171. Courtonne, I, 214.
119 *Ep.* 99.4: Deferrari, II, 181. Courtonne, I, 217. Basil's episcopal interventions in Armenia are depicted in *Epp.* 102–103 and 227–230. It is around this time in the early 370s that Valens became increasingly vigilant against the Persians who at the time were making threatening advances towards the Kingdom of Armenia. In the 380s relations became amicable when an agreement was reached based on the division of Armenia into a smaller western zone, under Roman protectorate, and an eastern counterpart (Parsarmenia), which looked towards Persia. From the reign of Diocletian to that of Theodosius I (284–395) and especially after the Roman defeat of Persia in 298, emperors strenuously campaigned against internal rivals and defended their frontiers against external enemies. See Baynes, *Byzantine Studies and other Essays*, 201–208; Mitchell, *A History of the Later Roman Empire*, 52–55, 82.
120 See *Ep.* 120: Στάσεων ἐμπλῆσαι τὴν Ἀρμενίαν. Courtonne, II, 26. "Armenia has become filled with schisms". Deferrari, II, 249. For the complex relations between Cappadocia and Armenia as they are implicated in *Epp.* 120–122 see Rousseau, *Basil of Caesarea*, 278–287.

(τῇ κοινῇ καταστάσει τῶν Ἐκκλησιῶν βουλευόμενος).[121] Basil's concluding address to Count Terentius, the *comes* and *dux* of Armenia, indicates that Basil's commission to Armenia Minor was indeed successful: "I have established peace (εἰρηνεύσας) among the bishops of Armenia, and have argued with them in befitting terms to put aside their customary indifference, and to take up again the true zeal of the Lord in behalf of the churches".[122]

3.3 Basil as Father of the Poor

Basil's family was notable not only for its piety but also for its affluence and social status. Although it is difficult to determine whether anyone in Basil's family was of senatorial rank, it would not be an exaggeration to say that they were well within the elite minority of the upper class.[123] In an age where wealth was measured primarily by land holdings, Basil's family was indeed prosperous. Basil's privileged upbringing influenced his writings on how the wealthy should live, especially in terms of how they should look out for the poor. Writing in retrospect about the pivotal changes

---

121 *Ep.* 99.1: Deferrari, II, 173. Courtonne, I, 214. While this was desired, things did not always go to plan. Theodotus, bishop of Nicopolis in Armenia Minor, would refuse to cooperate with Basil when it came to placing bishops in Armenia based on the latter's association with Eustathius of Sebasteia (see *Ep.* 99.1) who Theodotus argued was of unsound faith. Basil believed he could get a written confession from Eustathius denying Theodotus' allegations, to which not only was he not able to but it was revealed, to Basil's surprise, that Eustathius had opposite (non-Nicene) views (see *Ep.* 99.3). Basil's *Ep.* 130 to Theodotus acknowledges that Theodotus was correct in his assumptions about Eustathius. If Basil's letters are any indication, it seems that he only got as far as Armenia Minor in the West with providing bishops.
122 *Ep.* 99.4: Deferrari, II, 181. Εἰρηνεύσας τοὺς τῆς Ἀρμενίας ἐπισκόπους καὶ διαλεχθεὶς αὐτοῖς τὰ πρέποντα, ὥστε ἀποθέσθαι τὴν συνήθη διαφορὰν καὶ ἀναλαβεῖν τὴν γνησίαν τοῦ Κυρίου ὑπὲρ τῶν Ἐκκλησιῶν σπουδήν. Courtonne, I, 217-218.
123 Thomas A. Kopecek, "The Social Class of the Cappadocian Fathers", presents the view that Basil's family belonged to the curial class of the aristocracy. See Kopecek, "The Social Class of the Cappadocian Fathers", 453-466. For a descriptive account of the privileges granted to the aristocracy in Basil's time, see Salzman, *The Making of a Christian Aristocracy: Social and Religious Change in the Western Roman Empire*, 24-68.

that he needed to make within his own life to serve the poor, Basil acknowledged that his commitment to serving the poor was the closest thing he could do to realise perfection within his own spiritual formation. In a confessional way he explained:

> Before all things my care was to make some amendment in my character, which had for a long time been perverted by association with the wicked. And accordingly, having read the Gospel, and having perceived therein that the greatest incentive to perfection is the selling of one's goods and the sharing of them with the needy of the brethren, and the being entirely without thought of this life, and that the soul should have no sympathetic concern with the things of this world.[124]

If there ever was a defining feature about Basil's ministry it would have to be his commitment to social justice and care for the poor. Finn in his monograph, *Almsgiving in the Later Roman Empire*, describes the situation of the poor as follows:

> A great many found themselves trapped in utter destitution, without home or savings, without a family to support them, unable to find sufficient work to feed and support themselves. In rural districts a few might join the bands of robbers who preyed on travellers [...] It was a fate which awaited in particular the sick, the aged, the crippled, the blind, or otherwise disabled.[125]

In Basil's era, the death of the poor through hunger, cold and exploitation was an unfortunate fact of everyday life as epitomised

---

124 *Ep.* 223.2: Deferrari, III, 293. Πρό γε πάντων ἐπιμελὲς ἦν μοι διόρθωσίν τινα τοῦ ἤθους ποιήσασθαι, πολὺν χρόνον ἐκ τῆς πρὸς τοὺς φαύλους ὁμιλίας διαστραφέντος. Καὶ τοίνυν ἀναγνοὺς τὸ Εὐαγγέλιον καὶ θεασάμενος ἐκεῖ μεγίστην ἀφορμὴν εἰς τελείωσιν τὴν διάπρασιν τῶν ὑπαρχόντων καὶ τὴν πρὸς τοὺς ἐνδεεῖς τῶν ἀδελφῶν κοινωνίαν, καὶ ὅλως τὸ ἀφροντίστως ἔχειν τοῦ βίου τούτου καὶ ὑπὸ μηδεμιᾶς συμπαθείας πρὸς τὰ ὧδε τὴν ψηχὴν ἐπιστρέφεσθαι. Courtonne, III, 10.
125 Finn, *Almsgiving in the Later Roman Empire*, 19–20.

by his words: "the hungry man is dying" (ὁ πεινῶν τήκεται).[126] Roman society at the time, even within an emerging Christian culture, offered no moral mandate which obligated anyone to help those who had no social affiliations. Without state-sponsored reliefs for the poor, what today would be considered as a type of "social security" or "pension", the only aid came in the form of appeals to charity from relatives, neighbours and friends.[127] Those with no kinship, friends or associates were expected to die, which highlighted the fact that need, on its own, was not enough to secure relief. Outside overt political and moral indifference towards the needy, the church had a unique calling to extend forth its hand and embrace the poor, especially as Sheather says "the poverty-stricken and ill who are not part of one's own household".[128] Donations were asked from richer members of the church and included offerings of the bishop's own possessions. Peter Brown explains:

> Nowhere was the Christian representation of the church's novel role in society more aggressively maintained than in the claim of the Christian bishops to act as "lovers of the poor". [....] In the fourth century conditions, "love of the poor" took on a new resonance. It was an activity that came to affect the city as a whole [...] In the name of a religion that claimed to challenge the values of the elite, upper class Christians gained control of the lower classes of the city.[129]

Church edifices and martyrs' shrines often created the public space for a bishop to interact with the poor and carry out his almsgiving through supervising lay people whom he committed

---

126 Basil, *I Will Tear Down My Barns*, 6. PG 31. 273D.
127 Describing the civil identity of the poor in the fourth century Peter Brown notes: "The homeless and destitute were excluded" from "the self-image of the traditional city". Brown, *Power and Persuasion in Late Antiquity*, 84.
128 Sheather, "Pronouncements of the Cappadocians on Issues of Poverty and Wealth", 380.
129 Brown, *Power and Persuasion in Late Antiquity*, 77-78.

towards this task.[130] Enrolled widows and their children became the principal beneficiaries of episcopal alms, as well as those who were among the poorest in the Christian and non-Christian communities. Christianity in its essential ideology unambiguously advocated for the poor, and with the injunction "love your neighbour" (ἀγαπήσεις τὸν πλησίον σου),[131] expected its followers to respond in practice to the predicament of the poor. Basil's *Ep.* 243 single-handedly points out what this involved: "Visits to the sick, the consolation of those who grieve, the assisting of those who are in distress, succour of all kinds".[132] Confronted with a moral challenge and a spur to action, the existence of the poor presented itself as an opportunity to highlight the public role of the bishop as a "governor of the poor".[133] From the second half of the fourth century hostels for the poor (πτωχοτροφία) where being established in major cities of the Eastern empire. Sozomen reports that by the time of Emperor Julian's reign in the early 360s, the prevalence of Christian hostels for the poor was well enough known for him to compete against them by imitating their operation along pagan lines.[134]

Basil's voice was heard loudest when he advocated for the needs of the poor and made their plight his own. This, according to Finn, was in line with a bishop's proper status as the "father of the poor" and "ultimate leader", with a claim to authority over the socially destitute, and where a bishop's "care for the poor was symbolic of his good government and orthodoxy".[135] On account of almsgiving, the donor, Basil maintained, was awarded the honour

---

130 Finn, *Almsgiving in the Later Roman Empire*, 11, 14. See Gain, *L'Église de Cappadoce*, 69–70.
131 Matt. 22:39, Mk. 12:31.
132 *Ep.* 243.4: Deferrari, III, 447. Ἐπισκέψεις τῶν ἀσθενούντων, παράκλησις τῶν λυπουμένων, βοήθεια τῶν καταπονουμένων, ἀντιλήψεις παντοδαπαί. Courtonne, III, 72–73.
133 Brown, *Poverty and Leadership in the Later Roman Empire*, 79.
134 See Sozomen, *Church History* 5.16; Gregory of Nazianzus, *Oration 4 (Against Julian* 1).
135 Finn, *Almsgiving in the Later Roman Empire*, 78, 213.

of being presented as a "father to countless children" (μυρίων παίδων πατέρα)[136] and furthermore acquired an enhanced status within the Christian community. Gregory of Nazianzus lauded Athanasius as the father of the orphans of Alexandria.[137] In Basil's view, to identify with the poor and afflicted (συμπαθείας τῶν θλιβομένων)[138] required the sensitivity to see their need as one's very own need. According to Florovsky, when this takes place, "the cold separation into 'mine' and 'thine' disappears".[139] Outside this sensitivity towards social responsibility, Basil held that a person was not true to himself or herself and consequently was inhibited from relating to the other. If this was the case, then, according to Basil, a person's possibility of salvation became compromised, since eternal judgement awaited a person who refused to help those who were suffering. At the very minimum, the promise of eternal bliss or punishment made social justice and philanthropy a core belief of Basil's Christian living, akin to an investment towards future (heavenly) rewards.[140] When Basil in his writings exposed the folly of greed, he was poignantly suggesting that human destinies lay beyond the ephemeral needs of the body and beyond the realms of a person's self-interest.[141]

Leading by example, Basil distributed much of his family inheritance to the needs of the poor, indeed the anonymous poor whom he viewed as instruments of God's justice. As Basil understood it, in precisely the same manner it behoved every Christian (not just the wealthy) to rid themselves of worldly possessions and offload them into the "stomachs of the poor" (τῶν πενήτων [...]

---

136 Basil, *I Will Tear Down My Barns*, 3. PG 31. 265C. See Gain, *L'Église de Cappadoce*, 89.
137 See Gregory of Nazianzus, *Oration* 21.10.
138 *Ep.* 31: Deferrari, I, 176. Courtonne, I, 73.
139 Florovsky, *Bible, Church, Tradition*, 41–42.
140 See Basil, *On Renunciation*, 8.
141 See Basil, *To the Rich*. PG 31. 292A; Sheather, *Pronouncements of the Cappadocians on Issues of Poverty and Wealth*, 384–387.

γαστέρας).¹⁴² Surpluses exist in the form of riches so that they can be of service to those in need. "For the just man", says Basil, "neither cares for wealth when it is present, nor seeks it when it is not present; for he is not inclined to the enjoyment of what is given but to its management (οἰκονομικός)".¹⁴³ Whatever one had that was over and beyond their actual need had to be distributed to those who had less, even to the point where Basil requested that "each should limit his possession to the last tunic".¹⁴⁴ In Basil's homilies, material possessions and spiritual gifts were considered to be not the private property of an individual but rather the common property of all. In one of his most often quoted social justice passages in support of this distributive mandate, Basil declares: "The bread you are holding back is for the hungry, the clothes you keep put away are for the naked, the shoes that are rotting way with disuse are for those who have none, the silver you keep buried in the earth is for the needy".¹⁴⁵

Such were the imperative needs of the poor, they could no longer continue to be ignored through the lifestyle choices of others, especially the rich, some of whom, according to Basil, were the ones who were "truly poor and deprived of all goodness" (πένης εἶ τῷ ὄντι, καὶ ἐνδεὴς παντὸς ἀγαθοῦ) through their being "poor in philanthropy" (πένης φιλανθρωπίας).¹⁴⁶ In a practical sense, there was a universal call from Basil for his people to simplify their life

---

142 Basil, *On Detachment from Wordly Things.* PG 31. 553A. See Gregory of Nazianzus, *Oration* 43.63.

143 *Ep.* 236.7: Deferrari, III, 405. Ὁ μέντοι δίκαιος οὔτε παρόντος ἐπιστρέφεται τοῦ πλούτου οὔτε μὴ παρόντα ἐπιζητεῖ· οὐ γὰρ ἀπολαυστικός ἐστι τῶν δεδομένων, ἀλλ᾽ οἰκονομικός. Courtonne, III, 54. See Basil, To the Rich. PG 31. 281B, 297C.

144 *Ep.* 150.3: Deferrari, II, 367. Εἰς τὸν ἔσχατον χιτῶνα ἕκαστον ἑαυτῷ περιστάναι τὴν κτῆσιν. Courtonne, II, 74.

145 Basil, *I Will Tear Down My Barns,* 7: Schroeder, Saint Basil the Great: On Social Justice, 69. Τοῦ πεινῶντός ἐστιν ὁ ἄρτος, ὃν σὺ κατέχεις· τοῦ γυμνητεύοντος τὸ ἱμάτιον, ὃ σὺ φυλάσσεις ἐν ἀποθήκαις· τοῦ ἀνυποδήτου τὸ ὑπόδημα, ὃ παρὰ σοὶ κατασήπεται· τοῦ χρῄζοντος τὸ ἀργύριον, ὃ κατορύξας ἔχεις. PG 31. 277A.

146 Basil, *I Will Tear Down My Barns,* 6. PG 31. 276A.

so as to create an opening where they could give of themselves to others through acts of mercy and charity. No one was considered exempt from this call towards a life of simplicity, especially since Basil argued that all are in need of receiving the benefits enacted by caring and sharing: rich and poor alike. Not least amongst the benefits was the freedom that was obtained from not being attached to possessions.

For Basil, if there was a language that was understood by all, it was not one that was necessarily spoken through words but rather one that was communicated primarily through the way that one lived his or her life. Schroeder points out that when it came to expressing religious faith "Basil was more than a man of words; he was also a man of action".[147] Rousseau maintains that Basil valued truth only when it could be qualified by actions – *praxis*, namely a visible response to Christian teaching through a display of behaviour.[148] In his own words the bishop of Caesarea firmly believed that "teaching a Christian how he ought to live does not call so much for words as for daily example".[149] Consequently, Basil considered himself to be "a man who both knows much from the experience of others, as well as from his own wisdom, and can impart it to those who come to him".[150]

Basil insisted on actions that are not just directed towards the building up of one's self, but rather on actions that are directed towards the benefit of others. Fasting in this context, for example, not only included abstinence from food but also abstinence from social discord so as to retain peace (εἰρήνη) and order (εὐταξία).[151]

---

147 Schroeder, *St Basil the Great: On Social Justice*, 33.
148 "It was how one lived that marked one out as a person of virtue and significance". Rousseau, *Basil of Caesarea*, 27. See 93–132, 181.
149 *Ep.* 150.4: Deferrari, II, 371. Ἡ περὶ τοῦ πῶς χρὴ ζῆν τὸν χριστιανὸν διδασκαλία οὐ τοσοῦτον δεῖται λόγου ὅσον τοῦ καθημερινοῦ ὑποδείγματος. Courtonne, II, 75. See *Homily* 327.1, 334.3, 337.1, 338.1.
150 *Ep.* 150.4: Deferrari, II, 371. Ἀνδρὶ πολλὰ καὶ ἐκ τῆς ἑτέρων πείρας καὶ ἐκ τῆς οἰκείας συνέσεως καὶ εἰδότι καὶ παρέχειν τοῖς προσιοῦσιν αὐτῷ δυναμένῳ. Courtonne, II, 75. See *Ep.* 190.1.
151 See *Homily* 330.10, 11; 331.5.

The *Apostolic Constitutions* expected that the money saved from fasting would be used for almsgiving.[152] In Basil's understanding, ascetic discipline was intrinsically linked to social harmony with each supporting and enhancing the other.[153] These types of actions, claims Rapp, are carried out in full public view and are considered to be a manifestation of one's ascetic sobriety.[154]

In all aspects of life but especially in times of crises, like the "famine of love" (λιμὸς ἀγάπης)[155] affecting Caesarea and central Anatolia in 369, Basil argued that there was an inexhaustible need "to offer in deed (ἔργῳ) examples (ὑποδείγματα) that are clear to all" and inclusive of all.[156] During the famine, Basil (who was not yet a bishop) wrote to Eusebius: "The famine has not yet released us, so that it is incumbent upon me to linger on in the city, partly to attend to distribution of aid, and partly out of sympathy for the afflicted".[157] Gregory of Nazianzus described Basil's response to the Cappadocian famine as follows: "Imitating the ministry of Christ [...] he ministered to the bodies and souls of the needy, combining marks of respect with the necessary refreshment, thus affording them relief in two ways".[158] Basil succeeded in prevailing upon the conscience of the wealthy so as to teach them to give to those less fortunate, namely the starving people of Caesarea. He maintained that the silent example of a bishop's deeds had to stand out more

---

152 Apostolic Constitutions 5.20.18.
153 Such is the understanding of Philip Rousseau after his reading of Basil's homilies. See Rousseau, *Basil of Caesarea*, 163.
154 Rapp, *Holy Bishops in Late Antiquity*, 23–55. See Sterk, *Renouncing the World Yet Leading the Church*, 52.
155 See *Ep*. 91: Deferrari, II, 129. Courtonne, I, 197.
156 *Ep*. 246: Deferrari, III, 477. Ἔργῳ πᾶσαν ἐναργῆ σπουδάσατε προσθεῖναι τὰ ὑποδείγματα. Courtonne, III, 85.
157 *Ep*. 31: Deferrari, I, 177. Οὔπω ἡμᾶς ὁ λιμὸς ἀνῆκε, διόπερ ἀναγκαία ἡμῖν ἐστιν ἡ ἐπὶ τῆς πόλεως διαγωγή, ἢ οἰκονομίας ἕνεκεν, ἢ συμπαθείας τῶν θλιβομένων. Courtonne, I, 73.
158 Gregory of Nazianzus, *Oration* 43.35: McCauley, 58. Τὴν τοῦ Χριστοῦ διακονίαν μιμούμενος [...] ἐθεράπευε μὲν τὰ σώματα τῶν δεομένων, ἐθεράπευε δὲ τὰς ψυχάς, συμπλέκων τῇ χρείᾳ τὸ τῆς τιμῆς καὶ ῥᾴους ποιῶν ἀμφοτέρους. SC 384. 204.

strongly than any of his words as a means of teaching. Concerning Bishop Dianius, who ordained Basil as a reader in 356, Basil made references to a man whom he "looked up to as majestic in appearance, magnificent and possessing great sanctity". Only from beholding Dianius' "spiritual" virtues which included "his gentleness of soul, his lofty spirit combined with mildness, his decorum, his control of temper, and his cheerfulness and affability mingled with dignity", did Basil really come to recognise Dianius and embrace his message.[159] In analogy to the conduct between a shepherd and his sheep, Basil held that the spiritual shepherd of the flock of Christ must be an example of moral teaching, through his holy way of life, for those entrusted to his pastoral care.[160]

In Basil's view, neither the cleric nor the lay person can ever aim too high in their pursuit of the spiritual life, but where the ordained minister did differ was in his pastoral responsibility before God. With respect to social justice, Basil firmly believed that the bishop was God's agent "to whom the management of the alms of the poor had been entrusted".[161] Notwithstanding his view of the coordinating role of the bishop, Basil considered charity to be a responsibility that all people had and he went to great lengths

---

159 Ep. 51.1: Deferrari, I, 325. Ἀπέβλεπον πρὸς τὸν ἄνδρα, ὡς μὲν γεραρὸς ἰδεῖν, ὡς δὲ μεγαλοπρεπής, ὅσον δὲ ἔχων ἱεροπρεπὲς ἐν τῷ εἴδει [...] ἡ τῆς ψυχῆς ἡμερότης, τὸ μεγαλοφυές τε ὁμοῦ καὶ πρᾷον, τὸ εὐπρεπές, τὸ ἀόργητον, τὸ φαιδρὸν καὶ εὐπρόσιτον τῇ σεμνότητι κεκραμένον. Courtonne, I, 132.
160 This attitude is very much emphasised in the writings of his friend Gregory of Nazianzus, who in his capacity as a bishop held so many views in common with Basil. In Gregory one finds the articulation of Basil's mindset: Καθαραθῆναι δεῖ πρῶτον, εἶτα καθᾶραι, σοφισθῆναι, καὶ οὕτω σοφίσαι, γενέσθι φῶς, καὶ φωτίσαι, ἐγγίσαι Θεῷ καὶ προσαγαγεῖν ἄλλους, ἁγιασθῆναι, καὶ ἁγιάσαι, χειραγωγῆσαι μετὰ χειρῶν, συμβουλεῦσαι μετὰ συνέσεως. Gregory of Nazianzus, Oration 2.71. SC 247. 184. "A man must himself be cleansed, before cleansing others; himself become wise, that he may make others wise; become light and then give light, draw near to God, and so bring others near; be hallowed, then hallow them, be possessed of hand to lead others by the hand, of wisdom to give wisdom". Gregory of Nazianzus, Oration 2, In Defence of His Flight to Pontus: Browne and Swallow, NPNF, vol. 7, 219.
161 Ep. 150.3: Deferrari, II, 369. Τῷ τὰ τῶν πτωχῶν οἰκονομεῖν πεπιστευμένῳ. Courtonne, II, 74.

to sting the conscience of the faithful to give alms to the destitute. As a matter of principle Basil held that charity is expressed in its own unique ways, depending on the strengths and weaknesses of a person, and is lived out in the calling of salvation that God has for each person. His own expression of this was lived out in his *Basiliad*, through which his campaign for a social revolution received great impetus.

3.4 Basil's *Basiliad*

A person's commitment to the poor was regarded by Basil as following the teachings of the Scriptures and therefore as pleasing to God. Basil argued that "in the divinely inspired Scriptures many directions are set forth which must be strictly observed by all who earnestly wish to please God".[162] Basil's keeping of the Gospel commandment, "sell your possessions and give alms",[163] was so impressed on his brother Gregory of Nyssa that he remarked that Basil "ungrudgingly spent upon the poor his patrimony even before he was a priest, and most of all in the time of the famine, during which he was a ruler of the church, though still a priest in the rank of presbyters, and afterwards did not hoard even what remained to him".[164]

In redistributing his own wealth Basil was acting in the way that he expected a wealthy aristocrat to act in times of famine and food crisis. This explains why in 370, in response to the famine affecting Cappadocia after the particular dry winter of 369–370

---

162 *Ep.* 22.1: Deferrari, I, 129. Πολλῶν ὄντων τῶν ὑπὸ τῆς θεοπνεύστου Γραφῆς δηλουμένων καὶ τῶν κατορθοῦσθαι ὀφειλόντων τοῖς ἐσπουδακόσιν εὐαρεστῆσαι τῷ Θεῷ. Courtonne, I, 52.
163 Luke 12:33. Πωλήσατε τὰ ὑπάρχοντα ὑμῶν καὶ δότε ἐλεημοσύνη.
164 Gregory of Nyssa, *Against Eunomius* 1.10.103: Moore and Austin, NPNF, vol. 5, 45. Ὁ τὴν πατρῴαν οὐσίαν καὶ πρὸ τῆς ἱερωσύνης ἀφειδῶς ἀναλώσας τοῖς πένησι καὶ μάλιστα ἐν τῷ τῆς σιτοδείας καιρῷ, καθ᾽ ὃν ἐπεστάτει τῆς ἐκκλησίας, ἔτι ἐν τῷ κλήρῳ τῶν πρεσβυτέρων ἱερατεύων, καὶ μετὰ ταῦτα μηδὲ τῶν ὑπολειφθέντων φεισάμενος. SC 521. 188–190.

caused the grain crop to fail,[165] Basil set up and formalised his own philanthropic centre on the outskirts of Caesarea which in time took on the renowned name Βασιλείας *Basiliad* after Basil himself – the city of Basil or otherwise known as "new city".[166] Basil considered food shortages to be a matter of the highest priority in his own actions as well as in his preaching on mercy and justice.[167] Sheather notes that homilies in church congregations on social justice that chastised incorrect behaviours and attitudes often shared the same ethical concerns raised by pagan philosophers.[168] Clothed in a distinct Christian context however, there was a general call in these homilies for all people to get involved according to their means in social welfare and see Christ in the poor. Clergy, monastics and prominent citizens, in particular, were encouraged in imitation of Christ to undertake selfless acts of charity.

Anecdotal evidence suggests that bishops and monastics in monasteries actively participated in making sure that they had provisions ready in times of famine or shortage.[169] In Basil's *Basiliad*,

---

165 For an excellent account see Holman, *The Hungry are Dying*, 64–134. Included in Holman's book is a translation of Basil's *Homily 8, In Time of Famine and Drought* (183–192).
166 The epithet "new city" comes from Gregory of Nazianzus' *Oration* 43.35. In subscribing to Gregory's "city" image, Liebeschuetz comments: "This was a city in itself, with a church in the centre and around it the house of the bishop, streets of houses for the clergy, hostels for the clergy, and hospitals for the sick". Liebeschuetz, *Antioch*, 240. See Rousseau, *Basil of Caesarea*, 139–143; Daley, "Building a New City: The Cappadocian Fathers and the Rhetoric of Philanthropy", 431–461. The 75th canon of the Council of Nicaea exhorts the establishment of homes for the destitute. See *Epp.* 94, 150, 176.
167 Two of Basil's letters, *Epp.* 27 and 31, addressed to Eusebius and Eusebonas show how Basil cancelled his much anticipated pastoral visits to them in response to the famine affecting Caesarea. Basil considered it a greater need to stay in Caesarea so that together with his co-workers he could attend to and feed the starving. He wrote four homilies in response to the drought affecting Caesarea. In a loose chronological order these are: *Homily 8, In Time of Famine and Drought*, PG 31. 303–328; *Homily 9, God is Not the Author of Evils*, PG 31. 329–354; *Homily 6, I Will Tear Down My Barns*, PG 31. 261–277; *Homily 7. To the Rich*, PG 31. 277–304.
168 See Sheather, *Pronouncements of the Cappadocians on Issues of Poverty and Wealth*, 377.
169 Rapp, *Holy Bishops in Late Antiquity*, 232–234.

the poor, sick and marginalised of Caesarea were gathered together in one place (or rather found the one place) of suburban Caesarea where they received food, clothing,[170] medical attention and shelter free of charge. Gregory of Nyssa says that all this would not have been made possible if Basil had not sold his paternal inheritance and others of like mind had not dispensed their surplus food and goods to the needy under Basil's supervision. However, Basil did not give gave away all his possessions arbitrarily and without judging "one to be in need of aid" (τινα χρήζοντα βοηθείας).[171] Rather he made sure that his almsgiving took place with discernment based on past experiences and after some form of an examination that would determine the sincerity of the case in need. While charity was open to all, specific decisions needed to be made by Basil as to who justified inclusion in the category of the destitute.

> Experience was necessary for distinguishing between the man who is truly in need and the man who begs through avarice. And while he who gives to the afflicted has given to the Lord, and will receive his reward from him, yet he who gives to every wanderer casts it to a dog, that is troublesome on account of his shamelessness, but not pitiable because of his need.[172]

During Basil's episcopal ministry (370–379) Basil's *Basiliad* expanded significantly and took on the form of a whole range of buildings with various programs. Basil's *Epp.* 94, 150 and 176 provide the chronological framework within which his entire project developed, as well as descriptions of a church edifice, hospital

---

170 See *Ep.* 286.1.
171 *Ep.* 22.2: Deferrari, I, 137. Courtonne, I, 55.
172 *Ep.* 150.3: Deferrari, II, 369. Ἐμπειρίας χρῄζειν τὴν διάγνωσιν τοῦ ἀληθῶς δεομένου καὶ τοῦ κατὰ πλεονεξίαν αἰτοῦντος. Καὶ ὁ μὲν τῷ θλιβομένῳ διδοὺς τῷ Κυρίῳ ἔδωκε καὶ παρ' αὐτοῦ λήψεται τὸν μισθόν, ὁ δὲ τῷ περιερχομένῳ προσέρριψε κυνὶ φορτικῷ μὲν διὰ τὴν ἀναίδειαν, οὐκ ἐλεεινῷ δὲ διὰ τὴν ἔνδειαν. Courtonne, II, 75.

(ξενοδοχεῖον), poorhouse (πτωχοτροφεῖον),[173] living quarters for the bishop and other clerics, hostel for travellers, and workshops contained therein. Such facilities would require significant financial investment just to stay open. It is because of these many functionalities that Sterk argues that it would be "erroneous" to refer to Basil's *Basiliad* as strictly speaking a "monastic" institution; even when it emphasised a life of poverty, charity to the needy and general asceticism with clear monastic overtones.[174]

The expansion and success of the *Basiliad* would not have occurred if Basil had not garnered support from the general populous as well as the elite, whom Basil characteristically labelled as "those who have much" since it was they who had influence over the grain houses with surplus stock. The fact that the distribution of surplus grain was not available in sufficient amounts and at affordable prices, and that there was widespread crop failure, effected a political and moral crisis. No one was immune from the devastating effects of food shortages. In the name of public interest that was linked to the affairs of the empire, all citizens had a part to play. The prefect Modestus was requested by Basil to exempt his clergy from paying taxes so that that the financial "relief" (παραμυθίαν) granted to his clergy could be used for the needs of "those who are at any time in distress" (τοῖς ἀεὶ καταπονουμένοις τὴν ἀπὸ τῆς ἀτελείας).[175] Officials such as Modestus, who had status and authority, were invited to ascertain for themselves the nature of Basil's welfare for the poor. Through paying Basil a visit, they could witness the functioning of his "homes for the poor" (πτωχοτροφία, πτωχοτροφεῖον), which by then were under the supervision of rural

---

173 See Holman, *The Hungry are Dying*, 74–76.
174 Sterk, *Renouncing the World Yet Leading the Church*, 71. Basil did have cenobitic monasteries that he did oversee and which routinely formed part of the agenda items discussed at his annual episcopal gatherings in Caesarea. Monastics, for Basil, occupied a key area in his pastoral ministry. *Epp.*123, 226, 256, 257, 259, 262 and 295 exhibit his correspondence with monks. See Silvas, *The Asketikon of St. Basil the Great*, 356; Rousseau, *Basil of Caesarea*, 140.
175 *Ep.* 104: Deferrari, II, 197. Courtonne, III, 5.

bishops. In this way imperial officials remained satisfied in their assessments that the tax exemptions granted to Basil's charitable homes were indeed justified.[176]

At the highest level, in 372, approximately two years after the conception of the *Basiliad*, Basil won the confidence of Emperor Valens whom Basil declared "has allowed us to govern the churches ourselves" (ἐᾶσαι ἡμᾶς ἐφ' ἑαυτῶν τὰς Ἐκκλησίας οἰκονομεῖν).[177] The benefactors of the *Basiliad* were increasingly coming from influential stakeholders within the empire, including "rulers and other most powerful people of the city".[178] Given the close proximity of the imperial estates to the *Basiliad*, it would not be hard to imagine Basil tapping into their resources and revenue.[179] In a letter addressed to the governor Elias, Basil recalled that all these initiatives "concerning [his] government of the churches" (ἐκ τῆς ἡμετέρας περὶ τὰς ἐκκλησίας οἰκονομίας) had taken place for the "common good of all" (τῶν κοινῶν) and in the interests of the social and moral wellbeing of the state.[180] To the slanderous accusations against Basil that were brought to the attention of the governor Elias, Basil responded in his defence that all his humanitarian works were an act of common interest that were an "ornament to the locality, and a source of pride to the governor" (τῷ μὲν τόπῳ κόσμος, τῷ δὲ ἄρχοντι [...] σεμνολόγημα).[181]

Central to the running of the *Basiliad* was the existence of a "house of prayer" (οἶκον εὐκτήριον),[182] namely a church or chapel

---

176 *Epp.* 142, 143. Basil was in particular strict on maintaining financial accountability. See *Ep.* 224: Οἱ ταμίαι τῶν ἱερῶν χρημάτων ἕτοιμοι δοῦναι τὸν λόγον τῷ βουλομένῳ. Courtonne, III, 22. "The treasuries of the church funds are here ready to give an accounting to him who wishes". Deferrari, III, 323.
177 *Ep.* 94: Deferrari, II, 151. Courtonne, I, 205.
178 Gregory of Nazianzus, *Oration* 43.34. Ἄρχοντας, τούς τε ἄλλους καὶ τοὺς δυνατωτάτους τῆς πόλεως. SC 384. 200.
179 Van Dam, *Bishops and Friends in Late Antique Cappadocia*, 74–76.
180 *Ep.* 94: Deferrari, II, 151. Courtonne, I, 205.
181 *Ep.* 94: Deferrari, II, 151. Courtonne, I, 206.
182 *Ep.* 94: Deferrari, II, 151. Courtonne, I, 205.

(ἐκκλησία)[183] of some kind for worship and spiritual formation. According to the study of Anne Keidel,[184] this contemplative side of Basil as a man of prayer is overlooked by most scholars, whose general reflections on Basil seem to reveal a portrait of person who is primarily an advocate for actions and good works. Contrasting him against his younger brother and renowned mystic, Gregory of Nyssa, only enhances this impression.[185] Although not strictly speaking a mystical theologian, Basil was *par excellence* a spiritual man concerned indeed with the spiritual life and the edification of the Christian faith. "Communion in prayer" (ταῖς προσευχαῖς κοινωνίαν), declares Basil, "brings great gain" (πολὺ κέρδος φέρουσαν).[186]

Accordingly, Basil's letters suggest that the *Basiliad* did not stop at merely helping the poor. More to the point, the *Basiliad* concerned itself with promoting a virtuous way of life (πρὸς εὐσχήμονα βίου διαγωγήν)[187] through nurturing personal morality and spirituality. Presumably the first encounter with the *Basiliad* began with a humanitarian need, but for Basil this need became the catalyst for receiving instruction on how to be immersed in "the way that is in accordance with Christ's polity" (τῆς ὁδοῦ τῆς κατὰ Χριστὸν πολιτείας).[188] Many came to the *Basiliad* with various needs and from a diversity of backgrounds. In the *Basiliad* they took on a new way of life that was founded upon prayer and lived out in a communal life of caring and sharing. The success of the *Basiliad* motivated Basil to attempt to implement its new and proven social order of existence in society at large. Here was a call from Basil to get back to the basics and live the life of the first

---

183 See *Ep.* 176: Deferrari, II, 461. Courtonne, II, 113.
184 Anne Keidel, "*Hesychia*, Prayer and Transformation in Basil of Caesarea". *Studia Patristica* 39 (Leuven: Peeters, 2001), 110–120.
185 Sheather recognises a "certain uniformity" in the theology, spirituality and ministry of the Cappadocians "despite differences in personality and gifts... tone and emphasis". Sheather, *Pronouncements of the Cappadocians on Issues of Poverty and Wealth*, 375, 390.
186 *Ep.* 150.2: Deferrari, II, 367. Courtonne, II, 73.
187 *Ep.* 94: Deferrari, II, 151. Courtonne, I, 206.
188 *Ep.* 150.1: Deferrari, II, 361. Courtonne, II, 71.

church of Jerusalem "whose members were together and had all things in common".[189] Basil exhorted everyone to "zealously imitate the early Christian community, where everything was held in common – life, soul, concord, a common table, indivisible kinship – while unfeigned love constituted many bodies as one and joined many souls into a harmonious whole".[190]

3.5 Basil's *Basiliad* as a Paradigm for Social Change

Living in an era that was burdened by social inequalities and fiscal mismanagement, the demarcation between the rich and the poor, the "haves" and the "have-nots", became increasingly sharpened. The prevailing social structure enriched the few at the expense of the many, who lacked the means to attend to their daily needs. The disproportionate concentration of land in the hands of the rich, accompanied by the heavy taxation of the lower classes (to support the military), were just some of the injustices that the overwhelming majority had to contend with.[191] At the sight of such overt injustices, Basil refused to remain silent and, in fact, felt

---

189 Fedwick, *The Church and the Charisma of Leadership*, 20.
190 Basil, *In Time of Famine and Drought*, 8: Schroeder, *Saint Basil the Great: On Social Justice*, 86. Τὸ πρῶτον τῶν Χριστιανῶν ζηλώσωμεν σύνταγμα· ὅπως ἦν αὐτοῖς ἅπαντα κοινά, ὁ βίος, ἡ ψυχὴ, ἡ συμφωνία, ἡ τράπεζα κοινὴ, ἀδιαίρετος ἀδελφότης, ἀγάπη ἀνυπόκριτος, τὰ πολλὰ σώματα ἓν ἐργαζομένη· τὰς διαφόρους ψυχὰς εἰς μίαν ὁμόνοιαν ἁρμόζουσα. PG 31. 325A–B. Georges Florovsky makes a point of stating that "Christianity from the very beginning existed as a corporate reality, as a community. To be Christian meant just to belong to the community. Nobody could be Christian by himself, as an isolated individual, but only together with 'the brethren', in a 'togetherness' with them. [...] Christianity means a 'common life', a life in common". Florovsky, Bible, Church, Tradition, 59.
191 The onslaught of barbarian invasions between the second and fourth centuries almost doubled the size of the military. From a fiscal point of view it has been estimated that over two-thirds of the annual state budget was absorbed by the army. Funding such an expansion of military strength occurred through tax revenue and the lease of imperial lands. The demands of heavily increased taxes forced many small farmers to sell their land into the hands of the wealthier classes. See Jones, *The Later Roman Empire*, 1045–1046; MacMullen, "The Roman Emperor's Army Costs", 571–580; Elton, *Warfare in Roman Europe AD 350–425*, 118–127.

a sense of growing responsibility towards implementing change for the "edification of the church" (οἰκοδομὴν τῆς Ἐκκλησίας)[192] and the good of society. Nothing short of a conversion to a new way of being in the world was required to respond to the needs of the "have-nots" who did not enjoy the same legal rights as the wealthy.[193] The way of life enshrined by the *Basiliad*, with its model Christian life, aimed to present the church as the centre of one's existence that was inclusive of all people, especially the poor and destitute. Basil's charitable centre stood as a countersign to social inequality in all its forms and was directed at invoking change. Rousseau in a few short words aptly states what Basil had in mind:

> Care of the sick, provision for the needy, formation in asceticism, together with "political" elements (the "new city", "Christ's polity", the engagement of elite support), heralded nothing less than a major social revolution, setting in place patterns of collaboration and of economic and political patronage that challenged directly the hypocrisy, corruption, and uncontrolled self-interest governing, in Basil's eyes, the society in which he had to operate.[194]

There was a need for a radical reorientation and transformation of one's mode of existence. In Basil's view, beginning with the Christian, the absence of generosity constituted a major sin.[195] He envisioned a new social order that saw principles of simplicity and sharing replace competition and private ownership, and he wanted to break once and for all the structures that create and reinforce the cycle of poverty. According to Gregory of Nazianzus, "By his word and exhortation he [Basil] opened the stores of those who possessed them" (λόγῳ γὰρ τὰς τῶν ἐχόντων ἀποθήκας ἀνοίξας καὶ παραινέσεσι)[196] through convincing the wealthy that God's provi-

---

192 *Ep.* 205: Deferrari, III, 177. Courtonne, II, 181.
193 See Rapp, *Holy Bishops in Late Antiquity*, 223-226.
194 Rousseau, *Basil of Caesarea*, 145.
195 In *Homily* 324.8 Basil considers almsgiving to be the surest release from sin.
196 Gregory of Nazianzus, *Oration* 43.35. SC 384. 202-204.

dence allowed the accumulation of their wealth so that it could be shared with others. In this way Basil believed that it behoved the rich to see themselves as stewards of God who were equipped for a ministry of relief towards their destitute fellow servants. If the rich could not see in themselves an innate calling towards charity, Basil argued they were living a life of fantasy. In any event, as part of Basil's agenda for social reform, it was time for the ideal of a community of shared life and resources associated with cenobitic monasticism to take on broader overtones. This was to be achieved through introducing the principles of monastic living into society at large.[197] In Basil, the virtues of monastic life forged a bond with active pastoral care which culminated in social morality. He aimed to bring about a social revolution in moral propriety, that is to say, a complete overturning of the self-interest and indulgence that was entrenched in the standard of living of the time.[198]

In Basil's understanding, the pursuit for personal holiness could no longer be realised if it was not social in character; heavenly blessings could not be acquired without the distribution of charity below.[199] According to Aristotle, "the person is by nature a social being" (ὁ ἄνθρωπος φύσει πολιτικὸν ζῷον)[200] in that we need one another and want to live with one another. In the words of Fedwick, "only through communion (κοινωνία) with God and his

---

197 See Basil's treatise *On the Renunciation of the World*: Ἆρά σοι δοκεῖ καὶ τοῖς ὑπογυναίοις τεθεῖσθαι τὰ Εὐαγγέλια; Ἰδού, σεσαφήνισταί σοι, ὡς πάντες ἄνθρωποι ἀπαιτηθησόμεθα τὴν πρὸς τὸ Εὐαγγέλιον ὑπακοήν, μοναχοί τε καὶ οἱ ἐν συζυγίαις. Ἀρκέσει γὰρ τῷ ἐπὶ γάμον ἐλθόντι ἡ συγγνώμη τῆς ἀκρασίας καὶ τῆς πρὸς τὸ θῆλυ ἐπιθυμίας τε καὶ συνουσίας· τὰ δὲ λοιπὰ τῶν ἐντολῶν πᾶσιν ὁμοίως νενομοθετημένα οὐκ ἀκίνδυνα τοῖς παραβαίνουσι. PG 31. 629A. "Does it not seem to you, then, that the Gospel applies to married persons also? Surely, it has been made clear that obedience to the Gospel is required for all of us, both married and celibate. The man who enters the married state may well be satisfied in obtaining pardon for his incontinency and desire for a wife and marital existence, but the rest of these precepts are obligatory for all alike and are fraught with peril for transgressors". *Saint Basil: Ascetical Works*, Wagner, 17.
198 See *Epp*. 94, 150, 176.
199 See Brown, *Poverty and Leadership in the Later Roman Empire*, 26–73.
200 Aristotle, *Politics*, 1.2 [1253a].

neighbours can man achieve perfection".²⁰¹ Basil drew explicit parallels between individual actions and their cosmic consequences such that membership of the Christian church had immediate social and economic consequences. Christians were expected by Basil to be participants in "the exercise of justice" (τῶν ἔργων τῆς δικαιοσύνης),²⁰² especially with regard to improving the lot of those in need. The Greek adjective κοινός, meaning shared or common, that is employed throughout Basil's writings is bereft of all meaning if that which is shared and common does not materialise into its fullest expression as exemplified by the noun κοινωνία or "communion". Consequently, those who do not live by this rule are called ἀκοινώνητοι, meaning not just unsociable with other human beings but also without (outside) communion. Basil uses κοινός to underscore his fundamental premise that all things are to be used for the common benefit of all. A κοινωνικὸς ἄνθρωπος (a person in communion) is a person who lives through relating to the needs of the other and considers others as equals (ὁμόδουλος)²⁰³ to himself or herself. Importantly this equality was founded upon an equality of honour (ὁμοτιμίας ἰσότης) which Basil claimed naturally existed amongst all people and therefore was the essential ingredient for which communion was realised. Basil explains:

> For we understand ourselves and realise that to every man belongs by nature equality of like honour with all men (πρὸς πάντας ὁμοτιμία), and that superiorities in us are not according to family, nor according to excess of wealth, nor according to the body's constitution, but according to the superiority of our fear of God.²⁰⁴

201 Fedwick, *The Church and the Charisma of Leadership*, 97.
202 *On the Holy Spirit*, 8.18: SC 17. 310. See Homily 320.3, 328.6.
203 Essentially what Basil implies by this term is that "we are all fellow slaves". See Basil, *On the Holy Spirit*, 20.51.
204 *Ep.* 262.1: Deferrari, IV, 85. Γνωρίζομεν γὰρ ἑαυτοὺς καὶ οἴδαμεν ὅτι παντὶ ἀνθρώπῳ πρὸς πάντας ὁμοτιμία ἔστι κατὰ τὴν φύσιν· ὑπεροχαὶ δὲ ἐν ἡμῖν οὐ κατὰ γένος οὐδὲ κατὰ περιουσίαν χρημάτων οὐδὲ κατὰ τὴν τοῦ σώματος κατασκευήν, ἀλλὰ κατὰ τὴν ὑπεροχὴν τοῦ φόβου τοῦ πρὸς τὸν Θεόν. Courtonne, III, 119.

The opposite to being a κοινονικὸς ἄνθρωπος is to be a ἀκοινώνητος ἄνθρωπος, in other words a person who is not aware of his or her common bond with all human beings. Without this fundamental understanding of one's innate calling to be a κοινονικὸς ἄνθρωπος, Basil accused his readers of being "hoarders" since they wilfully kept for themselves what rightfully belonged equally to "others". The type of hoarder sanctioned by Basil unjustly deprived the poor of material goods and social power, while being deliberately intent on making a profit. They kept exclusively for themselves what in essence was for common use, as if they were its permanent possessors. Basil relates: "It is as if someone were to take the first seat in the theatre, then bar everyone else from attending, so that one person alone enjoys what is offered for the benefit of all in common".[205]

Basil's specific choice of the word "common" (κοινή) in his writings aimed to emphasise the one "nature" (φύσις) that by birthright the rich and poor share.[206] This point, in particular, was augmented in Basil's homily *In Time of Famine and Drought* which apparently he delivered to a congregation composed mainly of landowners and farmers, and where he made his point by reflecting on the observations of physical nature. If the plant and animal kingdom is able to share nature's resources, Basil argued, why cannot human beings respond to the promptings of nature and do the same? Basil's conclusion: "We hoard what is common, and keep for ourselves what belongs to many others"[207] resulting in neglecting our nature and severing our natural ties with each other.[208] In

---

205 Basil, *I Will Tear Down My Barns*, 7: Schroeder, *Saint Basil the Great: On Social Justice*, 69. Ὥσπερ ἂν εἴ τις, ἐν θεάτρῳ θέαν καταλαβών, εἶτα ἐξείργοι τοὺς ἐπεισιόντας, ἴδιον ἑαυτοῦ κρίνων τὸ κοινῶς πᾶσι κατὰ τὴν χρῆσιν προκείμενον. PG 31. 276B.
206 See Basil, *I Will Tear Down My Barns*, PG 31. 264A.
207 Basil, *In Time of Famine and Drought*, 8: Schroeder, *Saint Basil the Great: On Social Justice*, 86. Ἡμεῖς δὲ, ἐγκολπιζόμεθα τὰ κοινά, τὰ τῶν πολλῶν μόνοι ἔχομεν. PG 31. 325A. This homily is carefully analysed in Holman, "The Hungry Body: Famine, Poverty and Basil's Homily 8", 337–363.
208 See Basil, *To the Rich*, PG 31. 297B–297C.

this homily Basil explicitly described famine as a living death, which he considered to be a death of the worst kind since it consisted of a social death that in essence exceeded biological death. As illustrated in Holman's comments: "The tragedy of this inner disease of hunger was that it destroyed the body, both the individual body of the person and the interconnecting social tissue with which it was linked to the community".[209]

For Basil, the directions found in Scripture that relate to giving and serving[210] are part and parcel of the heavenly vocation that the Christian has received and are constituent of the conduct found in the "Gospel of Christ". Such a heavenly vocation incorporated monastic principles of self-renunciation and charity as the ideal for the Christian life. Famine, for example, with all its difficulties, invited one to better living. Basil counselled:

> The Christian [...] ought not to hold or store up as his own what is given to all for their own use; but he should take heed for all things carefully as belonging to the Master. [...] He should not consider himself as his own master, but as having been delivered by God into servitude to his brethren of like spirit, so he should always think and act.[211]

Ascetic discipline and temperance allowed Christians to acquire a sense of mastery over their senses, which in turn allowed their senses to become vehicles of the Holy Spirit that would emit divine grace. People in need were called to demonstrate patience in response to their humbled predicament, especially when faced with what Sheather describes as "obvious inequalities".[212] Those

---

209 Holman, *The Hungry are Dying*, 97.
210 E.g. Luke 12:33.
211 *Ep.* 22.1: Deferrari, I, 133. Ὅτι δεῖ τὸν χριστιανόν [...] τῶν διδομένων ἑκάστῳ εἰς χρῆσιν οὐδὲν ὡς ἴδιον ἔχειν δεῖ ἢ ταμιεύεσθαι, ἐν μέντοι τῇ φροντίδι, πᾶσιν ὡς δεσποτικοῖς προσέχοντα [...] Ὅτι οὐ δεῖ οὔτε αὐτὸν ἑαυτοῦ κύριον εἶναί τινα, ἀλλ᾽ ὡς ὑπὸ Θεοῦ παραδεδομένον εἰς δουλείαν τοῖς ὁμοψύχοις ἀδελφοῖς, οὕτω καὶ φρονεῖν πάντα καὶ ποιεῖν. Courtonne, I, 53-54.
212 Sheather, *Pronouncements of the Cappadocians on Issues of Poverty and Wealth*, 381.

people who were better off were called to alleviate the needs of others through the practice of generosity. Poverty, as understood by Basil, was no disgrace and therefore there was no excuse for neglecting those in need. In a rhetorical question addressed to the rich, Basil asked: "Why then are you wealthy while another is poor? Why else, but so that you might receive the reward of benevolence and faithful stewardship, while the poor are honoured for patient endurance in their struggles?"[213] Implicit in this understanding of reciprocal blessings brought about by charity and patience was the understanding that divine grace is not contained but rather flows freely from one person to the other in accordance to one's personal disposition. Provided a person does not "grieve the Holy Spirit" (μὴ λυπῆται τὸ πνεῦμα τὸ ἅγιον), then grace will proceed, leading to the "edification of the faith" (οἰκοδομὴν τῆς πίστεως).[214]

In Basil's letters, ascetic discipline and the struggle (ἀγῶνα) associated with a life of purification, implied that the edification of a person's faith came as a direct consequence of serving the other. Furthermore Basil's letters show that love, charity and good works can only be realised when a person's life is lived in continuous communion with others. All people have a responsibility to care for their fellow human beings, especially since they are endowed with a conscience and free will. For this reason Basil argued that Christians or communities can never be said to be healthy and taking care of themselves if they are ignoring the interests and needs of others. Ignoring these needs constitutes sin, and all suffer because of the sins of the few. As a consequence Basil infers that all creation is pained, as expressed through, but not limited to, natural disasters (famine). To his friend Bishop Eusebius of Samosata, Basil lamented:

---

213 Basil, *I Will Tear Down My Barns*, 7: Schroeder, *Saint Basil the Great: On Social Justice*, 69. Διὰ τί σὺ μὲν πλουτεῖς, ἐκεῖνος δὲ πένεται; Ἢ πάντως, ἵνα καὶ σὺ χρηστότητος καὶ πιστῆς οἰκονομίας μισθὸν ὑποδέξῃ, κἀκεῖνος τοῖς μεγάλοις ἄθλοις τῆς ὑπομονῆς τιμηθῇ; PG 31. 276C.
214 See Eph. 4:30.

As for the interests of the churches – how they have gone to ruin and have been lightly sacrificed, while we, consulting our own personal safety, neglect the good of our neighbours and are unable to see even this, that the ruin of each of us is involved in the common disaster.[215]

3.6 Conclusion

From the above it can be seen that the role of the bishop in late antiquity included a multitude of spheres that interconnected with each other. The demographics of an episcopal see, its civil personalities and a bishop's engagement with these personalities, determined the outcomes of a bishop's ministry. For Basil, in spite of an antithetical imperial religious regime, doctrinal orthodoxy was inseparable from pastoral outreach in that both aimed to preserve the dignity of human life and its realisation in communion with God and with other people. Basil was convinced that a person could not truly "recognise God" (Θεὸν ἐπιγνώσεται) if he or she did not attend to his or her fellow human being. Only when this became the "first concern of the mind" (προηγούμενόν ἐστι τῷ νῷ) did a person become receptive to "the assistance of the Spirit" (τῇ τοῦ Πνεύματος [...] βοηθείᾳ) so as to "know truth" (ἀλήθειαν γνωρίσει) and live out God's ways.[216] As this chapter has shown, throughout his ministry Basil never lost sight of his social vision of a community of shared life and of shared resources, as modelled in cenobitic monasticism and as proven successful in his *Basiliad*. It was never Basil's intention to limit the virtues of monasticism to the confines of a monastic centre but rather to allow such virtues to flow out onto society at large. Although private ownership, prestige and wealth were dominant aspirations of the day, this did

---

215 *Ep.* 136: Deferrari, II, 315. Τὰ δὲ τῶν Ἐκκλησιῶν ὅπως οἴχεται καὶ προπέποται, ἡμῶν τῆς οἰκείας ἀσφαλείας ἕνεκεν τὰ τῶν πλησίον περιορώντων καὶ οὐδὲ τοῦτο συνορᾶν δυναμένων ὅτι τῇ τοῦ κοινοῦ κακοπραγίᾳ καὶ τὸ καθ' ἕκαστον συναπόλλυται. Courtonne, II, 52. See 1 Cor. 12-25-26.
216 *Ep.* 233.2: Deferrari, III, 369-71. Courtonne, III, 40-41.

not stop Basil from advocating for simplicity and charity. His four surviving homilies in response to the famine plaguing Caesarea had this focus in mind. It was through charity and his regard for social issues that Basil would find his voice and become one of the greatest orators in the Christian East on matters of social justice. His letters served to make his voice heard as vociferously as possible and as far and wide as possible.

Part Two: Basil's Letters

Chapter Four: Church as Communion in the Letters of Basil

Chapter Three, with its historical and social portrait of a bishop in late antiquity, shed much light into just how vast Basil's ministry was. Motivated by his desire for ecclesiastical communion, Basil chose to engage with all personalities of the empire, irrespective of their social status or their civil prominence. The very existence of his diverse and numerous letters are indicative of his realistic aspirations for communion. This chapter commences by looking generally at how Basil used letters as instruments of communion within the context of his own ministry. This then allows Basil's correspondence with Bishop Athanasius of Alexandria specifically to be showcased as an example of Basil's efforts to uphold and safeguard communion in a pro-Nicene church. An examination of the technical term for communion, "κοινωνία", follows, a word which features prominently in Basil's correspondence, as well as other metaphors and indicators of its manifestation. Basil exemplifies that the act of letter-writing and the receiving of letters by bishops was important in both serving as witnesses that reveal the bishops' communion with one another and in building up this communion. In a similar way, signed written confessions of Nicene statements of faith by bishops are treated by Basil as proofs of the bishops' allegiance to Nicene Christianity. The final part of this chapter will focus on Basil's ecclesiology, with a particular emphasis on κοινωνία in the church and κοινωνία in the Trinity. This section shifts focus from Basil's letters to his treatise *On the Holy Spirit*. Here it will become evident that Basil's ecclesiology is centred on the church as having its existence in communion, and that it is through the inspiration of the Holy Spirit that the church's "being in communion" is realised and participated.

4.1 Basil's Use of Letters: Instruments of Communion

Letters brought Basil into contact with others when he was not able physically to visit or receive people. "Long sickness" (χρονίας νόσου)¹ and the threat of persecution from "rapacious wolves" (λύκοι ἅρπαγες) caused Basil to admit: "of necessity I have been reduced to visit you by letter" (ἀναγκαίως ἐπὶ τὴν διὰ τοῦ γράμματος ἐπίσκεψιν ἦλθον).² As in all the ancient letter-writing corpora, and as will be shown in the examples below, these are topoi of genre.³ Basil turned his lack of physical communication and human contact into a positive. In his letter to the people of Beroea, who very much desired his visitation, Basil stated:

> Great is the consolation the Lord has given to those who are deprived of converse face to face, namely, intercourse by letter, whereby it is possible to perceive, not the physical appearance, but the disposition of the soul itself.⁴

Basil opens his letter to Bishop Ambrose of Milan with a proclamation of gratitude for being granted "one of the greatest gifts" (μία δὲ τῶν μεγίστων δωρεῶν), namely that of being "united to each other through communication by letter" (ἀλλήλοις συνάπτεσθαι διὰ τῆς ἐν τοῖς γράμμασι προσφωνήσεως):

> Ever great and many are the gifts of our Master, and neither can their greatness be measured nor their multitude enumerated. And one of the greatest gifts to those who are sensible of receiving his benefits is this present one – that he has granted us who are very widely separated by an

---

1 See *Ep.* 203.1 Ἐκ τῆς πρώτης ἡλικίας μέχρι τοῦ γήρως τούτου. Courtonne, II, 167. "From early manhood to my present old age". Deferrari, III, 143.
2 *Ep.* 139.3: Deferrari, II, 331. Courtonne, II, 59.
3 In Basil's letters, the discussion of a letter-writer's illnesses is considered to be part of the standard rhetoric of the time.
4 *Ep.* 220: Deferrari, III, 275–277. Μεγάλην ὁ Κύριος ἔδωκε παραμυθίαν τοῖς ἀπολιμπανομένοις τῆς κατ᾽ ὀφθαλμοὺς συντυχίας, τὴν διὰ τοῦ γράμματος ὁμιλίαν ἐξ ἧς ἐστι μανθάνειν οὐ τὸν σωματικὸν χαρακτῆρα, ἀλλ᾽ αὐτῆς τῆς ψυχῆς τὴν διάθεσιν. Courtonne, III, 3.

interval of space to be united to each other through communication by letter.[5]

In his episcopal ministry at Caesarea, Basil turned to letters also as a means of receiving comfort. It was obvious that Basil experienced much anguish as a bishop, something he considered to be common knowledge: "there is no part of the world which is now ignorant of our misfortunes",[6] and so receiving a letter was therapeutic for him. Coming from those close to him, "such letters" (γραμμάτων τοιούτων), Basil claims, "help us in our search for the knowledge of God" (δι' ὧν ἡ Θεοῦ γνῶσις ἐπιζητεῖται).[7] To his friend and protégé Amphilochius, Basil writes: "When I took into my hands the letter of your piety I straight away became forgetful of everything", referring to his "broken body and being considerably afflicted in soul".[8] When trouble befell him, the comfort Basil received from letters was augmented:

> For everything here is full of distress, and my only refuge from my troubles is the thought of your holiness; and this is brought more vividly to my mind by the intercourse which your letters, so full of wisdom and grace, give me.[9]

5 *Ep.* 197: Deferrari, III, 91. Μεγάλοι καὶ πολλαὶ τοῦ Δεσπότου ἡμῶν αἱ δωρεαὶ καὶ οὔτε τὸ μέγεθος αὐτῶν μετρητὸν οὔτε τὸ πλῆθος ἀριθμητόν. Μία δὲ τῶν μεγίστων δωρεῶν ἐστι τοῖς εὐαισθήτως δεχομένοις τὰς χάριτας καὶ ἡ παροῦσα αὕτη, ὅτι πλεῖστον ἡμᾶς τῇ θέσει τοῦ τόπου διῃρημένους ἔδωκεν ἀλλήλοις συνάπτεσθαι διὰ τῆς ἐν τοῖς γράμμασι προσφωνήσεως. Courtonne, II, 149-150.
6 *Ep.* 243.3: Deferrari, III, 441. Οὐδὲν μέρος ἐστὶ τῆς οἰκουμένης ὃ τὰς ἡμετέρας λοιπὸν ἠγνόησε συμφοράς. Courtonne, III, 70. Although Basil does readily admit that, with regards to his fellow churchmen from the West, ἀγνοοῦσι παντελῶς τὰ ἐνταῦθα. *Ep.* 214.2: Courtonne, II, 203.
7 *Ep.* 159.1: Deferrari, II, 395. Courtonne, II, 86.
8 *Ep.* 217: Deferrari, III, 241-243. Τὸ σῶμά μου συντετριμμένον ἐπαναγαγὼν καὶ τὴν ψυχὴν μετρίως κεκακωμένος, ἐπειδὴ τὸ γράμμα τῆς εὐλαβείας σου ἐπὶ χεῖρας ἔλαβον, πάντων ἀθρόως ἐπελαθόμην. Courtonne, II, 208-209.
9 *Ep.* 57: Deferrari, I, 355. Πάντα γὰρ ὀδύνης τὰ τῇδε πεπλήρωται, καὶ μόνη ἡμῖν ἐστιν ἀποστροφὴ τῶν δεινῶν ἡ τῆς σῆς ὁσιότητος ἔννοια· ἥν ἐναργεστέραν ἡμῖν ἐμποιεῖ ἡ διὰ τῶν πάσης σοφίας καὶ χάριτος πεπληρωμένων γραμμάτων σου ὁμιλία. Courtonne, I, 144.

Basil's overwhelming responsibilities, his experience of frequent illnesses,[10] and the challenges of the winter weather saw him depend on the ministry of letters all the more. During his darkest moments, the mere act of writing a letter had the same therapeutic results as being the recipient of a letter. The effect was instant; the moment Basil committed to write something in a letter was the moment that he felt alleviated of its troubling contents: "How great a weight of grief do we cast off, as we narrate our manifold misfortunes".[11]

There was no principle of the evangelic life that Basil could not explain through his letters. It made no difference whether he wrote to comfort the persecuted and the afflicted, the widowed and the bereaved, or whether he wrote to clarify essential articles of faith such as the consubstantiality of the Father and the Son, and the non-createdness of the Holy Spirit. Provided there was a recipient and the writing seemed "to befit the purpose of a Christian, who writes not so much for display as for general edification",[12] all subject-matter acquired a voice through Basil's letters.[13]

---

10 See *Epp.* 141.1, 162. For a list of Basil's illnesses see Gain, *L'Église de Cappadoce*, 397. Concerning his illnesses, Basil in a short letter that he wrote to Eusebius of Samosata admits: Οὐδὲ σχόντι ποτὲ τοσαύτην τοῦ λόγου δύναμιν ὥστε παντοδαπὴν οὕτω καὶ ποικίλην νόσον ἐναργῶς ἐξαγγεῖλαι. Πλὴν ὅτι [...] πυρετοὶ καὶ διάρροιαι καὶ σπλάγχνων ἐπαναστάσεις, ὥσπερ κύματά με ἐπιβαπτίζονται, ὑπερσχεῖν οὐκ ἐᾷ. "I never gained a command of language sufficient to enable me to describe clearly my varied and complex sickness. But the truth is [...] fevers, dysenteries, and rebellions of my bowels, drenching me like recurring waves, have not permitted me to emerge". *Ep.* 162: Courtonne, II, 95–96. Deferrari, II, 419. In an earlier letter to Eusebius, Basil had already mentioned: Ἐμὲ δὲ ἐπέλειπε παντελῶς τὸ σῶμα, ὡς μηδὲ τὰς σμικροτάτας κινήσεις δύνασθαι ἀλύπως φέρειν. "My body has failed me so completely that I am unable to make even slightest movement without pain". *Ep.* 100: Courtonne, I, 219. Deferrari, II, 185.
11 *Ep.* 243: Deferrari, III, 443. Οἷον ἀποσκευαζόμεθα τῆς λύπης τὸ βάρος, δι' ὧν πρὸς τὴν ὑμετέραν ἀγάπην τὰς πολυειδεῖς ἡμῶν συμφορὰς διαγγέλομεν. Courtonne, III, 70–71.
12 *Ep.* 135.1: Deferrari, II, 307. Προθέσει χριστιανοῦ οὐ πρὸς ἐπίδειξιν μᾶλλον ἢ κοινὴν ὠφέλειαν γράφοντος. Courtonne, II, 49.
13 See Gain, *L'Église de Cappadoce*, 298–304.

Amongst the recipients of Basil's letters were members of the clergy and charitable institutions,[14] magistrates,[15] civil[16] and military[17] officials, ascetics, youth, pagans[18] and of course friends, many of whom included the aforementioned.[19] There are eighteen surviving letters of Basil that are consolatory in character (παραμυθητικὴ ἐπιστολή), of which eight were addressed to widows,[20] four to bereaving parents or grandparents,[21] three to congregations who had lost their bishop,[22] and three to men or women in affliction.[23] In Basil's era it was common for bishops to write to one another as an expression of fellowship and communion, but also as a means by which they could discuss all matters such as sensitive pastoral questions or controversial points of doctrine.

Creating a network of social interactions allowed Basil to provide a context in which he could establish meaningful relationships with his correspondents that exemplified his pastoral leadership, friendship and patronage. To assist him in his correspondence, and as a way of removing any barriers to communica-

14 See *Epp.* 36, 37, 104, 142-144, 284.
15 See *Epp.* 72, 73, 111, 177-180.
16 Basil observed all protocols when writing to civil officials and often adorned his letters with complementary remarks. An example of this is seen in Basil's letter to his "Magnanimity" the prefect Modestus, which begins with the salutation: Αὐτὸ τὸ γράφειν πρὸς ἄνδρα τοσοῦτον, κἂν μηδεμία πρόφασις ἑτέρα προσῇ, μέγιστόν ἐστι τῶν εἰς τιμὴν φερόντων τοῖς αἰσθανομένοις, διότι αἱ πρὸς τοὺς παμπληθὲς τῶν λοιπῶν ὑπερέχοντας ὁμιλίαι μεγίστην τοῖς ἀξιουμένοις τὴν περιφάνειαν προξενοῦσιν. *Ep.* 104: Courtonne, II, 4-5. "The very act of writing to so great a man, even if there be no other excuse, is most conducive to honour in the eyes of the discerning; for intercourse with men who are overwhelmingly superior to the rest of mankind affords the greatest distinction to such as are deemed worthy of it". Deferrari, II, 195. See *Epp.* 35, 36, 63, 72, 74-77, 83, 84, 86, 88, 96, 104, 109, 114, 142, 225, 269, 280, 284, 299, 311,313, 317, 331.
17 See *Epp.* 148, 149, 152, 153, 179.
18 See *Epp.* 63, 112, 174.
19 For general examples see *Epp.* 15, 36, 37, 111, 177-180, 192, 273, 275, 279, 308, 312.
20 *Epp.* 107, 174, 269, 283, 196, 297, 301, 302.
21 *Epp.* 5, 6, 206, 300.
22 *Epp.* 28, 29, 62.
23 *Epp.* 101, 289, 316.

tion, Basil frequently gave the impression of being on the best possible terms with his correspondent. He used this flexible and somewhat opportunistic approach particularly when he saw that it would benefit his ministry and when it was aligned with his fundamental desire for peace. Basil showed that he could not only address and communicate with various people, but also be a voice for them as well, so that Gain describes him as their *defensor plebis*.[24]

In an age of "legal" Christianity, where the distinction between church and society was fluid, and the duties of civil and ecclesiastical servants overlapped,[25] it is no surprise to find that Basil called on politicians and not just members of the clergy for aid. Often in these situations, when duty compelled him, Basil was not afraid to upbraid episcopal, imperial or other personalities.[26] Writing to the bishops of Italy and Gaul, Basil appealed to a sense of shared destiny and mutual responsibility: "Our common possession – our treasure, inherited from our Fathers, of the sound faith".[27] Earlier on in the same letter he writes:

> Since the gospel of the kingdom, having begun in our region, has gone forth to the whole world, on this account the common enemy of our souls strives that the seeds of apostasy, having taken their beginning in the same region, may be distributed to the whole world. For upon whom the light of the knowledge of Christ has shone, upon these the darkness of impiety also contrives to come [...] Stretch forth your hand to those of the churches that are being tossed about, lest, if they are abandoned, they may endure

---

24 Gain, *L'Église de Cappadoce*, 304. See *Epp*. 72, 73, 178, 278. According to Gregory Nazianzus, people of all social standings saw in Basil's works guidelines to correct thinking and persuasive speech. In particular, candidates to the priesthood sought spiritual edification in Basil's writings which they used to enhance their vocation. See Gregory of Nazianzus, *Oration* 43.66.
25 Rousseau, *Basil of Caesarea*, 170.
26 See *Epp*. 61, 85, 99, 129, 237, 247.
27 *Ep*. 243.4: Deferrari, III, 445. Τοῦ κοινοῦ κτήματος, τοῦ πατρικοῦ θησαυροῦ τῆς ὑγιαινούσης πίστεως. Courtonne, III, 71.

complete shipwreck of the faith. Sigh for us because the only begotten is blasphemed, and there is no one to utter objection. The Holy Spirit is denied, and he who can offer refutation is driven into exile.[28]

In his letters Basil shows that he can be severe but also merciful. According to Deferrari, "he is the father who grieves no less than the judge who condemns or the bishop who uses his authority to maintain the discipline of the church".[29] His writings are filled with the frequent citation of Scripture and are coloured with illustrations. He explicitly tells his correspondents: "By proofs taken from Scripture you may recognise the strength of the truth and the rottenness of heresy".[30] Throughout his correspondence it becomes evident that Basil's letters are shaped not only by his classical education, but also by his familiarity with Scripture.

4.2 Basil's Letters to Athanasius: An Example of Κοινωνία

From the correspondence that took place between Athanasius and Basil there are only six extant letters. From these six letters found in the corpus of Basil's 365 letters, one can infer the loss of Athanasius' letters to Basil. Basil's letters *Epp.* 61, 66, 67, 69, 80, and 82, are addressed to "Athanasius, Bishop of Alexandria" (Ἀθανασίῳ ἐπισκόπῳ Ἀλεξανδρείας). In each of these letters to his brother bishop, Basil made his characteristic appeal to a sense

---

28 *Ep.* 243.3-4: Deferrari, III, 443-445. Ἐπειδὴ τὸ Εὐαγγέλιον τῆς βασιλείας ἀπὸ τῶν ἡμετέρων τόπων ἀρξάμενον εἰς πᾶσαν ἐξῆλθε τὴν οἰκουμένην, διὰ τοῦτο ὁ κοινὸς τῶν ψυχῶν ἡμῶν ἐχθρὸς τὰ τῆς ἀποστασίας ῥήματα, ἀπὸ τῶν αὐτῶν τόπων τὴν ἀρχὴν λαβόντα, εἰς πᾶσαν τὴν οἰκουμένην διαδοθῆναι φιλονεικεῖ. Ἐφ᾽ οὓς γὰρ ἔλαμψεν ὁ φωτισμὸς τῆς γνώσεως τοῦ Χριστοῦ, ἐπὶ τούτους ἐλθεῖν καὶ τὸ τῆς ἀσεβείας σκότος ἐπινοεῖ... Ταῖς χειμαζομέναις τῶν Ἐκκλησιῶν χεῖρα ὀρέξατε, μήποτε ἐγκαταλειφθεῖσαι παντελὲς ὑπομείνωσι τῆς πίστεως τὸ ναυάγιον. Στενάξατε ἐφ᾽ ἡμῖν ὅτι ὁ Μονογενὴς βλασφημεῖται καὶ ὁ ἀντιλέγων οὐκ ἔστι. Τὸ Πνεῦμα τὸ Ἅγιον ἀθετεῖται, καὶ ὁ δυνάμενος ἐλέγχει ἀποδιώκεται. Courtonne, III, 71-72.
29 Deferrari, I, ix-x.
30 *Ep.* 105: Deferrari, II, 201. Μετ᾽ ἀποδείξεων γραφικῶν καὶ τὸ τῆς ἀληθείας ἰσχυρὸν καὶ τὸ σαθρὸν τῆς αἱρέσεως ὑμᾶς ἐπιγνῶναι. Courtonne, II, 7.

of shared destiny and mutual responsibility. Basil insisted that it behoved the office of the bishop to safeguard and uphold the Nicene communion of the church. In this same series of letters Basil also requested help in getting the support of the collegiality of bishops from the West, who, being of the same Nicene faith as the bishops of Cappadocia and its neighbouring Armenia, were called to give witness to the communion of the church through denouncing heresy.[31] Basil's interest in enhancing and encouraging the communion of the church was not only limited to Cappadocia and its adjacent sees but also included any church where he perceived that this communion was being compromised or threatened. To Basil, a schism arising in any local church had consequences for the entire communion of the church. In line with the Pauline expression he readily admits: "when one member suffers all the members suffer with it".[32] To his brotherhood of monks he laments: "All churches are being tossed about, and all souls are being sifted".[33]

The first of Basil's letters to Athanasius, *Ep.* 61, was a reply to a notification that Basil had received from Athanasius and others about the excommunication of the governor of Libya. Basil's letter to Athanasius described the Libyan governor as "a man who spends his life equally in cruelty and licentiousness".[34] Basil assures Athanasius that he is aware of the governor's excommunication and that he will convey this information to others:

> He [the governor] has become known to our church also through the letter of your reverence, and all men will

---

31 In *Ep.* 242.3 Basil praises the West for: ἄσυλον τὴν ἀποστολικὴν παρακαταθήκην διαφυλάξαντας (having preserved unharmed the sacred trust of the apostles). Courtonne, III, 67. Deferrari, III, 433.
32 *Ep.* 242.1: Deferrari, III, 431. Εἴπερ πάσχοντος μέλους ἑνὸς συμπάσχει πάντα τὰ μέλη. Courtonne, III, 63. See 1 Cor. 12:26.
33 *Ep.* 226.1: Deferrari, III, 329. Πᾶσαι μὲν Ἐκκλησίαι ἐσαλεύθησαν, πᾶσαι δὲ ψυχαὶ σινιάζονται. Courtonne, III, 24.
34 *Ep.* 61: Deferrari, II, 15. Ἀνδρὸς ὠμότητί τε ὁμοῦ καὶ ἀκολασίᾳ συζῶντος. Courtonne, I, 151.

account him abominable, sharing with him neither fire, nor water, nor shelter; if in truth anything can be of avail to those who have thus won for themselves a common and unanimous condemnation. But sufficient is a published bulletin, and your letter itself read everywhere. For we shall not cease to show it to everyone who has to do with him, to relatives or family or strangers.[35]

The remaining correspondence between Athanasius and Basil discusses two matters which will be written about in greater detail below. First, the correspondence had to do with the continuance of a schism[36] in Antioch, and with Antioch having more than one bishop claiming to be its presiding hierarch. Although Basil failed to heal the schism in Antioch and bring about communion, his letters do reveal how important he regarded communion and what processes he believed were required for it to be achieved. Second, Basil's correspondence with Athanasius consisted of concerns and objections that Basil had over the Western bishops' acceptance of one of the bishops contending for Antioch, namely Paulinus, whom Basil regarded as non-Nicene. On both occasions Basil turned to Athanasius as someone who had "great solicitude

---

35 *Ep.* 61: Deferrari, II, 15. Ἐγνωρίσθη δὲ καὶ τῇ Ἐκκλησίᾳ ἡμῶν ἐκ τῶν γραμμάτων τῆς σῆς θεοσεβείας, καὶ ἀποτρόπαιον αὐτὸν πάντες ἡγήσονται, μὴ πυρός, μὴ ὕδατος, μὴ σκέπης αὐτῷ κοινωνοῦντες, εἴπερ τι ὄφελος τοῖς οὕτω κεκρατημένοις κοινῆς καὶ ὁμοψήφου καταγνώσεως. Ἀρκοῦσα δὲ αὐτῷ στήλη καὶ αὐτὰ τὰ γράμματα ἀναγινωσκόμενα πανταχοῦ. Οὐ γὰρ διαλείψομεν πᾶσιν αὐτοῦ καὶ οἰκείοις καὶ φίλοις καὶ ξένοις ἐπιδεικνύντες. Courtonne, I, 152.

36 The term schism first appears in the earliest texts of the New Testament (see 1 Cor. 1:10; 1:11; 11:18; 12:25). Its meaning though is limited to only being that of a temporary disagreement, and that between individuals as opposed to groups or congregations. By the third century "schism" was used interchangeably or even confused with heresy. In Basil's time, a more prudent difference necessitated which defined heresy as wrong belief, and schism as a division based on moral and subsequently administrative grounds. From an ecclesiological viewpoint there is no essential distinction between schism and heresy as they both constitute positions held outside the communion of the church.

for all the churches",[37] and therefore as a kind of divinely appointed "physician to heal the maladies of the churches".[38] In Athanasius, Basil recognised a personality who did not "cease to discourse, to admonish, to write, and on each occasion to send out men who give the best advice".[39] Basil considered Athanasius' "perfection" (τελειότητα) to be "highest of all" (κορηφὴν τῶν ὅλων), and for this reason wanted to use him as the "adviser and director" of his "actions" (χρησαίμεθα καὶ ἡγεμόνι τῶν πράξεων).[40]

The Antiochian schism involved Meletius and Paulinus, who both presented themselves as the presiding hierarchs of the church of Antioch. Consequently, as Basil sternly put it to Athanasius, this meant that Antioch "has not only been completely divided by heretics, but it is also being torn asunder by those who affirm that they hold identical opinions with one another".[41] Now friend and foe were at odds with each other in defence of Christianity. Thus, "in addition to the open war waged by heretics", Basil explains that "the other war that has come upon us from those who are supposed to be orthodox has reduced the churches to the last degree of weakness".[42]

The schism in Antioch came about following the death of Bishop Eustathius, under whom the church of Antioch became a strong proponent of Nicene Christianity. Finding a replacement for Eustathius became a difficult task as several bishops were

---

37 Ep. 69.1: Deferrari, II, 39. Ἡ μέριμνά σοι πασῶν τῶν Ἐκκλησιῶν τοσαύτη. Courtonne, I, 161.
38 Ep. 82: Deferrari, II, 97. Ἰατρὸν τῶν ἐν ταῖς Ἐκκλησίαις ἀρρωστημάτων. Courtonne, I, 184.
39 Ep. 69.1: Deferrari, II, 39. Οὐδένα χρόνον διαλείπεις διαλεγόμενος, νουθετῶν, ἐπιστέλλων, ἐκπέμπων τινὰς ἑκάστοτε τοὺς ὑποτιθεμένους τὰ βέλτιστα. Courtonne, I, 161.
40 Ep. 69.1: Deferrari, II, 41. Courtonne, I, 162.
41 Ep. 66.2: Deferrari, II, 33. Ἥ γε οὐχ ὑπὸ τῶν αἱρετικῶν διατέτμηται μόνον, ἀλλὰ καὶ ὑπὸ τῶν τὰ αὐτὰ φρονεῖν ἀλλήλοις λεγόντων διασπᾶται. Courtonne, I, 158.
42 Ep. 92.3: Deferrari, II, 143. Ἡμῖν δέ, πρὸς τῷ φανερῷ πολέμῳ τῶν αἱρετικῶν, ἔτι καὶ ὁ παρὰ τῶν δοκούντων ὁμοδοξεῖν ἐπαναστὰς εἰς ἔσχατον ἀσθενείας τὰς Ἐκκλησίας κατήγαγεν. Courtonne, I, 202.

judged to be unsuitable for the office, resulting in dissension within the diocese. Finally Meletius was chosen, a candidate considered by scholars to be a "compromise" despite the accolades attributed to him by the likes of St. John Chrysostom, St. Gregory of Nazianzus, St. Gregory of Nyssa and of course St. Basil himself, who describes the former *homoiousian* as one who is "not open to censure as regards his faith, and in respect to his life admits no comparison with the rest".[43] Meletius had been a bishop in Roman Armenia prior to being transferred to Antioch in 360. Regardless of Meletius' credentials, the churches of the West and Egypt tended to support Paulinus. The problem with Meletius for bishops such as Athanasius and Damasus was that he had been ordained by non-Nicene bishops and thus his reputation had been tainted because of his previous associations with opponents of Nicaea. Basil, however, must have felt assured in his own mind that Meletius had since adhered to a Nicene confession of faith.[44] Paulinus, on the other hand, held views that according to Mitchell "were dangerously Sabellian",[45] presumably because Basil accused Paulinus of being inclined towards the teachings of Marcellus of Ancyra.[46] This may explain why Paulinus, an aged priest who secured consecration from Roman Westerners in 363, was considered unfavourably by the churches of the East (excluding Egypt), who instead supported Meletius.

---

43 *Ep.* 67: Deferrari, II, 35. Τῇ τε πίστει ἀνεπίληπτον ὄντα καὶ τῷ βίῳ οὐδεμίαν πρὸς τοὺς ἄλλους ἐπιδεχόμενον σύγκρισιν. Courtonne, I, 159. There are six letters that survive and which are dated from 371 to 375 that Basil wrote to Meletius. Each of these letters reveals Basil's support for Meletius. These letters that Basil wrote as a bishop are identified as *Epp.* 57, 68, 89, 120, 129, 216; they give accounts of the problems that Meletius was facing.
44 Discernible proofs that indicate a bishop's faith allegiance will be discussed in chapters Five and Six. Of course in Basil's life time theological statements that purported to respond to orthodoxy, truth and Nicenism were not necessarily a given but rather an entire process that took much effort, revision and tension to be worked out.
45 Mitchell, *A History of the Later Roman Empire*, 287.
46 See *Ep.* 263.5. Τοῖς Μαρκέλλου προσπεπονθὼς δόγμασι. Courtonne, III, 125.

The schism in Antioch meant that once again a major town had more than one claimant to the episcopal office. The important difference in Antioch was that both its bishops, Meletius and Paulinus, claimed to identify with a Nicene position of faith. Notwithstanding their Nicene allegiance, mutual distrust and non-Nicene suspicion still existed amongst both bishops and their supporters. As a result, Nicene bishops were divided in their support of the rival orthodox bishops of Antioch,[47] which meant that, as advocates of Nicene faith, they were no longer united in their external witness. At a local level both Meletius and Paulinus cultivated their own loyal followers, which brought about much instability through the factionalism and rivalry that ensued. The factionalism ceased momentarily, however, when Valens moved to Antioch in 370 and forced Meletius into exile,[48] a move that Basil decried and did all that he could to overturn.[49] In wanting Meletius established as the sole bishop for the diocese of Antioch, Basil was hoping to achieve a united Nicene theological front in Antioch.[50]

At all times Basil sided with the "man of God" (ἀνθρώπῳ τοῦ Θεοῦ)[51] Meletius, and in his endeavours to uphold the cause of Meletius, he asked for the mediation of Athanasius. Basil argued that it was as a result of ignorance regarding the affairs of the church in the East that Meletius had been falsely represented by the Westerners as adhering to non-Nicene theological positions.[52] Basil's correspondence with Athanasius is virtually dominated by

47 See Basil *Epp.* 82, 92.3, 226.1, 258.1.
48 See Rochelle Snee, "Valens' Recall of the Nicene Exiles and Anti-Arian Propaganda". *Greek, Roman and Byzantine Studies*, vol. 26, no. 4 (1985): 414.
49 See *Epp.* 67–69, 92, 156, 258.
50 Radde-Gallwitz, *Basil of Caesarea*, 137.
51 *Ep.* 210.5: Deferrari, III, 207. Courtonne, II, 194.
52 See *Ep.* 214.2.

appeals for Athanasius to heal the schism affecting Antioch. He writes: "The people of the holy church of Antioch [...] ought to be brought into a single harmony and union, my purpose being to show clearly that those who are not divided into several parties should unite with the bishop Meletius".[53] Basil calls upon Athanasius' past, where theological conflicts for the most part were kept at bay, and for this reason appeals to him "who has experienced the pristine tranquillity and concord of the churches of the Lord touching the faith".[54] He asks him to help bring about "communion and unity with those of like belief" (ὁμοδόξους κοινωνίαν καὶ ἕνωσιν).[55] Specifically Basil writes that he had "entered upon this embassy and mediation" with Athanasius, out of earnest "desire for peace and mutual union among those who hold the same beliefs about the Lord".[56] Basil's letter to Bishop Ascholius of Thessalonica gives the reader an indication of what Basil had in mind when referring to the peace and concord of the churches in times gone past:

> In the olden times (ἀρχαίων καιρῶν) when the churches of God flourished, taking root in the faith, united by charity, there being, as in a single body, a single harmony of the various members; when the persecutors indeed were in the open, but in the open were also the persecuted; when the laity, though harassed, became more numerous, and the blood of the martyrs watering the churches nurtured many times as many champions of religion, later generations stripping themselves for combat in emulation of their predecessors. Then we Christians had peace (εἰρήνην)

---

53 *Ep.* 67: Deferrari, II, 33–35. Τὴν ἁγίαν Ἐκκλησίαν Ἀντιοχείας λαοῦ εἰς μίαν συμφωνίαν χρὴ καὶ ἕνωσιν ἐναχθῆναι, πρὸς τὸ δηλῶσαι ὅτι τῷ θεοφιλεστάτῳ ἐπισκόπῳ Μελετίῳ δέοι τὰ εἰς μέρη πλείονα νῦν διῃρημένα συνάψαι. Courtonne, I, 159.
54 *Ep.* 66.1: Deferrari, II, 27. Τὸν τῆς ἀρχαίας εὐσταθείας καὶ ὁμονοίας περὶ τὴν πίστιν τῶν Ἐκκλησιῶν τοῦ Θεοῦ πεπειραμένον. Courtonne, I, 157.
55 *Ep.* 82: Deferrari, II, 99. Courtonne, I, 185.
56 *Ep.* 82: Deferrari, II, 101. Ἐπιθυμίᾳ τῆς εἰρήνης καὶ τῆς πρὸς ἀλλήλους ἡμῶν συναφείας τῶν ὁμονοούντων εἰς τὰ πρὸς Κύριον, ἐπὶ τὴν πρεσβείαν ταύτην καὶ μεσιτείαν ἀφικομένους. Courtonne, I, 185.

among ourselves, that peace which the Lord left to us, of which now not even a trace any longer remains to us, so ruthlessly have we driven it away for one another.[57]

Basil's request was for Athanasius to write a letter to the bishops in communion with Meletius, or, failing that, at least to use his influence on Paulinus so as to prevail upon him to withdraw from occupying the position of the bishop of Antioch. Having the support of Athanasius and the bishops of the West was crucial to Basil, because they represented solidarity of belief through their commitment to a Nicene faith, and so personified the communion that was indicative of a pro-Nicene church. With respect to the West, Basil declares:

> I recognise but one avenue of assistance to the churches in our part of the world – agreement (σύμπνοιαν) with the bishops of the West [...] Since our rulers are timid about the fidelity of the masses, and the peoples everywhere follow their bishops unquestionably.[58]

Basil looked to the West as a safe harbour since it was unaffected by heresy and because it possessed "apostolic zeal for orthodoxy" (ἀποστολικὸν [...] ζῆλον ὑπὲρ τῆς ὀρθοδοξίας).[59] To a certain extent, because of its geographical positioning within a pro-Nicene imperial regime, the West was considered to be shielded from the influ-

---

57 Ep. 164.1: Deferrari, II, 423. Ἐπὶ τῶν ἀρχαίων καιρῶν γεγενῆσαι, ἡνίκα ἤνθουν αἱ Ἐκκλησίαι τοῦ Θεοῦ ἐρριζωμένει τῇ πίστει, ἡνωμέναι τῇ ἀγάπῃ ὥσπερ ἐν ἑνὶ σώματι μιᾶς συμπνοίας διαφόρων μελῶν ὑπαρχούσης· ὅτε φανεροὶ μὲν οἱ διώκοντες, πολεμούμενοι δὲ οἱ λαοὶ πλείους ἐγίνοντο καὶ τὸ αἷμα τῶν μαρτύρων ἄρδον τὰς Ἐκκλησίας πολυπλασίονας τοὺς ἀγωνιστὰς τῆς εὐσεβείας ἐξέτρεφε, τῷ ζήλῳ τῶν προλαβόντων ἐπαποδυομένων τῶν ἐφεξῆς. Τότε Χριστιανοὶ μὲν πρὸς ἀλλήλους εἰρήνην ἤγομεν, εἰρήνην ἐκείνην ἣν ὁ Κύριος ἡμῖν κατέλειπεν, ἧς νῦν οὐδ᾽ ἴχνος ἡμῖν ὑπολέλειπται, οὕτως αὐτὴν ἀπηνῶς ἀπ᾽ ἀλλήλων ἀπεδιώξαμεν. Courtonne, II, 97–98.
58 Ep. 66.1: Deferrari, II, 27–29. Οἶδα καὶ αὐτός [...] μίαν ἐπιγνοὺς ὁδὸν βοηθείας ταῖς καθ᾽ ἡμᾶς Ἐκκλησίας, τὴν παρὰ τῶν δυτικῶν ἐπισκόπων σύμπνοιαν [...] Τῶν τε κρατούντων τὸ ἀξιόπιστον τοῦ πλήθους δυσωπουμένων καὶ τῶν ἑκασταχοῦ λαῶν ἀκολούντων αὐτοῖς ἀναντιρρήτως. Courtonne, I, 157.
59 Ep. 90.2: Deferrari, II, 127. Courtonne, I, 196.

ences of heresy. According to Rousseau, under the pro-Nicene emperor Valentinian "the West was seen as a contrasting territorial unit, where harmony and fearless proclamation of the truth were safely established".[60] Because the Western emperor Valentinian embraced Nicene Christianity, it followed that the Nicene churches under his imperial governance enjoyed "peace, freedom and unity".[61] These fortuitous factors contributed to the Western bishops being greater ambassadors of the Nicene expression of Christian faith and more free in their witness when presenting a united Nicene front. In the name of "communion of the spirit" (κοινωνία πνεύματος),[62] the West was called upon by Basil "to furnish the desired aid to the churches of God" (παρασχέσθαι τὴν ἐπιζητουμένην βοήθειαν ταῖς τοῦ Θεοῦ Ἐκκλησίαις).[63] Furthermore they were asked to "zealously endeavour to count all things secondary to peace (εἰρήνη), and above all they must be solicitous for the church of Antioch, lest the orthodox section of it be weakened by being divided (σχιζομένην)".[64] There is no doubt that Basil considered his Western counterparts to be blessed. Being in the same communion of faith with the West meant that Basil could call upon them for help and inspiration:

> We consider your agreement and unity with one another (πρὸς ἀλλήλους σύμπνοιάν τε καὶ ἑνότητα) as a special blessing for us, so too we beg you to sympathise with our dissensions and not, because we are separated by our respective geographical positions, to sever us from yourselves, but inasmuch as we are united in the communion of the Spirit

---

60 Rousseau, *Basil of Caesarea*, 300.
61 Fedwick, *The Church and the Charisma of Leadership*, 107.
62 *Ep.* 90.2: Deferrari, II, 127. Courtonne, I, 196.
63 *Ep.* 263.5: Deferrari, IV, 101. Courtonne, III, 126.
64 *Ep.* 69.2: Deferrari, II, 47. Πάντα γὰρ δεῖ σπουδάσαι δεύτερα ἡγήσασθαι τῆς εἰρήνης καὶ πρὸ πάντων τῆς κατὰ Ἀντιόχειαν Ἐκκλησίας ἐπιμεληθῆναι, ὡς μὴ ἀσθενεῖν ἐν αὐτῇ τὴν ὀρθὴν μερίδα περὶ τὰ πρόσωπα σχιζομένην. Courtonne, I, 164.

(ἑνούμεθα τῇ κατὰ τὸ Πνεῦμα κοινωνίᾳ), to take us into harmony (συμφωνίαν) of one single body.[65]

To the bishops of Italy and Gaul, Basil writes: "You will sympathise as much with our afflictions, to which we have been given over on account of our sins, as we rejoice with you who are glorifying in the peace with which the Lord has blessed you".[66] It becomes apparent that Basil's letters to the West pushed his rhetorical skills to the limit. No doubt this seemed needed as he required immediate action and help. He therefore used whatever niceties of language he could to elicit a response:

> But as for you [bishops of the West], inasmuch as you happen to live far away from them [the heretics], so much the greater is the confidence you enjoy in the eyes of the laity, in addition to the fact that God's grace cooperates with you in the care of those who labour.[67]

To his much admired Bishop Athanasius, Basil was forthright in his request: "Put an end to factional usurpations of authority, subject all men to one another in charity, and restore to the church her pristine strength".[68] In the end, Meletius himself, once freed from

---

65 *Ep.* 90.1: Deferrari, II, 125. Ἡμεῖς ἴδιον ἀγαθὸν ἑαυτῶν ποιούμεθα τὴν ὑμετέραν πρὸς ἀλλήλους σύμπνοιάν τε καὶ ἑνότητα, οὕτω καὶ ὑμᾶς παρακαλοῦμεν συμπαθῆσαι ἡμῶν ταῖς διαιρέσεσι καὶ μή, ὅτι τῇ θέσει τῶν τόπων διεστήκαμεν, χωρίζειν ἡμᾶς ἀφ' ἑαυτῶν, ἀλλ᾽, ὅτι ἑνούμεθα τῇ κατὰ τὸ Πνεῦμα κοινωνίᾳ, εἰς τὴν ἑνὸς σώματος ἡμᾶς συμφωνίαν ἀναλαμβάνειν. Courtonne, I, 195.
66 *Ep.* 243.1: Deferrari, III, 437. Συμπαθήσετε ἡμῶν ταῖς θλίψεσιν αἷς παρεδόθημεν διὰ τὰς ἁμαρτίας ἡμῶν, ὅσον καὶ ἡμεῖς συγχαίρομεν ὑμῖν δοξαζομένοις ἐν τῇ εἰρήνῃ ᾗ ἐχαρίσατο ὑμῖν ὁ Κύριος. Courtonne, III, 68.
67 *Ep.* 263.2: Deferrari, IV, 93. Ὑμεῖς δὲ ὅσον μακρὰν αὐτῶν ἀπῳκισμένοι τυγχάνετε, τοσούτῳ πλέον παρὰ τοῖς λαοῖς τὸ ἀξιόπιστον ἔχετε, πρὸς τῷ καὶ τὴν παρὰ τοῦ Θεοῦ χάριν συναίρεσθαι ὑμῖν εἰς τὴν ὑπὲρ τῶν καταπονουμένων ἐπιμέλειαν. Courtonne, III, 122.
68 *Ep.* 66.2: Deferrari, II, 33. Παῦσαι δὲ τὰς μερικὰς προστασίας, ὑποτάξαι δὲ πάντας ἀλλήλοις ἐν ἀγάπῃ καὶ τὴν ἀρχαίαν ἰσχὺν ἀποδοῦναι τῇ Ἐκκλησίᾳ. Courtonne, I, 159. There are no surviving letters from Athanasius that indicate any direct response to Basil's request for help in support of Meletius. Rather than leaving this to the realm of the unknown, Radde-Gallwitz conjectures: "He [Athanasius] probably perceived Basil as too compromising with former 'Homoians' such as Meletius". Radde-Gallwitz, *Basil of Caesarea*, 137.

exile,[69] approached his rival Paulinus and agreed to join congregations, with the mutual understanding being that whichever bishop passed away first they would bequeath sole episcopacy to the other.[70] In 381 the death of Meletius finally brought an ending to the almost twenty years of disputes over the bishopric of Antioch.

In his later correspondence to Athanasius concerning Marcellianism, Basil was disturbed by the failure of the Westerners to repudiate Marcellus of Ancyra, who, despite his old age, was still attracting masses of people (ἀναρίθμητον πλῆθος).[71] Perhaps this had to do with the fact that in the early 350s, under the non-Nicene emperor Constantius II, Marcellus and Athanasius had both experienced exile in the West.[72] While in exile for different reasons, they had the common task of gaining support for their lost positions. Originally Marcellus upheld the cause of Nicaea, later however, while attacking the errors of Asterius, he was seen to have taught that the Son had no real personhood but was rather a mere external image of the Father. For Marcellus, the second person of the Trinity, the Word, did indeed make his appearance in time, but did not exist in essence before this or after his return. Such an understanding, according to Basil, was not far from Sabellianism and for this reason was seen as the theological opposite extreme to Arianism. Through Athanasius, Basil was attempting to entice the bishops of Rome and the West to: "exterminate the heresy of Marcellus as being both dangerous and harmful, and foreign to true faith".[73] Basil wanted the bishops of the West to apply the same "censure" (μέμψιν) to Marcellus as they did to Arius:

---

69 See *Ep.* 57.
70 See Theodoret, *Church History* 5.3.
71 See *Ep.* 266.
72 The synods of Arles (353) and Milan (355) had condemned Athanasius and Marcellus.
73 *Ep.* 69.2: Deferrari, II, 45. Τὸ τὴν Μαρκέλλου αἵρεσιν αὐτοὺς ὡς χαλεπὴν καὶ βλαβερὰν καὶ τῆς ὑγιαινούσης πίστεως ἀλλοτρίως ἔχουσαν ἐξορίσαι. Courtonne, I, 163.

> For up to the present, in all the letters which they [the Romans] send, while they do not cease anathematising the abominable Arius up and down and banishing him from the churches, yet against Marcellus, who has exhibited an impiety diametrically opposed to that of Arius, who has in fact been impious concerning the very existence of the only begotten Godhead, and has accepted a false signification of "the Word", they have manifestly brought no censure whatever.[74]

In response to Basil's attempts to have Marcellus and his followers excommunicated,[75] the Marcellians in 371 sent a delegation to Alexandria with letters from the bishops of Achaia that testified to Marcellus' orthodoxy. The Marcellian delegation produced a statement of faith in solidarity with the Creed of Nicaea. In particular, the distinction between the "Word" (Λόγος) and the Son is rejected, and the belief that the Father existed before the Son is anathematised. Athanasius accepts this confession and re-establishes communion with Marcellus and his followers. Receiving Athanasius' verdict, Basil concedes that his attempts to have Marcellus condemned are dismissed.

From the above, one can see that Basil speaks with utmost respect and veneration about Athanasius. He considers Athanasius to be a beacon of light that unites all those who are sound in faith, while also exposing those who are not of true faith. The correspondence between Athanasius and Basil, concerning the religious controversy of the Antiochian schism and Marcellianism, had as its ultimate aim the recognition of truth and the establishment of communion. As Basil says to Athanasius: "The result will

---

74 *Ep.* 69.2: Deferrari, II, 45. Ἐπεί, μέχρι τοῦ νῦν, ἐν πᾶσιν οἷς ἐπιστέλλουσι γράμμασι, τὸν μὲν δυσώνυμον Ἄρειον ἄνω καὶ κάτω ἀναθεματίζοντες καὶ τῶν Ἐκκλησιῶν ἐξορίζοντες οὐ διαλείπουσι, Μαρκέλλῳ δέ, τῷ κατὰ διάμετρον ἐκείνῳ τὴν ἀσέβειαν ἐπιδειξαμένῳ καὶ εἰς αὐτὴν τὴν ὕπαρξιν τῆς τοῦ Μονογενοῦς θεότητος ἀσεβήσαντι καὶ κακῶς τὴν τοῦ Λόγου προσηγορίαν ἐκδεξαμένῳ, οὐδεμίαν μέμψιν ἐπενεγκόντες φαίνονται. Courtonne, I, 163.
75 See *Epp.* 125.1, 207.1, 263.5, 265.3, 266.1.

be that henceforth we shall be able to recognise those who are of one mind (ὁμόφρονας) with us".[76] Basil considered Athanasius to be someone on whom he could depend upon for the restoration of peace among the churches. The more serious the dissensions within the churches became, the more Basil turned to Athanasius so as to be saved "from the present fearful tempest" (ἐκ τοῦ φοβεροῦ τούτου χειμῶνας).[77] When Basil asked Athanasius the question: "Who is the helmsman capable of meeting these dangers?" (Πρὸς ταῦτα τίς ἱκανὸς κυβερνήτης;)[78] and therefore capable of safeguarding the communion of the church, Basil knew all too well that the prelate of Alexandria was not only capable of being such a helmsman but spent his entire life doing so.

4.3 The Term Κοινωνία and its Use in the Letters

The word "communion" (κοινωνία) is mentioned frequently in the letters of Basil. In its etymology κοινωνία denotes something that is held in common and in which all can share.[79] Scholars of Koine Greek refer to κοινωνία as "participation, impartation and fellowship",[80] implying a sharing by all for the benefit of all. In a Christian context, κοινωνία denotes a participation in, or fellowship with, the very person and life of Jesus Christ[81] that is made possible through fellowship with the Spirit of God.[82] As a noun, κοινωνία is used 302 times in Basil's works. Its root κοιν- is found 344 times in Basil's letters and in his treatise *On the Holy Spirit*. The equivalents of κοινωνία are: "agreement" (ὁμόνοια, συμφωνία), "unity" (ἕνωσις) and "association" (συνάφειαν). The opposite of κοινωνία

---

76   *Ep.* 69.2: Deferrari, II, 47. Ὥστε τοῦ λοιποῦ γνωρίζειν ἡμᾶς τοὺς ὁμόφρονας καὶ μή. Courtonne, I, 163.
77   *Ep.* 80: Deferrari, II, 91. Courtonne, I, 181.
78   *Ep.* 82: Deferrari, II, 99. Courtonne, I, 184.
79   See Liddell and Scott, *A Greek-English Lexicon*, 968.
80   Hauck, *Theological Dictionary of the New Testament*, 798.
81   See 1 Cor. 1:9.
82   See 2 Cor. 13:13.

is ἴδιον, which signifies that which is private, particular or specific, and therefore cannot be participated in or shared.[83] In Basil's theology, κοινωνία refers not only to the church's intimate unity, but also to its participation in the life of the Godhead. Furthermore Basil states that it is the "only one way leading to the Lord, and all who travel toward him are companions of one another and travel according to one agreement as to life".[84] This is why, for Basil, the most intimate relationship with God also includes a communion amongst people as well. In this sense, Basil sees κοινωνία as a fundamental component of human life and as a natural consequence of living out the will of God. He insisted that the person is a κοινωνικὸν ζῷον: "a being that is communal by nature",[85] and so, to those who were not in κοινωνία, Basil exhorted that every effort should be made, in fulfilment of "the laws of charity" (θεσμοὺς τῆς ἀγάπης), to be "united [...] in communion" (προσκαλεῖσθαι [...] εἰς συνάφειαν):

> It does not seem best to me to estrange ourselves entirely from those who do not accept the faith, but we should show some concern for these men according to the laws of charity and should with one accord write letters to them, offering every exhortation with kindliness, and offering to them the faith of the Fathers we should invite them to join us; and if we convince them, we should be united with them in communion.[86]

---

83 See Chapter Three.
84 *Ep.* 150.2: Deferrari, II, 365. Μίαν εἶναι ὁδὸν τὴν πρὸς τὸν Κύριον ἄγουσαν, καὶ πάντες τοὺς πρὸς αὐτὸν πορευομένους συνοδεύειν ἀλλήλοις, καὶ κατὰ μίαν συνθήκην τοῦ βίου πορεύεσθαι. Courtonne, II, 73.
85 See the third rule of Basil's *Longer Rules*. PG 32. 181A-C.
86 *Ep.* 128: Deferrari, II, 281. Οὐδὲ παντελῶς μοι δοκεῖ τῶν μὴ δεχομένων τὴν πίστιν ἀλλοτριοῦν ἑαυτούς, ἀλλὰ ποιήσασθαί τινα τῶν ἀνδρῶν ἐπιμέλειαν κατὰ τοὺς παλαιοὺς θεσμοὺς τῆς ἀγάπης, καὶ ἐπιστεῖλαι αὐτοῖς ἀπὸ μιᾶς γνώμης πᾶσαν παράκλησιν μετ᾽ εὐσπλαγχνίας προσάγοντες, καὶ τὴν τῶν Πατέρων πίστιν προτεινομένους προκαλεῖσθαι αὐτοὺς εἰς συνάφειαν· κἂν μὲν πείσωμεν, κοινῶς αὐτοῖς ἑνωθῆναι. Courtonne, II, 39.

It is important to note the connection Basil sees between κοινωνία and the term church (ἐκκλησία). Throughout Basil's letters there are constant references to being in communion with the church. In the same vein as the New Testament Scriptures, Basil uses the term ἐκκλησία in its communal connotation, that is to say, the calling together of God's chosen people into an assembly. Derived from the Greek verb to "call out" (ἐκ – καλέω), church (ἐκκλησία) was understood in New Testament times as a communal gathering that took place in response to a calling from God. It was only with the conviction that God was calling the Christian community in the name of Jesus Christ[87] that the early Christian community, and subsequent Christian communities thereafter, would hold to the confession of being in communion with the ἐκκλησία of God.

The letters themselves, apart from conveying what it is to be in communion, were also used as an instrument of maintaining communion or even restoring communion. Eustathius of Sebasteia, for example, prior to his final rupture with Nicene Christianity, was formerly restored to his see only when he could "display" that he was the recipient of a "letter" from his fellow bishops "restoring him" (ἐπιστολὴν ἐκόμισεν ἀποκαθιστῶσαν αὐτόν, ἣν ἐπιδείξας).[88] Basil, when writing to the exiled bishops Eulogius, Alexander and Harpocration, and in response to having become aware of their written confession refuting the teachings of Apollinarius,[89] proclaimed: "We have considered it right to come into communion with your good company and to join ourselves through this letter (διὰ τοῦ γράμματος) with your reverences".[90] Only once the faithful have "anathematised" a particular "heresy", declares Basil in the

---

87 See Acts 20:28; 1Cor 1:2, Τῇ ἐκκλησίᾳ τοῦ Θεοῦ [...] ἐν Χριστῷ Ἰησοῦ. "The church of God... in Jesus Christ".
88 *Ep.* 263.3: Deferrari, IV, 97. Courtonne, III, 124.
89 "Regarded by that time as a leading exponent of the Sabellian tradition". Rousseau, *Basil of Caesarea*, 242.
90 *Ep.* 265.1: Deferrari, IV, 107. Δίκαιον ἐνομίσαμεν κοινωνοὶ γενέσθαι τῆς ἀγαθῆς μερίδος ὑμῶν καὶ συνάψαι ἑαυτοὺς διὰ τοῦ γράμματος τῇ ὑμετέρᾳ εὐλαβείᾳ. Courtonne, III, 128.

same letter, do they become "acceptable for communion" (δεκτοὺς γενέσθαι τῇ κοινωνίᾳ).⁹¹

The decision as to who to "receive [...] into communion" (λαβεῖν κοινωνούς),⁹² and as to who is "in communion" (ἔχομεν κοινωνικόν),⁹³ was often left to the discretion of the synod of bishops, and was "canonically and legally promulgated" through a "synodical letter" (τῷ συνοδικῷ γράμματι κανονικῶς καὶ ἐνθέσμως δεδογματισμένοις).⁹⁴ It was not uncommon for letters to be drawn up for the sole purpose of being "signed by all those in communion" (ὑπογραφῆναι δὲ πάντων τῶν κοινωνικῶν).⁹⁵ These letters, if needed, acted like licenses which validated a bishop's canonicity and bore witness to his communion with the church. Such is the case with some of Basil's correspondents who were ordained to the episcopacy. They presented Basil with enthronement and synodical letters that bore witness to their Nicene orthodoxy, and which also served as proof of their communion with those of like faith.⁹⁶ Bishops who were involved in exchanging letters with Basil were called οἱ κοινωνικοί (lit. the ones in communion), in that they were in communion with him and each other.⁹⁷ For Basil, "those who confessed" the Nicene "faith" were included in "the party of the communicants" (τῇ μερίδι τῶν κοινωνικῶν).⁹⁸ To the charge that Basil was "in communion with Apollinarius", Basil amongst other things responds first and foremost to his "violent" accusers: "let them show [...] canonical letters (κανονικὰ γράμματα) sent by me

---

91   Ep. 265.3: Deferrari, IV, 107. Τοὺς ἑπομένους αὐτῷ ἀναγκαῖον ἀναθεματίσαντας ἐκείνην τὴν αἵρεσιν οὕτω δεκτοὺς γενέσθαι τῇ κοινωνίᾳ. Courtonne, III, 131.
92   Ep. 237.2: Deferrari, III, 411. Courtonne, III, 57.
93   Ep. 244.3: Deferrari, III, 457. Courtonne, III, 76.
94   Ep. 92.3: Deferrari, II, 145. Courtonne, I, 203.
95   Ep. 120: Deferrari, II, 245. Courtonne, II, 25.
96   See Epp. 65, 197.1, 203.
97   See Ep. 120: Courtonne, II, 26; Fedwick, *The Church and the Charisma of Leadership*, 74, 122.
98   Ep. 204.6: Deferrari, III, 171. Τοὺς ταύτην ὁμολογοῦντας τὴν πίστιν ἐγκατέτασσον τῇ μερίδι τῶν κοινωνικῶν. Courtonne, II, 179.

to him or by him to me".⁹⁹ An important proviso for Basil was that a canonical letter could only be written by a bishop. Anything written by bishops while they were still in a "lay state" (τῷ λαϊκῷ βίῳ)¹⁰⁰ was not considered as "proof" (ἀπόδειξιν)¹⁰¹ of a canonical letter and therefore should not be treated as one. Regarding himself and his former correspondence with Apollinarius, Basil states:

> No one while in the episcopate is accused, if through indifference he wrote anything inadvertently while in the lay state, and that too not even on faith, but a simple letter (ψιλὸν γράμμα) with a friendly greeting.¹⁰²

To the clergy and laity who did not espouse the same doctrinal faith and ethos as Basil and his fellow bishops, Basil declared himself not to be in communion with them (μηδὲ κοινωνικούς αὐτῶν εἶναι).¹⁰³ Writing to the educated of Neocaesarea, Basil asserts: "If they [the non-Nicene bishops] persist in these same [false] doctrines we must proclaim the misfortune among you to other churches also, and cause letters to be sent to you from many bishops to break down this mass of impiety".¹⁰⁴ To the priest Paregorius, Basil warns: "If you dare, without correcting your ways, to cling to your priestly office, you will be anathema to all the laity; and those who receive you will be excommunicated throughout the church

---

99 *Ep.* 224.2: Deferrari, III, 317. Δειξάτωσαν ἢ κανονικὰ γράμματα παρ᾽ ἐμοῦ πρὸς αὐτὸν διαπεμπόμενα, ἢ παρ᾽ ἐκείνου πρὸς ἐμέ. Courtonne, III, 19.
100 *Ep.* 224.2: Deferrari, III, 317. Courtonne, III, 19.
101 See *Ep.* 226.4: Deferrari, III, 339. Courtonne, III, 28.
102 *Ep.* 224.2: Deferrari, III, 317. Οὐδεὶς ἐν ἐπισκοπῇ ὢν ἐγκαλεῖται, εἴ τι κατὰ ἀδιαφορίαν ἐν τῷ λαϊκῷ ἀπαρατηρήτως ἔγραψε· καὶ τοῦτο μηδὲν περὶ πίστεως, ἀλλὰ ψιλὸν γράμμα φιλικὴν ἔχον προσηγορίαν. Courtonne, III, 19. See *Ep.* 226.4: λαϊκοὶ ὄντες πρὸς λαϊκοὺς ἐπεστέλλομεν (as laymen wrote to laymen). Courtonne, III, 28. Deferrari, III, 341.
103 *Ep.* 113: Deferrari, II, 225. Courtonne, II, 17.
104 *Ep.* 210.4: Deferrari, III, 207. Ἐὰν δὲ τοῖς αὐτοῖς ἐπιμένωσιν, ἀνάγκη καὶ πρὸς ἄλλας Ἐκκλησίας ἐκβοῆσαι ἡμᾶς τὴν καθ᾽ ὑμᾶς συμφορὰν καὶ ποιῆσαι παρὰ πλειόνων ἐπισκόπων γράμματα ὑμῖν ἀφικέσθαι, τὸ μέγεθος τοῦτο τῆς ὑποκατασκευαζομένης ἀσεβείας καταργηνύντα. Courtonne, II, 194.

(ἐκκήρυκτοι κατὰ πᾶσαν Ἐκκλησίαν γενήσονται)".[105]

In *Epp.* 113 and 114, Basil's addressees were asked to accept as communicants only those who adhere to the faith of Nicaea and who furthermore refuse to describe the Holy Spirit as a creature. Basil's general understanding was to "regard communion with these [as valid], as long as they were with the sound [Nicene] party".[106] This poignantly comes across in the introduction of Basil's letter to the exiled bishop Meletius of Antioch. To garner support against Meletius' unjustified exile to Armenia, and to complain about the uncanonical ordination of Faustus as the bishop of Antioch (an Armenian see under Basil's oversight), Basil informs Meletius about the need to create a letter which would only be signed by "all those in communion" (πάντων τῶν κοινονικῶν). The purpose of this letter was to rebut the uncanonical actions of one of Basil's staunch opponents, Anthimus of Tyana, whose subsequent ordination of Faustus, Basil declared void since it was never sanctioned by the communion of the church. Writing to Meletius, Basil explains:

> I have received a letter from the most God-beloved bishop Eusebius, enjoining that we write again to Westerners concerning certain ecclesiastical affairs. He wished further that the letter be drawn up by us and signed by all those in communion (πάντων τῶν κοινονικῶν) [...] for we are ready both to agree to this and to cause it to be sent to those in communion with us (τοῖς κοινωνικοῖς).[107]

---

105 *Ep.* 55: Deferrari, I, 351. Ἐὰν δὲ τολμήσῃς, μὴ διορθωσάμενος σεαυτὸν, ἀντέχεσθαι τῆς ἱερωσύνης, ἀνάθεμα ἔσει παντὶ τῷ λαῷ καὶ οἱ δεχόμενοί σε ἐκκήρυκτοι κατὰ πᾶσαν Ἐκκλησίαν γενήσονται. Courtonne, I, 142.
106 *Ep.* 245: Deferrari, III, 475. Ὧν ὅσου ἀξίαν ἐτιθέμεθα τὴν κοινωνίαν, ἕως ἦσαν ἐπὶ τῆς ὑγιαινούσης μερίδος. Courtonne, III, 84.
107 *Ep.* 120: Deferrari, II, 245-247. Γράμματα ἐδεξάμην παρὰ τοῦ θεοφιλεστάτου ἐπισκόπου Εὐσεβίου προστάσσοντα πάλιν γραφῆναι τοῖς Δυτικοῖς περὶ τινων ἐκκλησιαστικῶν. Καὶ ἐβουλήθη παρ' ἡμῶν τυπωθῆναι τὴν ἐπιστολήν, ὑπογραφῆναι δὲ παρὰ πάντων τῶν κοινωνικῶν [...] Ἡμῶν ἑτοίμως ἐχόντων καὶ αὐτῷ συνθέσθαι καὶ ταχέως ποιῆσαι περικομισθῆναι τοῖς κοινωνικοῖς. Courtonne, II, 25-26.

On another occasion, when speaking about his past mentor, Bishop Eustathius of Sebasteia, Basil warns: "If I find that he affirms his agreement in writing, I shall remain in communion with him; but if I catch him drawing back, I shall sever all connexions with him".[108] Reconciliation for Basil was instant and all so-called past wrongdoings, whether in conduct or doctrinal affiliation, were forgotten. As Basil affirms: "we do not consider the past, if only the present be sound".[109] The present state of believers, Basil argued, had to sincerely manifest their disposition of faith, "for either they may correct their hidden malady, or, if they still conceal it in the depth of their hearts, they will themselves bear the responsibility for their deception".[110] This was deemed necessary by Basil, "so that no one may be taken prematurely into communion".[111]

If all indicators showed true signs of repentance, Basil would not dwell on previous theological conflicts: "Better it is for us to be put out of the way and for the churches to agree with one another (τὰς δὲ Ἐκκλησίας ὁμονοεῖν πρὸς ἀλλήλας) than through our childish pettiness to bring so great an evil upon the people of God".[112] As support for his position Basil quotes from a letter that he received from Athanasius (no longer in existence), saying, "He [Athanasius] has clearly ordered that, if anyone wishes to come over from the heresy of the Arians by confessing the faith of Nicaea, we should receive him without making any discrimina-

---

108 *Ep.* 99: Deferrari, II, 179. Ἐὰν μὲν οὖν εὕρω αὐτὸν συντιθέμενον ἐγγράφως, ἐπιμενῶ τῇ κοινωνίᾳ· ἐὰν δὲ λάβω ἀναδυόμενον, ἀποστήσομαι αὐτοῦ τῆς συναφείας. Courtonne, I, 217.
109 *Ep.* 210.4: Deferrari, III, 207. Οὐ σκοποῦμεν τὰ παρελθόντα, τὰ παρόντα μόνον ὑγιαινέτωσαν. Courtonne, II, 194.
110 *Ep.* 125.1: Deferrari, II, 261. Ἢ γὰρ διορθώσαιντο ἑαυτῶν τὴν ἐν τῷ κρυπτῷ νόσον ἢ συγκαλύπτοντες αὐτὴν ἐν τῷ βάθει αὐτοὶ μὲν τὸ κρίμα τῆς ἀπάτης βαστάσουσιν. Courtonne, II, 31.
111 *Ep.* 240.3: Deferrari, III, 427. Ὡς μὴ προσληφθῆναί τινας εἰς κοινωνίαν. Courtonne, III, 64.
112 *Ep.* 204.7: Deferrari, III, 173. Βέλτιόν ἐστιν ἡμᾶς ἐκ ποδῶν γενέσθαι, τὰς δὲ Ἐκκλησίας ὁμονοεῖν πρὸς ἀλλήλας, ἢ διὰ τὰς μειρακιώδεις ἡμῶν μικροψυχίας κακὸν τοσοῦτον ἐκπάγεσθαι τοῖς λαοῖς τοῦ Θεοῦ. Courtonne, II, 180.

tion in his case".[113] Ultimately there was no foolproof method of ascertaining one's sincerity when it came to embracing the Nicene faith. The final word in this regard Basil left to the judgment of God. His interest was in reconciling, in the easiest possible way, people back into the communion of the church. A professed Nicene faith became for Basil a guarantor of Christian communion through offering a shared language that transcended divisions. For this reason he writes: "It is therefore fitting to receive them when they confess that they believe according to the words set forth by our Fathers at Nicaea and according to the meaning disclosed by those words when soundly interpreted".[114]

The exchanging of letters amongst canonical bishops also inspired reciprocal friendship and mutual good will central to Christian identity. Most of the year bishops were geographically separated from each other, and so a letter received was a welcomed alleviation of that separation. Well over a third of Basil's surviving letters are addressed to members of the clergy, the vast majority of these were diocesan bishops. When Basil addressed these bishops as "most loved by God" (θεοφιλέστατος),[115] they were reminded not only of their intimate bond of friendship, but also of the ideal of communion between people and God. To bond effectively in communion, bishops had only to make evident their common ground which was expressed through doctrinal statements of faith. General formulas reflecting the divinity and equality of the Trinity, for instance one *ousia* in three *hypostases*, were pivotal in forging communion amongst bishops. Such statements of faith were seen as unmistakable signs of loyalty, and were interpreted as

---

113 *Ep.* 204.6: Deferrari, III, 171. Φανερῶς διηγόρευσεν, εἴ τις ἐκ τῆς τῶν Ἀρειανῶν αἱρέσεως βούλοιτο μετατίθεσθαι ὁμολογῶν τὴν ἐν Νικαίᾳ πίστιν, τοῦτον προσίεσθαι μηδὲν διακρινομένους ἐπ᾽ αὐτῷ. Courtonne, II, 179.
114 *Ep.* 125.1: Deferrari, II, 261. Λαμβάνειν τοίνυν αὐτοὺς ὁμολογοῦντας προσήκει ὅτι πιστεύουσι κατὰ τὰ ῥήματα τὰ ὑπὸ τῶν Πατέρων ἡμῶν ἐκτεθέντα ἐν τῇ Νικαίᾳ καὶ κατὰ τὴν ὑγιῶς ὑπὸ τῶν ῥημάτων τούτων ἐμφαινομένην διάνοιαν. Courtonne, II, 31.
115 See Basil *Epp.* 32, 67, 92, 120, 127, 163, 215, 226, 227, 230.

an acknowledgment of belonging to the Nicene communion. Nearly all Nicene bishops where united in some way through official friendship and shared Nicene confessions of faith. Basil considered it his pastoral duty to keep within the communion of the church as many people as possible. To do this he remarked that great "labours" were needed "on behalf of the peace of the churches"[116] by both the clergy and laity alike. If there were divergences of opinions, Basil taught that these could be brought to harmony through "clarification" (τράνωσιν). According to him, "longer association together" (χρονιωτέρᾳ συνδιαγωγῇ) and "mutual experience without strife" (ἀφιλονείκῳ συγγυμνασίᾳ),[117] lead to an enriched communion. To the Neocaesareans who are on the brink of isolation, Basil makes a special appeal to bring them into the fold of the church's communion:

> From the letters which are being conveyed from those regions [the provinces of the empire], and from those which are being sent back to them from here, it is possible for you to learn that we are all of one mind, having the same ideas (σύμψυχοι πάντες ἐσμέν, τὸ ἓν φρονοῦντες). So let him who flees communion with us, who cuts himself off from the whole church, not escape the notice of your keen mind. Look around you, brethren, and see with whom you are in communion; once you are not received by us, who henceforth will acknowledge you?[118]

More often than not, any attempt to sever connections with bishops involved the immediate sending of "a letter containing a pro-

---

116 *Ep.* 99.2: Deferrari, II, 177. Ποιοῦσι τοὺς ὑπὲρ τῆς εἰρήνης τῶν Ἐκκλησιῶν καμάτους. Courtonne, I, 216.
117 *Ep.* 113: Deferrari, II, 225. Courtonne, II, 17.
118 *Ep.* 204.7: Deferrari, III, 173. Ὧν ἐστιν ἡμῖν ἔκ τε τῶν ἐκεῖθεν φερομένων γραμμάτων μαθεῖν καὶ ἐκ τῶν ἐντεῦθεν πάλιν ἀντιπεμπομένων αὐτοῖς διδαχθῆναι ὅτι σύμψυχοι πάντες ἐσμέν, τὸ ἓν φρονοῦντες. Ὥστε ὁ τὴν πρὸς ἡμᾶς κοινωνίαν ἀποδιδράσκων μὴ λανθανέτω ὑμῶν τὴν ἀκρίβειαν πάσης ἑαυτῶν τῆς Ἐκκλησίας ἀπορρηγνύς. Περιβλέψασθε, ἀδελφοί, πρὸς τίνας ἐστὶν ὑμῖν ἡ κοινωνία· ἐπειδὰν παρ' ἡμῶν μὴ δεχθῆτε, τίς ὑμᾶς λοιπὸν ἐπιγνώσεται; Courtonne, II, 180.

hibition (ἀγόρευσιν) of communion with us".[119] Here the "us" was a reference to the sender and those bishops in communion with him (οἱ κοινωνικοί). A visible sign of staying in communion was witnessed through affirming a creed in writing, which on a practical level included subscribing one's signature next to its formulation. When called upon, the κοινωνικοί promptly "subscribed their names" (ὑπέγραψαν)[120] to a written confession or creed. Without Eustathius' signature alongside a Nicene confession of faith, reconciliation between Basil and his former friend remained in abeyance. In Basil's understanding, a "succinct statement" (σύντομον [...] λόγον)[121] such as "a written confession" (ἔγγραφον [...] ὁμολογίαν), became the only "sufficient demonstration" (ἱκανήν [...] ἀπόδειξιν) of one's faith "convictions" (προαιρέσεως),[122] and, when required, served as a testimony of one's communion in the church. To Bishop Epiphanius, Basil emphasises the importance of checking a bishop's confession of faith before entering into communion with him when he states: "For manifestly you would not have accepted communion with them had you not made sure of this matter on this part most particularly (μάλιστα τὸ μέρος ἀσφαλισάμενος)".[123] Irrespective of all the concerns and complaints that Basil had made known to Eustathius, and not withstanding Basil's perseverance to "cling strongly to union" with him (σφοδρῶς ἀντέχομαι τῆς πρὸς ὑμᾶς ἑνώσεως),[124] Eustathius remained firm in his resolve not to sign a Nicene confession of faith and therefore broke communion with the Nicene church of his own

---

119 *Ep.* 244.2: Deferrari, III, 455. Γράμματα εὐθὺς ἀπογόρευσιν ἔχοντα τῆς πρὸς ἡμᾶς κοινωνίας. Courtonne, III, 76.
120 *Ep.* 224.3: Deferrari, III, 319. Courtonne, III, 20.
121 *Ep.* 128.2: Deferrari, II, 279. Courtonne, II, 38.
122 *Ep.* 99: Deferrari, II, 175–177. Courtonne, I, 215.
123 *Ep.* 258.3: Deferrari, IV, 45. Οὐ γὰρ ἂν εἵλου δηλονότι τὴν πρὸς αὐτοὺς κοινωνίαν μὴ τοῦτο αὐτῶν μάλιστα τὸ μέρος ἀσφαλισάμενος. Courtonne, III, 103.
124 *Ep.* 224.3: Deferrari, III, 321. Courtonne, III, 20.

accord.¹²⁵ Basil comments: "He set forth [...] a creed to which only an Arius could subscribe or a real disciple of Arius".¹²⁶

In Basil's era, those in communion were not readily distinguishable, and those who were not in communion, sometimes preferred to remain hidden. The mechanism of testing/checking one's confession of faith, employed by Basil and his contemporaries, managed at least to identify those who were in sincere communion with each other. To Patrophilus, the bishop of the diocese of Aegae, Basil notes:

> Indeed the creed had been composed, and was brought forward by us; and it was signed [...] so that our brethren throughout the diocese might come together and unite with one another, and so that our communion in the future might be genuine and without guile (γνησίαν καὶ ἄδολον [...] εἶναι τὴν κοινωνίαν).¹²⁷

Basil's vocations as a monk, priest and then bishop, made him both a participant and initiator of communion. As he saw it, the Trinitarian controversies¹²⁸ caused by non-Nicene theological positions made the fragmentation of the communion of the church an imminent reality. In one of his letters he observes:

> For there is no sight rarer than this, when all are now disposed to be suspicious of all. For nowhere is there mercy,

125 See *Ep.* 130.1. Τῆς μὲν οὖν κοινωνίας ἡμῶν αὐτὸς ἀπέρρηξεν ἑαυτόν. Courtonne, II, 42. From *Ep.* 125 one can see that Eustathius, at first, signed a written confession but then soon after renounced it. He and his followers would slander Basil and accuse him of heresy (Sabellianism), especially for introducing innovations regarding the Holy Spirit. See *Epp.* 98.2, 99.2, 130, 226, 244.2. Unfortunately there are no writings that survive in Eustathius' name that could be used to confirm his theological persuasions.
126 *Ep.* 130.1: Deferrari, II, 293. Πίστιν αὐτῷ ἐξέθετο ἣν μόνου ἣν Ἀρείου συγγράψαι καὶ εἴ τις αὐτοῦ γνήσιος μαθητής. Courtonne, II, 43.
127 *Ep.* 244.2: Deferrari, III, 453. Δὴ καὶ συγγέγραπτο μὲν ἡ πίστις, προσηνέχθη δὲ παρ' ἡμῶν, ὑπεγράφη δέ [...] Ὥστε καὶ τοὺς κατὰ τὴν παροικίαν ἀδελφοὺς ἡμῶν συνελθόντας ἑνωθῆναι ἀλλήλοις καὶ γνησίαν καὶ ἄδολον τοῦ λοιποῦ εἶναι τὴν κοινωνίαν. Courtonne, III, 75.
128 Namely: the Anomeans, Pneumatomachians, as well as the innovations of Apollinarius, Eunomius and Marcellus. See Chapter Two.

nowhere compassion, no brotherly tear for a brother in distress. No persecutions for truth's sake, no churches whose entire membership groans, not this long series of misfortunes that encompass us, can move us to solicitude for one another.[129]

Basil advocated for a consensus amongst those "who are supposed to share the same opinions" (οἱ δοκοῦντες τῷ αὐτῷ κοινωνεῖν φρονήματι ἐπιτείνομεν) and thus are "in harmony on the most important points" (οἱ ἐν τοῖς καιριωτάτοις ἔχοντες συμφωνίαν).[130] Basil's aim was to assert and protect the essential theological teachings of the Nicene faith in which communion is realised. In one of his letters to Eustathius, Basil explains what he was hoping to achieve:

> Those who have formerly been committed to an unorthodox confession of faith and wish to pass over into unity with the orthodox, or those who now for the first time wish to be instructed in the doctrine of truth, must be taught the articles of faith as drawn up by the blessed Fathers in the synod once convened in Nicaea.[131]

Basil faced a public challenge to communion that went beyond the theological and canonical requirement of a Nicene alignment of faith. Through his vocation as a bishop, in seeking to bring about communion, he had to employ a certain type of social diplomacy. It is true, for example, that he was up against influential person-

---

129 *Ep.* 258.1: Deferrari, IV, 37. Οὐδὲν γὰρ τούτου σπανιώτερον θέαμα, πάντων πρὸς πάντας λοιπὸν ὑπόπτως διακειμένων. Οὐδαμοῦ γὰρ εὐσπλαχνία, οὐδαμοῦ συμπάθεια, οὐδαμοῦ δάκρυον ἀδελφικὸν ἐπ᾽ἀδελφῷ κάμνοντι. Οὐ διωγμοὶ ὑπὲρ τῆς ἀληθείας, οὐκ Ἐκκλησίαι στενάζουσι πανδημεί, οὐχ ὁ πολὺς οὕτως τῶν περιεχόντων ἡμᾶς δυσχερῶν κατάλογος κινεῖν δύναται ἡμᾶς πρὸς τὴν ὑπὲρ ἀλλήλων μέριμναν. Courtonne, III, 100-101.
130 *Ep.* 258.1: Deferrari, IV, 37-39. Courtonne, III, 101.
131 *Ep.* 125: Deferrari, II, 259-261. Τοὺς ἢ προληφθέντες ἑτέρα πίστεως ὁμολογίᾳ καὶ μετατίθεσθαι πρὸς τὴν τῶν ὀρθῶν συνάφειαν βουλομένους ἢ καὶ νῦν πρῶτον ἐν τῇ κατηχήσει τοῦ λόγου τῆς ἀληθείας ἐπιθυμοῦντας γενέσθαι διδάσκεσθαι χρὴ τὴν ὑπὸ τῶν μακαρίων Πατέρων ἐν τῇ Νικαίᾳ ποτὲ συγκροτηθείσῃ συνόδῳ γραφεῖσαν πίστιν. Courtonne, II, 30.

alities from the imperial court, such as the prefect Modestus, whom Basil once described as acting "from peculiarly personal motives" (διαλεχθέντων ἰδιοπαθῶς) in supporting his enemies (τῶν ἐναντίων).[132] Even churchmen and colleagues of Basil struggled to maintain a unified Nicene position as a result of having "private reasons for differing with one another" (ἰδίας τῶν πρὸς ἀλλήλους διαφορῶν ἀφορμάς).[133] Basil was not blind to the fact that there were some who "concealing their private enmities, pretend that they still hate one another for religion's sake".[134] Being at his lowest ebb, he later reflected: "I almost fell into suspicion of everybody, thinking that there was nothing trustworthy in anyone, because my very soul had been stricken by their treacherous wounds".[135]

Communion in Basil's understanding was meant to be both accessible to all and constitutive of the church's existence. In his letter to Amphilochius, Basil explains: "Since by the grace of God harmony in the faith (τὴν πίστιν συμφωνίας) is strengthened among us, there is nothing else to hinder our being one body and one spirit, even as we have been called in one hope of our calling".[136] For Basil, the very survival of the church and "peace among the churches" (εἰρήνην τῶν ἐκκλησίων)[137] was founded upon κοινωνία. To the bishops living in Italy and Gaul, who were geographically separated from him, he states:

> Our Lord Jesus Christ, having deigned to call the whole church of God his body and having declared us individ-

---

132 *Ep.* 79: Deferrari, II, 89. Courtonne, I, 181.
133 *Ep.* 69.2: Deferrari, II, 47. Courtonne, I, 164.
134 *Ep.* 92.2: Deferrari, II, 139. Τὰς ἰδίας ἔχθρας ἐπικρυψάμενοι ὑπὲρ τῆς εὐσεβείας ἐχθραίνειν κατασχηματίζονται. Courtonne, I, 200.
135 *Ep.* 223.3: Deferrari, III, 297. Μικροῦ γὰρ εἰς τὴν κατὰ πάντων ἐξέπεσον ὑποψίαν, οὐδὲν ἡγούμενος εἶναι παρ' οὐδενὶ πιστόν, ἐκ τῶν δολερῶν πραγμάτων τὴν ψυχὴν πεπληγμένος. Courtonne, III, 12.
136 *Ep.* 191: Deferrari, III, 79. Ὅτι, Θεοῦ χάριτι τῆς κατὰ τὴν πίστιν συμφωνίας ἐρρωμένης ὑμῖν, οὐδὲν ἕτερόν ἐστι τὸ ἐμποδίζον πρὸς τὸ εἶναι ἡμᾶς ἓν σῶμα καὶ ἓν πνεῦμα, καθὼς ἐκλήθημεν ἐν μιᾷ ἐλπίδι διὰ τῆς κλήσεως. Courtonne, II, 144.
137 *Ep.* 28.3: Deferrari, I, 169. Courtonne, I, 70. See Eph. 4:4.

ually members of each other, has granted also to us all to be on intimate terms with all according to the harmony of the members. Wherefore, even if we are separated very far from each other by habitation, yet by reason at least of our union (συναφείας) we are near each other.[138]

It is peace (εἰρήνην) amongst the churches that Basil desired first and foremost. Peace amongst the churches became the definitive mark of his episcopal ministry. Moreover Basil considered peace to be a defining attribute that is intrinsically present in every Christian believer: "For no activity is so peculiarly Christian as making peace (εἰρηνοποεῖν)".[139] Without peace, Basil would argue that communion was rendered impossible, since peace was an imperative condition for communion. From his own experiences as a bishop and shepherd of the church, Basil believed that with the absence of peace, division was able to be fuelled and the distortion of truth was left continually to increase.

4.4 Metaphors for Κοινωνία in Basil's Letters

Together with the word κοινωνία there are certain metaphors and phrases that Basil uses to denote ecclesial communion. Leading the way are the depictions of an unblemished "garment" (ἱμάτιον),[140] a "ship", vis-à-vis those sailing (οἱ πλέοντες),[141] and of course the most

---

138 *Ep.* 243.1: Deferrari, III, 435. Ὁ Κύριος ἡμῶν Ἰησοῦς Χριστὸς σῶμα ἑαυτοῦ καταδεξάμενος ὀνομάσαι τὴν πᾶσαν τοῦ Θεοῦ Ἐκκλησίαν, καὶ τοὺς καθ᾽ ἕνα ἡμῶν ἀλλήλων ἀποδείξας μέλη, ἔδωκε καὶ ἡμῖν πᾶσι πρὸς πάντας ἔχειν οἰκείως κατὰ τὴν τῶν μελῶν συμφωνίαν. Διόπερ εἰ καὶ πλεῖστον ἀλλήλων διωρίσμεθα ταῖς οἰκήσεσιν, ἀλλὰ τῷ γε λόγῳ τῆς συναφείας ἐγγὺς ἀλλήλων ἐσμέν. Courtonne, III, 68.
139 *Ep.* 114: Deferrari, II, 227. Οὐδὲν γὰρ οὕτως ἴδιόν ἐστι χριστιανοῦ ὡς τὸ εἰρηνοποιεῖν. Courtonne, II, 18. See *Ep.* 203.1 Οὐ δύναμαι πεῖσαι ἐμαυτὸν ὅτι ἄνευ τῆς εἰς ἀλλήλους ἀγάπης καὶ ἄνευ τοῦ εἰς ἐμὲ ἥκοντος εἰρηνεύειν πρὸς πάντας δύναμαι ἄξιος κληθῆναι δοῦλος Ἰησοῦ Χριστοῦ. Courtonne, II, 168. "I am unable to persuade myself that without love toward one another, and without, as far as I am concerned, being peaceful toward all, I can be called a worthy savant of Jesus Christ". Deferrari, III, 143.
140 See *Ep.* 113.
141 See *Ep.* 151.

obvious, that of "body" (σῶμα).¹⁴² This section will discuss this last depiction of "body" first and in greater detail, while only briefly touching on the metaphors of "garment" and "ship".

Basil's use of the metaphor "body" followed the Pauline expression of the church as being the "body of Christ" (σῶμα Χριστοῦ)¹⁴³ that embraces all members. Basil considered communion in the body of Christ, the church, to be the greatest of all goods: "For what could be more pleasant than to behold men who are separated from one another by so vast a diversity of places of residence, bound by the unity of love in the body of Christ?"¹⁴⁴ Basil's general understanding is that when Christians are united in communion with God, they become the body of Christ, the church, whereas when heresy sets in, Christians are no longer in communion but are "plainly cut off from the body of the church" (φανερῶς ἀπορραγὲν τοῦ σώματος τῆς Ἐκκλησίας).¹⁴⁵ According to Basil: "Those who confess the apostolic faith, having put an end to the schisms of their own devising, may henceforth become subject to the authority of the church, that the body of Christ, having returned to unity in all its parts, may be made perfect".¹⁴⁶

If Christians are to be part of the body of Christ, the church, it follows, says Basil, that they need each other: "For we all need each other in the communion of our members".¹⁴⁷ Indeed no part of the body is identical to any other, yet each has need of the other, and all serve the same purpose. Christians, says Basil, by virtue of being

---

142 See *Epp*. 28.2, 97, 161.2, 190.1, 199, 203.3, 222, 243.1.
143 See 1 Cor. 12:12-31; Col. 1:18; 2:18-20; Eph. 1:22-23; 3:19; 4:13.
144 *Ep*. 70: Deferrari, II, 49. Τί γὰρ ἂν γένοιτο χαριέστερον ἢ τοὺς τοσούτῳ τῷ πλήθει τῶν τόπων διῃρημένους τῇ διὰ τῆς ἀγάπης ἑνώσει καθορᾶν εἰς μίαν μελῶν ἁρμονίαν ἐν σώματι Χριστοῦ δεδέσθαι; Courtonne, I, 164-165.
145 *Ep*. 263.2: Deferrari, IV, 91. Courtonne, III, 122.
146 *Ep*. 92.3: Deferrari, II, 143. Τοὺς τὴν ἀποστολικὴν ὁμολογοῦντας πίστιν, ἅπερ ἐπενόησαν σχίσματα διαλύσαντας, ὑποταγῆναι τοῦ λοιποῦ τῇ αὐθεντίᾳ τῆς Ἐκκλησίας, ἵνα ἄρτιον γένηται τὸ σῶμα τοῦ Χριστοῦ, πᾶσι τοῖς μέλεσιν εἰς ὁλοκληρίαν ἐπανελθόν. Courtonne, I, 202-203.
147 *Ep*. 266.2: Deferrari, IV, 127. Χρῄζομεν γὰρ ἀλλήλων πάντες κατὰ τῶν μελῶν κοινωνίαν. Courtonne, III, 135.

dependent on each other and the fact that they are united in their diversity, have communion as a constituent of their existence. To push this point Basil argues that one only has to look into the constitution of their own bodies to see that communal interaction is a necessity for meeting the challenges of existence: "For whenever I look upon these very limbs of ours and see that no one of them is sufficient in itself to produce action, how can I reason that I of myself suffice to cope with the difficulties of life?"[148]

To be in communion with one another was the ideal for Basil, and indeed part and parcel of the God-given laws of nature, "since it was not possible from afar off (πόρρωθεν) to see the providence of God".[149] There was no place in Basil's mind for an individual monad but only for a communion of existence. Appealing once again to the human biological makeup, he conclusively declares: "Indeed, from the very constitution of our bodies the Lord has taught us the necessity of communion (ἀναγκαῖον τῆς κοινωνίας)".[150] The Christian therefore, as a personified communal being, becomes displaced when communion with the *other* is broken. For Basil, all things are related and have communion as their highest priority. Thus he readily admits: "We would truly be the most unnatural of all men, if we rejoiced in the schisms and divisions of the churches, and did not consider the union of the members of the body of Christ to be the greatest of all blessings".[151]

Likewise Basil says:

---

148 *Ep.* 97: Deferrari, II, 163. Ὅταν γὰρ πρὸς αὐτὰ ταῦτα ἀπίδω τὰ μέλη ἡμῶν, ὅτι ἓν οὐδὲν ἑαυτῷ πρὸς ἐνέργειαν αὔταρκες, πῶς ἐμαυτὸν λογίσομαι ἐξαρκεῖν ἑαυτῷ πρὸς τὰ τοῦ βίου πράγματα; Courtonne, I, 210.

149 *Ep.* 313: Deferrari, IV, 251. Οὐκ ἔστι πόρρωθεν ἰδεῖν τὰς οἰκονομίας τὰς τοῦ Θεοῦ. Courtonne, III, 187.

150 *Ep.* 97: Deferrari, II, 163. Ἐπεὶ καὶ ἐξ αὐτῆς τῆς τοῦ σώματος ἡμῶν κατασκευῆς τὸ ἀναγκαῖον τῆς κοινωνίας ὁ Κύριος ἡμᾶς ἐδίδαξεν. Courtonne, I, 210.

151 *Ep.* 156.1: Deferrari, II, 385. Καὶ γὰρ ἂν εἴμεν ὡς ἀληθῶς πάντων ἀνθρώπων ἀτοπώτατοι, σχίσμασι καὶ κατατομαῖς Ἐκκλησιῶν ἐφηδόμενοι καὶ μὴ τὴν συνάφειαν τῶν μελῶν τοῦ σώματος τοῦ Χριστοῦ τὸ μέγιστον τῶν ἀγαθῶν τιθέμενοι. Courtonne, II, 82.

I see that none of those things which are accomplished either by nature or by deliberate choice is completed without the union of the related forces, since, in truth, even prayer itself, if it be not voiced by many together, is much less efficacious than it might be, and the Lord has promised that he would be in the midst of two or three who should invoke him together.[152]

As mentioned above, in his correspondence Basil also uses the metaphors "ship" and "garment" in ways that allude to communion. He employs both these metaphors in a two-fold way to reveal successful and unsuccessful expressions of κοινωνία. For example, "ship", on the one hand, is indicative of the "ark of salvation" when one is with*in* the safety zone of the church. On the other hand, it also seeks to forewarn that all who have embarked on the "ship" are exposed to the volatility of the ocean (τρικυμίαις [...] ἐγειρομέναις). In this sense, one is called to protect themselves from the ocean's "sea of evils" (πελάγει κακῶν)[153] and its "bitter waves of error" (πικροῖς τῆς κακοδοξίας κύμασι).[154] In Basil's understanding, the whims and the tumults of the oceans were considered to be the "buffets of the blasts of heresy, which lead to drowning and shipwreck for souls".[155] Basil saw the tumultuous oceans as being the "fury of the heretical waves" (τὸν θυμὸν τῶν αἱρετικῶν κυμάτων)[156] that were attacking the church in the East through a "mighty storm and flood" (μεγάλῳ χειμῶνι καὶ κλύδωνι).[157] In contrast to the church in the East, the church in the West was described by Basil

---

152 *Ep.* 97: Deferrari, II, 163. Οὐδὲν οὔτε τῶν ἐκ φύσεως οὔτε τῶν ἐκ προαιρέσεως κατορθουμένων ὁρῶ ἄνευ τῆς τῶν ὁμοφύλων συμπνοίας ἐπιτελούμενον, ὅπου γε καὶ αὐτὴ ἡ προσευχὴ μὴ ἔχουσα τοὺς συμφωνοῦντας ἀδρανεστέρα ἐστὶ πολλῷ ἑαυτῆς καὶ ὁ Κύριος ἐπηγγείλατο μέσος γενήσεσθαι δύο ἢ τριῶν ἐπικαλουμένων αὐτὸν ἐν ὁμονοίᾳ. Courtonne, I, 210–210.
153 *Ep.* 242.1: Deferrari, III, 429. Courtonne, III, 65.
154 *Ep.* 161.2: Deferrari, II, 415. Courtonne, II, 93.
155 *Ep.* 28.1: Deferrari, I, 163. Αἱρετικῶν πνευμάτων ζάλη, καταποντισμοὺς ἐπάγουσα καὶ ναυάγια ταῖς εὐπεριτρέπτοις ψυχαῖς. Courtonne, I, 67.
156 *Ep.* 203.1: Deferrari, III, 143. Courtonne, II, 168.
157 *Ep.* 70: Deferrari, II, 49. Courtonne, I, 165.

as being complacent in their safe harbour.[158] Regarding the situation affecting the church in the East, Basil explains:

> For here all things are sick [...] and in the face of the continuous attacks of her enemies the church has given up the struggle – like a ship in mid-sea when it is buffeted by the successive blows of the waves – unless it receives some speedy visitation of the goodness of the Lord.[159]

The metaphor "garment" was also used in the same dual manner that "ship" was, that is, to describe positive and negative aspects of communion. Mostly, however, Basil used "garment" to describe the consequences of defective κοινωνία. Once upon a time, prior to the encroachment of heresy, the garment was strong and withstood any test of tension, but now, as a result of its defection, it is torn apart by every heresy, creating holes that increase in size with the passing of time. In this way, commenting on the "condition" (κατάστασις) of the church in the East, Basil remarks:

> The spirit of the times is much inclined to the destructions of the churches [...] The condition of the church now [...] is like that of an old garment, which, being easily torn by an ordinary strain, cannot be again restored to its original strength.[160]

---

158 See *Ep.* 243.
159 *Ep.* 90.1: Deferrari, II, 125. Κέκμηκε γὰρ ἐνταῦθα [...] καὶ ἀπείρηκε πρὸς τὰς συνεχεῖς προσβολὰς τῶν ἐναντίων ἡ Ἐκκλησία, ὥσπερ τι πλοῖον ἐν πελάγει μέσῳ ταῖς ἐπαλλήλοις πληγαῖς τῶν κυμάτων βασανιζόμενον, εἰ μή τις γένοιτο ταχεῖα ἐπισκοπὴ τῆς ἀγαθότητος τοῦ Κυρίου. Courtonne, I, 195. Metaphors from maritime vocabulary are the most popular in Basil's letters. They aim to depict the volatile state of the church's communion. See *Epp.* 28.1, 70, 90.1,2, 91, 113, 161.2, 196, 203.1, 210.2, 242.1, 243.1.
160 *Ep.* 113: Deferrari, II, 223. Ὁ καιρὸς πολλὴν ἔχει ῥοπὴν πρὸς καταστροφὴν τῶν Ἐκλησιῶν [...] Ἡ τῆς Ἐκκλησίας κατάστασις [...] ἱματίῳ παλαιῷ ὑπὸ τῆς τυχούσης προφάσεως ῥᾳδίως καταρρηγνυμένῳ, ὃ πρὸς τὴν ἐξ ἀρχῆς ἰσχὺν ἐπανελθεῖν πάλιν ἀδυνατεῖ. Courtonne, II, 16–17.

Basil's response to any form of division always took on pastoral overtones. In particular his goal was nothing short of reconciliation and communion, provided, of course, that no spiritual harm was caused in the process. To the priests of Tarsus he advises:

> In such times, therefore, as these there is need of great diligence and much care that the churches may be in some way benefited. And benefit it is that the parts which have hitherto been broken apart be united (ἑνωθῆναι) again. And a union might be effected if we should be willing to show indulgence to the weaker, whenever we can do so without causing harm to souls.[161]

4.5 The Witness of Κοινωνία in the Struggles of Basil's Church

Having explored the use of the word "communion" and its associated metaphors in Basil's letters, it will be helpful now to look at the structural ways in which "communion" is realised in the Basilian letters. In the first place, communion is realised at a local level and at a diocesan level.[162] Communion at a local level consists of one's personal communion in a local church, and has as its hallmarks baptism, repentance and, most importantly, the Eucharist. Communion at a diocesan level is realised when a local church is under the pastoral jurisdiction of a canonical bishop. A bishop's canonicity is made evident when he and his diocese are in communion with all the dioceses of the whole church. During Basil's

---

161 *Ep.* 113: Deferrari, II, 223. Ὡς οὖν ἐν καιρῷ τοιούτῳ μεγάλης χρεία τῆς σπουδῆς καὶ πολλῆς τῆς ἐπιμελείας εὐεργετηθῆναι τι τὰς Ἐκκλησίας. Εὐεργεσία δέ ἐστιν ἑνωθῆναι τὰ τέως διεσπασμένα. Ἕνωσις δ᾽ ἂν γένοιτο, εἰ βουληθείημεν ἐν οἷς μηδὲν βλάπτομεν τὰς ψυχὰς συμπεριενεχθῆναι τοῖς ἀσθενεστέροις. Courtonne, II, 17.

162 The whole of the next chapter (Chapter Five) will be dedicated to looking at communion within a local church and a diocesan setting. For now the aim is to highlight the pastoral dynamics of Basil and his clergy, and how these affected each other's ministry.

episcopal ministry (370–379), a key concern of his was to restore peace and order amongst the local churches in his diocese of Caesarea. At the same time, he wanted to bring about communion for all the churches of the East. In his understanding, communion amongst the dioceses in the East was indispensable for the solidarity and witness of the one church, and for protecting and continuing the church's mission. Basil views the fullness of the church as being lived out and manifested in a complete and organic way at the local and diocesan level, and only when the local church and diocese are in communion with the wider Nicene church. In this setting, the bishop and the diocese become the fundamental ecclesial reality through which the local church exists and functions.

Upon his election to the see of Caesarea, one of Basil's first tasks was to clean up the internal affairs of his diocese. His letters present a vivid picture of a church assailed by heresy and internecine rivalry, as well as inadequate and incompetent leadership. To Basil, "a subversion of faith" (πίστεως διαστροφή) was being contemplated that appeared to be "hostile to both apostolic and evangelical doctrines, and hostile to the tradition" (ἐχθρὰ μὲν τοῖς ἀποστολικοῖς καὶ εὐαγγελικοῖς δόγμασιν, ἐχθρὰ δὲ τῇ παραδόσει) of the Fathers of the church.[163] According to Basil, "the poor name of the episcopal office" (τὸ ἐλεεινὸν τῆς ἐπισκοπῆς [...] ὄνομα) was being insulted" (καθυβρίζοντο), especially since it had "fallen upon wretched men" (εἰς δυστήνους ἀνθρώπους [...] περιέστη).[164] All this prompted Basil to declare: "I do not recognise as bishop, nor would I number among the clergy, him who was promoted to a dignity by those profane hands to the destruction of the faith".[165] In one of the earliest letters of his episcopacy, Basil in anguish wrote to the rural bishops under his pastoral oversight:

---

163 *Ep.* 210.3: Deferrari, III, 201. Courtonne, II, 191.
164 *Ep.* 239.1: Deferrari, III, 415–417. Courtonne, III, 59–60.
165 *Ep.* 240.3: Deferrari, III, 425–427. Οὐκ οἶδα ἐπίσκοπον μηδὲ ἀριθμήσαιμι ἐν ἱερεῦσι Χριστοῦ τὸν παρὰ τῶν βεβήλων χειρῶν ἐπὶ καταλύσει τῆς πίστεως εἰς προστασίαν προβεβλημένον. Courtonne, III, 64.

It gives me great pain that the canons of the Fathers have lately fallen into neglect, and that all discipline has been banished from the churches. I fear that, as this indifference proceeds, the affairs of the church will gradually come to complete ruin.[166]

Basil saw that discipline was lacking in the clergy, and that this lack of discipline was influencing the laity, who, by "wicked teachings" (τὸν ταῖς πονηραῖς ταύταις διδασκαλίαις), were increasingly "being forced into destruction" (τὴν ἀπώλειαν συνωθούμενον).[167] Faced with the above pastoral challenges from members of his own clergy, together with the non-Nicene religious policy of Emperor Valens, which removed non-compliant clergy from their respective churches, Basil's working conditions were far from ideal.

> The teachings of the true faith have been overthrown and the ordinances of the church have been set at naught.
>
> The lust for office on the part of men who do not fear the Lord leaps upon the positions of high authority, and quite openly now the foremost prize is offered as a prize of impiety; and consequently that man who has uttered the more horrible blasphemies is accounted the more worthy of the episcopal direction of the people. Gone is the dignity of the priesthood. None are left to tend the flock of the Lord with knowledge, while ambitious men ever squander the sums collected for the poor on their own pleasures and for the distribution of gifts. The strict observance of the canons has been weakened. Licence to commit sin has become widespread [...] Just judgment is dead [...] Wickedness

---

166 *Ep.* 54: Deferrari, I, 343. Πάνυ με λυπεῖ ὅτι ἐπιλελοίπασι λοιπὸν οἱ τῶν Πατέρων κανόνες καὶ πᾶσα ἀκρίβεια τῶν Ἐκκλησιῶν ἀπελήλαται, καὶ φοβοῦμαι μή, κατὰ μικρὸν τῆς ἀδιαφορίας ταύτης ὁδῷ προϊούσης, εἰς παντελῆ σύγχυσιν ἔλθῃ τὰ τῆς Ἐκκλησίας πράγματα. Courtonne, I, 139.
167 *Ep.* 243.4: Deferrari, III, 447. Courtonne, III, 72.

goes beyond all bounds, the laity are deaf to admonition.¹⁶⁸

Basil in his observations about his current situation remarks to his brother bishops in the West:

> The wisdom of the world takes first place to itself, having thrust aside the glory of the cross. The shepherds are driven away, and in their places are introduced troublesome wolves who tear asunder the flock of Christ. The houses of prayer are bereft of those wont to assemble therein; the solitudes are filled with those who weep. The elders weep, comparing the past with the present; the young are more to be pitied, since they know not of what they have been deprived.¹⁶⁹

Even though Basil admitted, "my speech in comparison with the true state of things falls far short of a worthy presentation of them",¹⁷⁰ his verdict about the current "state of affairs" (ἐπὶ τούτοις) of the churches in "most of the cities" (πλείσταις τῶν πόλεων) under his pastoral oversight was all but conclusive:

> Hence this is a truceless war, for the perpetrators of these evil deeds dread a general peace on the ground that it will lay bare their hidden acts of shame. At this state of affairs

---

168 *Ep.* 92.2: Deferrari, II, 137–139. Ἀνατέτραπται μὲν τὰ τῆς εὐσεβείας δόγματα, συγκέχυνται δὲ Ἐκκλησίας θεσμοί. Φιλαρχίαι δὲ τῶν μὴ φοβουμένων τὸν Κύριον ταῖς προστασίαις ἐπιπηδῶσαι καὶ ἐκ τοῦ προφανοῦς λοιπὸν ἆθλον δυσσεβείας ἡ προεδρία πρόκειται, ὥστε ὁ τὰ χαλεπώτερα βλασφημήσας εἰς ἐπισκοπὴν λαοῦ προτιμότερος. Οἴχεται σεμνότης ἱερατική, ἐπιλελοίπασιν οἱ ποιμαίνοντες μετ' ἐπιστήμης τὸ ποίμνιον τοῦ Κυρίου, οἰκονομίας πτωχῶν εἰς ἰδίας ἀπολαύσεις καὶ δώρων διανομὰς παραναλισκόντων ἀεὶ τῶν φιλαρχούντων. Ἠμαύρωται κανόνων ἀκρίβεια, ἐξουσία τοῦ ἁμαρτάνειν πολλή [...] Ἀπόλωλε κρίμα δίκαιον [...] Ἡ πονηρία ἄμετρος, οἱ λαοὶ ἀνουθέτητοι. Courtonne, I, 200.

169 *Ep.* 90.2: Deferrari, II, 125–127. Ἡ τοῦ κόσμου σοφία τὰ πρωτεῖα φέρεται, παρωσαμένη τὸ καύχημα τοῦ σταυροῦ. Ποιμένες ἀπελαύνονται, ἀντεισάγονται δὲ λύκοι βαρεῖς, διασπῶντες τὸ ποίμνιον τοῦ Χριστοῦ. Οἶκοι εὐκτήριοι ἔρημοι τῶν ἐκκλησιαζόντων, αἱ ἐρημίαι πλήρεις τῶν ὀδυρομένων. Οἱ πρεσβύτεροι ὀδύρονται, τὰ παλαιὰ συγκρίνοντες τοῖς παροῦσιν· οἱ νέοι ἐλεεινότεροι, μὴ εἰδότες οἵων ἐστέρηνται. Courtonne, I, 196.

170 *Ep.* 90.2: Deferrari, II, 127. Συγκρινόμενος δὲ τῇ ἀληθείᾳ τῶν πραγμάτων ὁ λόγος ἀξίας πολὺ τῆς αὐτῶν ἀπολείπεται. Courtonne, I, 200.

> unbelievers laugh, those of little faith waiver; the true faith is ambiguous; ignorance is poured down upon souls by reason of the fact that those who maliciously falsify doctrine imitate truth. For the lips of the pious are silent, yet every blasphemous tongue is let loose. Holy things have been profaned; those of the laity who are sound in faith flee the houses of prayer as schools of impiety.[171]

Writing to the bishops of Italy and Gaul, Basil bewails the condition of his local church and, in particular, its state of confusion. The majority of the laity, perhaps unaware, had no other choice but to go along and comply with what Basil describes as "a long standing deception" (χρονίας ἀπάτης).[172]

> The nurslings of the church are being brought up in the doctrines of ungodliness. For what are they indeed to do? Baptisms are in the heretics' hands, attendance upon those who are departing this life, visits to the sick, the consolation of those who grieve, the assisting of those who are in distress, succour of all kinds, communion of the mysteries; all of these things, being performed by them, become a bond of agreement between them and the laity.[173]

Compounding the crises was the fact that the persecution carried out by the non-Nicenes had the added difficulty of being invoked

---

171 *Ep.* 92.2: Deferrari, II, 139. Διὸ καὶ ἄσπονδός ἐστιν ὁ πόλεμος οὗτος, τῶν τὰ πονηρὰ εἰργασμένων τὴν κοινὴν εἰρήνην ὡς ἀποκαλύπτουσαν αὐτῶν τὰ κρυπτὰ τῆς αἰσχύνης ὑφορωμένων. Ἐπὶ τούτοις γελῶσιν οἱ ἄπιστοι, σαλεύονται οἱ ὀλιγόπιστοι· ἀμφίβολος ἡ πίστις, ἄγνοια κατακέχυται τῶν ψυχῶν, διὰ τὸ μιμεῖσθαι τὴν ἀλήθειαν τοὺς δολοῦντας τὸν λόγον ἐν κακουργίᾳ. Σιγᾷ μὲν γὰρ τὰ τῶν εὐσεβούντων στόματα, ἀνεῖται δὲ πᾶσα βλάσφημος γλῶσσα· ἐβεβηλώθη τὰ ἅγια, φεύγουσι τοὺς εὐκτηρίους οἴκους οἱ ὑγιαίνοντες τῶν λαῶν ὡς ἀσεβείας διδασκαλεῖα. Courtonne, I, 201.
172 *Ep.* 243.4: Deferrari, III, 447.
173 *Ep.* 243.4: Deferrari, III, 447. Συνεκτρέφεται τὰ νήπια τῆς Ἐκκλησίας τοῖς λόγοις τῆς ἀσεβείας. Τί γὰρ καὶ ποιήσωσι; Βαπτίσματα παρ' ἐκείνων, προπομπαὶ τῶν ἐξοδευόντων, ἐπισκέψεις τῶν ἀσθενούντων, παράκλησις τῶν λυπουμένων, βοήθεια τῶν καταπονουμένων, ἀντιλήψεις παντοδαπαί, μυστηρίων κοινωνίαι· ἃ πάντα δι' ἐκείνων ἐπιτελούμενα σύνδεσμος γίνεται τοῖς λαοῖς τῆς πρὸς αὐτοὺς ὁμονοίας. Courtonne, III, 72-73.

in the *name* of Christ and in defence of *true* Christianity. This meant that those being persecuted were persecuted for introducing innovations that were considered to be against the doctrinal tradition of the church. For his part, Basil did all he could to allay any suspicions that he was introducing doctrinal innovations. He was adamant that he maintained "the precepts of the Gospel, which change neither with seasons nor with vicissitudes of human affairs, but continue the same, as they were pronounced by truthful and blessed lips, thus abiding always".[174]

Faced with onslaughts by non-Nicene clergy and their sympathisers, Basil warns his faithful living in Caesarea to "beware" (βλέπετε) of the relentless attacks coming from such non-Nicene advocates. Basil exhorts his faithful to take "guard" (φυλακτέον) and remain steadfast under the pastoral protection (ἐπιστασία) of their bishop.

> "Beware of dogs, beware of evil workers". The dogs are many. Why do I say dogs? Nay, rather ravenous wolves who hide their deceit under the guise of sheep, and everywhere in the world scatter Christ's flock. Against these you must guard, under the care of a watchful shepherd.[175]

Speaking to the monks under his patronage, Basil lets them know about the negative state of affairs affecting Caesarea and the church in the East in general:

> Certain men have unsparingly opened their mouth against their fellow servants. Falsehood is spoken fearlessly; truth is covered up. And those who are accused are condemned

---

174 *Ep.* 244.8: Deferrari, III, 469. Τῶν εὐαγγελικῶν ἐντολῶν [...] αἳ οὔτε καιροῖς οὔτε περιστάσεσιν ἀνθρωπίνων πραγμάτων συμμεταβάλλονται, ἀλλ᾽ αἱ αὐταὶ διαμένουσιν, ὡς προηνέχθησαν ἀπὸ τοῦ ἀψευδοῦς καὶ μακαρίου στόματος οὕτω διαιωνίζουσαι. Courtonne, III, 82.

175 *Ep.* 28.2: Deferrari, I, 167. «Βλέπετε, λέγων, τοὺς κύνας, βλέπετε τοὺς κακοὺς ἐργάτας». Πολλοὶ οἱ κύνες. Τί λέγω κύνες; Λύκοι μὲν οὖν βαρεῖς, ἐν ἐπιφανείᾳ προβάτων τὸ δολερὸν ὑποκρύπτοντες, πανταχοῦ τῆς οἰκουμένης τὸ Χριστοῦ ποίμνιον διασπῶσιν. Οὓς φυλακτέον ὑμῖν ἐγρηγορικοῦ τινος ποιμένος ἐπιστασίᾳ. Courtonne, I, 69.

without trial; those who accuse are trusted without inquiry.[176]

In an obvious change to the form of persecution, Christianity was no longer being attacked by those outside the Christian faith as it once was during the first three centuries of Christianity. Now, as has been mentioned above, friend and foe were fighting within the arena of professed Christianity. Fellow-countrymen were opponents of each other in defence of what they considered to be the true witness of the church. Basil says that the non-Nicenes looked up to their spiritual leaders "as if they were saints and in communion" (ὡς ἅγιοι παρ' αὐτῶν καὶ κοινωνικοὶ παραπεμπόμενοι).[177] In Basil's eyes, the crown of martyrdom was now devalued, since the non-Nicene offensive conducted in the name of Christ had overshadowed the Nicene persecution endured in the name of Christ. Consequently, the persecuted, among whom Basil considered himself and his flock, were not counted as confessors or even as martyrs if they had been executed. Basil explains: "Though grievous are our afflictions, yet nowhere is martyrdom, because those who harm us have the same appellation as ourselves".[178] To his monks, Basil wrote:

> For I judge war brought by fellow-countrymen to be more difficult [...] to deceive the many they put forward the name of Christ, that those who are persecuted may not even have the consolation of being confessors, for the many and simpler folk, while acknowledging that we are being wronged, yet do not account to us as martyrdom our

176 *Ep.* 226.1: Deferrari, III, 329. Ἤνοιξαν γάρ στόματά τινες ἀφειδῶς κατὰ τῶν ὁμοδούλων. Λαλεῖται τὸ ψεῦδος ἀφόβως, ἡ ἀλήθεια συγκεκάλυπται. Καὶ οἱ μὲν κατηγορούμενοι καταδικάζονται ἀκρίτως, οἱ δὲ κατηγοροῦντες πιστεύονται ἀνεξετάστως. Courtonne, III, 24.
177 *Ep.* 250: Deferrari, IV, 7. Courtonne, III, 88.
178 *Ep.* 164.2: Deferrari, II, 427. Καὶ αἱ μὲν θλίψεις βαρεῖαι, μαρτύριον δὲ οὐδαμοῦ διὰ τὸ τοὺς κακοῦντας ἡμᾶς τὴν αὐτὴν ἡμῖν ἔχειν προσηγορίαν. Courtonne, II, 99. See Gain, *L'Église de Cappadoce*, 359.

death for the sake of truth.[179]

For Basil, the prolongation of schisms and heresies meant that true episcopal representatives of Nicene Christianity were becoming increasingly difficult to discern. Furthermore the prevailing non-Nicene status quo imposed by imperial policy, made it easy for Basil and his fellow pro-Nicene advocates to be "charged with deception and want of principle, corruption of churches, and destruction of souls".[180] Speaking on behalf of his fellow Nicene proponents, Basil would despairingly cry out: "[Our persecutors] are now reviling us, on the ground that we proceed craftily, and under the guise of charity play the part of plotters!"[181] Basil regarded such persecution from the *inside*, "from amongst ourselves" (τὸ ἐξ ἡμῶν ὡρμῆσθαι),[182] as hardest to bear.

Basil believed that the Nicene church of his era was attacked by a double-sided impiety (ἀσέβεια). On the one hand, there was the overt doctrinal manifestation of the non-Nicene theological position, which was set on categorically denying the divinity of Christ as well as the divinity of the Holy Spirit. On the other hand, there was the less obvious warfare arising from what Basil considered to be the inherently evil actions of some church leaders within the non-Nicene camp. Basil's concern was that non-Nicene church leaders could get away with practising evil through professing Christ. Basil regarded this less obvious warfare involving active sin to be more serious, since it involved misappropriating goodness to satisfy evil: "For if anyone does an evil thing under

---

179 *Ep.* 257.1: Deferrari, IV, 31–33. Χαλεπώτερον γὰρ κρίνω ἐγὼ τὸν παρὰ τῶν ὁμοφύλων πόλεμον [...] εἰς δὲ τὴν τῶν πολλῶν ἀπάτην τὸ τοῦ Χριστοῦ προβάλλονται ὄνομα, ἵνα μηδὲ τὴν ἐκ τῆς ὁμολογίας παραμυθίαν ἔχωσιν οἱ διωκόμενοι, τῶν πολλῶν καὶ ἀκεραιοτέρων ἀδικεῖσθαι μὲν ἡμᾶς ὁμολογούντων, εἰς μαρτύριον δὲ ἡμῖν τὸν ὑπὲρ τῆς ἀληθείας θάνατον μὴ λογιζομένων. Courtonne, III, 98–99.
180 *Ep.* 244.5: Deferrari, III, 461. Ἡμᾶς κατηγορουμένους δόλον καὶ ῥᾳδιουργίαν, φθορὰν Ἐκκλησιῶν καὶ ψυχῶν ἀπώλειαν. Courtonne, III, 78–79.
181 *Ep.* 244.5: Deferrari, III, 463. Νῦν λοιδοροῦνται ἡμᾶς ὡς δολίως πορευομένους καὶ ἐν σχήματι ἀγάπης τὰ τῶν ἐπιβουλευόντων ποιοῦντας. Courtonne, III, 79.
182 *Ep.* 263.2: Deferrari, IV, 91–93. Courtonne, III, 122.

the guise of good, he deserves a twofold punishment, because he not only does what is in itself not good, but also makes use of the good as a co-worker, so to speak, for the accomplishment of his sin".[183]

Basil maintained that sin leading to moral failure was the ultimate reason for widespread heresy in the East. He also saw this as the cause of the Western bishops' reluctance to come to the aid of their Eastern counterparts.[184] Based on this logic, Basil believed that it was because of his own personal sins that he was not able to establish unity with Bishop Theodotus of Nicopolis.[185] Within his diocese, Basil saw himself as confronted with a doctrinal and moral anarchy. The lack of unity and cooperation amongst the churches of his diocese caused him to emphasise the ascetic ideal in the life of his bishopric. It was always his intention to have asceticism influence every aspect of church life and not just formal monasticism. According to Rousseau, Basil endeavoured to "incorporate the ascetic regime more obviously into the life of the church as a whole".[186] Thus, for Basil, the need for an ascetic fervour among Christian leaders was equally important with strict adherence to the doctrines of Nicaea. Basil's clergy were expected to hold monastic life and ecclesiastical authority in tandem. To achieve this, episcopal identity needed to be reframed in accordance with monastic values, just as it was in Basil who would become for many the epitome of the moderate bishop-monk ideal. Basil had learnt from his former mentor Eustathius of Sebasteia that active ministry within the church needed to be aligned with the values and practices of the monk, neither of

---

183 *Ep.* 53.1: Deferrari, I, 339. Ἐὰν γάρ τις τὸ κακὸν ἐν προσχήματι τοῦ ἀγαθοῦ ποιῇ, διπλασίονος τιμωρίας ἐστὶν ἄξιος, διότι αὐτό τε τὸ οὐκ ἀγαθὸν ἐργάζεται καὶ κέχρηται εἰς τὸ τελέσαι τὴν ἁμαρτίαν, ὡς ἂν εἴποι τις, τῷ καλῷ συνεργῷ. Courtonne, I, 138.
184 See *Epp.* 92.1, 164.2.
185 See *Ep.* 99.1.
186 Rousseau, *Basil of Caesarea*, 74.

which can be abandoned entirely in favour of the other.[187] In this sense, asceticism was viewed as being essential to the efficaciousness of church ministry. Without asceticism, Fedwick observes that "with the indiscriminately swelled ranks, the church's awareness of being a sacred community distinct from earthly society was in danger of disappearing".[188]

Lewis Patsavos makes reference to an established custom, dating back to the first half of the fourth century, of choosing bishops from within the cloister of a monastic brotherhood.[189] Although Basil has no extant treatise on the nature of the model Christian bishop, his *Ep.* 150 lays out his expectations as to what attributes a church leader needed to have.[190] Since monastic discipline and Christian formation rated high on Basil's list, the moral authority of the clergy depended upon the active demonstration of Christian virtues and holiness. The attributes alluded to in Basil's *Ep.* 150 are applicable to the Christian leader and disciple alike, and include renunciation of worldly ambitions, growth in asceticism, commitment to charity, and obedience to a spiritual adviser. Basil saw it as important that these attributes apply first to the Christian leader, since it was the cleric's example and practical teaching that was expected to edify the laity. Basil's *Ep.* 2, for example, argues that Christian moral life is founded upon living examples where virtue is learnt through imitation. Rapp makes a point of emphasising that personal holiness must accompany the priestly office for its ministry to be effective.[191] Basil's comments to Amphilochius say the same:

> For him who should heal his own wounds to bless another is unfitting. For benediction is the communication of sanctification (εὐλογία γὰρ ἁγιασμοῦ μετάδοσις ἐστιν). But

---

187 See Finn, *Almsgiving in the Later Roman Empire*, 85.
188 Fedwick, *The Church and the Charisma of Leadership*, 18.
189 Patsavos, *A Noble Task*, 111–112.
190 Basil's *Ep.* 232.2 mentions role models of clerical and ascetical life that he encountered in Palestine, Coele Syria, Mesopotamia as well as Egypt. *Ep.* 207.2 makes reference to these same areas.
191 Rapp, *Holy Bishops in Late Antiquity*, 16.

how will he who does not possess this because of transgression through ignorance impart it to another! Therefore, let him bless neither publicly nor privately [...] nor perform any other function.[192]

Rapp maintains that a bishop's ascetic virtues are authentically realised when they are evident in his appearance, lifestyle and conduct.[193] According to Basil, ascetic virtues play a vital role in the episcopal ministry, and are considered to be the foundation and inspiration to a bishop's actions. Furthermore they validate episcopal actions with spiritual authority and convey that a path to holiness is open and accessible to all.

When Basil raised the quality of Christian life amongst the clergy (καθηγούμενοι), he saw it as only natural for the laity to follow "in accord" (μετὰ συμπνοίας).[194] According to Rapp, on some occasions, since the mid-fourth century, bishops purposely went out to recruit monks into their line-up of clergy so as to combat the corruption that was present within their existing clergy.[195] Basil was more interested in adopting monastic values into the priesthood rather than bringing monks into its ranks. Faced with a spiritual leadership crisis, he felt the need for the calibre of his current body of clergy to dramatically change and improve. He found that bishops were not immune to greed or the misappropriation of church funds for their own private uses. Basil viewed such corruption amongst the clergy to be contagious, affecting the members of the faithful whom they served. "Whatever the rulers are", claims Basil, "such for the most part are the characters of those governed

192 *Ep.* 199.27: Deferrari, III, 119. Εὐλογεῖν δὲ ἕτερον, τὸν τὰ οἰκεῖα τημελεῖν ὀφείλοντα τραύματα, ἀνακόλουθον. Εὐλογία γὰρ ἁγιασμοῦ μετάδοσίς ἐστιν. Ὁ δὲ τοῦτο μὲ ἔχων δία τὸ ἐκ τῆς ἀγνοίας παράπτωμα πῶς ἑτέρῳ μεταδώσει; Μήτε τοίνυν δημοσίᾳ μήτε ἰδίᾳ εὐλογείτω [...] μήτε τι ἄλλο λειτουργείτω. Courtonne, II, 159.
193 Rapp, *Holy Bishops in Late Antiquity*, 16.
194 *Ep.* 222: Deferrari, III, 285. Courtonne, III, 7. See *Ep.* 150.4; Fedwick, *The Church and the Charisma of Leadership*, 97.
195 Rapp, *Holy Bishops in Late Antiquity*, 137, 147.

accustomed to become".¹⁹⁶ Basil says that ill-disposed clergy "have gained such control over the laity" (οἳ τοσοῦτον κατεκράτησαν τῶν λαῶν)¹⁹⁷ that they "cast the word into contempt by reason of the unworthiness of those called, and engender the practice of indifference among the laity".¹⁹⁸ In the same way that sick limbs cause harm to organs that are still healthy,¹⁹⁹ Basil acknowledges that a life of sin (especially amongst Christian leaders) can only bring disharmony and much suffering into the Christian community.

> For the just judge in accordance with our works has given us "an angel of Satan" who sufficiently buffets us and vehemently defends the heresy; and he carries on the war against us to such a degree that he does not even spare the blood of those who have placed their trust in God.²⁰⁰

When Basil reflected upon the sad state of affairs that he found in the Nicene church, he sincerely felt, at least for a time, that the church had been forsaken by God. In sheer desperation he once conceded: "The Lord has clearly abandoned us, seeing that we have grown cold in our love on account of the widespread increase of lawlessness".²⁰¹ Very quickly Basil turned his despair into a "trial of hope",²⁰² which then allowed him to acknowledge that the mercy of God is available to restore communion and love within the church: "For what we have suffered we have suffered because

---

196 *Ep.* 190.1: Deferrari, III, 71. Ὅτι ὁποῖοι δ' ἂν ὦσιν οἱ προεστῶτες, τοιαῦτα, ὡς ἐπὶ τὸ πολύ, καὶ τὰ ἤθη τῶν ἀρχομένων γίνεσθαι εἴωθεν. Courtonne, II, 141.
197 *Ep.* 239.1: Deferrari, III, 415. Courtonne, III, 59.
198 *Ep.* 190.1: Deferrari, III, 71. Λάθωμεν διὰ τὸ τῶν καλουμένων ἀδόκιμον εἰς εὐτέλειαν τὸν λόγον καταβαλόντες ἀδιαφορίας μελέτην τοῖς λαοῖς ἐμποιεῖν. Courtonne, II, 141.
199 See *Ep.* 263.2.
200 *Ep.* 248: Deferrari, III, 481. Ἔδωκε γὰρ ἡμῖν κατὰ τὰ ἔργα ἡμῶν ὁ Δικαιοκρίτης ἄγγελον Σατὰν ἱκανῶς ἡμᾶς κατακονδυλίζοντα καὶ σφοδρῶς μὲν ἐδικοῦντα τὴν αἵρεσιν, μέχρι τοσούτου δὲ τὸν πρὸς ἡμᾶς ἐξαγαγόντα πόλεμον ὦτε μηδὲ αἵματος φείσασθαι τῶν εἰς Θεὸν πεπιστευκότων. Courtonne, III, 86.
201 *Ep.* 141.2: Deferrari, II, 343. Προδήλως τοῦ Κυρίου ἐγκαταλιπόντος ἡμᾶς τοὺς διὰ τὸ πληθυνθῆναι τὴν ἀνομίαν ψύξαντας τὴν ἀγάπην. Courtonne, II, 64.
202 Rousseau, *Basil of Caesarea*, 156.

of our sins, but his succour shall the loving God show forth his love and compassion for the churches".[203] When Basil bewails the loss of respect within the priestly vocation, he is often referring principally to the growing number of non-Nicene allegiances that were taking place amongst members of the clergy: "Every bold and blasphemous tongue of those who speak iniquity against God has been loosed".[204] Imperial support of non-Nicene Christianity, and personal gain acquired from allegiances with those in political power, tempted many to renounce their Nicene faith. In doing so, Basil remarks such people have "forgotten everything" (πάντων ἐπιλαθόμενι), including their once very active "protest" that they "avoid communion with them [the heretics (αἱρετικῶν)] as death to their souls".[205] Basil had found it inexcusable that people could so easily renounce their Nicene faith just for the sake of appeasing those in power. Intent on exposing the vulnerabilities of those who changed from their Nicene position, Basil comments:

> For those who accuse us of heterodoxy are now revealed as openly in alliance with the party of the heretics [...] Consider the practice of those who dare this, that it is their habit always to change over to the party in power, and to trample upon those of their friends who are weak but to court those who are strong.[206]

Basil was firm in his conviction that moral and doctrinal errors

203 *Ep.* 247: Deferrari, III, 479. Ὁ μὲν γὰρ πεπόνθαμεν διὰ τὰς ἁμαρτίας ἡμῶν πεπόνθαμεν, τὴν δὲ αὐτοῦ βοήθειαν διὰ τὴν περὶ τὰς Ἐκκλησίας ἑαυτοῦ ἀγάπην καὶ εὐσπλαγχνίαν ὁ φιλάνθρωπος ἐπεδείξεται. Courtonne, III, 85.
204 *Ep.* 243.4: Deferrari, III, 445. Ἠνοίγη δὲ πᾶσα θρασεῖα καὶ βλάσφημος γλῶσα τῶν λαλούντων κατὰ τοῦ Θεοῦ ἀδικίαν. Courtonne, III, 72.
205 *Ep.* 226.2: Deferrari, III, 331. Διαμαρτυρόμενοι φεύγειν τὴν κοινωνίαν αὐτῶν ὡς ὄλεθρον τῶν ψυχῶν. Courtonne, III, 25.
206 *Ep.* 226.2: Deferrari, III, 331. Οἱ γὰρ ἡμῖν κακοδοξίαν ἐγκαλοῦντες ἐφάνησαν νῦν ἐκ τοῦ προφανοῦς τῇ μερίδι τῶν αἱρετικῶν προστιθέμενοι... Νοήσατε τὴν συνήθειαν τῶν ταῦτα τολμώντων, ὅτι ἔθος αὐτοῖς ἀεὶ πρὸς τὸ δυνατὸν μετατίθεσθαι μέρος, καὶ τοὺς μὲν ἀσθενοῦντας τῶν φίλων κατεπατεῖν, θεραπεύειν δὲ τοὺς κρατοῦντας. Courtonne, III, 24–25.

were inter-related: "For neither can a soiled mirror receive the reflections of images, nor can a soul that is already beset with the cares of life and darkened by the passions due to arrogance of the flesh receive the rays of the Holy Spirit".[207] In his letter to Ambrose, the bishop of Milan, Basil exhorts: "Correct the infirmities of the people, in case the disease of the Arian madness has indeed touched any".[208] Correction for Basil required one to accept Nicene Christianity and keep away from "the faction of those not in communion with us [Basil and his fellow bishops]" (οἱ τῆς μερίδος τῶν ἀκοινωνήτων ἡμῖν).[209]

Breaking communion with state endorsed non-Nicenism was not without its difficulties. Many were persecuted for remaining uncompromising in their acceptance of Nicene Christianity. Some even faced death. Martyrdom was a real phenomenon for the followers of Nicene Christianity, and as in so many cases of Jewish and Christian history it was sometimes considered to be inevitable. Basil reminds his disciple Amphilochius that Asclepius paid with his life in the Old Testament book of Kings[210] for refusing communion with Doeg: "For surely it has not escaped your charity that a certain Asclepius, for not having chosen communion with Doeg, was struck by them and died of the blows, or rather by means of the blows was translated to life".[211]

On a positive note, Basil's letter "To the Neocaesareans" relates how their spiritual wellbeing is due to the fact that they have been

---

207 Ep. 210.6: Deferrari, III, 213. Οὔτε γὰρ κατόπτρῳ ῥυπῶντι δυνατὸν τῶν εἰκόνων δέξασθαι τὰς ἐμφάσεις, οὔτε ψυχὴν ταῖς βιωτικαῖς προειλημμένην μερίμναις καὶ τοῖς ἐκ τοῦ φρονήματος τῆς σαρκὸς ἐπισκοτουμένην πάθεσι δυνατὸν ὑποδέξασθαι τοῦ Ἁγίου Πνεύματος τὰς ἐλλάμψεις. Courtonne, II, 196.
208 Ep. 197.1: Deferrari, III, 93. Διόρθωσαι τὰ ἀρρωστήματα τοῦ λαοῦ, εἴ τινος ἄρα τὸ πάθος τῆς Ἀρειανῆς ὕψατο. Courtonne, II, 150.
209 Ep. 250: Deferrari, IV, 5. Courtonne, III, 88.
210 See 1 Kings 21:7.
211 Ep. 248: Deferrari, III, 481. Πάντως γὰρ οὐκ ἔλαθέ σου τὴν ἀγάπην ὅτι Ἀσκληπιός τις διὰ τὸ μὴ ἑλέσθαι τὴν πρὸς τὸν Δωὴκ κοινωνίαν τυπτόμενος παρ' αὐτῶν ταῖς πληγαῖς ἐναπέθανεν, μᾶλλον δὲ διὰ τῶν πληγῶν εἰς τὴν ζωὴν μετετέθη. Courtonne, III, 86.

untouched by heresy: "For you have not been reached by buffets of the blasts of heresy, which lead to drowning and ship-wreck for souls".[212] According to Basil these were the fruits of being in communion with people of like faith (ὁμοδοξούντων κοινωνία). As expected, belonging to the correct confession of faith was insufficient if this faith was not supported by good works. Faith and works, he insisted, are inseparably linked and are mutually accountable:

> Neither strictness of life in itself, except it be illumined by faith in God, availeth aught, nor will right confession of faith, if devoid of good works, be able to bring you into the presence of the Lord, but both should go together (δεῖ ἀμφότερα συνεῖναι), that the man of God may be perfect.[213]

Some church leaders in Basil's diocese were isolating themselves from their fellow concelebrants and therefore were informally breaking communion with them. When this took place, such church leaders became easy targets for non-Nicene advocates and subsequently broke communion with the Nicene church in an official way. Basil realised that to prevent this predicament from arising with his clergy, a spiritual renewal was needed that was to be characterised by an ascetic disposition. Basil had hoped that this spiritual renewal would lead to a stronger Nicene acceptance of faith amongst all churches and, furthermore, would have ecclesiastical communion as its lasting expression. It was this internal renewal and commitment towards communion within his flock, namely to "show the greatest possible solicitude for the unity of the churches",[214] that positioned Basil to elevate his vision from

---

212 *Ep.* 28.1: Deferrari, I, 163. Οὐ γὰρ ὕψατο ὑμῶν αἱρετικῶν πνευμάτων ζάλη, καταποντισμοὺς ἐπάγουσα καὶ ναυάγια ταῖς εὐπεριτρέπτοις ψυχαῖς. Courtonne, I, 67.
213 *Ep.* 295: Deferrari, IV, 209. Οὔτε πολιτείας ἀκρίβεια καθ' ἑαυτὴν μὴ διὰ τῆς εἰς Θεὸν πίστεως πεφωτισμένη ὠφέλιμος, οὔτε ὀρθὴ ὁμολογία ἀγαθῶν ἔργων ἄμοιρος οὖσα παραστῆσαι ἡμᾶς δυνήσεται τῷ Κυρίῳ, ἀλλὰ δεῖ ἀμφότερα συνεῖναι, ἵνα ἄρτιος ᾖ ὁ τοῦ Θεοῦ ἄνθρωπος. Courtonne, III, 170.
214 *Ep.* 65: Deferrari, II, 25. Τὴν ἐνδεχομένην μέριμναν ὑπὲρ τῆς ἑνώσεως τῶν Ἐκκλησιῶν ἐπιδειξαμένους. Courtonne, I, 156.

its local manifestation and extend it to include all the Christian churches of the East.²¹⁵ Commenting on Basil's ability to pursue a loftier vision beyond the boundaries of his diocese, Basil's friend Gregory notes that he acted in this way only to safeguard and protect the dignity of the communion of the church. The communion of the church was too significant to be treated arbitrarily or to be taken for granted, since, for Basil, there always was and always would be only one communion within the church. Simply put, the church is communion. Gregory knew that Basil considered communion to be the greatest priority in his ministry and therefore worthy of every sacrifice:

> Basil, though he observed moderation in other respects, in this knew no measure. But lifting his head high and casting the eye of his soul in every direction, he obtained a mental vision of the whole world through which the word of salvation had been spread. He saw the great heritage of God, purchased by his own words and laws and sufferings, the holy nation, the royal priesthood, in a miserable plight and torn asunder into an infinity of doctrines and errors [...] He did not think it enough to lament misfortune in silence and merely lift up his hands to God to implore deliverance from the pressing evils, himself remaining asleep. Rather he thought he was bound to render aid and to make some personal contribution.²¹⁶

---

215 Basil was instrumental in restoring unity to the church of Armenia. See *Ep.* 190.
216 *Oration* 43.41: McCauley, 62–63. Καίτοι τἄλλα μέτριος ὢν ἐν τούτοις οὐ μετριάζει, ἀλλ᾽ ὑψοῦ τὴν κεφαλὴν διάρας καὶ κύκλῳ τὸ τῆς ψυχῆς ὄμμα περιαγαγών, πᾶσαν εἴσω ποιεῖται τὴν οἰκουμένην ὅσην ὁ σωτήριος λόγος ἐπέδραμεν. Ὁρῶν δὲ τὸν μέγαν τοῦ Θεοῦ κλῆρον καὶ τοῖς αὐτοῦ λόγοις καὶ νόμοις καὶ πάθεσι περιποιηθέντα, τὸ ἅγιον ἔθνος, τὸ βασίλειον ἱεράτευμα, κακῶς διακείμενον, εἴς τε μυρίας δόξας καὶ πλάνας διεσπασμένον [...] Οὐκ αὔταρκες ὑπολαμβάνει θρηνεῖν ἡσυχῇ τὸ πάθος καὶ πρὸς Θεὸν μόνον αἴρειν τὰς χεῖρας καὶ παρ᾽ ἐκείνου τῶν κατεχόντων κακῶν λύσιν ζητεῖν, αὐτὸς δὲ καθεύδειν, ἀλλά τι καὶ βοηθεῖν καὶ παρ᾽ ἑαυτοῦ συνεισφέρειν ᾤετο δεῖν. SC 384. 214–216.

4.6 The Κοινωνία of the Church and the Κοινωνία of the Trinity

The reality of κοινωνία: communion or more precisely ecclesial communion, was fundamental to Basil's concept of the church. "Communion" as a term for Basil is used in an equivocal way. Thus when Basil is speaking about Trinitarian communion and ecclesial communion, vastly different realities are implied. For this reason all comparisons of ecclesial communities with the Holy Trinity need to take into account Radde-Gallwitz's remark that the unity of the Holy Trinity is "infinitely greater" than the unity of human (ecclesial) communities.[217] The perfect divine persons of the simple God cannot serve as a model for limited, created, imperfect human beings. Divine personhood cannot be anthropomorphised. According to Basil, "the infinitely great" (τὸν ἀπειρομεγέθη) God can only be known "by the very small" (ὑπὸ τοῦ μικροτάτου) and limited person.[218] Consequently, there is an infinite difference between divine/uncreated and human/created reality.

Communion at its greatest level is essentially expressed in the Eucharist, in which God communicates himself to the person, and the person enters into communion with him. Outside a relationship with God, communion with God and through God with each other cannot take place. Experiencing the other and regarding the other becomes the prerequisite to understanding oneself

---

217 Radde-Gallwitz, *Basil of Caesarea*, 70. Contrary to the views of some patristic scholars from the twentieth century, Radde-Gallwitz challenges the notion of Basil having a "social doctrine" of the Holy Trinity, namely "in which human community provides a paradigm for reflection on the Trinity". Radde-Gallwitz, *Basil of Caesarea*, 69. For further critiques of social trinitarianism see Leftow, "Anti Social Trinitarianism", 203-250; Coakley, "'Persons' in the 'Social' Doctrine of the Trinity: A Critique of Current Analytic Discussion", 123-144. Kilby, "Perichoresis and Projection: Problems with Social Doctrines of the Trinity", 432-445.
218 *Ep.* 233.2: Deferrari, III, 369. Courtonne, III, 40.

and the source of one's meaningful existence.[219] Increasing communion with others is a natural outpouring of grace that is found when one is in communion with God, and also further perpetuates participation in the eternal life of the Triune God. Where there is no communion with God as Trinity, there is no church. In communing with the very life of the Trinity, the person's being becomes by grace the "image and likeness"[220] of God. Following the words of the Apostle Paul, the church becomes "the body of Christ" (σῶμα Χριστοῦ),[221] where the Eucharist constitutes its core being.

According to Zizioulas, in the life of the church, communion with the other reflects fully the relations between communion and otherness in the Holy Trinity.[222] Here Zizioulas is trying to pick up on Basil's notion of communion being an ontological reality, where the very nature of God is communion or rather the communion of "the persons of the Godhead" (τῶν προσώπων).[223] As the prototype of ecclesial existence, the Holy Trinity, for Zizioulas, becomes the icon *par excellence* of communion amongst the members of the "body of Christ" the church.[224] Indeed it would be an eisegesis to apply this type of thinking to Basil. His understanding of human interrelatedness and interdependence mentioned above, as an expression of ecclesial life that is intrinsically relational and communal, makes no suggestion that these relations are modelled on the Trinity.

The unity that is manifested in plurality in the relations of the three persons of the Holy Trinity is essentially otherness in com-

---

219 A person left to him or herself and without the ability to relate to the other cannot be a person. The Scottish philosopher John MacMurray summarised this reality with his famous: "I need you in order to be myself". MacMurray, *Persons in Relation*, passim. According to MacMurray, "We become persons in community in virtue of our relations to others. Human life is inherently a common life". MacMurray, *The Conditions of Freedom*, 37.
220 Gen. 1:26.
221 1 Cor. 12:27.
222 Zizioulas, *Communion and Otherness*, 263.
223 *Ep.* 52.3: Deferrari, I, 333. Courtonne, I, 135.
224 See 1 Cor. 12:27.

munion and communion in otherness. In the words of Basil: "Nothing is itself of like substance (ὁμούσιον) with itself, but one thing is of like substance (ὁμούσιον) with another thing".²²⁵ Clearly for Basil, in the Father's love for the Son, the Father does not forget the Holy Spirit, thus any possibilities of confusing the Father with the Son are avoided. The Holy Spirit acts not only as a bond between the Father and the Son, but also preserves the distinctions of the three persons while maintaining their unity. In Basil's understanding, the Holy Spirit is eternally with the Father and the Son, and he is united with the Father through the Son. The eternal and inseparable presence of the Holy Spirit with the Father and the Son conveys the Father's love for the Son, and the Son's response to the Father's love. This interpenetrating communion of love existing amongst the three persons of the Holy Trinity was later known as *perichoresis*.²²⁶ Father, Son and Holy Spirit, with their distinct personal attributes, exist in unceasing interpersonal communion through reciprocating a movement of love. Perichoretic love, as lived out in communion, is central to the very being of God.

In *On the Holy Spirit* Basil affirms, in a clear and dynamic way, that the reality of the hypostatic differences amongst the persons of the Holy Trinity does not invoke separation or plurality in the Godhead: "Since the divine nature is not composed of parts, union of the persons is accomplished by partaking of the whole".²²⁷ From the image of the Holy Trinity, Basil views otherness as the *sine qua non* of unity. Otherness, Basil emphasises, is no distortion to communion but rather constitutive of it, in the same way that the modes of being within the Holy Trinity maintain their per-

225 *Ep.* 52.3: Deferrari, I, 333. Οὐ γὰρ αὐτὸ τί ἐστιν ἑαυτῷ ὁμοούσιον, ἀλλ᾽ ἕτερον ἑτέρῳ. Courtonne, I, 135–136.
226 As a noun this terms first appears in the writings of St. Maximus the Confessor (d. 662).
227 *On the Holy Spirit*, 18.45: Anderson, 72. Ὥσπερ ἐπὶ τῶν τεχνικῶν κατὰ τὴν μορφὴν ἡ ὁμοίωσις, οὕτως ἐπὶ τῆς θείας καὶ ἀσυνθέτου φύσεως, ἐν τῇ κοινωνίᾳ τῆς θεότητός ἐστιν ἡ ἕνωσις. SC 17. 406.

sonal *hypostasis* through their relationship with each other. Conversely, unity that emanates from communion with the Holy Trinity does not destroy otherness but rather affirms and realises its ontological presence. God is not first One and then Three, but rather simultaneously One and Three,[228] since the *hypostases* of the Father, Son and Holy Spirit are both particular and relational.[229] In this way communion is not antithetical towards otherness, it generates and manifests it.[230]

Upon further reading the Basilian understanding of *hypostasis*, it becomes apparent that being (as opposed to substance) is existentially connected to being in relationship with the other. According to Basil, there is no area of church life where communion and togetherness co-exist so deeply as in the church's ministry. In his ministry Basil wants the life of the Christians to be the same, and for them to be united in indivisible kinship through "communion in prayer" (ταῖς προσευχαῖς κοινωνίαν)[231] that has its realisation in God. When the "other" is rejected, the testimony of Christ's Gospel is falsified, the witness of the church is destroyed, and, according to Basil, a person ceases to live "the way that is in accordance with Christ's polity" (τῆς ὁδοῦ τῆς κατὰ Χριστὸν πολιτείας).[232] With respect to being "ecclesiastical members" (ἐκκλησιαστικῶν μελῶν) of the body of Christ, Basil tells his maritime bishops, "You cannot say to us who have been placed in the same body: 'We have no need of you.'" He continues: "For the hands need each other, and the feet steady each other, and it is through their working in concert (συμφωνίᾳ) that the eyes possess

---

228 See *Against Eunomius* 1.14–15; *On the Holy Spirit*, 18.47.
229 See *Ep.* 236.6; Zizioulas, *Communion and Otherness*, 137.
230 See Zizioulas, *Communion and Otherness*, 6. In the context of personhood, Zizioulas maintains that from the image of the Trinity, "*otherness* is incompatible with *division*". Zizioulas, *Being as Communion*, 107.
231 *Ep.* 150.2: Deferrari, II, 367. Courtonne, II, 73.
232 *Ep.* 150.1: Deferrari, II, 361. Courtonne, II, 71.

their clearness of perception".[233] For Basil, communion between the person and God is realised in Christ without division but at the same time without confusion, that is, perfect unity which does not remove but affirms and realises otherness. In patristic terminology, the person is an identity that emerges through relationship (*schesis*). In contemporary language one might say it is an "I" that can exist only as long as it relates to a "Thou" which affirms its existence and otherness.[234] For Basil, in the case of God the Father, an eternal *schesis* with the Son and the Holy Spirit exists, without which Fatherhood would not be possible.[235] That is to say, the Father was never alone in his divinity as this would imply that he was not always "Father", and assert, contrary to Nicaea, that there was a time when he *was not*. To isolate the "I" from the "Thou" is to lose not only the otherness of the "I" but also its very existence; it simply cannot *be* without the other, just as God the Father cannot be without the Son and the Holy Spirit. There can be no other way, insists Basil, but that of a trihypostatic God in which "natural goodness, inherent holiness and royal dignity reaches from the Father through the only begotten to the Spirit".[236] God's existence in this sense is constitutive of the communal relations that is realised within the three persons of the Holy Trinity, whose unique *hypostases* remain distinct and unconfused since they are united in essence through freedom and love.

Having looked at the concept of communion amongst the divine persons of the Holy Trinity, it remains for Basil to point out what it is that the persons of the Holy Trinity and the mem-

---

233 *Ep.* 203.3: Deferrari, III, 149. Εἴτε καὶ ἐν ἄλλῃ τάξει τῶν ἐκκλησιαστικῶν μελῶν ἑαυτοὺς τάσσετε, οὐ δύνασθε λέγειν τοῖς ἐν τῷ αὐτῷ σώματι κατατεταγμένοις ἡμῖν τό· χρείαν ὑμῶν οὐκ ἔχομεν. Αἵ τε γὰρ χεῖρες ἀλλήλων δέονται καὶ οἱ πόδες ἀλλήλους στηρίζουσι καὶ οἱ ὀφθαλμοὶ ἐν τῇ συμφωνίᾳ τὸ ἐναργὲς τῆς καταλήψεως ἔχουσιν. Courtonne, II, 170.
234 Zizioulas, *Being as Communion*, 240.
235 See *Against Eunomius* 1.14–15.
236 *On the Holy Spirit*, 18.47: Anderson, 75. Ἡ φυσικὴ ἀγαθότητης, καὶ ὁ κατὰ φύσιν ἁγιασμός, καὶ τὸ βασιλικὸν ἀξίωμα, ἐκ Πατρός, διὰ τοῦ Μονογενοῦς, ἐπὶ τὸ Πνεῦμα διήκει. SC 17. 412.

bers of the church are in communion with. Is communion simply an expression of the oneness of essence that exists amongst the Godhead, and a manifestation of the moral values shared amongst the communicants? Patristic sources of theology, most notably Sts. Ignatius, Irenaeus, Athanasius and the Cappadocians, maintain that communion is a question of being united with the very person of God the Father. Basil's consensus in this area has already been stated above in that he maintains that God "exists" fundamentally as a person, the person (*hypostasis*) of the Father, and not simply as his substance (essence).[237] Basil holds that communion is a union with the person of God the Father, who is inseparably and coeternally united in freedom and love with the *hypostases* of the Son and the Holy Spirit. Outside this Trinitarian relationship, in which the Father begets the Son and brings forth the Holy Spirit, there is no God. Thus, for Basil, it is the personal existence of God the Father as a person that constitutes the very being of God, which in turn allows the being to co-eternally hypostasise and give life to its substance.

4.7 Κοινωνία in the Holy Spirit

Since the time of the Apostle Paul, the Holy Spirit has always been associated with the notion of communion.[238] It is from the third person of the Holy Trinity, the Holy Spirit, that the event of communion is realised. In the Holy Trinity, it is the Holy Spirit which connects the Father and Son as well as the person with divine life. To participate in the communion of the Holy Trinity (*theosis*) "is the personal gift of the Spirit, as the gift of adoption to the Father in Christ".[239] Whereas Christ became incarnate and gave the church

---

237 See *On the Holy Spirit*, 16:38: Ἀρχὴ γὰρ τῶν ὄντων μία, δι Υἱοῦ δημιουργοῦσα, καὶ τελειοῦσα ἐν Πνεύματι. SC 17. 378. "The originator of things is one, he creates through the Son and he perfects through the Spirit". Anderson, 62; *Against Eunomius* 1.14–15, 2:22. See also Chapter Two.
238 See 2 Cor. 13:13.
239 Meyendorff, *Catholicity and the Church*, 19.

its "body", it was the Holy Spirit who consecrated and mobilised the church. This enabled the effects of the incarnation to be communicated throughout the church in history. Unity with God as it existed before the fall of Adam, is now re-established once and for all in Christ the *new* Adam.²⁴⁰ Through the operations of the Holy Spirit, Christ is manifested and the experience of union with Christ is lived out as being in the Holy Spirit. For Basil this understanding was founded upon the Pauline proclamation that, "no one can say 'Jesus is Lord' except by the Holy Spirit".²⁴¹ Basil considered this statement of faith to be an admission of the person's inability to contemplate God without the presence of God: "We are not capable of glorifying God on our own; only *in* the Spirit is this made possible. In him we are able to thank God for the blessings we have received".²⁴²

According to Basil, the church as the Body of Christ exists where the Holy Spirit is present. The Holy Spirit "comes to rest" (alights) upon the church and in the church.²⁴³ It does this because he comes to rest upon Christ, its head, and because the church is united with Christ. In each person's relation to Christ, the Holy Spirit, argues Basil, is not simply an assistance to the individual in reaching Christ, but the *in* ("κοινωνία"),²⁴⁴ in which he or she are participants in Christ, "since the Spirit in himself reveals the divinity of the Lord".²⁴⁵ Basil exhorts:

> If you remain outside the Spirit, you cannot worship at all, and if you are *in* him you cannot separate him from God. Light cannot be separated from what it makes visible, and

---

240 See 1 Cor.15:20-24, 45-48.
241 1 Cor. 12:3. Οὐδεὶς δύναται εἰπεῖν, Κύριος Ἰησοῦς, εἰ μὴ ἐν πνεύματι ἁγίῳ.
242 *On the Holy Spirit*, 26.63: Anderson, 96. Οὔτε δοξάσαι ἀφ᾽ ἑαυτῶν ἱκανοί ἐσμεν, ἀλλ᾽ ἡ ἱκανότης ἡμῶν ἐν τῷ Πνεύματι τῷ ἁγίῳ, ἐν ᾧ δυναμωθέντες, τὴν ὑπὲρ ὧν εὐεργετήθημεν, τῷ Θεῷ ἡμῶν εὐχαριστίαν ἀποπληροῦμεν. SC 17. 474.
243 See Fedwick, *The Church and the Charisma of Leadership*, 90.
244 Ep. 90.1: Courtonne, I, 195. See Eph. 6:18.
245 *On the Holy Spirit*, 26.64: Anderson, 97. Ὡς ἐν ἑαυτῷ δεικνύντι τὴν τοῦ Κυρίου θεότητα. SC 17. 476.

it is impossible for you to recognise Christ, the image of the invisible God, unless the Spirit enlightens you. Once you see the image, you cannot ignore the light; you see the light and the image simultaneously.[246]

Baptism according to Basil was from the outset considered to be "*in* the Spirit" and "*into* Christ". When the Holy Spirit is present and "blows where it wills" (ὅπου θέλει πνεῖ),[247] a movement takes place where the individualisation of the human being is transfigured to that of communal living. In this way the other becomes an ontological part of one's identity. To question the divinity of the Holy Spirit, for Basil, had faith implications and therefore was tantamount to repudiating the very engagement entered into at baptism:

> If someone rejects the Spirit, his faith in the Father and Son is made useless; it is impossible to believe in the Father and the Son without the presence of the Spirit. He who rejects the Spirit rejects the Son, and he who rejects the Son rejects the Father [...] Such a person has no part in true worship. It is impossible to worship the Son except in the Holy Spirit; it is impossible to call upon the Father except in the Spirit of adoption.[248]

Basil regarded one's baptismal engagement as a lifetime imitation of Christ. By imitating the humility of Christ, one rejected "the life that went before" and through the Holy Spirit had the guaran-

---

246 *On the Holy Spirit*, 26.64: Anderson, 97. Ἔξω μὲν γὰρ ὑπάρχων αὐτοῦ, οὐδὲ προσκυνήσεις τὸ παράπαν· ἐν αὐτῷ δὲ γενόμενος οὐδενὶ τρόπῳ ἀποχωρίσεις ἀπὸ Θεοῦ· οὐ μᾶλλόν γε, ἢ τῶν ὁρατῶν ἀποστήσεις τὸ φῶς. Ἀδύνατον γὰρ ἰδεῖν τὴν εἰκόνα τοῦ Θεοῦ τοῦ ἀοράτου, μὴ ἐν τῷ φωτισμῷ τοῦ Πνεύματος. Καὶ τὸν ἐνατενίζοντα τῇ εἰκόνι, ἀμήχανον τῆς εἰκόνος ἀποχωρίσαι τὸ φῶς. Τὸ γὰρ τοῦ ὁρᾶν αἴτιον, ἐξ ἀνάγκης συγκαθορᾶται τοῖς ὁρατοῖς. SC 17. 476.
247 John 3:8.
248 *On the Holy Spirit*, 11.27, Anderson, 48. Τῷ τὸ Πνεῦμα παραιτουμένῳ, ὅτι ἡ εἰς Πατέρα καὶ Υἱὸν πίστις αὐτῷ εἰς κενὸν ἀποβήσεται, ἣν οὐδὲ ἔχειν δύναται, μὴ συμπαρόντος τοῦ Πνεύματος. Οὐ πιστεύει μὲν γὰρ εἰς Υἱὸν ὁ μὴ πιστεύων τῷ Πνεύματι· οὐ πιστεύει δὲ εἰς Πατέρα ὁ μὴ πιστεύσας τῷ Υἱῷ [...] Ἄμοιρός ἐστι καὶ τῆς ἀληθινῆς προσκυνήσεως ὁ τοιοῦτος. Οὔτε γὰρ Υἱὸν προσκυνῆσαι δυνατόν, εἰ μὴ ἐν Πνεύματι ἁγίῳ, οὔτε ἐπικαλέσασθαι δυνατὸν τὸν Πατέρα, εἰ μὴ ἐν τῷ τῆς υἱοθεσίας Πνεύματι. SC 17. 342.

tee of life promised to humanity "from the beginning":

> This is what it means to be born of water and the Spirit: the water accomplishes our death, while the Spirit raises us to life [...] The Lord describes in the Gospel the pattern of life we must be trained to follow after the (baptismal) resurrection: gentleness, endurance, freedom from the defiling love of pleasure, and from covetousness. We must be determined to acquire in this life all the qualities of the life to come.[249]

Basil made it clear that holiness was an enduring state that was not achieved at the expense of human freedom and commitment. Implied in his teachings was the understanding of a constant communion (κοινωνία) with the Holy Spirit which naturally led to an ordered life. In this sought-after communion lay the realisation of the restoration of the close friendship (οἰκείωσις) of the person with God. Progress in virtue, through communion with the Holy Spirit (τῇ πρὸς ἑαυτὸ κοινωνίᾳ), led to the participation of eternal realities. Basil explains:

> From this comes knowledge of the future, understanding of mysteries, apprehension of hidden things, distribution of wonderful gifts, heavenly citizenship, a place in the choir of angels, endless joy in the presence of God, becoming like God, and, the highest of all desires, becoming God (θεὸν γενέσθαι).[250]

---

249 *On the Holy Spirit*, 15.35: Anderson, 59. Τοῦτο οὖν ἐστι τὸ ἄνωθεν γεννηθῆναι ἐξ ὕδατος καὶ Πνεύματος· ὡς τῆς μὲν νεκρώσεως ἐν τῷ ὕδατι τελουμένης· τῆς ζωῆς ἡμῶν ἐνεργουμένης διὰ τοῦ Πνεύματος [...] Πρὸς οὖν τὸν ἐξ ἀναστάσεως βίον καταρτίζων ἡμᾶς ὁ Κύριος, τὴν εὐαγγελικὴν πᾶσαν ἐκτίθεται πολιτείαν, τὸ ἀόρτον τοῦ τρόπου νομοθετῶν· ὥστε ἅπερ ὁ αἰὼν ἐκεῖνος κατὰ τὴν φύσιν κέκτηται, ταῦτα προλαβόντας ἡμᾶς ἐκ προαιρέσεως κατορθοῦν. SC 17. 368-370.
250 *On the Holy Spirit*, 9.23: Anderson, 44. Ἐντεῦθεν, μελλόντων πρόγνωσις, μυστήριον σύνεσις, κεκρυμμένων κατάληψις, χαρισμάτων διανομαί, τὸ οὐράνιον πολίτευμα, ἡ μετὰ ἀγγέλων χορεία, ἡ ἀτελεύτητος εὐφροσύνη, ἡ ἐν Θεῷ διαμονή, ἡ πρὸς Θεὸν ὁμοίωσις, τὸ ἀκρότατον τῶν ὀρεκτῶν, θεὸν γενέσθαι. SC 17. 328.

The Holy Spirit as the "paraclete" (παράκλητον) of "truth" (ἀληθείας),[251] through uniting into a single body all the faithful, is the creator and sustainer of the ecclesial community. Being in the whole church and wholly in each member, the Holy Spirit is the one who bestows the various unrepeatable gifts on each member of the ecclesial community. All unique gifts of each member, when used properly, become common gifts for the sake of the whole. Equality of membership is preserved through the differentiation of gifts that exists within the organic whole. In this sense, the Holy Spirit does not maintain uniformity but "a symphony of personalities in which the mystery of the Holy Trinity is reflected".[252] As the "spirit of communion" (κοινωνία πνεύματος), the Holy Spirit which "builds the churches" (οἰκοδομοῦν δὲ τὰς ἐκκλησίας), proclaims Basil, is invoked to lead the church unto all truth.[253] The Holy Spirit is the living force of unity among the faithful and between the faithful and the Holy Trinity. All the faithful become present in the Holy Spirit, the communion that it affects with them and among them, inseparably takes place with the Father and the Son. Although the faithful are not natural sons begotten by the Father, a relation attributed to Christ alone, the faithful are sons (children) by grace adopted through the Holy Spirit.[254]

In line with Basil's understanding, the Holy Spirit qualifies the very ontology of the church; it makes the church *be* not in the sense that it animates it, but in the sense that it is the very being of the church.[255] By being constitutive of both Christology and ecclesiology, the Holy Spirit makes it impossible to think of Christ as

---

251 See John 14:16; 16:13.
252 Lossky, *In the Image and Likeness of God*, 178.
253 *Ep.* 90.2: Deferrari, II, 127. Courtonne, I, 196.
254 Primarily the intra (immanent) relations of the persons of the Holy Trinity become the paradigm of one's relationship with God in which the Son's eternal reception of the gift of the Holy Spirit from God the Father is the key to one's adoption as a child of God. What God the Son possesses by nature, believers can now receive by grace when they are united to him, since it was Christ's incarnation that became the guarantee of this reality once and for all.
255 Zizioulas, *Being as Communion*, 136.

an individual not being in communion with the "many", his body; or to think of the church as one without simultaneously thinking of her as many. In this sense, multiplicity is not subordinate to oneness, rather it is constitutive of it. Each eucharistic community, therefore, is identical and in communion with each other by virtue of the whole presence of Christ contained in them. Being inseparably united to Christ, the church incarnates Christ's very presence in history.

4.8 Conclusion

Although this last section has taken up Basil's theology in his *On the Holy Spirit* — which is itself a letter addressed to Bishop Amphilochius containing a doctrinal treatise — the main work of this chapter has been to explore the concept of Basil's letters as instruments of communion. Basil, through his letters, aimed to restore into the communion of the Nicene church all dioceses within the Eastern Roman Empire that were forced to conform to the Empire's non-Nicene legislation. Basil's correspondence with Athanasius and other bishops exemplified his efforts to bring about and protect communion "κοινωνία" within a Nicene church. Κοινωνία and its associated metaphors in Basil's letters are aligned with Nicene statements of faith, and essentially embody the Nicene church's identity. According to Basil, communion in the Holy Spirit is constitutive of the church's existence. Nicene theology made this possible, which through its proclamation of the divinity of the Holy Spirit declared that communion is accessible to all. For Basil, communion in the Holy Spirit brought about communion in otherness, which was realised in the life of the church. In its practical application, communion as understood by Basil was participated in through the Eucharist. The head of each eucharistic community was Christ, who in each ecclesiastical diocese was made manifest through its presiding bishop. Basil used every opportunity to encourage the church as a communion of believers. His letters showcase his efforts and in many ways are indicative of his success in restoring peace and communion in the church.

Chapter Five:
The Bishop and the Communion of the Local Church in Basil's Letters

After having explored in the previous chapter Basil's theological, ecclesiological and metaphorical understanding of communion from his letters, this current chapter examines what Basil's letters reveal about the practical manifestation of the communion of the church as it appears in a parochial and a diocesan setting. The first section takes up Basil's view of communion in the life of the parochial church as founded and realised in the three sacraments of Baptism, Repentance and the Eucharist. This is followed by a reflection on the ministry of the bishop as the agent who makes communion possible and accessible for the faithful in the life of the church. In this regard, a bishop's adherence to a Nicene confession of faith is important, as is his acceptance into the Nicene communion of churches by his brother bishops who adhere to the same faith. Finally, this chapter explores the ministry of the assistant bishop in Basil's church and Basil's attempts to change its functioning so that it is more accountable to the oversight of a diocesan bishop.

5.1 The Bishop and the Sacraments

5.1.1 Baptism

According to Basil, the baptism of a Christian marked his or her "birth" (γενέσεως) into the communion of the church. Without baptism, entrance into the communion of the church was not permissible. Basil's twentieth canon comments upon the spiritual state of those outside the communion of the church (the unbaptised), and calls upon all catechumens to be "received by the church" (δεκταί εἰσι τῇ Ἐκκλησίᾳ) through baptism:

> Those who have not yet come under the yoke of Christ do not recognise the laws of the Lord. Therefore, they should be received by the church, sharing with all the remission that is accorded in these things because of their faith in Christ. And in general such things as are committed in the catechumenal state are not called into account. But these persons, of course, the church does not receive without baptism. Therefore, it is most necessary in these cases to observe the rights of birth.[1]

Between the years 374–375 Basil wrote three long canonical letters[2] to Bishop Amphilochius of Iconium. These letters were intended to assist Amphilochius with the pastoral direction of the baptised faithful within his diocese.[3] In Basil's canonical letters, extensive references are made to the rules, customs and expectations that he considered to be applicable to the orderly functioning of the clergy and laity alike. Unlike Basil's other letters to Amphilochius, which offer insight on more theological issues, these three long letters are called canonical letters because they contain eighty four binding canons or rules in response to Amphilochius' "practical

---

1   Canon 20 in *Ep.* 199.20: Deferrari, III, 111. Αἱ δὲ μήπω ὑπελθοῦσαι τὸν ζηγὸν τοῦ Χριστοῦ οὐδὲ τὴν νομοθεσίαν ἐπιγινώσκουσι τοῦ Δεσπότου. Ὥστε δεκταί εἰσι τῇ Ἐκκλησίᾳ μετὰ πάντων καὶ τὴν ἐπὶ τούτοις ἄφεσιν ἔχουσαι ἐκ τῆς πίστεως τῆς εἰς Χριστόν. Καὶ καθόλου τὰ ἐν τῷ κατηχουμένῳ βίῳ γενόμενα εἰς εὐθύνας οὐκ ἄγεται. Τούτοις δέ, δηλονότι, ἄνευ βαπτίσματος ἡ Ἐκκλησία οὐ παραδέχεται. Ὥστε ἀναγκαιότατον ἐπὶ τούτοις τὰ πρεσβεῖα τῆς γενέσεως. Courtonne, II, 157.
2   See *Epp.* 188, 199, 217.
3   See Canon 47: Ὥστε, ἐὰν ἀρέσῃ τοῦτο, δεῖ πλείονας ἐπισκόπους ἐν ταὐτῷ γενέσθαι καὶ οὕτως ἐκθέσθαι τὸν κανόνα, ἵνα καὶ τῷ ποιήσαντι τὸ ἀκίνδυνον ᾖ καὶ ὁ ἀποκρινόμενος τὸ ἀξιόπιστον ἔχῃ ἐν τῇ περὶ τῶν τοιούτων ἀποκρίσει. *Ep.* 199.47: Courtonne, II, 163. "Accordingly, if this be acceptable, more bishops ought to come together and afterwards publish a canon, in order that there may be no danger to him who has acted, and that he who replies may have some authority in making answer about such things". Deferrari, III, 133.

theological queries"⁴ on church discipline.⁵ In his responses, Basil relied either on canons already published by the Fathers gathered in council, or on custom and tradition: "We must resort again to custom, and must follow the fathers who have dispensed legislation that pertains to us".⁶

Within the environment of the local church, one is spiritually born through baptism into the world-wide communion of the church. When baptism was conducted in the name of the three divine *hypostases*, it was understood by Basil that one became united to God and to everyone else in the communion of the church. This union was believed to be modelled, albeit in a human and limited way, on the eternal and pure union of the three divine *hypostases*.⁷ Basil states, for example, that as a result of one's baptism, one undergoes living a life that is separated from sin and puts on an "immortal garment" which "annihilates death in the flesh and swallows up mortality in the garment of incorruptibility".⁸ Accordingly, baptism also endowed the newly baptised with gifts of the Spirit, since, as has already been mentioned in Chapter Four, the ontological unity of the church is brought about by the life-giving (ζωοποιόν) presence and activity of the Holy Spirit.

Because baptism constituted membership into the communion of the church, Basil saw baptism and Nicene faith as being intrinsically linked and inseparable. In his letter on the canons that he wrote to his disciple Amphilochius, Basil is quick to

---

4   Holman, *The Hungry are Dying*, 109.
5   See also *Epp.* 233-236, which "sum up in a remarkable and unusual way his [Basil's] theological position on almost every fundamental point he ever addressed". Rousseau, *Basil of Caesarea*, 261. The division of these three long letters into "canons" occurred at a later date, see Rousseau, *Basil of Caesarea*, 260, n. 136.
6   Canon 1 in *Ep.* 118.1: Deferrari, III, 19. Πάλιν τῷ ἔθει χρηστέον καὶ τοῖς οἰκονομήσασι τὰ καθ᾽ ἡμᾶς Πατράσιν ἀκολουθητέον. Courtonne, II, 123.
7   See Chapter Four.
8   *Ep.* 292: Deferrari, IV, 199. Τὸν ἐν τῇ σαρκὶ θάνατον ἐξηφάνισε καὶ κατεπόθη τὸ θνητὸν ἐν τῷ τῆς ἀφθαρσίας ἐνδύματι. Courtonne, III, 166.

remind his spiritual child[9] that it was the inherent tradition of the church to accept as a baptismal creed that which in no way differed from the faith of Nicaea. Basil explains to Amphilochius that in the past certain labels were used by their predecessors to identify those outside the communion of the Nicene church:

> The ancients (οἱ παλαιοί) [...] employed the names: heresies, schisms and illegal congregations; those who are completely broken off and, as regards the faith itself, alienated; schisms, those at variance with one another for certain ecclesiastical reasons and questions that admit of a remedy; illegal congregations, assemblies brought into being by insubordinate presbyters or bishops, and by uninstructed laymen.[10]

Basil justifies his stance on Nicene faith by appealing to the "the traditions of the fathers" (τῶν πατέρων αἱ παραδόσεις) who gathered at Nicaea or elsewhere.[11] It was always his policy to heed what had been confessed by "holy men" (τῶν ἁγίων), to "walk in their footsteps" (ἴχνη βαίνειν ἐκείνοις)[12] and therefore "not to betray the sound faith" (τὴν ὑγιαίνουσαν πίστιν μὴ καταπροδοῦναι).[13] Indeed the core of Basil's episcopal ministry was based on his continuous desire to "restore the creed which was written" by the Fathers of the Nicene Council, to "banish heresy" and ultimately to "speak to the churches a message of peace by bringing those of like con-

---

9 Basil viewed Amphilochius as his very own son. See *Epp.* 161.2, 176.
10 *Ep.* 188.1: Deferrari, III, 9–11. Ὅθεν τὰς μὲν αἱρέσεις ὠνόμασαν, τὰ δὲ σχίσματα, τὰς δὲ παρασυναγωγάς. Αἱρέσεις μὲν τοὺς παντελῶς ἀπερρηγμένους καὶ κατ᾽ αὐτὴν τὴν πίστιν ἀπηλλοτριωμένους, σχίσματα δὲ τοὺς δι᾽ αἰτίας τινὰς ἐκκλησιαστικὰς καὶ ζητήματα ἰάματα πρὸς ἀλλήλους διενεχθέντας, παρασυναγωγὰς δὲ τὰς συνάξεις τὰς παρὰ τῶν ἀνυποτάκτων πρεσβυτέρων ἢ ἐπισκόπων καὶ παρὰ τῶν ἀπαιδεύτων λαῶν γινομένας. Courtonne, II, 121.
11 *Ep.* 261.3: Deferrari, IV, 83. Courtonne, III, 118. See *Ep.* 243.2.
12 *Ep.* 159.1: Deferrari, II, 395. Courtonne, II, 86.
13 *Ep.* 114: Deferrari, II, 227. Courtonne, II, 18.

victions into unity" (φρονοῦντας συνάγοντες εἰς ὁμόνοιαν).[14]

When Basil sensed a divergence from tradition, he proclaimed: "This was not what that holy and God-beloved synod had in mind".[15] Consequently, literary expressions employed by Basil such as "what has been handed down to us by the Fathers", "the sound doctrine of faith" or "doctrine of truth" (τοῦ λόγου τῆς ἀληθείας),[16] referred to what had been agreed upon at the Council of Nicaea and other local councils leading up to and following on from Nicaea. Specifically Basil exhorted Amphilochius that they "must follow the fathers who have dispensed legislation (οἰκονομήσασι)"[17] that pertained to their current circumstances. Included in this legislation was "a canon of communion" (κανόνα τινὰ τῆς πρὸς αὐτοὺς κοινωνίας)[18] that was based on baptism and that was validated "through the acceptance of the bishops" (διὰ τῆς τῶν ἐπισκόπων παραδοχῆς)[19] which, more often than not, was expressed through "a canonical synodical letter" (συνοδικῷ γράμματι κανονικῶς).[20] Safeguarding the Nicene faith by Basil and his contemporaries also meant proclaiming that they kept the faith of the Fathers unadulterated. For Basil this was nothing short of the apostolic faith that kept one in communion with the church:

> Those who confess the apostolic faith, having put an end to schisms of their own devising, may henceforth become subject to the authority of the church, that the body of Christ, having returned to unity in all its parts, may be

---

14 *Ep.* 92.3: Deferrari, II, 141. Τὴν ἐν Νικαίᾳ γραφεῖσαν παρὰ τῶν Πατέρων ἡμῶν πίστιν ἀνανεώσονται καὶ τὴν αἵρεσιν ἐκκηρύξουσι καὶ ταῖς Ἐκκλησίαις τὰ εἰρηνικὰ διαλέξονται τοὺς τὰ αὐτὰ φρονοῦντας συνάγοντες εἰς ὁμόνοιαν. Courtonne, I, 202.
15 *Ep.* 226.3: Deferrari, III, 337. Οὐ γὰρ τοῦτο ἐνόησεν ἡ ἁγία ἐκείνη καὶ θεοφιλής σύνοδος. Courtonne, III, 26.
16 *Ep.* 114: Deferrari, II, 227. Courtonne, II, 18.
17 *Ep.* 188.1: Deferrari, III, 19. Τοῖς οἰκονομήσασι τὰ καθ' ἡμᾶς Πατράσιν ἀκολουθητέον. Courtonne, II, 123.
18 *Ep.* 188.1: Deferrari, III, 21. Courtonne, II, 124.
19 *Ep.* 188.1: Deferrari, III, 21. Courtonne, II, 124.
20 *Ep.* 92.3: Deferrari, II, 145. Courtonne, I, 203.

made perfect [...] and that we may see our own churches recover their ancient glory of orthodoxy [...] and proclaim the faith of the fathers without evasion. This faith we too have received, and we recognised it from the apostolic traits with which it was characterised, having submitted ourselves both to it and to all the doctrines which have been canonically and legally promulgated in the synodical letter.[21]

5.1.2 Repentance

If the sacrament of baptism was considered to be a person's entrance into the communion of the church, it was the sacrament of repentance that reconciled a person into the communion of the church if he or she had departed. It was understood that personal sin caused one to be cut off from the communion of the church. When the whole person was directed back to communion with God after personal sin, Basil believed that the original beauty and harmony of that person bestowed at baptism was restored. In Basil's era, the church had at its disposal the formal means to receive back into its communion those who had removed themselves because of sin. Although baptism brought complete absolution from sins, it still was possible to sin after baptism. The exercise of a person's God-given freedom meant that the newness of life provided through the sacrament of baptism could be lost. Even with Basil's projection of a monastic ethos — which he had intended for all and which had as its goal a life of sanctification within the callings of one's environment — it was still possible (if

---

21 *Ep.* 92.3: Deferrari, II, 143-145. Τοὺς τὴν ἀποστολικὴν ὁμολογοῦντας πίστιν, ἅπερ ἐπενόησαν σχίσματα διαλύσαντας, ὑποταγῆναι τοῦ λοιποῦ τῇ αὐθεντίᾳ τῆς Ἐκκλησίας, ἵνα ἄρτιον γένηται τὸ σῶμα τοῦ Χριστοῦ, πᾶσι τοῖς μέλεσιν εἰς ὁλοκληρίαν ἐπανελθόν [...] ἀλλὰ καὶ τὰς ἡμετέρας αὐτῶν Ἐκκλησίας ἐπίδωμεν τὸ ἀρχαῖον καύχημα τῆς ὀρθοδοξίας ἀπολαβούσας [...] τὴν δὲ τῶν Πατέρων πίστιν ἄνευ τινὸς ὑποστολῆς κηρύσσειν, ἣν καὶ ἡμεῖς ἐδεξάμεθα καὶ ἐπέγνωμεν ἐκ τῶν ἀποστολικῶν χαρακτήρων μεμορφωμένην, συνθέμενοι καὶ αὐτῇ καὶ πᾶσι τοῖς ἐν τῷ συνοδικῷ γράμματι κανονικῶς καὶ ἐνθέσμως δεδογματισμένοις. Courtonne, I, 202-203.

not expected) for the believer to fall short of this ideal. Through repentance however, believers had access to the state of renewal that they formerly received on the day of their baptism. For Basil, the discipline of repentance was an important aspect of his ministry and was closely tied to the monastic attitudes that he wanted applied to the broader ecclesial community of his episcopate. At certain times Basil departed from the line offered by the canons of the Fathers and offered a severer penance.[22] Basil wanted to teach Amphilochius about the acute discernment required when exercising pastoral care within the episcopal ministry. Basil was more severe than the rule of the canon only when there was a need to "give strict attention both to the act as it appears to us on reflection, and to the meaning of Scripture as it is possible to discover it through inference".[23] At most other times, however, Basil was cautious about applying the full force of the canons, realising that "we may by the severity of our decision stand in the way of those who are being saved".[24] Likewise he writes, "Since we are not judges of the human heart, but judge what we hear, let us leave vengeance to the Lord and ourselves receive him [the penitent] without discrimination granting pardon".[25] The canons for the large part were concerned with those who broke away from the communion of the church for reasons other than denying the core tenets of the faith. Specifically Basil mentioned the sins of the clergy and the laity which included amongst others: theft, usury, murder, magic, oaths and apostasy. As a result, the majority of the canons were penitential and took on the form of rules that a

---

22 For example in the case of fallen virgins, see Canon 18.
23 Canon 18 in *Ep.* 199.18: Deferrari, III, 107. Προσέχειν ἀκριβῶς τῷ τε κατ᾽ ἔννοιαν φαινομένῳ πράγματι καὶ τῆς Γραφῆς διανοίᾳ ἣν δυνατὸν ἐξευρεῖν ἀπὸ τοῦ ἀκολούθου. Courtonne, II, 155.
24 Canon 1 in *Ep.* 118.1: Deferrari, II, 19. Ἐμποδίσωμεν τοῖς σωζομένοις διὰ τὸ τῆς προτάσεως αὐστηρόν. Courtonne, II, 123.
25 *Ep.* 188.10: Deferrari, III, 43. Ἐπειδὴ δὲ οὔκ ἐσμεν καρδιῶν κριταί, ἀλλ᾽ ἐξ ὧν ἀκούομεν κρίνομεν, δῶμεν τῷ Κυρίῳ τὴν ἐκδίκησιν, αὐτοὶ δὲ ἀδιακρίτως αὐτὸν δεξώμεθα συγγνώμην δόντες. Courtonne, II, 130.

bishop could use when he was required to allocate penances for particular sins.

Basil resorted to οἰκονομία (pastoral dispensation) as his guiding principle in determining the penance for each sin. *Economia*, literally meaning "law of the house", referred to a way in which canons were applied by bishops in the pastoral ministry of the church, generally in a more lenient and flexible way. Its opposite was ἀκρίβεια (precision, exactness), which was considered to be a rigid and strict application of a canon. *Economia* allowed for a flexibility or dispensation of the canon in question in response to human weakness and had as its primary purpose the facilitating of God's plan (*economia*) for a person's salvation. For Basil, *economia* involved applying the rule leniently, especially when the rule was not conducive to the penitent's correction and growth. Since Basil's main focus was to assist the penitent on his or her path to salvation, he took much care in applying *economia* within a pastoral setting.

The whole aim of Basil in instituting penitential canons was to seek the correction of the penitent, namely their "withdrawal from sin" (ἁμαρτίας ἀναχώρησις),[26] which was interpreted as a sincere repentance for the sin committed and a resolve to refrain from it in the future. Sometimes with severe sins, penitential canons were enforced to exclude the penitent from the Eucharist. The emphasis here too was on the repentance of the penitent. Excluding the penitent from the Eucharist was considered by Basil to be therapeutic since it aimed at increasing the penitent's desire for Christ. Regarded as a "truer remedy" (ἀληθέστερον ἴαμα),[27] reform of the penitent was the only reason why, according to Basil, the penitent

---

26 Canon 3 in *Ep.* 188.3: Deferrari, III, 25. Courtonne, II, 125. In other words, to tip the scales towards the side of repentance and less to that of punishment, see *Ep.* 188.4,7. Forgiveness always followed repentance, see *Ep.* 260. Rousseau appropriately summarises: "One should not press too hard upon those in theological error, if they showed signs of repentance". Rousseau, *Basil of Caesarea*, 277.
27 Canon 3 in *Ep.* 188.3: Deferrari, III, 25. Courtonne, II, 125

"was not restored immediately to communion" (οὐκ εὐθὺς δὲ εἰς τὴν κοινωνίαν ἀποκαθίστανται).[28] If a bishop, however, saw that the penitent was properly disposed before the completion of the time of his or her penance, the bishop could waive the penance imposed on the penitent. In Basil's mindset, it is not the time of the penance that counts but rather the quality of the penance as seen through its ability to reform the penitent.[29] In his advice to Amphilochius on the application of the canons, Basil presents his guiding principle: "We should not determine the treatment according to time but according to the manner of repentance".[30]

In Basil's day, an important aspect of penance was that it was public in character. Its liturgical setting aimed at enhancing personal and social morality. While undergoing his or her penance, the penitent was excluded from public worship (κοινωνία) and its ideal expression, the Eucharist. It was a gradual process, sometimes spanning many years,[31] before the penitent could be received again as a communicant (δεκτοὺς γενέσθαι εἰς τὴν κοινωνίαν).[32] Generally speaking, in the East and especially within the dioceses of Asia Minor, the penitents were divided into four categories: namely, the weepers, the hearers, the prostrates, and the standers.[33]

Deferrari provides a concise description of each of the four stages of the penitential process, which will now be summarised.[34]

---

28 Canon 38 in *Ep.* 199.38: Deferrari, III, 127. Courtonne, II, 162.
29 See Canons 2, 3, 74, 84.
30 Canon 2 in *Ep.* 118.2: Deferrari, II, 23. Ὁρίζειν δὲ μὴ χρόνῳ ἀλλὰ τρόπῳ τῆς μετανοίας τὴν θεραπείαν. Courtonne, II, 124. See Canons 3, 74, 84.
31 Sins that were considered grievous such as fornication, adultery, abortion, murder and apostasy carried heavier penances where the penitent was deprived from the Eucharist for ten or twenty years. Canon 13 of the Council of Nicaea decreed that no penitent at the hour of his or her death should be deprived of the Eucharist if they sincerely request it with repentance.
32 Canon 81 in *Ep.* 217.81: Deferrari, III, 261. Courtonne, II, 215.
33 Deferrari makes a point of saying that the division of the penitents into four categories is only found in the East. In the West all penitents were treated like the catechumens or hearers. Deferrari, III, xviv. See Gain, *L'Église de Cappadoce*, 16-18.
34 Deferrari, III, xviii–xxiv.

The weepers, according to Deferrari, were forbidden from entering the church edifice. Instead they were made to stand at the courtyard of the church where, in a public display of their penance, they had to entreat the faithful to pray for them as they entered the church. The hearers, Deferrari says, had the same treatment as the catechumens who were being instructed in the faith. They were allowed to stand only in the narthex (entrance area) of the church and only up until the Liturgy of the Word, which included Scripture readings and instruction. Together with the catechumens, the hearers were dismissed from the church at the appropriate time so as not to participate in the Liturgy of the Faithful which was centred on the Eucharist. The prostrates, according to Deferrari, were allowed to enter the church but had to appear in the penitential posture of a prostration during the liturgical moments at which the rest of the congregation generally stood. The standers were permitted to attend church like everybody else, without any public display of penance during worship. Deferrari is quick to point out, however, that they were prohibited from receiving the Eucharist (which did not remain unnoticed). Of course, not every penitent had to pass through all four categories as some penitents skipped the "weepers" stage and were classed automatically in the category of the "hearers", while others simply were asked to refrain from receiving the Eucharist.

The penitential canons were considered by Basil to be pedagogical in character "that the fruits of penance may be tested"[35] and, despite their disciplinary nature, they conveyed a sense of optimism to the penitent. Simply put, any sin irrespective of its gravity can be forgiven because it is God who forgives. Basil understood that since at various times throughout their lives people sin, all are in need of forgiveness. Keeping a communicant away from the worshipping community and the Eucharist was aimed at

---

35   Canon 84 in *Ep.* 217.84: Deferrari, III, 265. Ὥστε τοὺς καρποὺς δοκιμάζεσθαι τῆς μετανοίας. Courtonne, II, 216.

instilling in the communicant the necessary disposition that was needed to be a part of the worshipping community. Only after "a truly worthy penance" (ἀξιόλογον [...] τὴν μετάνοιαν ἐπιδειξάμενοι) was one granted to be "restored to the communion of the body of Christ" (ἀποκαταστήσονται εἰς τὴν κοινωνίαν τοῦ σώματος τοῦ Χριστοῦ).[36] The tangible sign that one had been reconciled with God and henceforth with the worshipping community was manifested in his or her ability to receive the Eucharist. Those who chose not to repent and be reconciled with God brought upon themselves the act of excommunication and therefore were "banished from ecclesiastical communion" (ἐξορίσας [...] τῆς ἐκκλησιαστικῆς κοινωνίας).[37] Basil explains in a letter to his maritime bishops: "Nothing separates us from one another, brethren, unless we establish the separation by deliberate choice".[38] Along the same lines of the Pauline admonition of the unrepentant being "turned over to Satan, so that they may learn not to blaspheme",[39] Basil too did not mince his words when he spoke about a person's wilful decision not to embrace repentance: "Perhaps when he has become a thing to be shunned he will change".[40] Writing about an unnamed unrepentant male, Basil comments:

> Those whom public punishments do not chasten, nor debarment from prayers lead to repentance, must submit to the canons handed down by the Lord [...] Since, then, we have protested to him, and he has not accepted, let him henceforth be excommunicated (ἐκκήρυκτος). And let it be proclaimed to the entire district that he must not be received in any of the ordinary relations of life

---

36 Canon 82 in *Ep.* 217.82: Deferrari, III, 263. Courtonne, II, 215-216.
37 *Ep.* 289: Deferrari, IV, 183. Courtonne, III, 159.
38 *Ep.* 203.3: Deferrari, III, 149. Οὐδὲν ἡμᾶς χωρίζει ἀπ᾽ ἀλλήλων, ἀδελφοί, ἐὰν μὴ τῇ προαιρέσει τὸν χωρισμὸν ὑποστῶμεν. Courtonne, II, 170.
39 1 Tim. 1:20. Οὓς παρέδωκα τῷ Σατανᾷ, ἵνα παιδευθῶσιν μὴ βλασφημεῖν. See also 1 Cor. 5:5.
40 *Ep.* 287: Deferrari, IV, 179. Ἴσως παραφύλαγμα γενόμενος ἐντραπήσεται. Courtonne, III, 158.

(ἀπρόσδεκτον αὐτὸν εἶναι πρὸς πᾶσαν κοινωνίαν χρήσεως βιοτικῆς), so that by our not associating with him, he may become entirely food for the devil.[41]

5.1.3 Eucharist

The most distinctive act that bore witness to a person's communion (κοινωνία) with the church was expressed through his or her partaking of the Eucharist (μεταλαμβάνειν τοῦ ἁγίου σώματος καὶ αἵματος τοῦ Χριστοῦ).[42] In his letters Basil admonished that one should partake of the Eucharist almost "every day [...] for who can doubt that sharing continually in the life is nothing else than living in many ways?"[43] Basil employed this rule in his own spiritual life and encouraged his spiritual children to do the same: "We for our part, however, take communion four times each week – on Sunday, on Wednesday, on Friday, and on Saturday – and on the other days only when there is a commemoration of a saint".[44] If, because of the "very force of circumstances" (δι' αὐτῶν τῶν πραγμάτων),[45] it was not possible to attend church and receive the Eucharist from the ordained minister, the faithful were encouraged to partake of the Eucharist themselves after previously having received it from church. Consequently, when there was "no priest" present (μὴ ἔστιν ἱερεύς), or accessing the church was not possible, the faithful

---

41 Ep. 288: Deferrari, IV, 181. Οὓς τὰ κοινὰ ἐπιτίμια οὐ σωφρονίζει οὔτε τὸ εἰρχθῆναι τῶν εὐχῶν ἄγει εἰς μετάνοια ἀνάγκη τοῖς παρὰ τοῦ Κυρίου δοθεῖσι κανόσι ὑποβάλλειν [...] Ἐπεὶ οὖν διεμαρτυράμεθα αὐτῷ καὶ οὐ κατεδέξατο, λοιπὸν ἔστω ἐκκήρυκτος. Καὶ διαγγελήτω πάσῃ τῇ κώμῃ ἀπρόσδεκτον αὐτὸν εἶναι πρὸς πᾶσαν κοινωνίαν χρήσεως βιοτικῆς, ὡς ἐκ τοῦ μὴ συναναμίγνυσθαι ἡμᾶς αὐτῷ γένηται παντελῶς κατάβρωμα τοῦ διαβόλου. Courtonne, III, 158.
42 Ep. 93: Courtonne, I, 203.
43 Ep. 93: Deferrari, II, 145. Καὶ τὸ κοινωνεῖν δὴ καθ᾽ ἑκάστην ἡμέραν [...] Τίς γὰρ ἀμφιβάλλει ὅτι τὸ μετέχειν συνεχῶς τῆς ζωῆς οὐδὲν ἄλλο ἐστὶν ἢ ζῆν πολλαχῶς; Courtonne, I, 203.
44 Ep. 93: Deferrari, II, 145. Ἡμεῖς μέντοιγε τέταρτον καθ᾽ ἑκάστην ἑβδομάδα κοινωνοῦμεν, ἐν τῇ Κυριακῇ, ἐν τῇ Τετράδι καὶ ἐν τῇ Παρασκευῇ καὶ τῷ Σαββάτῳ καὶ ἐν ταῖς ἄλλαις ἡμέραις, ἐὰν ᾖ μνήμη Ἁγίου τινός. Courtonne, I, 203-204.
45 Ep. 93: Deferrari, II, 147. Courtonne, I, 204.

kept "communion at home" (κοινωνίαν οἴκοι κατέχοντες) so as to partake of it whenever they desired (ὅτε βούλεται).[46] With respect to receiving the Eucharist, Basil says that the communicant "has complete right of possession, and by such right raises it to his mouth with his own hand".[47]

Through being a participant in the Eucharist, Basil argues the believer becomes something different from he or she who wilfully refuses to participate in its sacramental expression. This *something different* is the one church. Irrespective of cultural, social and political differences, Basil says that through the Eucharist "all who have placed their hopes in Christ are one people and the followers of Christ are now one church".[48] According to Basil, the church united in the Eucharist is inseparably united with Christ in such a way that the two become one being. When there is "communion according to faith" (πίστιν κοινωνίας), Basil says there is no division amongst believers but only a "single union" (μίαν [...] ἕνωσιν) that is realised "not through the features of the body, but through the peculiarities of the soul" (οὐ διὰ σωματικῶν χαρακτήρων, ἀλλὰ διὰ τῶν τῆς ἀρετῆς ἰδιωμάτων).[49] For this reason Basil declares: "For though our bodies will be separated in space, yet the eye of God is assuredly gazing upon us [...] in common (κοινῇ)".[50] A key point, therefore, in Basil's understanding is that the church's communion consists of believers who, although dispersed throughout the world, are united in faith:

---

46   *Ep.* 93: Deferrari, II, 147. Courtonne, I, 204.
47   *Ep.* 93: Deferrari, II, 147. Μετ 'ἐξουσίας ἁπάσης καὶ οὕτω προσάγει τῷ στόματι τῇ ἰδίᾳ χειρί. Courtonne, I, 204.
48   *Ep.* 161.1: Deferrari, II, 413. Εἷς λαὸς πάντες οἱ εἰς Χριστὸν ἠλπικότες καὶ μία Ἐκκλησία νῦν οἱ Χριστοῦ. Courtonne, II, 93.
49   *Ep.* 133: Deferrari, II, 303. Τοῖς τῆς ψηχῆς ὀφθαλμοῖς καὶ περιπτύξασθαί σε τῇ ἀγάπῃ [...] καὶ οἱονεὶ συμφυῆναί σοι καὶ πρὸς μίαν ἐλθεῖν ἕνωσιν ἐκ τῆς κατὰ τὴν πίστιν κοινωνίας. Courtonne, II, 47.
50   *Ep.* 150.2: Deferrari, II, 365. Τὰ μὲν γὰρ σώματα ἡμῶν τόποις δισταθήσεται, ὁ δὲ τοῦ Θεοῦ ὀφθαλμὸς κοινῇ [...] ἐφορᾷ δηλονότι. Courtonne, II, 73.

Eyes are promoters of bodily friendship [...] But true love is formed by the gift of the Spirit, which brings together objects separated by a wide space, and causes loved ones to know each other, not through the features of the body, but through the peculiarities of the soul. This indeed the favour of the Lord has wrought [...] to enter into a single union [...] through communion according to faith.[51]

In the first of his three canonical letters[52] to Amphilochius, written in 374, Basil distinguished three ways in which a baptised person could be separated from the communion of the church. These three ways were expressed with the terms: "heresies" (αἱρέσεις), "schisms" (σχίσματα) and "parasynagogues" (παρασυναγωγάς).[53] Part of Basil's concern was that some people seemed unconcerned at being cut off from the communion of the church. Church leaders and their congregations seemed complacent about the presence of heresies, schisms and parasynagogues, and their effects on the Nicene communion of churches. Those who broke communion with the Nicene communion of churches refused to see a difference between what they once were and their new faith identity. Basil's aim was to promote the path established by "those fathers who decreed that by small signs the tokens of communion (χαρακτήρων τὰ τῆς ἐπιμιξίας) should be carried about from one end of the earth to the other, and that all should be fellow-citizens and neighbours to all".[54] For Basil, the "small signs" were to be manifested in the

---

51 *Ep.* 133: Deferrari, II, 303. Τῆς μὲν σωματικῆς φιλίας ὀφθαλμοὶ πρόξενοι γίνονται [...] Τὴν δὲ ἀληθινὴν ἀγάπην ἡ τοῦ Πνεύματος δωρεὰ συνίστησι συνάπτουσα μὲν τὰ μακρῷ διεστῶτα τῷ τόπῳ, γνωρίζουσα δὲ ἀλλήλοις τοὺς ἀγαπητούς, οὐ διὰ σωματικῶν χαρακτήρων, ἀλλὰ διὰ τῶν τῆς ἀρετῆς ἰδιωμάτων. Ὃ δὴ καὶ ἐφ᾽ ἡμῶν ἡ τοῦ Κυρίου χάρις ἐποίησε [...] πρὸς μίαν ἐλθεῖν ἕνωσιν ἐκ τῆς κατὰ τὴν πίστιν κοινωνίας. Courtonne, II, 47.
52 See *Epp.* 188, 199, 217.
53 See *Ep.* 188.1: Deferrari, III, 11. Courtonne, II, 121.
54 *Ep.* 203.3: Deferrari, III, 151. Ἐκείνων ὄντες τῶν πατέρων, οἳ ἐνομοθέτησαν διὰ μικρῶν χαρακτήρων τὰ τῆς ἐπιμιξίας σύμβολα ἀπὸ περάτων τῆς γῆς εἰς πέρατα περιφέρεσθαι καὶ πάντας πᾶσι πολίτας καὶ οἰκείους εἶναι. Courtonne, II, 170-171. Instead of τὰ τῆς κοινωνίας σύμβολα (the tokens of communion) that is found in Deferrari, Courtonne has the expression τὰ τῆς ἐπιμιξίας σύμβολα.

partaking of the Eucharist in the Nicene communion of churches. Although it is common to see the technical terms for a breach of communion used as loose synonyms (and not just in Basil's writings), strictly speaking each term has a different usage that is determined by whether a disagreement falls on actual faith in God, on church discipline, or on ecclesiastical rulings. While it is important to acknowledge the distinctiveness of each term, heresy, schism and parasynagogue are not mutually exclusive. In many instances one of these terms becomes the precursor to the other. An example of this will be seen below where "schism" can be seen as a precursor to "parasynagogue". What follows comments briefly on the concepts of heresy, schism and parasynagogue as they appear in Basil's letters.

In the context of his explanation to Amphilochius on heresy, Basil describes heretics as people "who were completely broken off" (παντελῶς ἀπερρηγμένους) from the church, and are "as regards the faith itself, alienated" (κατ' αὐτὴν τὴν πίστιν ἀπηλλοτριωμένους).[55] Heresy was seen as a disagreement (διαφορά), a discrepancy on vital issues of faith which led to the negation of the unity of the church. Basil argues that the causes of separation (χωρισμός, ἀλλοτρίωσις) within the communion of the church arise from pride and arrogance (μεγαλοφροσύνη), and therefore come from free choice (προαίρεσις). In this regard, because heresy was considered to be an act of deliberate choice, Basil had no tolerance for its presence in his churches. All non-Nicene hierarchs and their followers were cautioned first. If they refused to change their faith position, they were then excommunicated from the Nicene communion of churches.

Bishops of the fourth century tended to view schism (σχίσμα) as a disagreement (διαφορά) between church members concerning ecclesiastical questions capable of mutual solution. According to Basil, schisms were the result of "those at variance with one another

---

55   *Ep.* 188.1: Deferrari, III, 11. Courtonne, II, 121.

for certain ecclesiastical reasons and questions that admit of remedy".[56] Often these disagreements were not of such a serious nature so as to warrant a lasting division among members of church communities. Of the three types of separations, schisms and parasynagogues were the easiest to deal with for Basil especially since the baptism of their constituents was still deemed to be valid. With schisms and parasynagogues, Basil was more concerned with the lifestyle of the proponents of these movements, which he considered to be problematic (sinful) and in need of repentance. Consequently, unlike the heretics who in some circumstances needed both repentance and baptism to be brought into the communion of the church, those from schismatic (σχίσματα) or para-ecclesial groups (παρασυναγωγάς) only needed to repent so as to be restored into the communion of the church.[57] The same holds true for the ordained orders of both these groups. Clerical orders from heretical groups (αἱρέσεις) were not always accepted by Basil, whereas the clerical orders of those leaving a schism or a parasynagogue, after a strict examination that revealed "adequate repentance and change of heart" (μετανοίᾳ ἀξιολόγῳ καὶ ἐπιστροφῇ βελτιωθέντες),[58] were accepted by him. The ordained orders of those coming over from schisms and parasynagogues, however, if they were to be accepted, needed to have been originally bestowed by a church in communion with Nicaea.

In all cases Basil accepts the validity of holy orders only if they are aligned with the Nicene church. Outside Nicene Christianity, Basil argued that holy orders had no validity. What once was, no longer is. Basil explains: "Those who had been cut off, becoming laymen, possessed the power neither of baptizing nor of ordain-

---

56 *Ep.* 188.1: Deferrari, III, 11. Τοὺς δι 'αἰτίας τινὰς ἐκκλησιαστικὰς καὶ ζητήματα ἰάματα πρὸς ἀλλήλους διενεχθέντας. Courtonne, II, 121.
57 With the non-Nicene faith position of Eustathius of Sebasteia, should he have wanted to re-enter the Nicene communion of churches, it would have been acceptable by Basil for Eustathius simply to sign a Nicene confession of faith. See *Ep.* 99; Chapter Four.
58 *Ep.* 188.1: Deferrari, III, 13. Courtonne, II, 122.

ing, being able no longer to impart to others the grace of the Holy Spirit for which they themselves had fallen away".[59] As always, in his handling of ecclesiastical affairs and in his concern for communion, Basil claimed to be doing nothing else but upholding the tradition of the "ancients". That is to say, the tradition of the Fathers who had at various times and in various places gathered in council, and who had subsequently "dispensed legislation" (οἰκονομήσασι).[60] Consequently, Basil observes:

> The ancients, accordingly, decided to reject completely the baptism of heretics, but to accept that of schismatics on the ground that they were still of the church (ἔτι ἐκ τῆς Ἐκκλησίας ὄντων); and as to those in illegal congregations, to join these again to the church (συνάπτεσθαι πάλιν τῇ Ἐκκλησίᾳ) after they had been improved by adequate repentance and change of heart (μετανοίᾳ ἀξιολόγῳ καὶ ἐπιστροφῇ βελτιωθέντες); hence they often received into the same rank, whenever they have repented, even those in orders who have gone off with the insubordinate.[61]

Through dialogue, compassion, acts of mercy and good will, Basil did whatever he could to win over dissident believers into the fold of the church. As in his pastoral canons, so also here, Basil veered away from the strictness of the rule only "for the sake of the pastoral care of the many" (οἰκονομίας ἕνεκα τῶν πολλῶν).[62] According to Basil, communion in the church needed to remain as accessible as possible, while at the same time being safeguarded from the

---

59 *Ep.* 188.1: Deferrari, III, 17. Οἱ δὲ ἀπορραγέντες, λαϊκοὶ γενόμενοι, οὔτε τοῦ βαπτίζειν οὔτε τοῦ χειροτονεῖν εἶχον τὴν ἐξουσίαν, οὐκέτι δυνάμενοι χάριν Πνεύματος Ἁγίου ἑτέροις παρέχειν ἧς αὐτοὶ ἐκπεπτώκασι. Courtonne, II, 123.
60 *Ep.* 188.1: Deferrari, III, 19. Courtonne, II, 123.
61 *Ep.* 188.1: Deferrari, III, 13. Ἔδοξε τοίνυν τοῖς ἐξ ἀρχῆς τὸ μὲν τῶν αἱρετικῶν παντελῶς ἀθετῆσαι· τὸ δὲ τῶν ἀποσχισάντων, ὡς ἔτι ἐκ τῆς Ἐκκλησίας ὄντων, παραδέξασθαι· τοὺς δὲ ἐν ταῖς παρασυναγωγαῖς, μετανοίᾳ ἀξιολόγῳ καὶ ἐπιστροφῇ βελτιωθέντες, συνάπτεσθαι πάλιν τῇ Ἐκκλησίᾳ, ὥστε πολλάκις καὶ τοὺς ἐν βαθμῷ συναπελθόντας τοῖς ἀνυποτάκτοις, ἐπειδὰν μεταμεληθῶσιν, εἰς τὴν αὐτὴν παραδέχεσθαι τάξιν. Courtonne, II, 122.
62 *Ep.* 188.1: Courtonne, II, 123.

"wicked action" (κακούργημα) of people that was "unacceptable to the church" (ἀπροσδέκτους ποιήσωσι τῇ Ἐκκλησίᾳ).[63] Both Basil's leniency and severity were in keeping with his desire to "observe the canons scrupulously" (δουλεύειν ἀκριβείᾳ κανόνων).[64] It was the prerogative of every bishop to make this judgement and perhaps one of the most important responsibilities that befitted his office. Basil believed that church leaders who resisted his request to come back into the communion of the church, did so not out of ignorance or unwillingly, but rather purposely and even ambitiously. Their motive according to Basil was to set up rival congregations (parasynagogues, παρασυναγωγάς).

Parasynagogues at the time of Basil's letters were considered to be "rival" or "counter-assemblies" and were so called by Basil because they were "assemblies brought into being by insubordinate presbyters or bishops, and by uninstructed laymen".[65] Basil remarks:

> If someone [deacon, priest or bishop] who has been apprehended in error (πταίσματι: "fault", "sin") has been forbidden the exercise of his office and has not submitted to the canons, but has unjustly arrogated to himself the episcopal and priestly functions, and certain people, abandoning the catholic church, have gone along with him,— such an affair is illegal congregation (παρασυναγωγή).[66]

In describing the impropriety of those who set up rival assemblies, Basil used the term "disobedient" (ἀνυπότακτος), the opposite of εὐταξία which implied the good order and discipline of the church. Each parasynagogue was understood by Basil as a breach of ecclesiastical unity and therefore as involving exclusion from

---

63 *Ep.* 188.1: Deferrari, III, 17–19. Courtonne, II, 123.
64 *Ep.* 188.1: Deferrari, III, 19. Courtonne, II, 123.
65 *Ep.* 188.1: Deferrari, III, 11. Συνάξεις τὰς παρὰ τῶν ἀνυποτάκτων πρεσβυτέρων ἢ ἐπισκόπων καὶ παρὰ τῶν ἀπαιδεύτων λαῶν γινομένας. Courtonne, II, 121.
66 *Ep.* 188.1: Deferrari, III, 11. Εἴ τις ἐν πταίσματι ἐξετασθεὶς ἐπεσχέθη τῆς λειτουργίας καὶ μὴ ὑπέκυψε τοῖς κανόσιν, ἀλλ᾽ ἑαυτῷ ἐξεδίκησε τὴν προεδρίαν καὶ τὴν λειτουργίαν καὶ συναπῆλθον τούτῳ τινὲς καταλιπόντες τὴν καθολικὴν Ἐκκλησίαν, παρασυναγωγὴ τὸ τοιοῦτο. Courtonne, II, 121.

the eucharistic communion of the church.[67]

In an ideal setting, the local eucharistic community would consist of all the Nicene faithful living in an area, city or province, united in the house of worship in which the Eucharist was celebrated. The organisation of the local church arose naturally out of the eucharistic assembly, through which it maintained canonical unity with all the local churches. However, in Basil's day, the harsh realities of state-endorsed non-Nicenism often meant that the faithful were forced to worship away from their church edifices and even outdoors.[68] Basil says that "churches becoming unsound, like vessels that have become porous, have received the heretical corruption that has flowed upon them".[69] According to Basil, non-Nicene proponents, with the full support of the state, were granted an open license to "cast down... altars" (ἐπανιόντες τὰ θυσιαστήρια) and "set up their own tables" (ἑαυτῶν τραπέζας ἐτίθεσαν).[70] Basil accuses Apollinarius of sending men "to the churches governed by the orthodox to tear them asunder and to vindicate some peculiar illegal service".[71] In the thirteenth year of Emperor Valens' reign in 376, Basil wrote "To the Westerners" (Τοῖς δυτικοῖς) about the systematic displacement of his congregations because of their allegiance to Nicene Christianity. Summarising what he described as

---

67 Canon 5 of the Council of Nicaea in 325 speaks of breaches of church unity caused by unruly clergy. According to the canon, the end result for the unruly clergy is ἀκοινωνήτων γενομένων, "to become excommunicated". The cleric becomes excommunicated, not necessarily in the juridical term, but in the sense that unless he repents he can no longer receive the Eucharist in the church. See Ραφτάνη, Πηδάλιον, 128.
68 See *Ep.* 164.2: Λαοὶ τῶν εὐκτηρίων οἴκων ἐξελαθέντες ἐν τῷ ὑπαίθρῳ πρὸς τὸν ἐν τοῖς οὐρανοῖς Δεσπότην τὰς χεῖρας αἴρουσι. Courtonne, II, 99. "The laity driven from the houses of prayer raise in the open their hands to the master in heaven". Deferrari, II, 427.
69 *Ep.* 242.3: Deferrari, III, 435. Αἱ Ἐκκλησίαι, σαθρωθεῖσαι ὥσπερ ἀγγεῖα ἀραιωθέντα τὴν αἱρετικὴν διαφθορὰν εἰσρυεῖσαν ἐδέξαντο. Courtonne, III, 67.
70 *Ep.* 226.2: Deferrari, III, 333. Courtonne, III, 25.
71 *Ep.* 265.2: Deferrari, IV, 109–111. Ταῖς παρὰ τῶν ὀρθοδόξων κυβερνωμέναις ἐπιπεμφθέντων παρ' αὐτοῦ πρὸς τὸ σχίσαι καὶ ἰδίαν παρασυναγωγὴν ἐκδικῆσαι. Courtonne, III, 129.

the "wickedness" (πονηρίας)[72] sanctioned by imperial authority, Basil wrote:

> The laity have abandoned the houses of prayer and are congregating in desert places, a pitiable sight—women, and children, and old men, and the otherwise infirm, in most furious rains, and in snowstorms, and in winds and frost of winter, and likewise also in summer suffering under the heat of the sun in the open air! And this they suffer for not consenting to become a part of the wicked leaven of Arius.[73]

In Basil's understanding, the wholeness of the church is reflected in the institution of the Eucharist where communion is realised. For communion to exist in the church, Basil maintained that there was a correlative need for him and his brother bishops to "govern the churches" (τὰς ἐκκλησίας οἰκονομήσωμεν) by "the grace of God" (Θεοῦ χάριτι).[74] The Eucharist became the vehicle through which canonical unity and thereby communion was expressed. Through the Eucharist the "many" are united in the One. As contemporary theologian John Zizioulas says, and in view of Basil's teachings, the ordained ministry and especially the office of the bishop are considered the *sine qua non* for the eucharistic community to exist and express the church's unity.[75] In this way, for Basil and his contemporaries, the unity of the church in the Eucharist became synonymous with the unity of the church in the bishop.

---

72 *Ep.* 242.1: Deferrari, III, 429. Courtonne, III, 65.
73 *Ep.* 242.2: Deferrari, III, 433. Οἱ λαοὶ τοὺς τῶν προσευχῶν καταλιπόντες οἴκους ἐν ταῖς ἐρήμοις συνάγονται. Θέαμα ἐλεεινόν· γυναῖκες καὶ παιδία καὶ γέροντες καὶ οἱ ἄλλως ἀσθενεῖς ἐν ὄμβροις λαβροτάτοις καὶ νιφετοῖς καὶ ἀνέμοις καὶ παγετῷ τοῦ χειμῶνος, ὁμοίως δὲ καὶ ἐν θέρει ὑπὸ τὴν φλόγα τὴν τοῦ ἡλίου, ἐν τῷ ὑπαίθρῳ ταλαιπωροῦντες. Καὶ ταῦτα πάσχουσι διὰ τὸ τῆς πονηρᾶς ζύμης Ἀρείου γενέσθαι μὴ καταδέχεσθαι. Courtonne, III, 66–67. The forced disposition on the faithful was not limited to houses of prayer but also included their very homes. See *Ep.* 243.2: Ἀπελαύνονται μὲν τῶν πατρίδων οἱ εὐσεβεῖς, πρὸς δὲ τὰς ἐρημίας μετοικίζονται. Courtonne, III, 69. "The pious are driven from their native places, and are exiled to desert regions". Deferrari, III, 437–439.
74 *Ep.* 191: Deferrari, III, 81. Courtonne, II, 144.
75 Zizioulas, *Being as Communion*, 240.

Bishops of the early church would say that just as unity in the Eucharist or in the local church was essential, so too was maintaining unity in the communion that exists in the local bishop. Since "the episcopate is one", wrote St. Cyprian of Carthage, "the parts of which are held together (*in solidum*) by the individual bishops".[76] In his letter *To the Ephesians*, St. Ignatius of Antioch wrote: "I have received in God's name your whole congregation in the person of Onesimus [...] your earthly bishop".[77] As the voice of the church, the bishop offered the Eucharist to God in the name of the church, and thus brought before God the communion of believers, the body of Christ. Basil encouraged the laity of Nicopolis to "deign heartily to cleave to the bishop" so as "to repel vigorously the assaults from without" and "that the genuineness of your love for God may be proclaimed among all".[78]

The most obvious way to undermine the unity and harmony of the church was to use calumny against its bishop. Where this was not possible, violence was often used to displace and persecute the bishop, even to the point of death. Once the bishop was undermined or attacked, lower orders of clergy and the laity could suffer a similar fate. "My personal experience shows", recalls Basil, "the inclination of accusers towards calumny".[79] Basil laments: "Oh, strange fabrication" (Ὦ τοῦ καινοῦ δράματος),[80] over the harsh

---

76 Cyprian of Carthage, *The Unity of the Church*, 5: Deferrari, 99. "Episcopatus unus est, cuius a singulis in solidum pars tenetur". SC 500. 182–184.
77 Ignatius of Antioch, *To the Ephesians*, 1.3: Holmes, 183–185. Τὴν πολυπληθίαν ὑμῶν ἐν ὀνόματι Θεοῦ ἀπείληφα ἐν Ὀνησίμῳ, τῷ [...] ὑμῶν δὲ ἐν σαρκὶ ἐπισκόπῳ. Holmes, *The Apostolic Fathers*, 182–184.
78 *Ep.* 230: Deferrari, III, 357. Καταξιώσητε ἐκθύμως περιέχεσθαι τοῦ δεδομένου ὑμῖν ἐπισκόπου καὶ τὰς παρὰ τῶν ἔξωθεν πείρας ἰσχυρῶς ἀποκρούεσθαι [...] ὥστε διαβοηθῆναι παρὰ πᾶσι τὸ γνήσιον ὑμῶν τῆς εἰς Θεὸν ἀγάπης. Courtonne, III, 35–36.
79 *Ep.* 223.5: Deferrari, III, 307. Ἡ κατ' ἐμοῦ πεῖρα τὸ πρὸς συκοφαντίαν εὔκολον τῶν κατηγορούντων συνίστησι. Courtonne, III, 15. In *Ep.* 24 Basil declares: Κρείττονα εἶναι διαβολῶν ἀνθρώπου βίον τῶν χαλεπωτάτων ἐστίν, ἵνα μὴ τῶν ἀδυνάτων εἴπω. Courtonne, I, 59. "For a man's life to be above slander is one of the most difficult things in the world, not to say an impossibility". Deferrari, I, 145.
80 *Ep.* 223.4: Deferrari, III, 301. Courtonne, III, 13.

personal affairs affecting his ministry and that of his fellow bishops, and he continues: "we are charged with deception and want of principle, corruption of churches, and destruction of souls".[81] In his explanation, Basil states:

> Bishops have been convicted on the strength of calumny alone, and, although no proof has supported the charges, they are given over to the punishments. And some have neither known accusers, nor seen courts of law, nor been falsely accused at all, but seized by violence late at night they have been exiled to foreign lands, given over to the cruel sufferings of the desert unto death. And what follows this is known to everyone, even if we are silent about it – flight of presbyters, flight of deacons, and harassing of all the clergy.[82]

According to Basil, getting rid of the church's leaders (the bishops), "the pillars and foundation of the truth",[83] meant that the ecclesiastical communities remained orphaned, disconnected from one another and left to disintegrate. Writing to the bishops of Italy and Gaul, Basil comments: "Persecution has laid hold of us, most honoured brethren, and the most oppressive of persecutions (διωγμῶν ὁ βαρύτατος). For shepherds are being persecuted that their flocks may be scattered".[84] Later on in the same letter Basil says:

---

81 *Ep.* 244.5: Deferrari, III, 461. Ἡμᾶς κατηγορουμένους δόλον καὶ ῥᾳδιουργίαν, φθορὰν Ἐκκλησιῶν καὶ ψυχῶν ἀπώλειαν. Courtonne, III, 78–79.
82 *Ep.* 243.2: Deferrari, III, 439. Ἐπίσκοποι δὲ ὑπὸ μόνης συκοφαντίας ἑάλωσαν καὶ μηδεμιᾶς ἀποδείξεως τοῖς ἐγκλήμασιν ἐπεχθείσης ταῖς τιμωρίαις ἐκδίδονται. Τινὲς δὲ οὔτε ἔγνωσαν κατηγόρους οὔτε εἶδον δικαστήρια οὔτε ἐσυκοφαντήθησαν τὴν ἀρχήν, ἀλλ᾽ ἀωρὶ τῶν νυκτῶν βιαίως ἀναρπασθέντες εἰς τὴν ὑπερορίαν ἐφυγαδεύθησαν ταῖς ἐκ τῆς ἐρημίας κακοπαθίαις παραδοθέντες εἰς θάνατον. Τὰ δὲ τούτοις ἑπόμενα γνώριμα παντί, κἂν ἡμεῖς σιωπήσωμεν· φυγαὶ πρεσβυτέρων, φυγαὶ διακόνων, παντὸς τοῦ κλήρου λεηλασία. Courtonne, III, 69. See *Ep.* 25.2, 263.3.
83 *Ep.* 243.4: Deferrari, III, 445. Οἱ στῦλοι καὶ τὸ ἑδραίωμα τῆς ἀληθείας. Courtonne, III, 72.
84 *Ep.* 243.2: Deferrari, III, 437. Διωγμὸς κατείληφεν ἡμᾶς, ἀδελφοὶ τιμιώτατοι, καὶ διωγμῶν ὁ βαρύτατος. Διώκονται γὰρ ποιμένες, ἵνα διασκορπισθῶσι τὰ ποίμνια. Courtonne, III, 69.

Spiritual joy and gladness have been taken away. Our feasts have been turned into mourning; houses of prayer have been closed; idle are the altars of spiritual service. No longer are there gatherings of Christians, no longer precedence of teachers, no teachings of salvation, no assemblies, no evening singing of hymns, nor that blessed joy of souls which arises in the souls of those who believe in the Lord at the gatherings for Holy Communion (ἐπὶ ταῖς συνάξεσι καὶ τῇ κοινωνίᾳ) and when the spiritual blessings are partaken of.[85]

The bishop's ministry in Basil's day was seen as a fundamental aspect of his ecclesiology that involved both a consciousness of belonging to the one church of Christ and an agreement as to what that church was in her very being. The bishop was seen as the provider, facilitator and realisation of communion within his diocese, as well as throughout the whole universal church.

5.2 The Bishop as the Criterion of Communion for the Local Church

For Basil and his fellow bishops, the Eucharist in the life of the church constituted the most perfect criterion that manifested the church's communal existence. Within the life of the eucharistic community, its members were called upon, through the guidance of the Holy Spirit, to preserve and continue the communion (κοινωνία) realised in the eucharistic synaxis.[86] In this vein, the Eucharist was regarded as an act conducted by the *whole* church and not something done *only* by the clergy on behalf of the laity. For this reason Basil would state in his letters that the presence of

---

85 *Ep.* 243.2: Deferrari, III, 441. Ἐξῆρται χαρὰ καὶ εὐφροσύνη πνευματική. Εἰς πένθος ἐστράφησαν ἡμῶν αἱ ἑορταί, οἶκοι προσευχῶν ἀπεκλείσθησαν, ἀργὰ τὰ θυσιαστήρια τῆς πνευματικῆς λατρείας. Οὐκέτι σύλλογοι Χριστιανῶν, οὐκέτι διδασκάλων προεδρίαι, οὐ διδάγματα σωτήρια, οὐ πανηγύρεις, οὐχ ὑμνῳδίαι νυκτεριναί, οὐ τὸ μακάριον ἐκεῖνο τῶν ψυχῶν ἀγαλλίαμα ὃ ἐπὶ ταῖς συνάξεσι καὶ τῇ κοινωνίᾳ τῶν πνευματικῶν χαρισμάτων ταῖς ψυχαῖς ἐγγίνεται τῶν πιστευόντων εἰς Κύριον. Courtonne, III, 70.
86 See Elert, *Eucharist and Church Fellowship in the First Four Centuries*, 24.

the laity was constitutive to the ministry of the clergy.[87] Without lay people there could not be any clergy, especially since it was from the laity that the clergy were chosen.

Once a cleric was chosen, the laity were expected to support and strengthen him in his ministry. In the words of Basil: "The management of the churches is in the hands of those who have been entrusted with their guidance, but they are strengthened by the laity".[88] The fundamental role of the laity took on liturgical connotations as well, because the Eucharist could not be performed unless members of the laity were present. Consequently, the local church for Basil was comprised of two basic components that were bound together in complete unity and order: the clergy (κλῆρος) and the laity/people (λαός). Although for the clergy there existed various degrees of pastoral and administrative responsibility, this was not the case for the laity. All the faithful, however, were dependent on the bishop as the possessor of the highest office of responsibility, and owed obedience to him. In this way, the bishop was seen as the instrument that expressed the catholicity of the local church. It is he who offered to God the Eucharist in which the church in its local place was united, thus becoming the very body of Christ. When Basil writes to a local church, he writes to its bishop alone, since it is the bishop who represents the communion of the local church.

According to Basil, it is God himself who calls and chooses, through the intervention of the church hierarchy, an individual for the ministry of the church. In the case of the "most God-beloved bishops" (θεοφιλεστάτων ἐπισκόπων), Basil proposes that God, through the mediation of another member of the church and in "accordance to God's wish" (κατὰ βούλησιν Θεοῦ γενομένην),[89] calls

---

87 See *Ep*. 230.
88 *Ep*. 230: Deferrari, III, 357. Αἱ περὶ τὰς Ἐκκλησίας οἰκονομίαι γίνονται μὲν παρὰ τῶν πεπιστευμένων τὴν προστασίαν αὐτῶν, βεβαιοῦνται δὲ παρὰ τῶν λαῶν. Courtonne, III, 35.
89 See *Ep*. 227: Deferrari, III, 349. Courtonne, III, 32.

and chooses an individual to undertake a ministry within the life of the church. By extension, every person, irrespective of the nature of their calling, is a chosen instrument destined to be disposed towards the service of others. It follows that the response to one's calling from God is manifested as an activity of service within the Christian community, where, once someone is faced with the calling of God, Basil makes it clear that there is no shying away from "the inescapable nets of his grace" (τοῖς ἀφύκτοις δικτύοις τῆς χάριτος). On the occasion of Amphilochius' consecration to the episcopacy, Basil assured his modest spiritual child of the following:

> Blessed is God, who selects those in each generation who are pleasing to him and makes known the vessels (σκεύη) of his election, and uses them for the ministry (λειτουργία) of the saints; he who even now has ensnared you with the inescapable nets of his grace, when, as you yourself admit, you are trying to escape, not us, but the expected call through us, and who has brought you into the midst of Pisidia, so that you may take men captive for the Lord and bring those who had already been taken captive by the devil from the depths into the light according to his will. Therefore, you also may speak the words of the blessed David: "Whither shall I go from the spirit? or wither shall I flee thy face?"[90]

As Basil makes clear in the above quotation, it is not only because

---

90 *Ep.* 161.1: Deferrari, II, 411–413. Εὐλογητὸς ὁ Θεὸς ὁ τοὺς καθ 'ἑκάστην γενεὰν εὐαρεστοῦντας αὐτῷ ἐκλεγόμενος καὶ γνωρίζων τὰ σκεύη τῆς ἐκλογῆς καὶ κεχρημένος αὐτοῖς πρὸς τὴν λειτουργίαν τῶν ἁγίων, ὁ καὶ νῦν σε φεύγοντα, ὡς αὐτὸς φῄς, οὐχ ἡμᾶς, ἀλλὰ τὴν δι' ἡμῶν προσδοκωμένην κλῆσιν, τοῖς ἀφύκτοις δικτύοις τῆς χάριτος σαγηνεύσας καὶ ἀγαγὼν εἰς τὰ μέσα τῆς Πισιδίας, ὥστε ἀνθρώπους ζωγρεῖν τῷ Κυρίῳ καὶ ἕλκειν ἀπὸ τοῦ βυθοῦ εἰς τὸ φῶς τοὺς ἐζωγρημένους ὑπὸ τοῦ διαβόλου εἰς τὸ ἐκείνου θέλημα. Λέγε οὖν καὶ σὺ τὰ τοῦ μακαρίου Δαβίδ· «Ποῦ πορευθῶ ἀπὸ τοῦ Πνεύματός σου; καὶ ἀπὸ τοῦ προσώπου σου, που φύγω;» Courtonne, II, 92–93. See *Ep.* 188. Fedwick hints that this quote with its biblical references is a "paraphrase" of a prayer used for the service of ordination conducted in Basil's diocese. Given the pastoral nature of this letter that Basil addressed to Amphilochius, it would seem quite odd for Basil to be paraphrasing from the ordination service. From the liturgy that bears Basil's name, one would assume a paraphrase to include an invocation of God's name or the calling upon of the Holy Spirit. Fedwick, *The Church and the Charisma of Leadership*, 79.

of a person's own choosing that he becomes a leader entrusted with the exercise of ministry, but it is also (and more importantly) through the providence of God that the ordained minister has been given the charisma to fulfil his calling. Elsewhere Basil proclaims: "For the Lord knows who are his, and will bring forward those whom we perhaps do not expect".[91] In a letter to Ambrose, who at the time was recently ordained bishop of Milan, Basil affirms: "We have glorified our God who chooses in every generation those who are pleasing to him".[92] One senses that for Basil, the ordained minister's spiritual authority, which is not his own but has been entrusted to him to bring about "obedience to the faith" (ὑπακοὴν πίστεως),[93] binds him with an accountability to exercise his ministry worthily. According to Basil, true guidance of those entrusted to the spiritual care of the cleric allowed no room for pride or love of authority. On the contrary, Basil argued that to be a leader in the church was to participate in the works which directly manifested Christ's own authority of love. In this way, to be in the ordained ministry meant to be a living proof of Christ's love. Ultimately, for Basil, the cleric became the vessel that was used to impart divine grace amongst the communion of believers in the life of the church. For this reason Basil insisted that it behoved the cleric to manifest Christ, as this was proof of the cleric's spiritual disposition to work in communion with God, where all things were seen to "be done for edification" (πρὸς οἰκοδομὴν γινέσθω).[94] In his self-reflective advice to the Maritime bishops, Basil admonishes: "As long as we draw breath, we are obliged to overlook nothing that leads to the edification (οἰκοδομήν) of the

---

91 *Ep.* 28.2: Deferrari, I, 167–169. Οἶδε γὰρ Κύριος τοὺς ὄντας αὐτοῦ, καὶ ἀγάγοι ἂν εἰς τὸ μέσον τοὺς παρ' ἡμῶν τυχὸν οὐ προσδοκωμένους. Courtonne, I, 69.
92 *Ep.* 197.1: Deferrari, III, 91. Ἐδοξάσαμεν τὸν Θεὸν ἡμῶν τὸν καθ' ἑκάστην γενεὰν ἐκλεγόμενον τοὺς αὐτῷ εὐαρεστοῦντας. Courtonne, I, 150.
93 Rom. 1:5.
94 1 Cor. 14:26.

churches of Christ".⁹⁵

Basil regarded the office of the bishop (ἐπίσκοπος) to be the chosen vessel within the body of the church that was entrusted with proclaiming the correct teachings that were contained within the conscience of the church. Such a sacred task of being the "voice" of the church, of being responsible for expressing (as opposed to formulating), and of passing on the conscience of the church (tradition), Basil accepted was not for all.⁹⁶ As a chosen instrument of God, the bishop was called upon by Basil to maintain the pastoral care (ἐπιμέλεια) and solicitude (φροντίς) of Christ's flock.⁹⁷ When required, Basil also insisted that the bishop must "with all outspokenness refute those who do not walk uprightly according to the Gospel".⁹⁸

Within the ranks of the clergy, Basil considered the proclaimers of the Gospel to be the lips and eyes of the body of Christ. The clergy and specifically the bishops, through their lips, place their voices at the disposal of the Holy Spirit so that "words of eternal life" can be inscribed "in the hearts of the faithful".⁹⁹ The eyes of the clergy become instruments of the Holy Spirit "discerning good and evil, and guiding the members of Christ as circumstances require with regard to each one".¹⁰⁰ Through the liturgical and sacramental activity of the ordained minister, Basil believed that grace entered into physical existence, which in turn made possible the transformation of life onto a path that leads to salva-

---

95 *Ep.* 203.4: Deferrari, III, 153. Ἕως ἀναπνέομεν ὑπεύθηνοί ἐσμεν μηδὲν ἐλλιμπάνειν τῶν εἰς οἰκοδομὴν τῶν Ἐκκλησιῶν τοῦ Χριστοῦ. Courtonne, II, 171-172.
96 See *Ep.* 28.2.
97 See *Ep.* 197.
98 *Ep.* 250: Deferrari, IV, 7. Ἐν πάσῃ παρρησίᾳ ἔλεγχε τοὺς μὴ ὀρθοποδοῦντας πρὸς τὴν ἀλήθειαν τοῦ Εὐαγγελίου. Courtonne, III, 89. See Gal. 2:14.
99 Basil, *On Psalm 44*, 3: Way, *Saint Basil Exegetical Homilies*, 281. ῥήματα τῆς αἰωνίου ζωῆς ταῖς καρδίαις τῶν πιστευόντων. PG 29. 396A. See *Epp.* 50, 244.8.
100 Basil, *Herewith Begins the Morals*, 80.14: Wagner, *Saint Basil: Ascetical Works*, 201. Διακριτικοὺς μὲν ἀγαθῶν καὶ τῶν φαύλων, κατευθύνοντας δὲ τὰ μέλη τοῦ Χριστοῦ πρὸς τὰ ἑκάστῳ ἐπιβάλλοντα. PG 31. 865A.

tion. In the end Basil understood that it was Christ himself, as the initiator, provider and protector of ministry, who helped carry out the extraordinary work of the clergy. Basil was convinced that without Christ's input, there would be no ministry. When faced with the vocation of priesthood, Basil told his clerics not to be overwhelmed by its seemingly insurmountable burden, but rather instead to press on and continue commanding the ship God had entrusted to them, so as "to guide those who are on the way to salvation" (καθηγεῖσθαι τῶν σωζομένων).[101]

> Play the man, then, and be strong, and go before the people whom the Most High has entrusted to your right hand. And like a wise helmsman who has assumed the command of a ship, rise superior in your resolution to every blast [...] Do not lament that the weight is beyond your strength. For if it were you alone that were to bear this burden, it would not be merely heavy but utterly unendurable. But if it is the Lord who helps you bear it, "cast your care upon the Lord",[102] and he himself shall do it.[103]

Basil began his episcopal ministry in 370 amidst concerns that he had for the fate of Nicene Trinitarian doctrines in the East. Crucial to eliminating these concerns was ensuring doctrinal harmony first and foremost within his own ecclesiastical jurisdiction of Cappadocia and Armenia, and then by extension with presiding bishops in key seats elsewhere. Amongst the leading bishops of Nicene theology were Bishop Athanasius of Alexandria,[104] the principal defender of Nicaea, Peter of Alexandria (Athanasius'

---

101 *Ep.* 161.2: Deferrari, II, 415. Courtonne, II, 94.
102 See Ps. 55:23, 1Pet. 5:7.
103 *Ep.* 161.2: Deferrari, II, 413-415. Ἀνδρίζου τοίνυν καὶ ἴσχυε, καὶ προπορεύου τοῦ λαοῦ ὃν ἐπίστευσε τῇ δεξιᾷ σου ὁ Ὕψιστος. Καὶ ὡς νοήμων κυβέρνησιν ποιησάμενος, πάσης ζάλης [...] Βάρος δὲ ὑπερβαῖνον τὴν δύναμιν μὴ ὀδύρου. Εἰ μὲν γὰρ αὐτὸς ἦς ὁ μέλλων φέρειν τὸ βάσταγμα τοῦτο, οὐδὲ οὕτως ἂν ἦν βαρύ, ἀλλὰ φορητὸν παντελῶς. Εἰ δὲ Κύριος ὁ συνδιαφέρων, «Ἐπίρριψον ἐπὶ Κύριον τὴν μέριμνάν σου, καὶ αὐτὸς ποιήσει». Courtonne, II, 93-94.
104 See Chapter One.

successor), and Bishop Damasus of Rome. Together with the Nicene leaders from the East, such as Meletius of Antioch and Eusebius of Samosata, these bishops were called upon by Basil to present a united front in defence of Nicene Christianity. Basil asked that they "not let schisms loose among the churches", and that they should "by every means urge into unity (ἕνωσις) those who hold identical doctrines" to Nicaea.[105]

It has been already pointed out that the Alexandrians and Westerners supported Paulinus as the canonical bishop of Antioch since they esteemed him as a more trustworthy theologian than Meletius, and that this began a damaging schism among the Nicenes in the heartland of the Eastern capital.[106] Harmony within Cappadocia, the wider territory of the Antiochian church, as well as within the Alexandrian circle of influence, came about only when the semantics behind terms and definitions did not interfere with a common advocacy of Nicene Christianity.[107] In any event, one of Basil's main accusations against his opponents was their fickleness in oscillating (εὐμετάβολον) from one creedal confession to another. It was not that their credal changes ran along the same trajectory, resulting in an enhanced confession of faith, but rather that each new creed of theirs found itself in opposition to its predecessor. "These creeds", states Basil, "are opposed to one another". And as for the adherents to these creeds, Basil says, "they alike give proof of their fickleness of character, because of that fact that these men never stand by the same words".[108]

Amongst Nicene bishops, that which remained indisputable and unchangeable was the affirmation of the divinity of the Son

---

105 *Ep.* 69.2: Deferrari, II, 47. Μὴ ἐναφῶσι ταῖς Ἐκκλησίαις τὰ σχίσματα, ἀλλὰ τοὺς τὰ αὐτὰ φρονοῦντας παντὶ τρόπῳ εἰς ἕνωσιν συνελάσωσι. Courtonne, I, 164.
106 See Chapter Four.
107 See Gain, *L'Église de Cappadoce*, 374.
108 *Ep.* 244.9: Deferrari, III, 471. Τούτων δὲ τῶν πίστεων [...] πρὸς ἀλλήλας ἔχουσιν ἐναντίως, ἀλλ᾽ οὖν τὸ εὐμετάβολον τοῦ τρόπου ὁμοίως συνιστῶσι διὰ τὸ μηδέποτε αὐτοὺς ἐπὶ τῶν αὐτῶν ἑστάναι ῥημάτων. Courtonne, III, 83.

and the Holy Spirit. *Homoousios* never claimed to exhaust this affirmation but only to identify it. Its philosophical point was to establish that "being" is the same in the Father as it is in the Son and in the Holy Spirit. From a theological point of view, this is all that Basil was seeking. Although in Basil's letter *To the Deaconesses, Daughters of Count Terentius*, no mention is made of the term *homoousios*, nevertheless the Nicene faith is still affirmed because that alone testifies to the baptismal doxology of the entire church:

> You have believed in Father, Son, and Holy Spirit; do not prove false to this sacred trust: Father, the beginning of all things; only begotten Son, born from him, true God, perfect from perfect, living image, displaying the Father entirely in himself; Holy Spirit, with his subsistence from God, fount of holiness, power that gives life, grace that gives perfection, whereby man is adopted, and the mortal made immortal, joined to the Father and the Son in every phase of glory and eternity, of power and royalty, of sovereignty and divinity, as even the tradition of the baptism of salvation does testify.[109]

A key strategy in Basil's episcopal ministry was to fill up the dioceses where he could, especially in Eastern Anatolia, Armenia and Syria, with bishops that were loyal to Nicene faith through their doctrinal disposition, "that we may know with whom we shall be in agreement" (ἵνα γνῶμεν πρὸς τίνας ἡμῖν ἔσται ἡ συμφωνία).[110] This was to be achieved, firstly, through replenishing episcopal vacancies with suitable candidates and, secondly, through the

---

109 *Ep.* 105: Deferrari, II, 199–201. Εἰς Πατέρα καὶ Υἱὸν καὶ Ἅγιον Πνεῦμα πεπιστεύκατε· μὴ προδῶτε ταύτην τὴν παρακαταθήκην. Πατέρα τὴν πάντων ἀρχήν. Υἱὸν Μονογενῆ, ἐξ αὐτοῦ γεννηθέντα, ἀληθινὸν Θεόν, τέλειον ἐκ τελείου, εἰκόνα ζῶσαν, ὅλον δεικνύτα ἐν ἑαυτῷ τὸν Πατέρα· Πνεῦμα Ἅγιον, ἐκ Θεοῦ ὕπαρχον, τὴν πηγὴν τῆς ἁγιότητος, δύναμιν ζωῆς παρεκτικήν, χάριν τελειοποιόν, δ' οὗ υἱοθετεῖτε ἄνθρωπος καὶ ἀπαθανατίζεται τὸ θνητόν, συνημμένον Πατρὶ καὶ Υἱῷ κατὰ πάντα, ἐν δόξῃ καὶ ἐν ἀϊδιότητι, ἐν δυνάμει καὶ βασιλείᾳ, ἐν δεσποτείᾳ καὶ θεότητι, ὡς καὶ ἡ τοῦ σωτηρίου βαπτίσματος παράδοσις μαρτυρεῖ. Courtonne, II, 6–7.
110 *Ep.* 191: Deferrari, III, 81. Courtonne, II, 145.

creation of additional Nicene episcopal sees.¹¹¹ Difficulties arose when there were vacancies in episcopal sees, such as would occur when a hierarch passed away, because an uncertainty loomed over the doctrinal fidelity of a bishop's successor. When Bishop Athanasius of Ancyra passed away, Basil in his anguish cried out: "To whom shall we transfer the cares of the churches? [...] A man has fallen, who was in truth a pillar and foundation of the church". Basil warned the faithful: "There is no little danger that many will fall together with this support which has been taken from under them, and that the rottenness of certain persons will be laid bare".¹¹² Basil considered the death of Athanasius of Ancyra to be a great loss for the Nicene church, "a mouth has been sealed" (κέκλεισται στόμα). "The struggle", he concluded, "is not slight, that we may prevent the springing up again, over the election of a superintendent (τὴν ἐκλογὴν τοῦ προστατοῦντος), of strifes and dissentions, and the utter overturning, as the result of a petty quarrel, of all our labours".¹¹³

Basil hoped for a "fellowship of men of like faith (ὁμοδοξούντων κοινωνία), or, more truly, of the fellowship of men who obey the law of love and shun the peril of silence".¹¹⁴ Notwithstanding his

111 See *Ep.* 190.1: Σπουδὴ γενέσθω ἡμῖν πρότερον ταῖς μικροπολιτείαις ἤτοι μητροκωμίαις ταῖς ἐκ παλαιοῦ ἐπισκόπων θρόνον ἐχούσαις δοῦναι τοὺς προϊσταμένους. Courtonne, 142. "Let our zeal be, first to appoint overseers for the small towns and villages which of old had an episcopal seat". Deferrari, III, 73. There was great variation in the geographical and population sizes of the various sees under Basil's oversight. The larger the see in terms of its population, the more care Basil exerted in finding a replacement when there was a vacancy. See Gain, *L'Église de Cappadoce*, 80.
112 *Ep.* 29: Deferrari, I, 171-173. Πρὸς τίνα λοιπὸν τὰς φροντίδας τῶν ἐκκλησιαστικῶν ὑπερθώμεθα;... Πέπτωκεν ἀνήρ, στῦλος τῷ ὄντι καὶ ἑδραίωμα τῆς ἀληθείας [...] Κίνδυνος δὲ οὐ μικρὸς μὴ πολλοὶ τῷ ἐρείσματι τούτῳ ὑπεξαιρεθέντι συγκαταπέσωσι καὶ τὰ σαθρά τινων φανερὰ γένηται. Courtonne, I, 71.
113 *Ep.* 29: Deferrari, I, 173-175. Ὁ ἀγὼν οὐ μικρὸς μή τινες πάλιν ἔριδες καὶ διχοστασίαι, ἐπὶ τὴν ἐκλογὴν τοῦ μεταστάντος ἀναφυεῖσαι, πάντα ὁμοῦ τὸν κόπον ἐκ τῆς τυχούσης ἔριδος ἀνατρέψωσιν. Courtonne, I, 71.
114 *Ep.* 28: Deferrari, I, 169. Ὁμοδοξούντων κοινωνίαν, εἴτε καί, ὅπερ ἀληθέστερόν ἐστι, τῷ τῆς ἀγάπης πειθομένων νόμῳ καὶ τὸν ἐκ τοῦ σιωπῆσαι κίνδυνον ἐκκλινόντων. Courtonne, I, 69-70.

friends with ascetic dispositions who were in monasteries,[115] it became apparent that Basil was lacking a visible group of supporters in the world that he could call upon to fight for what he believed to be the church's theological causes. His search for new supporters was a constant aspect of his episcopal ministry, as were his sojourns within and outside his own province so as to strengthen ties amongst his own and neighbouring bishops. In the name of the communion of the church, Basil sought to promote his own ideas which revolved around the confession of a Nicene faith. Writing to Eusebius of Samosata, in response to Eusebius' concern about why he has not done more to present a greater defence of Nicene orthodoxy, he explained: "While ostensibly the majority of us are united with another [...] yet in reality they render us no assistance in the most urgent matters".[116] Some supporters of Basil, for example, irrespective of their elevation to ecclesiastical hierarchy, like his friend Gregory of Nazianzus, stayed attached to the ascetic and contemplative life.

The demand for the establishment of an orthodox consensus, a neo-Nicene coalition of Christian bishops, was so overpowering for Basil that in the end he utilised unconventional means to achieve his desired aim. Such measures could be interpreted as a breach of the canons. He was not afraid to chastise others who transgressed the same canonical laws. Despite obvious inconsistencies in his policies, Basil's actions were influenced by his crusade to get more Nicene bishops and especially those with suitable leadership. At one time he even agreed to the ordination of a neophyte, on the proviso that the neophyte was receiving spiritual guidance

---

115 See *Ep.* 207.2: Ἀνθρώπους ἔχουμεν τῆς εὐσεβείας ἀσκητάς, ἀποταξαμένους τῷ κόσμῳ καὶ πάσαις ταῖς βιωτικαῖς μερίμναις. Courtonne, II, 185. "We have men practised in piety, who have withdrawn from the world and earthly cares". Deferrari, III, 185.

116 *Ep.* 141.2: Deferrari, II, 341. Ἀλλὰ σχήματι μὲν δῆθεν οἱ πλείους ἐσμὲν μετ' ἀλλήλων [...] ἀληθείᾳ δὲ πρὸς οὐδὲν ἡμῖν τῶν ἀναγκαιοτάτων συναίρονται. Courtonne, II, 63.

from the bishop ordaining him.¹¹⁷ In *Ep.* 225 he defends his actions by emphatically denying that he breached any canons through his choice of ordinations. As was often the case, Basil believed that the "harm being done to the churches" (βλάβας τῶν ἐκκλησιῶν) was just too great for him not to act otherwise. Especially since "the harm is not confined to one or two men, but whole cities and peoples get the benefit, indirectly, of our misfortunes".¹¹⁸

Much to the resentment of his fellow hierarchs (particularly Bishop Anthimos of Tyana), Basil's drive for bishops saw him enter into areas outside his immediate ecclesiastical jurisdiction of Cappadocia Prima (Caesarea).¹¹⁹ In particular, the neighbouring ecclesiastical province of Cappadocia Secunda (Tyana) proved to be a resource of new bishops for him.¹²⁰ At times Basil moved and transferred bishops with little or no notice¹²¹ if he determined that they were needed to fulfil his responsibility of "the burden of looking out for the churches" (τὸ βάρος τῆς φροντίδος τῶν ἐκκλησιαστικῶν).¹²² Basil maintained that the sacrifices made by a local church, in having its bishop transferred, were for the benefit of the communion of the church. His understanding was that the faithful should "not look to the present" (μὴ τὸ παρὸν ὁρᾶν)¹²³ and thus the local, but rather to the eternal and lasting needs of the whole church. Basil had no qualms in enacting these transfers since with confidence and assertiveness he insisted that "the

---

117 See *Ep.* 217.
118 *Ep.* 59.3: Deferrari, II, 7–9. Ἡ βλάβη οὐκ εἰς ἕνα ἢ δεύτερον περιορίζεται, ἀλλὰ πόλεις ὅλαι καὶ δῆμοι τῶν ἡμετέρων παραπολαύουσι συμφορῶν. Courtonne, I, 149.
119 See *Epp.* 99.3-4, 190, 216.
120 It is true that Basil struggled to accept Cappadocia as being divided into two provinces (see Chapter Three). Ecclesiastically he saw Caesarea and thus himself as having jurisdictional oversight over Tyana (Cappadocia Secunda) since this was constitutive to maintaining "peace" and "harmony" within his own diocese and by extension within the general Christian communion. See *Ep.* 97: Deferrari, II, 161.
121 See *Epp.* 227, 228.
122 *Ep.* 227: Deferrari, III, 347. Courtonne, III, 31.
123 *Ep.* 240: Deferrari, III, 423. Courtonne, III, 62.

arrangement of the most God-beloved bishops [...] has been according to God's wish"[124] and "with the counsel of the Spirit" (τῇ συμβουλίᾳ τοῦ Πνεύματος).[125] In 375, Euphronius, the much loved prelate of Colonia,[126] was transferred from the "distant spot" of Colonia in Lesser Armenia[127] and positioned in the diocesan see of Nicopolis.[128] This took place so as to challenge the unrecognised Fronto, a rival bishop with Sabellianist persuasions whom Basil described as "a common abomination to all Armenia" (κοινὸν βδέλυγμα πάσης τῆς Ἀρμενίας).[129] Fronto had appeared to fill the episcopal vacancy created by the death of Theodotus, the metropolitan of Nicopolis. "Who will doubt", explains Basil to the clergy of Nicopolis about the pro-Nicene Euphronius' swift transfer to Nicopolis, that these "plans came into being by communion with our Lord Jesus Christ".[130]

In his quest for the unity and strength of the Nicene communion of churches, Basil took it upon himself unilaterally to ordain bishops without synodal approval,[131] and furthermore to coerce some of his closest friends and associates to accept ordination. He began a successful campaign of gerrymandering through establishing new bishoprics in his province of Caesarea. In defence of Nicaea, Basil created episcopal allies whom he could then use to acquire much needed votes at synodical meetings. This certainly

---

124 *Ep.* 227: Deferrari, III, 349. Τὴν τῶν θεοφιλεστάτων ἐπισκόπων οἰκονομίαν κατὰ βούλησιν Θεοῦ γενομένην. Courtonne, III, 32.
125 *Ep.* 229.1: Deferrari, III, 353. Courtonne, III, 33.
126 The clergy and laity of Colonia were so upset at losing their beloved bishop that they even threatened to take legal action ("have recourse to the courts" – τὰ δικαστήρια καταληψόμεθα) so as to contest the decision of having their bishop removed. See *Ep.* 227: Deferrari, III, 347. Courtonne, III, 31.
127 Today North-eastern Turkey.
128 See *Ep.* 227. Nicopolis (today Koyulhisar in North-eastern Turkey) was the capital of the Roman province of Lesser Armenia and was located some forty kilometres south-east of Colonia.
129 *Ep.* 239.1: Deferrari, III, 417. Courtonne, III, 60.
130 *Ep.* 229.1: Deferrari, III, 353. Κοινωνίᾳ τῇ τοῦ Κυρίου ἡμῶν Ἰησοῦ Χριστοῦ [...] τὴν βουλὴν γεγενῆσθαι. Courtonne, III, 34.
131 See *Epp.* 81, 99.4, 102, 103.

was the case with his former school friend Gregory, by then a priest in Nazianzus, who in 372 was consecrated as the bishop of Sasima, a tiny village with only twenty-two residents.[132] Although a village, Sasima was strategically located in that in was situated on the border between the two newly divided provinces of Cappadocia Prima and Cappadocia Secunda. Winning the village's episcopal loyalty was a key to strengthening Basil's jurisdiction and thus supporting his Nicene theological causes.[133] Basil's younger brother, Gregory, received similar treatment to Gregory of Nazianzus when he was made the newly ordained bishop of Nyssa towards the end of the same year in 372. The initial call for both these men was to act as warriors in support of Basil's causes and to support his authority in the face of theological division amongst Cappadocian bishops. In the end it was only Gregory of Nyssa who paid heed to Basil's summons, even if this was somewhat short-lived. Gregory of Nazianzus, on the other hand, never turned up to resume responsibilities in Sasima. Gregory acted in this way both as a protest against his forced ordination and because he wanted to remain firm in his resolve to live out a solitary life of prayer and contemplation.[134] Unperturbed, Basil's determination for ecclesial fellowship and communion continued at all costs.

In his endeavour to bring about unity within the Christian church, Basil identified that this unity could only be maintained through hierarchal officers and their jurisdictional connections. In other words, unity and therefore ecclesiastical communion are to be demonstrated through harmony and concord amongst the bishops who were called by Basil to conduct their ministry "in harmony and accord with all the churches of God" (ταῖς τοῦ Θεοῦ

---

132 See *Epp.* 48–50 for an overview of these events.
133 Sterk, *Renouncing the World Yet leading the Church*, 81–82.
134 See Gregory of Nazianzus, *Ep.* 49, *Oration* 10.1–2, 11.3. In his defence, Basil would argue that Sasima was just the place for Gregory in that it was small, relatively hassle free and outside the mainstream of ecclesiastical affairs. See *Ep.* 48.2–3.

ἐκκλησίαις συνῳδά ἐστι καὶ σύμφωνα).¹³⁵ Such a conviction is not abstract and relative, as Van Dam infers,¹³⁶ but rather is seen by Basil as being part and parcel of the natural and necessary characteristics of communion (χαρακτήρων τὰ τῆς ἐπιμιξίας σύμβολα).¹³⁷ In its most essential form, where there is fraternity and mutual recognition amongst the bishops, therein exists the communion of the Christian church. To the Neocaesareans, Basil explains: "It would be more just that our affairs be judged, not by one or two, who do not walk uprightly according to the truth, but by the multitude of bishops throughout the world who are united with us (τὴν οἰκουμένην ἐπισκόπων συνημμένων ἡμῖν) by the grace of the Lord".¹³⁸ Anyone thus separated from the communion of bishops was considered to be separated from the Lord and deprived of all truth. To certain Neocaesareans who were considered to be having allegiances to a Sabellian movement, Basil exhorts:

> For while I am deprived of you, you are being robbed of the truth; and while he who is responsible for this is separating me from you, he is alienating himself from the Lord; because it is not possible for one to become united with God through that which is forbidden. On your account, therefore, rather than my own do I utter these words, and to rescue you from an unbearable injury. For what greater evil could one suffer than the loss of truth, of all things the most precious?¹³⁹

---

135 *Ep.* 208.3: Deferrari, III, 187. Courtonne, II, 186.
136 Van Dam, *Emperors, Bishops and Friends in Late Antique Cappadocia*, 71.
137 *Ep.* 203.3: Deferrari, III, 151. Courtonne, II, 171.
138 *Ep.* 204.7: Deferrari, III, 171. Δικαιότερον δὲ τὰ καθ᾿ ἡμᾶς κρίνεσθαι μὴ ἐξ ἑνὸς ἢ δευτέρου τῶν μὴ ὀρθοποδούντων πρὸς τὴν ἀλήθειαν, ἀλλ᾿ ἐκ τοῦ πλήθους τῶν κατὰ τὴν οἰκουμένην ἐπισκόπων συνημμένων ἡμῖν χάριτι τοῦ Κυρίου. Courtonne, II, 179.
139 *Ep.* 204.3: Deferrari, III, 161. Ἐγὼ μὲν γὰρ ὑμᾶς ἀποστεροῦμαι, ὑμεῖς δὲ τὴν ἀλήθειαν ἀφαιρεῖσθε, καὶ ὁ τούτων αἴτιος ἐμὲ μὲν ὑμῶν διίστησιν, ἑαυτὸν δὲ ἀλλοτριοῖ τοῦ Κυρίου, διότι οὐκ ἔστι Θεῷ ἐκ τῶν ἀπογορευμένων οἰκειωθῆναι. Ὑμῶν οὖν μᾶλλον ἕνεκεν ἢ ἐμαυτοῦ ποιοῦμαι τοὺς λόγους καὶ τοῦ ὑμᾶς ἐξελέσθαι βλάβης οὐκ ἀνεκτῆς. Τί γὰρ ἂν καὶ μεῖζον πάθοι κακόν τις τὸ τιμιώτατον τῶν ὄντων ζημιωθεὶς τὴν ἀλήθειαν; Courtonne, II, 175.

The head of the Christian community for Basil was no one else but Christ himself, whereas the initiator and maintainer of communion came about through the inspiration of the Holy Spirit. Within the analogy of a "body",[140] one of the three main metaphors that he uses to depict the church ("garment" and "ship" being the other metaphors),[141] he maintained that the limbs and organs of this body where subordinate to its head. For Basil the bishops of the Christian church are only part of the body of the church when they are subordinate to Christ its head.

5.3 The Assistant Bishop in Basil's Church

Assistant or suffragan bishops (χωρεπίσκοποι) first see the light of ministry after the second half of the first century and initially in Italy.[142] After 249, the ordination of bishops for villages became increasingly more prominent. An obvious indication of this is the way that the number of bishops in a given province exceeds the number of cities contained within that province. Prior to this, it makes sense to assume that the village people would travel into the cities so as to participate in the Eucharist that was officiated by the local bishop. In his comprehensive study, F. Gillmann challenges this view by holding that already from the first century, when Christianity spread to regional areas, bishoprics were established in the countryside.[143] However, this as an unlikely possibility, since it presupposes that assistant bishops appeared automatically in

---

140 See *Ep.* 97.
141 See Chapter Four.
142 During the reign of Antonius (138–161), for example, Bishop Alexander had pastoral oversight over a country area called vicus Baccansis in Tuscany. In like manner, other country areas of Italy are recorded as having episcopal oversight. It would be anachronistic to assume that the bishops of these country areas were called χωρεπίσκοποι from as early as the first century. What is important here is that already from the first century there were some places like Italy that had bishops residing in country areas. See Hefele and Leclercq, *Histoire des Conciles*.
143 Gillmann, *Das Institut der Chorbischöfe im Orient*, 74. See Stewart, *The Original Bishops: Office and Order in the First Christian Communities*, 11–54.

villages where Christians were living. The fact that there is no mention of assistant bishops in first or even early second-century literature calls into question the assumption that assistant bishops appeared during this early Christian period.

It was not always easy for the Christians of the countryside to align themselves with the city bishop and his congregation. Detached from eucharistic communion in the city, such Christians in time were provided with their own bishops so as to form their own local churches to celebrate the Eucharist. As a result, new churches, each under the pastorship of a bishop, were established in villages. In this way the principle of one bishop serving one Eucharist in one church was preserved. Today this practice seems to be the function of a parish priest in that each parish priest, serving in the name of the bishop, presides over each eucharistic community.

Within his diocese Basil had assistant bishops at his disposal, and going by his *Epp.* 53 and 54, his first encounter with them upon his installation as their presiding hierarch proved to be unsettling as he instantly implemented changes to their responsibilities. As will be shown further below, these changes involved taking away a significant portion of their authority, while insisting that they attend to the oversight of poorhouses, act on his orders and, when required, be his proxy.[144] These moves by Basil raised questions about the jurisdictional authority of the assistant bishops. Assistant bishops, it seems, occupied an office inferior to that of the urban bishop but superior to that of the presbyter.[145] Rather than having full episcopal power and jurisdictional autonomy, the assistant bishops were treated by Basil more like presbyters, or at least like presbyters today. Conversely, this could also mean that the presbyters of today fulfil much the same role as the (assistant) bishops of Basil's time. The fact that the office of the presbyter today is con-

---

144 See *Epp.* 24, 142, 143, 291.
145 Cooper and Decker, *Life and Society in Byzantine Cappadocia*, 144.

ducted in the name of the bishop certainly adds weight to this understanding. Whatever the case may be, it is certainly true that for Basil the rights of the assistant bishop, even within his own territory (παροικία), closely depended upon the bishop of the city. A comparative study of the canons in effect during the years surrounding Basil's episcopacy[146] reveals a gradual decline in the rights and importance of assistant bishops. The tenth canon of the local Council of Antioch in 341, for example, confines the assistant bishops to ordaining only members of the lower clergy. Specifically the canon mentions that assistant bishops are to: "appoint readers, subdeacons and exorcists, and shall be content with [only] promoting these".[147] Conveniently, Basil relied on such and other "canons of the Fathers" (τῶν πατέρων κανόνες)[148] in his endeavours to curtail and limit the negative influences of his assistant bishops. By 381, at the Council of Laodicea, the institution of the assistant bishop was all but gone. According to its 57th canon: "Bishops must not be appointed in villages or country districts, but visitors [as in visiting priests – περιοδευτάς]".[149] Basil's two letters: "To the Suffragan Bishops" (χωρεπισκόποις),[150] written at the commencement of his episcopate in 370, did little in terms of promoting their cause:

> But now you, in the first place, thrusting me aside, and not even consenting to refer matters to me, have arrogated to yourselves the entire authority [...] Therefore, since I perceive that the situation is already approaching the incur-

---

146 Namely canons from the local councils: 13th of Ancyra (314), 14th of Neocaesarea (314–325), 10th of Antioch (341), 6th of Sardica (343–344) and 57th of Laodicea (343–385).
147 Synod of Antioch, Canon 10: Percival, NPNF, vol. 14, 113. Καθιστᾶν δὲ ἀναγνώστας, καὶ ὑποδιακόνους, καὶ ἐφορκιστὰς, καὶ τῇ τούτων ἀρκεῖσθαι προαγωγῇ. Ραφτάνη, Πηδάλιον, 412.
148 *Ep.* 54: Deferrari, I, 343. Courtonne, I, 139.
149 Synod of Laodicea, Canon 57: Percival, 158. Οὐ δεῖ ἐν ταῖς κώμαις καὶ ἐν ταῖς χώραις καθίστασθαι ἐπισκόπους, ἀλλὰ περιοδευτάς. Ραφτάνη, Πηδάλιον, 441.
150 *Epp.* 53, 54.

able [...] I have been compelled to resort to the renewal of the canons of the Fathers.¹⁵¹

It is beyond dispute that Basil's elevation into the ranks of the episcopacy brought with it changes to the administrative running of his diocese. In particular, changes were introduced in the way that candidates to the priesthood were elected, with special emphasis given to the episcopacy. Scrutiny for a start was applied to all candidates for the clergy, as also a written recommendation from Basil's episcopal colleagues testifying to the ethical conduct of the candidates, especially those seeking elevation to the episcopacy.¹⁵² Basil's *Moralia* details his concerns over the necessity of church leaders to have an impeccable reputation that is beyond reproach.¹⁵³ In his endeavours to examine the lives of prospective candidates, Basil would readily admit that "it is not easy to find worthy men" (οὐκ εὔκολον εὑρεῖν ἄνδρας ἀξίους).¹⁵⁴ Deeply rooted in Basil's mind was the question: What is it that a candidate priest must do and possess so as to embrace worthily the ministry of the priesthood? Basil's intention was to "purge the church by excluding those [candidates] who are unworthy of her".¹⁵⁵ His statements speak for themselves: "Gone is the dignity of the priesthood. None are left to tend the flock of the Lord with knowledge (μετ᾿ ἐπιστήμης)".¹⁵⁶ Basil declared: "The wisdom of the world takes first place to itself, having thrust aside the glory of the Cross".¹⁵⁷

151 *Ep.* 54: Deferrari, I, 345. Νῦν δὲ πρῶτον μὲν ἡμᾶς παρωσάμενοι καὶ μηδὲ ἐπαναφέρειν ἡμῖν κατεδεχόμενοι, εἰς ἑαυτοὺς τὴν ὅλην περιεστήσατε αὐθεντίαν [...] Ἐπεὶ οὖν ὁρῶ τὸ πρᾶγμα λοιπὸν εἰς ἀνήκεστον προϊόν [...] ἀναγκαίως ἦλθον εἰς τὸ ἀνανεώσασθαι τοὺς τῶν Πατέρων κανόνας. Courtonne, I, 140.
152 See *Ep.* 121.
153 See *Moralia* 70.37: PG 31. 844D-845A.
154 *Ep.* 190.1: Deferrari, III, 71. Courtonne, II, 141.
155 *Ep.* 54: Deferrari, I, 347. Ἐπικαθαρίσατε τὴν Ἐκκλησίαν τοὺς ἀναξίους αὐτῆς ἀπελαύνοντες. Courtonne, I, 140.
156 *Ep.* 92.2: Deferrari, II, 137-139. Οἴχεται σεμνότης ἱερατική, ἐπιλελοίπασιν οἱ ποιμαίνοντες μετ᾿ ἐπιστήμης τὸ ποίμνιον τοῦ Κυρίου. Courtonne, I, 200.
157 *Ep.* 90.2: Deferrari, II, 125. Ἡ τοῦ κόσμου σοφία τὰ πρωτεῖα φέρεται, παρωσαμένη τὸ καύχημα τοῦ σταυροῦ. Courtonne, I, 196.

It is true that in Basil's day, clerics were often promoted to higher levels of ordination and ecclesiastical honours in haste, without being conscientiously examined beforehand, and without any experience in the lower clerical orders. In particular, one is led to infer that there were unrestrained and ambitious candidates who attained ecclesiastical offices at the expense of worthy candidates. Often the worthy candidates, because of their humility (as seen through their commitment to Christian virtue or their pursuit of a monastic life), were overlooked and totally excluded. Such humility and selflessness were esteemed as first among the virtues for Basil: "For this indeed is the law of victory among Christians, and it is he who has consented to hold an inferior place that is crowned".[158] The office of the priesthood for Basil required a humble person, and personal qualifications which were so essential to the ministry of the cleric had to be demonstrated indirectly. Consequently, for Basil, the unacceptable motive of ambition was regarded as a dangerous impediment to the spiritual disposition of the priest and was guaranteed to have negative repercussions on the effectiveness of his ministry. It was no wonder then that Basil viewed disturbances in the church as also arising from the negligent and unrestricted manner in which members of the clergy were elected. Against a background of heresy, factionalism and alleged incompetence in the ordained orders, Basil sought a reform in the church that was to be empowered by ascetic virtues.

Prior to Basil assuming episcopal responsibility in Caesarea, all candidates to the priesthood in Caesarea were accepted based on the recommendation of the assistant bishop (χωρεπίσκοπος). The problem that Basil encountered with this was that the assistant bishops would chose candidates to the priesthood from within their family networks or, where this was not possible, from within the circle of their family friends. In one of his letters to his

---

158 *Ep.* 191: Deferrari, III, 79. Καὶ γὰρ οὗτος νόμος τῆς ἐν χριστιανοῖς νίκης καὶ ὁ ἔλαττον ἔχειν καταδεξάμενος στεφανοῦται. Courtonne, II, 144.

assistant bishops, Basil remarks:

> You have allowed priests and deacons, selecting whomsoever they pleased, without examining into their lives, through motives of partiality based either upon kinship or upon some other friendly relationship, to introduce into the church unworthy men (ἐπεισάγειν τῇ Ἐκκλησίᾳ τοὺς ἀναξίους).[159]

Basil found that every candidate to the priesthood was also expected to come up with a gift of some monetary value which was given to the elector bishop. This gift was somehow assessed by the ordaining bishop as being evidence of the candidate's piety. Hence Basil's comment: "The report is that some of you take money from candidates for ordination, and cover it up under the name of piety (εὐσεβείας)".[160] In response to such overt simony, he made use of the Pauline text: "We and the churches of God have no such custom".[161] He also warned his assistant bishops: "If you sell what you have received as a free gift, you will be deprived of all its grace, as if you yourself were sold to Satan".[162] Basil wasted no time in reproving assistant bishops guilty of simony. In particular he laid all blame for the atrocities affecting the church on the careless ordination selections of assistant bishops. Although, as has been shown above, Basil had no problem ordaining to the bishopric personal friends or even members within his own family such as his brother Gregory, he clearly was not afraid of avoiding such ordinations if they would in any way interfere with

---

159 *Ep.* 54: Deferrari, I, 345. Πρεσβυτέροις καὶ διακόνοις ἐπετρέψατε οὓς ἂν ἐθέλωσιν ἀπὸ ἀνεξετάστου βίου, κατὰ προσπάθειαν, ἢ τὴν ἀπὸ συγγενείας, ἢ τὴν ἐξ ἄλλης τινὸς φιλίας, ἐπεισάγειν τῇ Ἐκκλησίᾳ τοὺς ἀναξίους. Courtonne, I, 140.
160 *Ep.* 53.1: Deferrari, I, 339. Φασί τινές ὑμῶν παρὰ τῶν χειροτονουμένων λαμβάνειν χρήματα, ἐπισκιάζειν δὲ ὀνόματι εὐσεβείας. Courtonne, I, 137–138.
161 1 Cor. 11:16. Ἡμεῖς τοιαύτην συνήθειαν οὐκ ἔχομεν οὐδὲ αἱ ἐκκλησίαι τοῦ Θεοῦ.
162 *Ep.* 53.1: Deferrari, I, 339. Ὃ σὺ δωρεὰν ἔλαβες, ἐὰν πωλῇς, ὡσανεὶ πεπραμένος τῷ Σατανᾷ ἀφαιρεθήσῃ τοῦ χαρίσματος. Courtonne, I, 138.

the edification of the communion of the church or with service to God. Basil insisted that holy orders must transcend personal friendships. Ecclesiastical appointments, he argued, needed to be decided upon without contention, through prayer and with complete trust in God.[163] It was precisely because of expedient ordinations and the ensuing spiritual deterioration and moral degradation created within the Christian communion that Basil asserted, by right of being the metropolitan bishop, that he would have the final say when it came to the appointment of any member of the clergy.[164] By calling upon the tradition of the "canons of the Fathers" and thus "the practice that has long been followed in God's Churches",[165] Basil was able to keep at bay the ambitions and briberies that were previously associated with some candidates to the priesthood. Specifically the 13th canon of Ancyra in 314 stands out: "It is not lawful for assistant bishops (χωρεπίσκοποι) to ordain presbyters or deacons [...] without written permission from the bishop".[166] From now on, anyone received into the holy orders without Basil's approval "will be still a layman" (λαϊκὸς ἔσται).[167]

Basil understood the priesthood as being an extension of the

---

163 See *Ep.* 290.10-13.
164 *Epp.* 120-122, 126, 127, 216 all talk about ecclesiastical disputes of various kinds and most importantly bear witness to Basil's attempts to prevent non-canonical ordinations.
165 *Ep.* 54: Deferrari, I, 343. Ἡ πάλαι ταῖς τοῦ Θεοῦ Ἐκκλησίαις ἐμπολιτευμένη συνήθεια. Courtonne, I, 139. Basil opens his letter "To the Assistant Bishops" with the criticism that they have neglected church canon law: Πάνυ με λυπεῖ ὅτι ἐπιλελοίπασι λοιπὸν οἱ τῶν Πατέρων κανόνες καὶ πᾶσα ἀκρίβεια τῶν Ἐκκλησιῶν ἀπελήλαται, καὶ φοβοῦμαι μή, κατὰ μικρὸν τῆς ἀδιαφορίας ταύτης ὁδῷ προϊούσης, εἰς παντελῆ σύγχυσιν ἔλθῃ τὰ τῆς Ἐκκλησίας πράγματα. *Ep.* 54: Courtonne, I, 139. "It gives me great pain that the canons of the Fathers have lately fallen into neglect, and that all discipline has been banished from the churches. I fear that, as this indifference proceeds, the affairs of the church will gradually come to complete ruin". Deferrari, I, 343.
166 Council of Ancyra, Canon 13: See Percival, 68. Χωρεπισκόποις μὴ ἐξεῖναι, πρεσβυτέρους ἢ διακόνους χειροτονεῖν [...] χωρὶς τοῦ ἐπιτραπῆναι ὑπὸ τοῦ ἐπισκόπου μετὰ γραμμάτων. Ραφτάνη, Πηδάλιον, 377.
167 *Ep.* 54: Deferrari, I, 347. Courtonne, 1, 140.

ministry and the salvific work of its prototype Christ. From the Scriptures he argued that Christ entrusted (πιστευθῆναι) the deposit of his message (εὐαγγέλιον)[168] to the chosen vessels (σκεῦος ἐκολογῆς)[169] of his divine grace, the apostles. Basil believed that so also should the ministry of the priesthood be allotted to those who are called, through a life of sanctity, to be a chosen vessel of God's divine grace. Here worldly attributes (which are not always evil in themselves), such as prestige, family and good standing in society, are not only a distant second but can also be vehemently opposed to the nature of priesthood. Basil saw that it was through the distractions and temptations attached to worldly attributes that the ministry of priesthood was misconstrued.

5.4 Conclusion

In Basil's letters, communion at a parochial and diocesan level is essentially one and the same thing. It is the diocese that gives life to the parochial church, while it is in the life of the parochial church where church life is mostly realised. As this chapter makes clear, the central idea of Basil in his letters is communion at a parochial and diocesan level. In this chapter it has been shown that communion in a parochial setting concerned itself with the believer and his or her relationship with God within the community of believers. What began at baptism was renewed through repentance, and had as its aim communion with God as expressed through participation in the Eucharist. All parochial churches under the spiritual oversight of a diocesan bishop were regarded by Basil as being in communion with each other by right of association with that bishop. A bishop and his churches were said to be in communion with God only when they adhered to a Nicene confession of faith. In Basil's letters, the communion of the church was essentially a communion of churches that confessed a Nicene faith. It was the

---

168 See 1 Thess. 2:4.
169 See Acts 9:15.

role of the diocesan bishop together with his assistant bishops, to lead their churches in accordance to the Nicene communion of churches. Basil exemplified this role. He argued that it behoved all his brother bishops to do the same.

Chapter Six:
Basil on Communion at a Universal Level: Inter-episcopal Communion

In many ways, up until now, communion in the church, according to Basil, has been looked at from a personal level. As just witnessed in Chapter Five, this specifically involved identifying the communion of the individual believer with his or her being in sacramental communion with the local bishop. It now remains for Basil to say what it is that makes a local bishop of a particular diocese to be in communion with all bishops and thus all dioceses of the universal church. This final chapter explores Basil's understanding of communion at a universal level as it is manifested through inter-episcopal communion letters. It begins by highlighting the importance of bishops meeting together at synodical gatherings. For Basil it was essential that such bishops shared a Nicene faith. Furthermore, this chapter considers Basil's view of the presence of heresy and its implications for the Nicene communion of churches, and focuses on Basil's claim that where heresy is present, communion remains unguarded. The last section of this chapter examines the collective authority of the Nicene communion of bishops and their innate responsibility to manifest the one church.

6.1 The Synods of the Bishops

Fundamental to Basil's understanding of the identity of the church was his unreserved notion that the church is one. According to Basil, all who belong to the one church, pray and believe in the same thing. Basil states: "Our Lord is one, our faith one, our hope the same".[1] The proceeding chapter noted how, for Basil, unity in the *one Lord* is manifested first and foremost in worship and pre-eminently in the Eucharist. The preservation of the *one Eucharist* in each church was guaranteed through the leadership of the presiding bishop. In a similar vein to the Ignatian ideal,[2] Basil subscribed to the view that where the bishop is, there also will be the Eucharist and the unity of the church:

> Yet assuredly the limbs of the church knitted together by his [the bishop's] superintendence (προστασίας) as by a soul, and joined into a union of sympathy and true communion (ἀκριβῆ κοινωνίαν), are not only steadfastly preserved by the bond of peace (συνδέσμου τῆς εἰρήνης) for the spiritual communion (πνευματικὴν ἁρμολογίαν), but will also be preserved for ever.[3]

Basil's exhortation was for all churches in a given ecclesiastical eparchy to remain united in one Eucharist, under one bishop "since he who by the grace of God is the bishop is the man upon whom the care of his church falls chiefly".[4] For Basil, the oneness of the church is expressed at its most authoritative and "best" (ἄριστον) level when the bishops of every local church are in "ecclesiastical communion"

---

1   *Ep.* 203.3: Deferrari, III, 149. Εἷς ἡμῶν Κύριος, μία πίστις, ἐλπὶς ἡ αὕτη. Courtonne, II, 170.
2   See Ignatius of Antioch, *To the Philadelphians*, 4: Μία γὰρ σὰρξ τοῦ Κυρίου ἡμῶν Ἰησοῦ Χριστοῦ, καὶ ἓν ποτήριον εἰς ἕνωσιν τοῦ αἵματος αὐτοῦ· ἓν θυσιαστήριον, ὡς εἷς ἐπίσκοπος. Holmes, *The Apostolic Fathers*, 238. "There is one flesh of our Lord Jesus Christ, and one cup that leads to unity through his blood; there is one altar, just as there is one bishop". Holmes, *The Apostolic Fathers*, 239.
3   *Ep.* 29: Deferrari, I, 173. Ἀλλὰ μὴν τά γε συναφθέντα μέλη τῆς Ἐκκλησίας, οἷον ὑπὸ ψυχῆς τινος, τῆς ἐκείνου προστασίας εἰς μίαν συμπάθειαν καὶ ἀκριβῆ κοινωνίαν συναρμοσθέντα, καὶ φυλάσσεται διὰ τοῦ συνδέσμου τῆς εἰρήνης πρὸς τὴν πνευματικὴν ἁρμολογίαν παγίως καὶ φυλαχθήσεται εἰς ἀεί. Courtonne, I, 71. Deferrari translates the word for κοινωνίαν as "fellowship", which inadvertently conveys a weaker connection than one conceived in the directly translated word "communion".
4   *Ep.* 156.2: Deferrari, II, 387. Ὄντος τοῦ ἐπισκόπου τῇ τοῦ Θεοῦ χάριτι, ᾧ ἡ φροντὶς ἀνήκει προηγουμένως τῆς Ἐκκλησίας. Courtonne, II, 83.

(κοινωνίας [...] ἐκκλησιατικῆς)⁵ with each other. Commenting on this, Fedwick states: "ecclesial unity would manifest itself chiefly in the Eucharist".⁶ Basil, in his letter to Patrophilus, the bishop of the church at Aegae, writes: "Now if you should remain in communion with me (εἰ μὲν οὖν ἐν τῇ πρὸς ἡμᾶς κοινωνίᾳ) this is best and worthy of most earnest prayer" (τοῦτο ἄριστον καὶ εὐχῆς τῆς ἀνωτάτω ἄξιον).⁷ Only when the bishop of Aegae was in communion with Basil could he still be regarded as a bishop, whereas outside this communion, in Basil's view, he ceased to be a bishop and his office within the church became defunct.

Bishops who were in communion with each other were called, where possible, to celebrate the Eucharist together. Basil considered this practice to be a necessary characteristic (χαρακτήρων)⁸ of communion and for this reason he spoke of "communion in prayer" (προσευχαῖς κοινωνίαν) as bringing about "great gain" (πολὺ κέρδος φέρουσαν).⁹ In his diocese of Caesarea, on the occasion of its local feast day in honour of St. Eupsychius celebrated on September the 7th, he made it a "custom to celebrate annually in honour of the martyrs" (δι' ἔτος ἄγειν ἐπὶ τοῖς μάρτυσιν ἔθος).¹⁰ When bishops celebrated the memory of a martyr, they were declaring their allegiance to the same faith of the martyr and in this way were manifesting their communion of faith.¹¹ On the feast of Basil's patron saint,¹² bishops came together to participate in the festivities honouring St. Eupsychius in a spirit of trust and fellowship which culminated in the celebration of the Eucharist. It was not uncommon for the bishops to come up to three days before

---

5   Ep. 265.3: Deferrari, IV, 117. Courtonne, III, 131.
6   Fedwick, The Church and the Charisma of Leadership, xiv.
7   Ep. 244.9: Deferrari, III, 473. Courtonne, III, 83.
8   203.3: Deferrari, III, 151. Courtonne, II, 171.
9   Ep. 150.2: Deferrari, II, 367. Courtonne, II, 73. In this instance Deferrari has translated the word for κοινωνίαν as "association", see n. 3.
10 Ep. 176: Deferrari, II, 459. Courtonne, II, 112. See Chapter One, n. 91.
11 See Finn, Almsgiving in the Later Roman Empire, 9.
12 See Epp. 100, 142, 252.

the feast day itself so as to participate in an episcopal synod.[13] In his invitation to his brother bishops, Basil wrote: "Accordingly we urge you to arrive three days beforehand, in order that you may also make great by your presence the memorial chapel of the house of the poor".[14]

Attendance at a synodical gathering of bishops meant inclusion in both doctrinal and social terms. It was Basil's principle that if a person agreed "with the sound doctrine of faith" (τῷ ὑγιαίνοντι λόγῳ τῆς πίστεως), then that person could be accepted as "sharing in communion with the saints" (κοινωνὸν ἡγήσασθαι τῶν ἁγίων).[15] Those who disagreed with the doctrinal affiliation of the synodical gathering of bishops, did so by refraining from the synaxis. From Basil's letters, one learns that some of those attending a Nicene gathering of bishops were Eusebius of Samosata, Amphilochius of Iconium, and the bishops of the diocese of Pontus.[16] Amongst other things, the purpose of Basil's gathering of bishops was to "converse at leisure with each other and be mutually consoled through the communion of spiritual gifts (διὰ τῆς κοινωνίας τῶν πνευματικῶν χαρισμάτων)".[17] In this environment, Basil took it upon himself to be a champion for the Nicene theological cause, especially for the region of Asia Minor: "We, being publicly exposed to all, like headlands jutting out into the sea, receive the fury of heretical waves, and that, although they break

---

13 See *Ep.* 100: Τῆς συνόδου γενέσθαι ἣν δι 'ἔτους ἄγομεν ἐπὶ τῇ μνήμῃ τοῦ μακαριωτάτου μάρτυρος Εὐψυχίου [...] κατὰ τὴν ἑβδόμην τοῦ Σεπτεμβρίου μηνός ἡμέραν. Courtonne, I, 219. "The synod which we convene every year on the seventh of September in memory of the blessed martyr Eupsychius". Deferrari, II, 185.

14 *Ep.* 176: Deferrari, II, 461. Διὸ παρακαλοῦμεν πρὸ τριῶν ἡμερῶν ἐπιστῆναι, ἵνα καὶ τοῦ πτωχοτροφείου τὴν μνήμην μεγάλην ποιήσῃς τῇ παρουσίᾳ. Courtonne, II, 113.

15 *Ep.* 214.2: Deferrari, III, 231. Courtonne, II, 204.

16 *Epp.* 100, 176, and 252, respectively.

17 *Ep.* 176: Deferrari, II, 459–461. Ἀλλήλοις συγγενέσθαι καὶ συμπαρακληθῆναι διὰ τῆς κοινωνίας τῶν πνευματικῶν χαρισμάτων. Courtonne, II, 113.

about us, they do not overflood what is behind us".[18]

Ecclesiastical concerns were discussed and decided at synodical gatherings of bishops, which, aside from theological clarifications and the resolution of conflicts, included deliberations about the election of future bishops and the discipline of current ones. Fedwick describes these gatherings of bishops as follows: "More than a legislative or executive body, they appear in Basil as a means of sharing anxieties with one's colleagues, of soliciting advice on urgent matters and as an expression of love and brotherhood".[19] For Basil, a united witness and confession of faith amongst the bishops of the church was indicative of a strong and resilient church, a church that was able to stand up to heresy but at the same time bring about the reconciliation of dissenters from the faith.

Basil commended his Western colleagues for their success in adhering to a united Nicene confession and sought to imitate their united witness of faith in his own diocese and, by extension, in all the Eastern dioceses struggling against heresy. At that time, Rome, in the Western empire, had no rivals as an apostolic see and its bishops were free from the challenges imposed by non-Nicene sympathisers.[20] To the Westerners Basil writes with admiration: "[Since] a considerable number of you together declare the same doctrines (τὰ αὐτὰ δογματίσετε) with one voice, it is clear that the multitude of those who have so declared will bring about for all the acceptance of the doctrine without contradiction".[21] Basil's aim was to evoke a council of Eastern and Western bishops together

---

18 Ep. 203.1: Deferrari, III, 145. Δημοσίᾳ προκείμενοι πᾶσιν, ὥσπερ οἱ ἐν τῇ θαλάσσῃ προβεβλημένοι σκόπελοι, ἡμεῖς τὸν θυμὸν τῶν αἱρετικῶν κυμάτων ὑποδεχόμεθα, καὶ περὶ ἡμᾶς ῥηγνύμενοι τὰ κατόπιν ἡμῶν οὐκ ἐπικλύζουσι. Courtonne, II, 168.
19 Fedwick, *The Church and the Charisma of Leadership*, 125. See Gain, *L'Église de Cappadoce*, 86-88; Epp. 92.3, 95, 98, 100, 126, 201, 203.1-4, 205, 227-230.
20 See Chapter Four.
21 Ep. 263.2: Deferrari, IV, 93. Ἐὰν δὲ καὶ συμφώνως πλείονες ὁμοῦ τὰ αὐτὰ δογματίσετε, δῆλον ὅτι τὸ πλῆθος τῶν δογματισάντων ἀναντίρρητον πᾶσι τὴν παραδοχὴν κατασκευάσει τοῦ δόγματος. Courtonne, III, 122-123.

(ἐν κοινῇ σκέψει)[22] so as to expose conclusively individuals (in particular, hierarchs) resisting Nicene communion. Those who would choose not to align themselves with the Nicene communion would effectively find themselves publicly excluded from the unity of the church.[23]

6.2 One Bishop, One Diocese, One Communion

The church in Basil's day was a federation or technically a communion of local churches, each led by a bishop and each centred in one of the cities of the Roman Empire (and sometimes beyond its territory). Each presiding bishop, as the head of his own eucharistic assembly, was the leader of a complete church which needed no complement, and so for every local diocese there was only one bishop. Such also was the insistence of the first Ecumenical Council: "that there may not be two bishops in the city".[24] With this in mind, Basil, when confronted with the problem of more than one diocesan bishop in a particular see, rhetorically asked the question: "How can there be two bishops?" (Πῶς δύνανται δύο εἶναι ἐπίσκοποι;) As he understood it, a bishop is either "consecrated" (κεχειροτονημένος) and remains, or "deposed" (καθῃρημένος) and replaced.[25] If the deposed bishop remains or someone else assumes the office of the bishop who is outside the communion of the church, the faithful should have "considered them as heretics" (ὡς αἱρετικοῖς ἐπέρχονται) and therefore must "avoid communion with them" (τὴν κοινωνίαν αὐτῶν οὐκ ἐκτρέπονται).[26]

Basil was immoveable in his stance that a second ruling bishop and a second Eucharist within the auspices of the same local church, constituted a situation that was uncanonical. According

---

22 *Ep.* 263.5. See *Ep.* 66.1.
23 See *Epp.* 204.7, 263.5.
24 Synod of Nicaea, Canon 8: Percival, 20. Ἵνα μὴ ἐν τῇ πόλει δύω ἐπίσκοποι ὦσιν. Ραφτάνη, Πηδάλιον, 133.
25 *Ep.* 243.6: Deferrari, III, 465. Courtonne, III, 80.
26 *Ep.* 226.2: Deferrari, III, 333. Courtonne, III, 25.

to Basil, if this occurred, it meant that the second diocesan bishop had "not submitted to the canons" (μὴ ὑπέκυψε τοῖς κανόσιν) and therefore was outside the communion of the "catholic church" (καθολικὴν Ἐκκλησίαν).[27] Consequently, only through the presence of a schism is there more than one presiding bishop in a local church. When Faustus appeared in Armenia as a rival to Bishop Cyril, Basil remarked: "Armenia has become filled with schisms" (Στάσεων ἐμπλῆσαι τὴν Ἀρμενίαν).[28] In response to Faustus' uncanonical presence, Basil was strict in his admonitions to his faithful that there should never be communion with a schismatic bishop and their congregation, since to do so was counterproductive to spiritual life: "We should avoid communion with these (ὧν φεύγειν προσήκει τὰς κοινωνίας) and turn away their words as being snares for the soul".[29] Basil admonished his faithful that they needed to be careful so as not to be "deceived by their falsehoods when they proclaim orthodoxy of faith. For such men are traffickers in Christ, and not Christians (Χριστέμποροι γὰρ οἱ τοιοῦτοι καὶ οὐ χριστιανοί), ever preferring that which profits them in this life to living according to truth".[30] Regarding the bishops in the West, Basil considered it his duty to exhort them:

> Not to receive indiscriminately the communion (μὴ ἀκρίτως δέχεσθαι τὰς κοινωνίας) of those coming from the East, but after once choosing a single portion of them, to accept the rest on the testimony of these already in communion (ἐκ τῆς μαρτυρίας τῶν κοινωνικῶν προσλαμβάνεσθαι); and of urging them not to take into communion everyone who

---

27 *Ep.* 188.1: Deferrari, III, 11. Courtonne, II, 121.
28 *Ep.* 120: Deferrari, II, 249. Courtonne, II, 26.
29 *Ep.* 105: Deferrari, II, 201. Ὧν φεύγειν προσήκει τὰς κοινωνίας καὶ ἐκτρέπεσθαι τοὺς λόγους ὡς δηλητήρια ὄντα ψυχῶν. Courtonne, II, 26.
30 *Ep.* 240.3: Deferrari, III, 425. Μὴ ἐξαπατηθῆτε ταῖς ψευδολογίαις αὐτῶν ἐπαγγελλομένων ὀρθότητα πίστεως. Χριστέμποροι γὰρ οἱ τοιοῦτοι καὶ οὐ χριστιανοί, τὸ ἀεὶ αὐτοῖς κατὰ τὸν βίον τοῦτον λυσιτελοῦν τοῦ κατ' ἀλήθειαν ζῆν προτιμώντες. Courtonne, III, 63.

writes down the Creed as supposed proof of Orthodoxy.³¹

In Basil's view, it became the responsibility of the bishop to manifest authentically the balanced sense of the church as a catalyst to safeguard and restore the church's communion. Undoubtedly the whole canonical unity of the church, which concerned itself with the church's external presence, was realised through the participation of eucharistic communion. As the visible centre and head of the eucharistic assembly, the bishop expressed in space and time the unity of the church of God.³² By nature of his "union with the Spirit" (συνεργείᾳ τοῦ πνεύματος),³³ the bishop was granted the ability to exercise his ministry within the life of the church. Clearly for Basil, the initiator of the bishop's ministry was God himself. The human element was called to work in communion with God and therefore become an instrument of God that was totally dedicated to the care of the church. Collectively all bishops are at the disposal of the Holy Spirit from whom they are empowered and directed in their service (διακονία) for the church. When writing to the clergy of Colonia in Lesser Armenia about their bishop's transfer forty kilometres south-east to the diocesan see of Nicopolis,³⁴ the synergy between the Holy Spirit and its chosen vessel, the bishop, became paramount for Basil:

> Do not consider this a human arrangement, nor that it has been prompted by the reasoning of men who think of earthly things, but be convinced that it is through union with the Spirit (τῇ συνεργείᾳ τοῦ Πνεύματος) that those who are committed with the care of the churches of God have done this [...] Those who do not receive from the churches of God what is commanded by the

31 *Ep.* 129.3: Deferrari, II, 289. Μὴ ἀκρίτως δέχεσθαι τὰς κοινωνίας τῶν ἐκ τῆς Ἀνατολῆς ἀφικνουμένων, ἀλλ᾽ ἅπαξ μίαν μερίδα ἐκλεξάμενους, τοὺς λοιποὺς ἐκ τῆς μαρτυρίας τῶν κοινωνικῶν προσλαμβάνεσθαι καὶ μὴ παντὶ τῷ πίστιν γράφοντι ἐπὶ προφάσει δὴ τῆς ὀρθοδοξίας προστίθεσθαι. Courtonne, II, 41.
32 See Chapter Five.
33 *Ep.* 227: Deferrari, III, 345. Courtonne, III, 30.
34 See Chapter Five, n. 126.

churches "resist the ordinance of God" (τοῦ Θεοῦ διαταγῇ ἀνθίστανται).³⁵

Cut off from the eucharistic assembly and its expression of communion *par excellence*, Basil maintained that the bishop "now becomes different from what he was" (οὗτος νῦν ἕτερον γέγονεν ἐξ ἑτέρου).³⁶ Amongst the litany of reasons for this new identity, he mentioned the following:

> [They] were not partakers of the Holy Spirit, and were not governing their churches by the grace of God, but had seized their dignity by human power and a desire of empty glory [...] Their aim is one, as it seems – to seek their own advantage everywhere, and to consider him a friend who assists in accomplishing their desires, but to judge him an enemy, and to spare no calumny (διαβολῆς) against him, who opposes their desires.³⁷

There was no place for diplomatic dealings with schismatic bishops, and for this reason Basil insisted that they were to be avoided at all costs. What may appear as uncharitable and antisocial was for Basil forgivable and, most importantly, a necessary witness in the name of saving truth. Thus, Basil states: "We do not follow with them [schismatic bishops], and if we avoid those who have the same ideas as they, we should with justice receive pardon, for

---

35 *Ep.* 227: Deferrari, III, 345. Ταύτην μὴ ἀνθρωπίνην νομίσητε, μηδὲ ἐκ λογισμῶν κεκινῆσθαι τὰ γήϊνα φρονούντων ἀνθρώπων, ἀλλὰ τῇ συνεργείᾳ τοῦ Πνεύματος τοὺς τὴν μέριμναν ἀνηρτημένους τῶν Ἐκκλησιῶν τοῦ Θεοῦ τοῦτο ποιῆσαι πέπεισθε [...] Οἱ μὴ δεχόμενοι παρὰ τῶν ἐκλεκτῶν τοῦ Θεοῦ τὰ ταῖς Ἐκκλησίαις διατυπούμενα τῇ τοῦ Θεοῦ διαταγῇ ἀνθίστανται. Courtonne, III, 30. See Rom. 13:2.
36 *Ep.* 244.1: Deferrari, III, 451. Courtonne, III, 74.
37 *Ep.* 244.6: Deferrari, III, 465. Οὐκ ἦσαν Πνεύματος Ἁγίου μέτοχοι οὐδὲ Θεοῦ χάριτι τὰς Ἐκκλησίας οἰκονομοῦντες, ἀλλ᾽ ἀνθρωπίνῃ δυναστείᾳ κατ᾽ ἐπιθυμίαν δόξης κενῆς τὰς προστασίας ἁρπάσαντες [...] Ἀλλ᾽ εἷς ὁ σκοπός, ὡς ἔοικε, τὸ ἑαυτῶν ζητεῖν πανταχοῦ, καὶ φίλον μὲν ἡγεῖσθαι τὸν ταῖς ἐπιθυμίαις αὐτῶν συνεργοῦντα, πολέμιον δὲ κρίνειν καὶ μηδεμιᾶς κατ᾽ αὐτοῦ διαβολῆς φείδεσθαι τὸν ταῖς ἐπιθυμίαις αὐτῶν ἀνθιστάμενον. Courtonne, III, 80.

we consider nothing to be preferable to truth and our salvation".[38] Reading into Basil's letters, it becomes obvious that unless heresy and schism are healed, frustration, pain and suffering are unavoidable. Writing to the Nicopolitans, Basil bemoaned the new troubles affecting their lives as a result of heresy: "Blows and insults against yourselves, and pillaging of homes, and devastation of the city, and upheaval of all the land, persecution of church and banishment of priests, attack of wolves and scattering of sheep".[39]

In no uncertain terms Basil charged all his faithful to "abstain from communion with heretics" (τοὺς αἱρετικοὺς κοινωνίας ὑμας ἀπέχεσθαι).[40] Basil ordered his monks to avoid all possible "meetings (συντυχίας) with them, which are deceitful means of perverting hearers, that you may keep undefiled your charity towards us, and may preserve the faith of the Fathers unharmed, and may be found honoured in the sight of the Lord as friends of the truth".[41] Basil's opposition to being complacent about the presence of heresy and the ensuring communion with heretics was clear to all Nicene Christians and their leaders: "Indifference in these matters takes away liberty in Christ" (Τὸ ἐν τούτοις ἀδιαφορεῖν τὴν ἐπὶ τοῦ Χριστοῦ παρρησίαν ἡμῶν ἀφαιρεῖται).[42]

---

38 *Ep.* 245: Deferrari, III, 475-477. Νῦν δὲ εἰ μήτε ἐκείνους συνεπόμεθα καὶ τοὺς τὰ αὐτὰ φρονοῦντας αὐτοῖς ἐκκλίνομεν, συγγνώμης ἂν δικαίως τύχοιμεν μηδὲν προτιμότερον τῆς ἀληθείας καὶ τῆς ἑαυτῶν ἀσφαλείας τιθέμενοι. Courtonne, III, 84.
39 *Ep.* 247: Deferrari, III, 477-479. Πληγὰς μὲν καὶ ὕβρεις εἰς ὑμᾶς αὐτούς, πόρθησιν δὲ οἴκων καὶ ἐρήμωσιν πόλεως καὶ πατρίδος ὅλης ἀνατροπήν, διωγμὸν Ἐκκλησίας καὶ φυγὴν ἱερέων, ἐπανάστασιν λύκων καὶ ποιμνίων διασποράν. Courtonne, III, 85.
40 *Ep.* 262.2: Deferrari, IV, 89. Courtonne, III, 120.
41 *Ep.* 226: Deferrari, III, 343. Τὰς μέντοι συντυχίας αὐτῶν τὰς δολερῶς ἐπὶ καταστροφῇ τῶν ἀκουόντων γινομένας ἐκκλίνειν, ἵνα καὶ τὴν πρὸς ἡμᾶς ἀγάπην ἀκεραίαν φυλάξητε καὶ τὴν τῶν Πατέρων πίστιν ἄθραυστον διασώσητε καὶ παρὰ τῷ Κυρίῳ εὐδόκιμοι φανῆτε ὡς φίλοι τῆς ἀληθείας. Courtonne, III, 29.
42 *Ep.* 262.2: Deferrari, IV, 89. Courtonne, III, 120.

6.3 The Unguarded Communion of Heresy

In his letters Basil went to great lengths to expose heresies and even to name them individually: "Heresies are, for example, those of the Manicheans, of the Valentinians, of the Marcionites, and of these very Pepuzeni; for here at once regarding faith in God itself disagreement exists".[43] Basil believed that there was an underlying need to expose the "impious doctrine of Arius" (τὸ δυσσεβὲς δόγμα τοῦ Ἀρείου)[44] who "begot Aetius, the heretic" (Ἀέτιον ἐγέννησε τὸν αἱρετικόν).[45] Basil feared the obvious threat of a "renewal of the ancient heresy of Sabellius" (ἀνανεωθείσης τῆς παλαιᾶς Σαβελλίου αἱρέσεως),[46] a renewal which he considered to be the latest "enemy of the church" (ἐχθροῦ τῆς Ἐκκλησίας).[47]

Through being aware of heresies, Basil was seeking to equip his readers with the knowledge to protect themselves "against the harm of depraved teachings" (ἀπὸ τῶν πονηρῶν διδαγμάτων

---

43 *Ep.* 188.1: Deferrari, III, 11. Αἱρέσεις δὲ οἷον ἡ τῶν Μανιχαίων, καὶ Οὐαλεντίνων, καὶ Μαρκιωνιστῶν, καὶ τούτων τῶν Πεπουζηνῶν· εὐθὺς γὰρ περὶ αὐτῆς τῆς εἰς Θεὸν πίστεως ἡ διαφορά. Courtonne, II, 122. See *Epp.* 199.47, 263.4. The Pneumatomachians, who later are called Macedonians in Basil's letters, were most active during Basil's ministry. Even though one finds Basil increasing his efforts to refute and counter them, they rarely get a mention in his correspondence, see *Epp.* 140.2, 263.3. The leading proponents of heresies whom Basil names and repeatedly castigates include: Arius, see *Epp.* 69.2, 70, 125.3, 130.1, 223.5, 226.4, 244.9, 263.3; and Sabellius, see *Epp.* 9.2, 126, 129.1, 210.3–5, 214.3, 223.6, 226.4, 265.2. Less often Basil cites the names of the disciples of Arius such as Aetius, the deacon of Antioch, see *Epp.* 223.5, 244.3 and Eunomius, the bishop of Cyzicus, see *Epp.* 210.4, 244.9. Other founders of sects from preceding centuries whom Basil mentions in his letters are: Valentinius, see *Ep.* 261.2; Paul of Samosata, see *Ep.* 52.1; Marcellus of Ancyra, see *Epp.* 69.2, 125.1, 239.2, 263.5, 265.3 and Apollinarius of Laodicea, see *Epp.* 129.1, 131.1,2, 224.1, 244.3, 263.4, 265.2.
44 *Ep.* 263.3: Deferrari, IV, 95. Courtonne, III, 123.
45 *Ep.* 223.5: Deferrari, III, 307. Courtonne, III, 15.
46 *Ep.* 126: Deferrari, II, 273. Courtonne, II, 36. See *Ep.* 224.2: Ἡ ἀσεβεστάτη αἵρεσις τοῦ Σαβελλίου ἀνενεώθη. Courtonne, III, 19. "The most impious heresy of Sabellius has been renewed". Deferrari, III, 317. See *Ep.* 210.3: "The evil of Sabellius" (Τοῦ Σαβελλίου κακόν), "The foolish-minded Sabellius" (Τοῦ ματαιόφρονος Σαβελλίου). Deferrari, III, 201, 203. Courtonne, II, 192.
47 *Ep.* 126: Deferrari, II, 273. Courtonne, II, 36.

βλάβας),⁴⁸ and to "silence innovations in the faith" (τὴν πίστιν καινοτομίας κατασιγάσετε).⁴⁹ Basil sensed that the church's identity was at stake, as was a person's participation in its communion (κοινωνίαν ἐκκλησιαστικήν). Basil asked, for example, that the "heresy of Marcellus" be "exterminated" (ἐξορίσαι), since he considered it to be "both dangerous and harmful, and foreign to the true faith".⁵⁰ In his letter to Bishop Athanasius of Alexandria regarding Marcellus, he writes:

> Of this man, therefore, the present circumstances demand that appropriate mention be made, so that those who seek an opportunity may have no opportunity, in consequence of our uniting with your holiness [Athanasius of Alexandria] all who are sound in the faith, and of our revealing to all men those who are slack in the true faith. The result will be that henceforth we shall be able to recognise those who are one mind with us (ὁμόφρονας), instead of being like those who fight a battle at night between friends and foes.⁵¹

Writing to the Westerners, Basil presented what seems to be his primary reason for naming "innovations in regard to the faith" (περὶ τὴν πίστιν καινοτομουμένων) and naming those advocating views "contrary to sound teaching" (ὑπεναντίως τῇ ὑγιαινούσῃ διδασκαλίᾳ).⁵² In his efforts to establish communion, Basil was seeking to either give those under the influence of heresy an opportunity to change their ways and be reconciled to the com-

---

48 *Ep.* 210.6: Deferrari, III, 211–213. Courtonne, II, 196.
49 *Ep.* 208.4: Deferrari, III, 193. Courtonne, II, 188.
50 *Ep.* 69.2: Deferrari, II, 45. Τὸ τὴν Μαρκέλλου αἵρεσιν αὐτοὺς ὡς χαλεπὴν καὶ βλαβερὰν καὶ τῆς ὑγιαινούσης πίστεως ἀλλοτρίως ἔχουσαν ἐξορίσαι. Courtonne, I, 163.
51 *Ep.* 69.2: Deferrari, II, 45–47. Ἐκείνου τε οὖν μνησθῆναι πρεπόντως ἀπαιτεῖ τὰ παρόντα, ὥστε μὴ ἔχειν ἀφορμὴν τοὺς θέλοντες ἀφορμήν, ἐκ τοῦ τῇ σῇ ὁσιότητι συνάπτειν τοὺς ὑγιαίνοντας καὶ τοὺς πρὸς τὴν ἀληθῆ πίστιν ὀκλάζοντας φανεροὺς πᾶσι ποιῆσαι· ὥστε τοῦ λοιποῦ γνωρίζειν ἡμᾶς τοὺς ὁμόφρονας καὶ μή, ὡς ἐν νυκτομαχίᾳ, μηδεμίαν φίλων καὶ πολεμίων ἔχειν διάκρισιν. Courtonne, I, 163.
52 *Ep.* 126: Deferrari, II, 273. Courtonne, II, 35. See Chapter Four.

munion of the church, or, at the very least, to limit the disturbances they cause to the communion of the church by having them exposed. Speaking as a churchman, Basil declares that this form of "protest" (προὔργου) towards those outside of the communion of the church "will either be of some avail toward our purpose or certainly will clear us of guilt at judgement".[53] Throughout his letters Basil was realistic, he acknowledged that his commitment to reconciling people into the communion of the church was not necessarily an easy task: "That the mouths of those who accuse us shall be checked through our letters is impossible; nay rather, is it likely that they are both irritated at our defence and are making greater and more serious preparations against us".[54]

Basil was determined, however, not to shy away from his desired objective of establishing and welcoming all efforts that lead towards communion. His letters had this objective in mind. As highlighted in Chapter Four, Basil repeatedly spoke about the need for unity, just as limbs and organs in a body are in need of one another.[55] Basil's position was that the communion of the church, although freely open to all, must still be guarded at all costs and shielded against the presence of heresy. In one of his final letters to the Westerners, Basil makes clear his intention to safeguard the communion of the church against "unguarded communion":

> It is these men that we would have made known publicly by your integrity to all the churches in the East, in order that either, mending their ways, they may truly be with us (ὦσι σὺν ἡμῖν), or, remaining in their perversity, they may keep

---

53 *Ep.* 210.4: Deferrari, III, 207. Ἡ γὰρ προὔργου τι ἔσται εἰς τὴν σπουδὴν ἢ πάντως ἡ παροῦσα διαμαρτυρία ἡμᾶς τῆς αἰτίας ἐπὶ τοῦ Κριτηρίου. Courtonne, II, 194.
54 *Ep.* 226.4: Deferrari, III, 341. Τὰ μὲν στόματα τῶν κακηγορούντων ἡμᾶς ἐπισχεθῆναι διὰ τῶν ἡμετέρων γραμμάτων ἀμήχανον· μᾶλλον μὲν οὖν εἰκὸς καὶ ἐρεθίζεσθαι αὐτοὺς ἐπὶ ταῖς ἀπολογίαις ἡμῶν, καὶ μείζονα καὶ χαλεπώτερα καθ᾽ ἡμῶν κατεσκευάζειν. Courtonne, III, 28–29.
55 See *Epp.* 29, 97, 263.2.

their harm to themselves alone, not being able through an unguarded communion (ἀφυλάκτου κοινωνίας) to share their own disease with their neighbours. And we must mention these by name, in order that you also may know who they are that cause disturbances among us (ταραχὰς παρ᾽ ἡμῖν ἐργαζομένους).⁵⁶

One of Basil's greatest lamentations, already mentioned in Chapter Five, was that no one felt ashamed from being cut off from the other as a result of unguarded communion. It was as if they thought that communion was an arbitrary matter and not an essential realisation of one's relationship with God and each other. Basil's rebuke was a warning to all: "Are we neither ashamed of our isolation, nor do we consider it a loss to endure the severance of our unanimity (διασπασμὸν τῆς ὁμονοίας), nor do we shudder that on us will come the fearful prophecy of our Lord, who said: 'Because iniquity has abounded, the charity of many shall grow cold.'"⁵⁷ Basil declared that "discord (ἀσυμφωνίαν) between one another is caused by the busy activity of the devil".⁵⁸ He deplored what he called "the wickedness of the age" (τοῦ καιροῦ τὴν κακότητα), since "those [churches] which from old have maintained a fraternal relationship toward one another, even those churches have now separated".⁵⁹ Basil fervently wanted a return to practices of earlier

---

56 *Ep.* 263.2: Deferrari, IV, 93. Οὓς ἀξιοῦμεν παρὰ τῆς ὑμετέρας ἀκριβείας πρὸς πάσας τὰς κατὰ τὴν Ἀνατολὴν Ἐκκλησίας δημοσιευθῆναι, ἵνα ἢ ὀρθοποδήσαντες γνησίως ὦσι σὺν ἡμῖν, ἢ μένοντες ἐπὶ τῆς διαστροφῆς ἐν ἑαυτοῖς μόνοις τὴν βλάβην ἔχωσι μὴ δυνάμενοι ἐκ τῆς ἀφυλάκτου κοινωνίας τῆς ἰδίας νόσου μεταδιδόναι τοῖς πλησιάζουσιν. Ἀνάγκη δὲ τούτων ὀνομαστὶ μνησθῆναι, ἵνα καὶ αὐτοὶ γνωρίσητε τοὺς τὰς ταραχὰς παρ 'ἡμῖν ἐργαζομένους. Courtonne, III, 122.
57 *Ep.* 203.3: Deferrari, III, 151. Οὔτε ἐπαισχυνόμεθα τῇ μονώσει οὔτε ζημίαν φέρειν τὸν διασπασμὸν τῆς ὁμονοίας τιθέμεθα οὔτε φρίσομεν ὅτι εἰς ἡμᾶς φθάνει ἡ φοβερὰ τοῦ Κυρίου ἡμῶν προφητεία εἰπόντος ὅτι «Διὰ τὸ πληθυνθῆναι τὴν ἀνομίαν φυγήσεται ἡ ἀγάπη τῶν πολλῶν». Courtonne, II, 171.
58 *Ep.* 99.4: Deferrari, II, 183. Διὰ τὴν ἐκ τῆς τοῦ διαβόλου περιεργίας ἡμῶν αὐτῶν πρὸς ἀλλήλους ἀσυμφωνίαν. Courtonne, I, 218.
59 *Ep.* 204: Deferrari, III, 173. Ἐκ παλαιοῦ πρὸς ἀλλήλας ἀδελφῶν τάξιν ἐπέχουσαι αὗται νῦν διεστήκασι. Courtonne, II, 180.

days (tradition), where communion in all areas was a distinguishing sign of the existence of the church. He explains:

> Question your fathers and they will tell you that even if the parishes seemed to be divided by geographical position, they were yet one mind and were governed by one counsel (φρονήματι ἓν ἦσαν, καὶ μιᾷ γνώμῃ ἐκυβερνῶντο). Continuous was association (ἐπιμιξίαι) among the people; continuous was mutual visiting (ἐπιδημίαι) among clergy; and among the pastors themselves there was such love for one another that each used the other as teacher and guide in matters pertaining to the Lord.[60]

Noting that in times past geographical distance was no deterrent to the spread of heresy, Basil pointed out that in his day heresy could reach across vast geographical distances.[61] As simple as it was for a letter to arrive from East to West, so easily could heresy also be spread. All a heresiarch needed to do was to send a "letter around everywhere" (τὰ γράμματα περιέπεμπον πανταχοῦ),[62] namely to his constituents (notably hierarchs of a church), for this letter to have a formula that equated to a written confession of faith, and finally for this letter to be signed. Consequently, those who agreed with non-Nicene confessions, Basil declared, "shall not be communicants with them [the church]" (μηδὲ κοινωνικοὺς αὐτῶν εἶναι).[63] Such measures, Basil claimed, were needed "in order that the church of God may be pure, having no weed mixed with it".[64] Concerning

---

60 Ep. 204.4: Deferrari, III, 173–175. Ἐρωτήσατε τοὺς πατέρας ὑμῶν καὶ ἀναγγελοῦσιν ὑμῶν ὅτι, εἰ καὶ τῇ θέσει τοῦ τόπου διῃρῆσθαι ἐδόκουν αἱ παροικίαι, ἀλλὰ τῷ γε φρονήματι ἓν ἦσαν καὶ μιᾷ γνώμῃ ἐκυβερνῶντο. Συνεχεῖς μὲν τοῦ λαοῦ αἱ ἐπιμιξίαι, συνεχεῖς δὲ τοῦ κλήρου ἐπιδημίαι, αὐτοῖς δὲ τοῖς ποιμέσι τοσοῦτον περιῆν τῆς πρὸς ἀλλήλους ἀγάπης ὥστε ἑκάτερον αὐτῶν διδασκάλῳ τῷ ἑτέρῳ καὶ ἡγεμόνι χρῆσθαι εἰς τὰ πρὸς Κύριον. Courtonne, II, 180.
61 See Ep. 188.1
62 Ep. 223.7: Deferrari, III, 311. Courtonne, III, 17.
63 Ep. 113: Deferrari, II, 225. Courtonne, II, 17.
64 Ep. 114: Deferrari, II, 229. Ἵνα καθαρὰ ᾖ τοῦ Θεοῦ ἡ Ἐκκλησία μηδὲν ζιζάνιον ἑαυτῇ παραμεμιγμένον ἔχουσα. Courtonne, II, 19.

the Pneumatomachian statements of Apollinarius, Basil remarked: "He has filled the world with his books" (ἐνέπλησε μὲν τῶν ἑαυτοῦ συνταγμάτων τὴν οἰκουμένην).⁶⁵ On another occasion Basil declared: "They [the heresiarchs] have taken over the altar, become leaven of the church there" (Παρέλαβον τὸ θυσιαστήριον, ζύμη ἐγένοντο τῆς ἐκεῖ Ἐκκλησίας).⁶⁶ A heresiarch, of course, would never identify himself as acting in the name of heresy, but instead would present himself as being a true shepherd who was acting out of necessity for the pastoral solicitude of Christ's church. Basil described such as a situation as a heresiarch "concealing his impious sentiments and screening himself behind a kind of orthodoxy of words".⁶⁷

Where heresy and schism were present, Basil argued that the very opposite of communion took place: "Those who make these false assertions, if they mend their ways, are in communion (εἶναι κοινωνικούς), but if they contentiously wish to abide in their innovations, are separated from those in communion".⁶⁸ Faced with counterparts adhering to heretical views, Basil admonished his faithful to "abstain from communion with those, as open blasphemers (ἀφίστασθαι δὲ τῆς κοινωνίας [...] ὡς φανερῶς βλασφημούντων) [...] We must avoid those [...] as being clearly enemies of religion" (ὅτι φεύγειν δεῖ [...] ὡς φανερῶς μαχομένους τῇ εὐσεβείᾳ).⁶⁹

6.4 The Universal Communion of the Bishops

As noted above, unity in the Eucharist, under the leadership of one bishop in each local church, was regarded by Basil as the supreme mark of remaining in communion with the catholic church.

65   *Ep.* 263.7: Deferrari, IV, 97. Courtonne, III, 124.
66   *Ep.* 244.7: Deferrari, III, 467. Courtonne, III, 81.
67   *Ep.* 263.3: Deferrari, IV, 95. Τὸ μὲν δυσσεβὲς ἐπικρυπτόμενος φρόνημα, ῥημάτων δέ τινα ὀρθότητα προβαλλόμενος. Courtonne, III, 123.
68   *Ep.* 263.5: Deferrari, IV, 101. Τοὺς ταῦτα παραχαράσσοντας, εἰ μὲν διορθοῖντο, εἶναι κοινωνικούς· εἰ δὲ ἐπιμένειν φιλονείκως βούλοιντο ταῖς καινοτομίαις, χωρίζεσθαι ἀπ᾽ αὐτῶν. Courtonne, III, 125.
69   *Ep.* 125.3: Deferrari, II, 269. Courtonne, III, 33–34.

Upon the foundation of a shared faith, bishops could recognise with which bishops they were in communion. Mutual recognition amongst the bishops ensured their legitimacy. In his letter to Amphilochius on the canons, Basil declared: "Through the acceptance of the bishops we have published a kind of canon of communion with them" (κανόνα τινὰ τῆς πρὸς αὐτοὺς κοινωνίας).[70] Where there is no communion with the local bishop and thereafter all bishops, there is no church. Consequently, for Basil, the Eucharist is valid only when it is united to the ministry of a canonical bishop.

Basil was equally convinced that the office of the bishops was meaningful only if the bishops occupying the espiscopacy were in communion with the rest of their brother bishops. Here unity is manifested in plurality. In this sense, the multiplicity of the bishopric (with their respective sees) is not subordinate to the oneness of the ministry that is realised in Christ, but constitutive of it. A bishop and his local church do not constitute a portion of the catholic church, but the place in which the fullness of the church dwells. Each local bishop and his church are esteemed by Basil as absolute equals within the catholic church. Furthermore, Basil maintains that a bishop is "a bulwark of the true faith" (ἔρεισμά τε ὀρθότητος)[71] only on the condition that he is united in faith with all other bishops and their churches. As the voice of the church and its most responsible witness entrusted to pass on the deposit of faith, the bishop is what he is, provided that what he has (the deposit of faith), he has "in strict harmony and unity" (ἐν ἀκριβεῖ συμφωνίᾳ καὶ ἑνότητι)[72] with all other bishops. The disruption of the communion of faith (τῇ τῆς πίστεως κοινωνίᾳ)[73] amongst bishops automatically brought about schism. Basil assures us in his letters that no amount of spirituality can ever be healthy for a bishop

---

70 *Ep.* 188.1: Deferrari, III, 21. Κανόνα τινὰ τῆς πρὸς αὐτοὺς κοινωνίας ἐκθέμενοι διὰ τῆς τῶν ἐπισκόπων παραδοχῆς. Courtonne, II, 124.
71 *Ep.* 25.1: Deferrari, I, 151. Courtonne, I, 62.
72 *Ep.* 91: Deferrari, II, 131. Courtonne, I, 197.
73 *Ep.* 154: Courtonne, II, 78. Deferrari translates κοινωνία as fellowship, see n. 3.

who has broken off from ecclesial communion.⁷⁴

Communion amongst the bishops, beyond its manifestation in the present of unity in faith and life with all other churches, also implied unity with the past (apostolic succession) and unity with the future (eschatology), through the operation of the Holy Spirit which guides the church into all truth.⁷⁵ Speaking about the bishops that gathered at Nicaea, Basil stated: "Realise that the three hundred and eighteen, coming together without strife, spoke not without the agency of the Holy Spirit".⁷⁶ According to Basil, since the bishop held a specific ministry of witnessing, declaring and guiding the church into all truth, there was an implicit responsibility placed on the bishop to manifest continuously the church's communion. It was for no other reason that Basil would exhort his fellow bishops to stand up "not for anything else of temporary things [...] but for our common possession – our treasure, inherited from our fathers, of the sound faith".⁷⁷ To bishops who, just because they were in the "calm harbours" (λιμέσιν εὐδίοις) of Nicene Christianity, thought that they did not need to react to the presence of non-Nicenism elsewhere, Basil wrote: "look not only to yourselves that you are moored in calm harbours".⁷⁸ Basil exhorted these bishops to be prepared and ready for any onslaughts arising from the storms of "heretical impiety" (αἱρετικῆς δυσσεβείας).⁷⁹ He stated: "Stretch forth your hand to those churches that are being tossed about lest, if they are abandoned, they may endure complete shipwreck of the

---

74 See *Epp.* 204.7, 226.2, 239.1.
75 John 16:13. See Zizioulas, *Lectures in Christian Dogmatics*, 154–157.
76 *Ep.* 114: Deferrari, II, 227–229. Εἰδέναι ὅτι τριακόσιοι δέκα καὶ ὀκτώ, ἀφιλονείκως συνιόντες, οὐκ ἄνευ τῆς τοῦ Ἁγίου Πνεύματος ἐνεργείας ἐφθέγξαντο. Courtonne, II, 18.
77 *Ep.* 243.4: Deferrari, III, 445. Οὐχ ὑπὲρ ἄλλου τινὸς τῶν προσκαίρων [...] ἀλλ᾿ ὑπὲρ τοῦ κοινοῦ κτήματος, τοῦ πατρικοῦ θησαυροῦ τῆς ὑγιαινούσης πίστεως. Courtonne, III, 71.
78 *Ep.* 243.4: Deferrari, III, 445. Μὴ τὸ καθ᾿ ἑαυτοὺς σκοπεῖτε μόνον ὅτι ἐν λιμέσιν εὐδίοις ὁρμίζεσθε. Courtonne, III, 72.
79 *Ep.* 243.4: Deferrari, III, 447. Courtonne, III, 72.

faith".⁸⁰ In a letter to Pope Damasus, Basil describes the situation of the church in the Eastern Roman Empire as follows:

> Almost the whole East [...] is being shaken by a mighty storm and flood, since the heresy, sown long ago by Arius, the enemy of truth, and now already grown up into shamelessness, and, like a bitter root, producing deadly fruit at last prevails because the champions of orthodox teaching in every diocese have been banished from their churches through slander and insult, and the administration of affairs has been surrendered to men who are making prisoners of the souls of those more pure in faith.⁸¹

As previously discussed, to help him overcome the problems caused by non-Nicene proponents, Basil called upon the help of Bishop Athanasius of Alexandria.⁸² In his correspondence with Athanasius, Basil expressed concern that Christianity was at risk, as was the life of the church: "If our affairs continue to ebb for the worse at this same speed, there will be nothing to prevent the churches from being completely changed into some other form within a brief period of time".⁸³ Communion amongst the dioceses in the East enabled the solidarity and witness of the one church, and was deemed indispensable by Basil for protecting and continuing the church's mission.

80 *Ep.* 243.4: Deferrari, III, 445. Ταῖς χειμαζομέναις τῶν Ἐκκλησιῶν χεῖρα ὀρέξατε, μήποτε ἐγκαταλειφθεῖσαι παντελὲς ὑπομείνωσι τῆς πίστεως τὸ ναυάγιον. Courtonne, III, 72.
81 *Ep.* 70: Deferrari, II, 40. Ἡ Ἀνατολὴ πᾶσαν σχεδόν [...] μεγάλῳ χειμῶνι καὶ κλύδωνι κατασείεται, τῆς πάλαι μὲν σπαρείσης αἱρέσεως ὑπὸ τοῦ ἐχθροῦ τῆς ἀληθείας Ἀρείου, νῦν δὲ πρὸς τὸ ἀναίσχυντον ἀναφανείσης καὶ οἱονεὶ ῥίζης πικρᾶς καρπὸν ὀλέθριον ἀναδιδούσης, κατακρατούσης λοιπὸν διὰ τὸ τοὺς μὲν καθ᾽ ἑκάστην παροικίαν προεστῶτας τοῦ ὀρθοῦ λόγου ἐκ συκοφαντίας καὶ ἐπηρείας τῶν Ἐκκλησιῶν ἐκπεσεῖν, παραδοθῆναι δὲ τοῖς αἰχμαλωτίζουσι τὰς ψυχὰς τῶν ἀκεραιοτέρων τὴν τῶν πραγμάτων ἰσχύν. Courtonne, I, 165.
82 See *Epp.* 61, 66, 67, 69, 80, and 82 which are addressed to Ἀθανασίῳ ἐπισκόπῳ Ἀλεξανδρείας – To Athanasius, Bishop of Alexandria. Chapter Four looks at some of the correspondence between Basil and Athanasius regarding certain types of non-Nicene faith movements.
83 *Ep.* 66.1: Deferrari, II, 27. Εἰ κατὰ τὴν αὐτὴν ὁρμὴν ἐπὶ τὸ χεῖρον ὑπορρέοι τὰ πράγματα, οὐδὲν ἔσται τὸ κωλῦον εἴσω ὀλίγου χρόνου πρὸς ἄλλο τι σχῆμα παντελῶς μεθαρμοσθῆναι τὰς Ἐκκλησίας. Courtonne, I, 156.

He maintained: "We would never attribute so much to ourselves as to consider that single-handed we could surmount our difficulties, for we know very clearly that we need the help of each and every brother more than one hand needs the other".[84] To curtail the spread of heresy, Basil appealed to the West "to write to all the churches in the East" (πάσαις ταῖς κατὰ τὴν Ἀνατολὴν Ἐκκλησίαις) about the "harm" (βλάβης) that is caused to the communion of the church once a heresy has "taken root" (ἐρριζωμένης).[85] If heresy is reduced "to a small number" (εἰς ὀλίγον ἀριθμὸν), chances were it "may be considered unworthy of belief by reason of the smallness of their number" (ἀναξιόπιστοι ὦσι διὰ τὴν ὀλιγότητα).[86] Despite the other implicit messages in Basil's letters, they never concealed their true purpose. With respect to his correspondence with his colleagues in the West, Basil used every opportunity to bring to their attention that imminent action was required so as to combat heresy, which was fast encroaching on their jurisdictions as well. He warned the Westerners to be attentive lest they too become victims of a non-Nicene onslaught. Writing to the bishops of Italy and Gaul, Basil states his concern:

> We fear lest the evil as it increases, like a flame passing through the burning forest, after it has consumed what is nearby, may lay hold of what is afar. For the evil of heresy is spreading; and there is fear lest, after consuming our churches, it may creep presently upon the portion of your district that is sound.[87]

---

84 *Ep.* 97: Deferrari, II, 163. Οὐκ ἄν ποτε τοσοῦτον ἑαυτοὺς ὑπολάβοιμεν ὥστε ἐν τῇ μονώσει δύνασθαι νομίσαι περιέσεσθαι τῶν πραγμάτων, ἀκριβῶς εἰδότες ὅτι πλέον ἡμεῖς τῆς ἑνὸς ἑκάστου τῶν ἀδελφῶν ἐπικουρίας δεόμεθα ἢ ὅσον ἡ ἑτέρα τῶν χειρῶν τῆς ἑτέρας. Courtonne, I, 210.
85 *Ep.* 263: Deferrari, IV, 101. Courtonne, III, 125–126.
86 *Ep.* 113: Deferrari, II, 223. Courtonne, II, 17.
87 *Ep.* 243.3: Deferrari, III, 443. Νῦν δὲ φοβούμεθα μή ποτε αὐξανόμενον τὸ κακόν, ὥσπερ τις φλὸξ διὰ τῆς καιομένης ὕλης βαδίζουσα, ἐπειδὰν καταναλώσῃ τὰ πλησίον, ἄψηται καὶ τῶν πόρρω. Ἐπινέμεται γὰρ τὸ κακὸν τῆς αἱρέσεως, καὶ δέος ἐστὶ μὴ τὰς ἡμετέρας Ἐκκλησίας καταφαγοῦσα ἕρψῃ λοιπὸν καὶ ἐπὶ τὸ ὑγιαῖνον μέρος τῆς καθ᾽ ὑμᾶς παροικίας. Courtonne, III, 71. A similar metaphor involving fire is found in *Ep.* 164.2.

In an untitled letter written in 371, that arguably was addressed to Pope Damasus, Basil put all the responsibility for assistance against heresy upon his shoulders. Desperate, Basil pleaded with the bishop of Rome as personifying "the one solution of these difficulties" (τούτων μίαν προσεδοκήσαμεν λύσιν).[88] He wrote:

> But since we have been cheated of our hope, unable to contain ourselves longer, we have had recourse to urging you by this letter to rouse yourself to our assistance, and to send us men of like mind (ὁμοψύχων) with us, who will either reconcile the dissenter, or restore the churches of God to friendship (εἰς φιλίαν τὰς Ἐκκλησίας τοῦ Θεοῦ ἐπανάγοντες), or will at least make more manifest to you those who are responsible for the confusion. It will thus be clear to you also for the future, with what men it is proper to have communion (ἔχειν τὴν κοινωνίαν).[89]

Time and time again Basil sought the help of "the bishop of Rome" (τῷ ἐπισκόπῳ Ῥώμης) "to examine the state of affairs" (ἐπισκέψασθαι τὰ ἐνταῦτα) of the church and exercise "full authority" (αὐθεντῆσαι) in combating heresy.[90] What this "full authority" implied is hard to determine. It is not likely that Basil had in mind an authority of power to enforce uniformity through doctrinal imperialism, but probably the bishop of Rome occupied a role of coordinating episcopal synods and of being the representative voice of those synods. In one instance, Basil makes reference to just simply asking for an "opinion" (γνώμη)[91] from Rome.

---

88   *Ep.* 70: Deferrari, II, 49. Courtonne, I, 165.
89   *Ep.* 70: Deferrari, II, 49-51. Ὡς δὲ διημάρτομεν τῆς ἐλπίδος, μηκέτι στέγοντες ἤλθομεν ἐπὶ τὴν διὰ τοῦ γράμματος ἡμῶν παράκλησιν διαναστῆναι ὑμᾶς πρὸς τὴν ἀντίληψιν ἡμῶν καὶ ἀποστεῖλαι τινας τῶν ὁμοψύχων, ἢ τοὺς συμβιβάζοντες τοὺς διεστῶτας, ἢ εἰς φιλίαν τὰς Ἐκκλησίας τοῦ Θεοῦ ἐπανάγοντες, ἢ τοὺς γοῦν αἰτίους τῆς ἀκαταστασίας φανερωτέρους ὑμῖν καθιστῶντας, ὥστε καὶ ὑμῖν φανερὸν εἶναι τοῦ λοιποῦ πρὸς τίνας ἔχειν τὴν κοινωνίαν προσῆκε. Courtonne, I, 165.
90   *Ep.* 69: Deferrari, II, 41-43. Courtonne, I, 162.
91   *Ep.* 69.1: Deferrari, II, 41. Courtonne, I, 162. Having said this, γνώμη can also mean "a decision".

It appears that the bishop of Rome enjoyed a primacy amongst his fellow bishops. There are other examples of bishops enjoying primacy within their own eparchies.[92] In Basil's doctrinal battles, the bishop of Rome was being summoned to "send men from Rome" (ἀποσταλῆναι τινας)[93] who were equipped with a synodical decree which gave testimony of the bishops from Rome and the rest of the West denouncing heresy. Consequently, bishops from other provinces could call upon Rome and its fellow Western sees for support in local disputes and help against heresy. Through its sheer size, the West was in a position to reinforce a Nicene position of faith against a non-Nicene adversary. What the West had to say, therefore, carried weight and furthermore exposed the geographical isolation and small size of those splintered communities not in communion with her. To those communities tempted by non-Nicenism, Basil comments:

> Look about on the world, and observe that this portion which is unsound [in orthodoxy] is small (μικρόν), but that the rest of the church, which from one end to the other has received the Gospel, abides by this sound and unchanged doctrine. And we pray that we may never be cast out from communion with these latter (τῆς κοινωνίας μὴ ἐκπεσεῖν).[94]

Writing to the Westerners in 376, Basil in true rhetorical fashion stated his case (not to be taken literally): "For it is the thirteenth year since the war of heresy arose against us; in this time more

---

92 In *Ep.* 28, Bishop Musonius of Neocaesarea was referred to as possessing a primacy amongst his fellow bishops. Not too much is said as to what this entailed. At the very least it is assumed that he was able to be the expression of a common voice on behalf of his brother bishops.
93 *Ep.* 69: Deferrari, II, 41. Courtonne, I, 162.
94 *Ep.* 251.4: Deferrari, IV, 17. Περιβλέψασθε εἰς τὴν οἰκουμένην καὶ ἴδετε ὅτι μικρόν ἐστι τοῦτο τὸ μέρος τὸ νενοσηκός· ἡ δὲ λοιπὴ πᾶσα Ἐκκλησία, ἡ ἀπὸ περάτων εἰς πέρατα δεξαμένη τὸ Εὐαγγέλιον, ἐπὶ τῆς ὑγιοῦς ἐστι ταύτης καὶ ἀδιαστρόφου διδασκαλίας. Ὧν καὶ ἡμεῖς εὐχόμεθα τῆς κοινωνίας μὴ ἐκπεσεῖν. Courtonne, III, 93. See *Ep.* 265.3

afflictions have happened to churches than are on record since the gospel of Christ was proclaimed".⁹⁵ It was not bricks and mortar, that is, the lost church edifices which were in the hands of the non-Nicenes, that Basil was worried about. With imperial support against him, he knew that battle was well and truly lost. His only concern had always been the human soul, which he believed was being harmed through the presence of heresy. Writing to Pope Damasus, Basil described what he considered to be the true "seizure of churches" (ἐκκλησιῶν ἅλωσιν):

> Indeed, it is not the destruction of earthly buildings that we mourn, but the seizure of churches; nor is it corporeal slavery that we behold, but the captivity of souls which is being brought about daily by the champions of the heresy. Accordingly, unless you immediately rouse yourself to our assistance, you will shortly not even find men to whom to stretch forth your hand, since all will have come under the dominion of heresy.⁹⁶

As mentioned above, the presence of heresy could not be ignored with complacency, especially by those who for the time being were geographically unaffected by its grip. For Basil, it was not "proximity of place" (οὐ γὰρ ἡ τῶν τόπων ἐγγύτης) that mattered most but "spiritual union" (ἡ κάτα πνεύμα συνάφεια),⁹⁷ that is to say, "to be in the same communion" (ἐν τῇ αὐτῇ συναφείᾳ).⁹⁸ Basil argued that care and discernment were needed so as "to escape the notice

---

95 *Ep.* 242.2: Deferrari, III, 431. Τρισκαιδέκατον γὰρ ἔτος ἐστιν ἀφ ' οὗ ὁ αἱρετικὸς ἡμῖν πόλεμος ἐπανέστη, ἐν ᾧ πλείους γεγόνασι ταῖς Ἐκκλησίαις αἱ θλίψεις τῶν μνημονευομένων ἀφ ' οὗ τὸ Εὐαγγέλιον τοῦ Χριστοῦ καταγγέλλεται. Courtonne, III, 66.
96 *Ep.* 70: Deferrari, II, 53. Οὐ γὰρ οἰκοδομημάτων γηΐνων καταστροφήν, ἀλλ ' Ἐκκλησιῶν ἅλωσιν ὀδυρόμεθα· οὐδὲ δουλείαν σωματικήν, ἀλλ 'αἰχμαλωσίαν ψυχῶν καθ 'ἑκάστην ἡμέραν ἐνεργουμένην παρὰ τῶν ὑπερμαχούντων τῆς αἱρέσεως καθορῶμεν. Ὥστε, εἰ μὴ ἤδη διανασταίητε πρὸς τὴν ἀντίληψιν, μικρὸν ὕστερον οὐδὲ οἷς ὀρέξετε τὴν χεῖρα εὑρήσετε, πάντων ὑπὸ τὴν ἐπικράτειαν τῆς αἱρέσεως γενομένων. Courtonne, I, 166.
97 *Ep.* 242.1: Deferrari, III, 431. Courtonne, III, 66.
98 *Ep.* 265.3: Deferrari, IV, 117. Courtonne, III, 132.

of the enemies of peace" (τοῦ φθάσαι τὴν αἴσθησιν τῶν ἐχθρῶν τῆς εἰρήνης).[99] Nothing short of an authentic struggle was needed to combat heresy head-on. In a letter that he wrote to Bishop Atarbius of Neocaesarea, a distant relative who was seemingly aloof about the dangers of Sabellianism, Basil exhorted him saying:

> Unless we assume a labour in behalf of the churches equal to that which the enemies of sound doctrine have taken upon themselves for their ruin and total obliteration, nothing will prevent truth from being swept away to destruction by our enemies, and ourselves from sharing in their condemnation, unless with all zeal and good will, in harmony with one another and in unison with God, we show the greatest possible solicitude for the unity of the churches.[100]

It behoved every Christian in good-standing, like Atarbius, not only to aspire towards communion, but also to do all that it took to preserve and maintain the unity of the church through communion. Any insinuation that was adverse to this objective, Basil considered "contrary to ecclesiastical law" (παρὰ τῶν ἐκκλησιαστικὸν θεσμόν).[101] Basil tells Bishop Atarbius that irrespective of one's tranquil circumstances, communion is to be desired at all times and in all places:

> Cast from your mind the thought that you have no need of communion with another (οἴεσθαι μηδενὸς ἑτέρου εἰς κοινωνίαν προσδεῖσθαι). For it does not befit the character of one who walks in charity, nor of one who fulfils the com-

---

99 *Ep.* 69.1: Deferrari, II, 43. Courtonne, I, 162.
100 6p. 65: Deferrari, II, 25. Εἰ μὴ τὸν ἴσον ἡμεῖς ἀγῶνα ὑπὲρ τῶν Ἐκκλησιῶν ἀναλάβοιμεν ὁπόσον ἔχουσιν οἱ ἀντικείμενοι τῇ ὑγιαινούσῃ διδασκαλίᾳ εἰς καθαίρεσιν αὐτῶν καὶ παντελῆ ἀφανισμόν, οὐδὲν τὸ κωλύον οἴχεσθαι μὲν παρασυρεῖσαν ὑπὸ τῶν ἐχθρῶν τὴν ἀλήθειαν, παραπολαῦσαι δέ τι καὶ ἡμᾶς τοῦ κρίματος, μὴ πάσῃ σπουδῇ καὶ προθυμίᾳ ἐν ὁμονοίᾳ τῇ πρὸς ἀλλήλους καὶ συμπνοίᾳ τῇ κατὰ Θεόν, τὴν ἐνδεχομένην μέριμναν ὑπὲρ τῆς ἑνώσεως τῶν Ἐκκλησιῶν ἐπιδειξαμένους. Courtonne, I, 155-156.
101 *Ep.* 126: Deferrari, II, 271. Courtonne, II, 35.

mand of Christ, to cut himself off from all connexion with his brethren (τοὺς ἀδελφοὺς συναφείας ἑαυτὸν ἀποτέμνειν). Consider this – that if the evil of war which now goes on all about us should sometime come upon ourselves likewise, and if we too along with others shall receive a share of its spitefulness, we shall find none to sympathise with us, because in the season of our own tranquillity we failed to pay betimes our contribution of sympathy to the victims of injustice.[102]

6.5 Conclusion

This chapter has shown that communion in Basil's church was identifiable, accessible and celebrated in its greatest possible way through the eucharistic synaxis. Basil essentially believed in a communion of churches that professed a Nicene faith. Each ruling bishop within a diocese was regarded as being in communion with the catholic church only when he possessed his jurisdictional authority alone. At the same time, each ruling bishop had to be recognised by every other ruling bishop within the Nicene communion of churches. Problems arose in the East when heresy introduced rival bishops into a diocese who subsequently set up their own parallel jurisdictions. Through his letters Basil called upon Rome and other Western sees to send representatives to combat the heresies he saw as destabilising the Nicene communion of churches in the East. Basil argued that no diocese was invulnerable to the presence of heresy. He believed that where there was

---

102 *Ep.* 65: Deferrari, II, 25–27. Ἔκβαλε τῆς σεαυτοῦ ψυχῆς τὸ οἴεσθαι μηδενὸς ἑτέρου εἰς κοινωνίαν προσδεῖσθαι. Οὐ γὰρ κατὰ ἀγάπην περιπατοῦντος οὐδὲ πληροῦντός ἐστι τὸν νόμον τοῦ Χριστοῦ τῆς πρὸς τοὺς ἀδελφοὺς συναφείας ἑαυτὸν ἀποτέμνειν. Ἅμα γὰρ κἀκεῖνο λογίζεσθαι τὴν ἀγαθήν σου προαίρεσιν βούλομαι, ὅτι τὸ τοῦ πολέμου κακόν, κύκλῳ περιιών, καὶ πρὸς ἡμᾶς ἔλθοι ποτέ, κἂν μετ' ἄλλον καὶ ἡμεῖς τῆς ἐπηρείας παραπολαύσωμεν, οὐδὲ τοὺς συναλγοῦντας εὑρήσομεν, διὰ τὸ ἐν καιρῷ τῆς εὐθηνίας ἡμῶν μὴ προκαταβαλέσθαι τοῖς ἠδικημένοις τὸν τῆς συμπαθείας ἔρανον. Courtonne, I, 156.

heresy, there too would a breach of communion be found. Inter-episcopal communion required each bishop to manifest and safeguard communion both within his own local diocese and across all the dioceses of the catholic church.

Conclusion:
Communion in Basil's Letters

This work has shown that, throughout Basil's episcopal ministry, his letters were a very important means of restoring, maintaining and expressing communion within a Christian church that was experiencing division because of differences in statements of faith. Basil had a real concern that the church's Christian identity was at risk of being eliminated and replaced with something "completely foreign to Christianity" (Χριστιανισμοῦ μὲν παντελῶς ἀλλοτρίαν).[1] He was also concerned about each person's participation in the church's communion (κοινωνίαν ἐκκλησιαστικήν), wherein, in his view, lay the realisation of their salvation. Basil maintained his episcopal post during an imperial regime that was theologically against him through its endorsement of non-Nicene Christianity. Despite what often appeared to be unfavourable socio-political and administrative factors under the reign of Emperor Valens (364–378), Basil remained dedicated to his vocation as a bishop of the church. He upheld Nicene Christianity and actively cultivated his belief that all forms of division could be overcome and permanently reconciled in the embrace of the church's communion.

The introduction of this book noted that the ecclesial communion, and the ecclesiology in general, of Basil's letters, had yet to be comprehensively studied. Having come to the end, the main aspects of Basil's theology of communion which appear in his letters, and which facilitated the use of Basil's letters as instruments of communion, can now be summarised. Basil's originality lay in his ability to present his view by appropriating new terms from the

---

1   *Ep.* 263.5: Courtonne, III, 125.

philosophical language and categories of his time. He thus contextualised scriptural mandates in the pre-existing norms of Graeco-Roman society. In this way he was able to present the truth of the Gospel in a manner that was both familiar and accessible to his listeners. As a bishop, Basil was always guided by what was needed in practice and to this extent his letters bear witness to his pastoral activities and his commitment to achieving communion in the church. In these letters Basil is seen to prioritise human dignity and worth through encouraging a person's communion with God in the life of the church.

Basil's letters served not only his quest for establishing communion in his diocese but also his attempt to build up inter-episcopal communion across the whole universal church (τὴν οἰκουμένην ἐπισκόπων συνημμένων).² Amongst Nicene bishops, that which remained indisputable and unchangeable was the affirmation of the divinity of the Son and of the Holy Spirit. Prompted by a spiritual renewal, the acceptance of pro-Nicene Christianity by churches had ecclesiastical communion as its lasting expression. Basil's correspondence with Bishop Athanasius of Alexandria, discussed in Chapter Four, exemplified his determination to uphold communion within the dioceses of a pro-Nicene church. He called upon Athanasius to help him bring about "communion and unity with those of like belief" (ὁμοδόξους κοινωνίαν καὶ ἕνωσιν).³ In Basil's judgement, a cessation of communion in any local church had negative consequences on the entire communion of the church. As exemplified by his own actions, he wanted his fellow hierarchs to "show the greatest possible solicitude for the unity of the churches".⁴

The proclamation of communion with God, although paramount in Basil's letters, was, he argued, most accurately expressed in

2 *Ep.* 204.7: Courtonne, II, 179.
3 *Ep.* 82: Courtonne, I, 185.
4 *Ep.* 65: Deferrari, II, 25. Τὴν ἐνδεχομένην μέριμναν ὑπὲρ τῆς ἑνώσεως τῶν Ἐκκλησιῶν ἐπιδειξαμένους. Courtonne, I, 156.

doxological worship. Doxology, in particular the glorification of the Trinity, could accommodate best the subtleties of human language, the limitations behind semantics, and the necessity to express transcendent truth in a coherent way. It is through doxological worship, Basil argued, that a person can best approach and convey the mystery of the church's experience of God. Basil's treatise *On the Holy Spirit*, discussed in Chapter Two, described how he defended his use of prepositions in doxological worship. When he ascribed glory to the Father *with* (μετά) the Son and *with* (σύν) the Holy Spirit,[5] he was defending the equality of worship, glory and honour of the persons of the Trinity, their "eternal communion and unceasing cooperation" (ἀϊδίου κοινωνίας καὶ ἀπαύστου συναφείας),[6] as well as the proper homage that was due to God.

For Basil's opponents, confusion arose in that he sometimes ascribed glory to the Father *with* (μετά) the Son and *with* (σύν) the Holy Spirit,[7] and sometimes to the Father, *through* (διά) the Son and *in* (ἐν) the Holy Spirit. When Basil used the formula "*with* (σύν) the Spirit" he was specifically advocating a theology of communion amongst the persons of the Trinity: "*With* reveals the communion among the persons more explicitly" (σὺν πρόθεσις τὴν κοινωνίαν πως συνενδείκνυται).[8] Basil used his letters to bring about a unity of faith and a unity of worship which he regarded as being inseparable. Belief and worship were inextricably bound together which, for "all those in communion" (πάντων τῶν κοινονικῶν),[9] implied eucharistic communion.

Basil's letters relate to the person's experience of communion from three interpenetrating perspectives: namely, communion in the local church, communion in the diocese, and finally communion between the dioceses. Importantly, communion in the local

---

5   Cf. *On the Holy Spirit*, 1.3, 7.16, 25.58.
6   *On the Holy Spirit*, 25.59: SC 17. 460.
7   See *On the Holy Spirit*, 1.3, 7.16, 25.58.
8   *On the Holy Spirit*, 25.59: Anderson, 91. SC 17. 460.
9   *Ep.* 120: Courtonne, II, 25.

church and the diocese only existed when the local church and the diocese were in communion with the wider Nicene church. Communion in the local church began (γενέσεως)[10] at baptism, was renewed through repentance, and had the Eucharist as its complete expression. Baptism conducted in the name of the Father, the Son and the Holy Spirit united the believer to God and to everyone else in the communion of the church. When Christians were united in communion with God, they became the body of Christ, the church, with the Eucharist constituting its core being. For Basil, the discipline of repentance aimed to seek the correction of the believer if he or she had fallen away from the communion of the church. The person who chose not to repent and be reconciled with God, brought upon him or herself the act of excommunication and therefore was "expelled from ecclesiastical communion" (ἐξορίσας [...] τῆς ἐκκλησιαστικῆς κοινωνίας).[11] While excommunicated, Basil claimed that a person could not be received back into the communion of the church (εἰς κοινωνίαν) until he or she ceased from sin (πρὶν ἢ παύσασθαι τῆς ἁμαρτίας).[12] When a person chose to be directed back to communion with God after personal sin, Basil believed that the original beauty and harmony of that person bestowed at baptism was restored. The greatest sign that a person had reconciled with God and henceforth with the worshipping community of the church was manifested in his or her ability to receive the Eucharist (μεταλαμβάνειν τοῦ ἁγίου σώματος καὶ αἵματος τοῦ Χριστοῦ).[13]

All local churches in a diocese acquired their validity to function through being aligned with the episcopal jurisdiction of a canonical bishop. Outside Nicene Christianity, according to Basil, those in holy orders had no canonicity and so were "not able to impart to others the grace of the Holy Spirit" (οὐκέτι δυνάμενοι

10   Canon 20 in *Ep.* 199.20: Courtonne, II, 157.
11   *Ep.* 289: Courtonne, III, 159.
12   *Ep.* 199.18: Courtonne, II, 156.
13   *Ep.* 93: Courtonne, I, 203.

χάριν Πνεύματος Αγίου ἑτέροις παρέχειν).[14] Placing a local church under the jurisdiction of a canonical bishop ensured that the faithful within that local church had access to eucharistic communion. By establishing and maintaining communion in the life of the local church, the bishop was charged with sanctioning or restoring eucharistic communion when it was absent, but also of dissolving it when its fundamental principles were not present in a person's way of life.

Communion in the diocese and between the dioceses had to do with the canonical standing of a bishop and his communion in faith (τῇ τῆς πίστεως κοινωνίᾳ)[15] with all other bishops. Essential doctrinal statements of faith (γραφεῖσαν πίστιν)[16] alluding to the divinity and equality of the Trinity, for instance one *ousia* in three *hypostases*, were necessary indicators that revealed a bishop's faith identity of belonging to a Nicene communion of churches. Where there was fraternity and mutual recognition among the bishops (διὰ τῆς τῶν ἐπισκόπων παραδοχῆς),[17] therein existed "a canon of communion" (κανόνα τινὰ τῆς πρὸς αὐτοὺς κοινωνίας),[18] indicating "ecclesiastical communion" (κοινωνίας ἐκκλησιαστικῆς)[19] on a universal level. Where there was heresy present, bishops and their congregations were separated from those in communion (χωρίζεσθαι ἀπ᾽ αὐτῶν)[20] and consequently were "plainly cut off from the body of the church" (φανερῶς ἀπορραγὲν τοῦ σώματος τῆς Ἐκκλησίας).[21]

In Basil's case, all non-Nicene hierarchs and their followers were asked to "correct their ways" (διορθοῖντο) so as to "be in com-

---

14 *Ep.* 188.1: Courtonne, II, 123.
15 *Ep.* 154: Courtonne, II, 78.
16 *Ep.* 125: Courtonne, II, 30.
17 *Ep.* 188.1: Courtonne, II, 124.
18 *Ep.* 188.1: Courtonne, II, 124.
19 *Ep.* 265.3: Courtonne, III, 131.
20 *Ep.* 263.5: Courtonne, III, 125.
21 *Ep.* 263.2: Courtonne, III, 122.

munion" (εἶναι κοινωνικούς).²² However, if they refused to change their faith position, they were excommunicated from the Nicene communion of churches. The process used to sever connections with non-Nicene hierarchs included the immediate sending of "a letter containing a prohibition (ἀπογόρευσιν) of communion with us".²³ Here the "us" was a reference to the sender and those bishops in communion with him (οἱ κοινωνικοί). Consequently, those who received deposed clergy found themselves "excommunicated throughout the whole church" (ἐκκήρυκτοι κατὰ πᾶσαν Ἐκκλησίαν γενήσονται).²⁴

During Basil's episcopal ministry, a key concern of his was to restore peace and order amongst the local churches in his diocese of Caesarea and throughout all his jurisdictional territory of Cappadocia Prima and Armenia. At the same time, Basil wanted to bring about communion for all the churches of the East. In Basil's mindset, a united witness and confession of faith amongst the bishops of the church was indicative of a strong and resilient church. When bishops were united in love and fellowship, they grew in strength through supporting each other and seeking each other's counsel. Basil believed that when bishops were in agreement with each other they could more readily give witness to the communion of the church, or when required and as befitted their office, defend the church's communion. The collective voice of the bishops on issues of faith, doctrine and morals placed them in a better position to expel heresy or to at least limit the disturbances caused to the communion of the church by having the heresy exposed. Basil's letters were meticulous in exposing heresies and even named them or their key followers individually. Those who chose not to accept a Nicene faith would effectively find themselves publicly excluded from the communion of the church. Basil

---

22 *Ep.* 263.5: Courtonne, III, 125.
23 *Ep.* 244.2: Deferrari, III, 455. Γράμματα εὐθὺς ἀπογόρευσιν ἔχοντα τῆς πρὸς ἡμᾶς κοινωνίας. Courtonne, III, 76.
24 *Ep.* 55: Courtonne, I, 142.

often referred to non-Nicene followers "as heretics" (ὡς αἱρετικοῖς) and admonished his faithful to abstain from having communion with them (τοὺς αἱρετικοὺς κοινωνίας ὑμᾶς ἀπέχεσθαι).[25]

By having the impact of heresy reduced "to a small number" of followers (εἰς ὀλίγον ἀριθμόν), Basil believed that the heresy would be "be considered unworthy of belief" (ἀναξιόπιστοι ὦσι)[26] and eventually disappear (ἐξορίσαι).[27] The numerical strength of Rome and its fellow Western sees was considered useful by Basil in his attempts to reinforce a Nicene position of faith against the non-Nicene adversary. In the name of "communion of the spirit" (κοινωνία πνεύματος),[28] the West was called upon by him "to give the desired aid to the churches of God" (παρασχέσθαι τὴν ἐπιζητουμένην βοήθειαν ταῖς τοῦ Θεοῦ Ἐκκλησίαις).[29] He advocated a consensus amongst those "who are supposed to share the same opinions" (οἱ δοκοῦντες τῷ αὐτῷ κοινωνεῖν φρονήματι ἐπιτείνομεν) and thus are "in agreement on the most important points" (οἱ ἐν τοῖς καιριωτάτοις ἔχοντες συμφωνίαν). Basil's aim was to assert and protect the essential theological teachings of the Nicene faith in which communion was realised.[30] He saw that when Nicene bishops were collectively united in faith and witness (ὁμοψύχων),[31] and in denouncing heresy, they had greater success in bringing about the reconciliation of dissenters from the faith.

As an indicative sign of their communion, bishops would often write letters to each other. Bishops who were involved in exchanging letters with Basil were called οἱ κοινωνικοί (lit. the ones in communion), in that they were in communion with him and each other.[32] For Basil, "those who confessed" the same Nicene "faith"

25 *Ep.* 262.2: Courtonne, III, 120.
26 *Ep.* 113: Courtonne, II, 17.
27 *Ep.* 69.2: Courtonne, I, 163.
28 *Ep.* 90.2: Deferrari, II, 127. Courtonne, I, 196.
29 *Ep.* 263.5: Courtonne, III, 126.
30 *Ep.* 258.1: Courtonne, III, 101.
31 *Ep.* 70: Courtonne, I, 165.
32 See *Ep.* 120: Courtonne, II, 26.

(τοὺς ταύτην ὁμολογοῦντας τὴν πίστιν) were considered to be part of the communion of the church.[33] When called upon, the κοινωνικοί promptly "signed their names" (ὑπέγραψαν)[34] to a written confession or creed. In Basil's understanding, a "succinct statement" (σύντομον [...] λόγον),[35] such as "a written confession" (ἔγγραφον [...] ὁμολογίαν), became the only "sufficient proof" (ἱκανήν [...] ἀπόδειξιν) of one's faith "convictions" (προαιρέσεως),[36] and when required, served as a testimony of one's communion in the church.

An affirmation of a creed in writing, done sincerely (γνησίαν καὶ ἄδολον [...] εἶναι τὴν κοινωνίαν)[37] and not just as "supposed proof of orthodoxy" (προφάσει δὴ τῆς ὀρθοδοξίας),[38] became the guarantor of a bishop's communion and a sign of his collegiality with all other bishops. This allowed bishops to be included in "the portion of the communicants" (τῇ μερίδι τῶν κοινωνικῶν)[39] and in this way to participate in eucharistic communion, which was mutually accepted by them as being the "best" (ἄριστον)[40] expression of communion. Correspondence between bishops through "letters of communion" (κανονικὰ γράμματα),[41] and the co-celebration of patronal feast days amongst bishops, served as forums where communion was expressed and practised. When Basil addressed these bishops as "most loved by God" (θεοφιλέστατος),[42] they were reminded not only of their intimate bond of friendship but also of the ideal of communion between people and God. Basil's patron feast day in memory of St. Eupsychius deliberately

33 *Ep.* 204.6: Courtonne, II, 179.
34 *Ep.* 224.3: Courtonne, III, 20.
35 *Ep.* 128.2: Courtonne, II, 38.
36 *Ep.* 99: Courtonne, I, 215.
37 *Ep.* 244.2: Deferrari, III, 453. Δὴ καὶ συγγέγραπτο μὲν ἡ πίστις, προσηνέχθη δὲ παρ᾽ ἡμῶν, ὑπεγράφη δέ [...] Ὥστε καὶ τοὺς κατὰ τὴν παροικίαν ἀδελφοὺς ἡμῶν συνελθόντας ἑνωθῆναι ἀλλήλοις καὶ γνησίαν καὶ ἄδολον τοῦ λοιποῦ εἶναι τὴν κοινωνίαν. Courtonne, III, 75.
38 *Ep.* 129.3: Courtonne, II, 41.
39 *Ep.* 204.6: Courtonne, II, 179.
40 *Ep.* 244.9: Courtonne, III, 83.
41 *Ep.* 224.2: Courtonne, III, 19.
42 See Basil *Epp.* 32, 67, 92, 120, 127, 163, 215, 226, 227, 230.

brought together Nicene bishops for a three-day celebration that culminated in eucharistic worship. Basil's rule was that if a bishop agreed "with the sound doctrine of faith" (τῷ ὑγιαίνοντι λόγῳ τῆς πίστεως), then that bishop could be received as "sharing in communion with the saints" (κοινωνὸν ἡγήσασθαι τῶν ἁγίων).[43]

As instruments of communion, Basil's letters confess, encourage, safeguard and ultimately facilitate communion in the life of the church. In this way, the letters, with the intention of prioritising participation in communion, reveal the characteristics needed for communion to take place (χαρακτήρων τὰ τῆς ἐπιμιξίας σύμβολα).[44] These characteristics have formed the main arguments of this volume, and so it is with reference to these characteristics that it will conclude.

---

43 *Ep.* 214.2: Courtonne, II, 204.
44 *Ep.* 203.3: Courtonne, II, 171.

The Characteristics of Communion in Basil Letters

Eucharistic

Communion in Basil's letters, at its greatest possible level, is realised as a eucharistic union with God. Through being a participant in the Eucharist, the believer becomes something different from what he or she was outside it. This *something different* is a communal being who is united in faith in the life of the church. According to Basil, the church united in the Eucharist is inseparably united with Christ in such a way that the two become one being (μίαν [...] ἕνωσιν).[1]

Through the Eucharist, God communicates himself to the person and in this way allows the person to enter into communion with him. Upon receiving the Eucharist, the person's being takes on by grace the "image and likeness"[2] of God. In the Eucharist, the transcendence of all division takes place and is replaced with communion. Basil says that all who participate in the Eucharist become "one people" (εἷς λαός) and "one church" (μία Ἐκκλησία).[3] Each eucharistic community, therefore, is identical and in communion with each other (φρονήματι ἕν)[4] by virtue of the whole presence of Christ contained in them.

The local eucharistic community would consist of all the Nicene faithful living in an area, city or province, united in the house of worship in which the Eucharist was celebrated. The

---

1   *Ep.* 133: Courtonne, II, 47.
2   Gen. 1:26.
3   *Ep.* 161.1: Courtonne, II, 93.
4   *Ep.* 204.4: Courtonne, II, 180.

Eucharist was preserved in each local church through the leadership of its presiding bishop. If the church's leaders (the bishops), "the pillars and foundation of the truth" (οἱ στῦλοι καὶ τὸ ἑδραίωμα τῆς ἀληθείας)[5] were absent, ecclesiastical communities remained orphaned, disconnected from one another and left to disintegrate. Within any given ecclesiastical community headed by a bishop, the Eucharist became the vehicle through which communion and canonical unity was expressed. In Basil's letters, the Eucharist is the most perfect criterion that manifests the church's communal existence.

1. In the Spirit, In Christ

Basil's letters tell the reader in no uncertain terms that communion is made possible through the inspiration of the Holy Spirit which "builds the churches" (οἰκοδομοῦν δὲ τὰς ἐκκλησίας).[6] The "Spirit of communion" (κοινωνία πνεύματος)[7] allows the communicant to see Christ and therefore be *in* the body of Christ, the church, where communion is sustained. Through the operations of the Holy Spirit, Christ is manifested since, according to Basil, "we are not capable of glorifying God on our own; only *in* the Spirit is this made possible".[8] In each person's relation to Christ, the Holy Spirit, argues Basil, is the *in* ("κοινωνία"),[9] in which he or she participates in Christ, "because the Spirit in himself reveals the divinity of the Lord".[10] As the sanctifier, teacher and revealer of mysteries, Basil sees the Holy Spirit as dwelling in Christians and guiding them towards salvation through a life of communion with

---

5 *Ep.* 243.4: Courtonne, III, 72.
6 *Ep.* 90.2: Courtonne, I, 196.
7 *Ep.* 90.2: Courtonne, I, 196.
8 *On the Holy Spirit*, 26.63: Anderson, 96. Οὔτε δοξάσαι ἀφ᾽ ἑαυτῶν ἱκανοί ἐσμεν, ἀλλ᾽ ἡ ἱκανότης ἡμῶν ἐν τῷ Πνεύματι τῷ ἁγίῳ, ἐν ᾧ δυναμωθέντες. SC 17. 474.
9 *Ep.* 90.1: Courtonne, I, 195.
10 *On the Holy Spirit*, 26.64: Anderson, 97. Ὡς ἐν ἑαυτῷ δεικνύντι τὴν τοῦ Κυρίου θεότητα. SC 17. 476.

God. In Basil's understanding, the Holy Spirit is eternally with the Father and the Son, and he is united with the Father through the Son. At the same time, the Holy Spirit is the living force of unity among the faithful and between the faithful and the Holy Trinity. For Basil, communion between God and the person is realised in Christ. When Christ became incarnate and gave the church its "body", he allowed the effects of the incarnation to be communicated throughout the church in history. As a result, unity with God as it existed before the fall of Adam, is now re-established once and for all in Christ the *new* Adam.[11] According to Basil, "all who have placed their hopes in Christ are one people and the followers of Christ are now one church".[12] To participate in the communion of the church was regarded by Basil to be the personal "gift of the Spirit" (ἡ τοῦ Πνεύματος δωρεά).[13] The eternal and inseparable presence of the Holy Spirit with the Father and the Son conveys the Father's love for the Son and the Son's response to this love.

In Basil's understanding, the Holy Spirit is intrinsic to God's divine activity, since the Holy Spirit is used as an instrument of sanctification that conveys God's love. Basil's treatise *On the Holy Spirit*, whose theology was discussed in Chapter Four, presented the church as having its existence in communion on the premise that it is through the Holy Spirit that the church's "being in communion" is realised and participated. By being constitutive of both Christology and ecclesiology, the Holy Spirit makes it impossible to think of Christ as an individual not being in communion with the "many", his body; or to think of the church as one without simultaneously thinking of her as many. Basil's theological understanding of communion is that a person is united with the very person of God the Father, through the Son and in the Holy Spirit.

---

11 See 1 Cor.15:20-24, 45-48.
12 *Ep.* 161.1: Deferrari, II, 413. Εἷς λαὸς πάντες οἱ εἰς Χριστὸν ἠλπικότες καὶ μία Ἐκκλησία νῦν οἱ Χριστοῦ. Courtonne, II, 93.
13 *Ep.* 133: Courtonne, II, 47.

2. Trinitarian

Basil's understanding of communion was immersed in his Trinitarian theology where he advocated the equal worship, glory and honour of the persons of the Trinity. Essentially, for Basil, the "Holy Trinity is one God" (εἷς Θεὸς ἡ Τριάς).[14] He holds that communion is a union with the person of God the Father, who is inseparably and coeternally united in freedom and love with the *hypostases* of the Son and the Holy Spirit. Chapter Two explored how the *monarchia* of the Father guarantees the unity and *homotimia* of the Trinity through locating the Father as the eternal source of the Son and the Holy Spirit. Basil's Trinitarian theology was expressed as a continuous and uninterrupted communion of divine persons, which was foundational to his ecclesiology.

According to Basil, when it comes to "the persons of the Godhead" (τῶν προσώπων),[15] otherness in the divine *hypostases'* distinctive features (ἰδιότητες), upholds their common essence and inseparable communion, and therefore does not undermine or threaten their equality. In the same way that the *hypostases* of the Father, Son and Holy Spirit are both common (κοινόν) and particular (ἴδιον),[16] so also are members within the communion of the church equal in honour and dignity through their common human nature, yet different in their personal characteristics through their individual distinctive features. Father, Son and Holy Spirit, with their distinct personal attributes, exist in interpersonal communion through reciprocating a movement of love. Although the hypostatic properties within the Holy Trinity are not communicated, the notion of person is inconceivable outside a relationship (σχέσις). Father, Son and Holy Spirit are names that indicate a relationship and therefore imply that "being" for the Holy Trinity is simultaneously relational and hypostatic.

---

14 *Ep.* 129.1: Courtonne, II, 40.
15 *Ep.* 52.3: Courtonne, I, 135.
16 See *Ep.* 236.6.

Basil regarded ecclesial communion as a communion of believers who in every way possible were encouraged to live in communion with the Trinitarian God. In this regard, however, there is no explicit reference in Basil's letters to a direct connection where communion in the life of the church was modelled on communion in the life of the Holy Trinity. Basil's letters do specifically mention that communion consists of a participation in the life of the church, which through the Holy Spirit consists of a life that is in direct communion with God. Basil's inherent message throughout his letters, for those belonging to the communion of the church, is to live in communion with God. In this sense, for Basil, personal being within the church is intrinsically relational and communal.

3. Inspired by the New Testament

Basil's reference to the New Testament community in Jerusalem served as proof that communion is not only possible but indeed always necessary. He exhorted his followers to: "accept the community life in imitation of the apostolic manner of living".[17] The apostolic community of Jerusalem found in Acts conveyed the ecclesial reality of the church as being that of communion, and Basil encouraged believers to "zealously imitate the early Christian community, where everything was held in common – life, soul, concord, a common table, indivisible kinship – while unfeigned love constituted many bodies as one and joined many souls into a harmonious whole".[18]

In the early Christian church of Jerusalem, believers partici-

---

17 *Ep.* 295: Deferrari, IV, 207. Τὴν ἐπὶ τὸ αὐτὸ καταδέξασθαι εἰς μίμημα τῆς ἀποστολικῆς πολιτείας. Courtonne, III, 169–170.
18 Basil, *In Time of Famine and Drought*, 8: Schroeder, *Saint Basil the Great: On Social Justice*, 86. Τὸ πρῶτον τῶν Χριστιανῶν ζηλώσωμεν σύνταγμα· ὅπως ἦν αὐτοῖς ἅπαντα κοινά, ὁ βίος, ἡ ψυχὴ, ἡ συμφωνία, ἡ τράπεζα κοινὴ, ἀδιαίρετος ἀδελφότης, ἀγάπη ἀνυπόκριτος, τὰ πολλὰ σώματα ἓν ἐργαζομένη· τὰς διαφόρους ψυχὰς εἰς μίαν ὁμόνοιαν ἁρμόζουσα. PG 31. 325A–B.

pated in a common life (κοινὸς βίος) of prayer and worship, and all things were held for the common good. In Basil's understanding, the faithful from the Jerusalem church in Acts lived their lives in such a way where they could "give to those who have need" (ματαδιδόναι τοῖς χρείαν ἔχουσι).[19] To him this was the best way of life and he likened it to heavenly worship where the faithful "imitate on earth the choir of the angels" (τὴν ἀγγέλων χορείαν ἐν γῇ μιμεῖσθαι).[20] New Testament communal living, according to Basil, consisted of a mode of existence amongst Christians that anticipated as much as possible the second *parousia* of Christ.

4. Traditional

Basil's letters equate "following the traditions of the fathers" (τῶν πατέρων αἱ παραδόσεις)[21] with "the practice that has long been followed in God's churches"[22] and which brought about communion in the church. According to Basil, it is the church's tradition to manifest communion in every area of the church's existence. His letters sought to defend communion or restore communion when it was broken by calling upon tradition which upheld apostolic faith. Basil was often accused of not standing by the tradition of the church and of introducing unscriptural elements into the liturgical life of the church. Throughout his letters, he vehemently rebutted any accusations that presented him as untraditional or as acting contrary to the Gospel commandments.

The basis of Basil's theological teaching on communion was founded upon the dual authority of Scripture and tradition, especially when the latter had to do with the lives of holy men and women of the past. Tradition, for Basil, was the culmination of the

---

19 *Ep.* 207.2: Courtonne, II, 157.
20 *Ep.* 2.2: Courtonne, I, 7–8.
21 *Ep.* 261.3: Courtonne, III, 118.
22 *Ep.* 54: Deferrari, I, 343. Ἡ πάλαι ταῖς τοῦ Θεοῦ Ἐκκλησίαις ἐμπολιτευμένη συνήθεια. Courtonne, I, 139.

written and the unwritten (ἄγραφα)[23] sources of witness, which he regarded as belonging to the whole church. It was Basil's firm belief that the communion of the church depended on maintaining "the precepts of the Gospel, which change neither with seasons nor with vicissitudes of human affairs, but continue the same, as they were pronounced by truthful and blessed lips, thus abiding always".[24] He spent much time in his letters exposing those church leaders accusing him by declaring that they were "contradicting themselves" (ἐναντιούμενοι)[25] and that "this was not what that holy and God-beloved [Nicene] synod had in mind".[26] Basil argued that it was his critics who were not adhering to a traditional Nicene position of faith but instead were "always changing" in their theological persuasions based on the political "party in power" (ἀεὶ πρὸς τὸ δυνατὸν μετατίθεσθαι μέρος).[27]

5. Nicene

In Basil's letters, communion with God and pastoral outreach are made possible only within the context of a professed Nicene faith (πίστιν κοινωνίας).[28] Above all, he had in mind the creed of Nicaea. He proclaimed: "the creed of the Fathers who assembled at Nicaea has been honoured by us" (ἡ τῶν ἐν Νικαίᾳ συνελθόντων Πατέρων πίστις […] προτετίμηται).[29] To enter and remain in the communion of the church, it was imperative for him that a person accepted a creed that in no way differed from the faith of Nicaea and that had

---

23 See *Epp.* 70, 204.
24 *Ep.* 244.8: Deferrari, III, 469. Τῶν εὐαγγελικῶν ἐντολῶν […] αἳ οὔτε καιροῖς οὔτε περιστάσεσιν ἀνθρωπίνων πραγμάτων συμμεταβάλλονται, ἀλλ᾿ αἱ αὐταὶ διαμένουσιν, ὡς προηνέχθησον ἀπὸ τοῦ ἀψευδοῦς καὶ μακαρίου στόματος οὕτω διαιωνίζουσαι. Courtonne, III, 82.
25 *Ep.* 226.2: Courtonne, III, 25.
26 *Ep.* 226.3: Deferrari, III, 337. Οὐ γὰρ τοῦτο ἐνόησεν ἡ ἁγία ἐκείνη καὶ θεοφιλὴς σύνοδος. Courtonne, III, 26.
27 *Ep.* 226.2: Courtonne, III, 25.
28 *Ep.* 133: Courtonne, II, 47.
29 *Ep.* 159.1: Courtonne, II, 86.

been confessed by "holy people" (τῶν ἁγίων) of the past.³⁰ The core of Basil's episcopal ministry was based on his continuous desire to "restore the creed which was written by the Fathers of the Nicene Council" (τὴν ἐν Νικαίᾳ γραφεῖσαν παρὰ τῶν Πατέρων ἡμῶν πίστιν ἀνανεώσονται);³¹ to "walk in their footsteps" (ἴχνη βαίνειν ἐκείνοις)³² and ultimately to "speak to the churches a message of peace by bringing those of like convictions into unity" (ταῖς Ἐκκλησίαις τὰ εἰρηνικὰ διαλέξονται τοὺς τὰ αὐτὰ φρονοῦντας συνάγοντες εἰς ὁμόνοιαν).³³

For Basil, Nicene Christianity was connected to salvation, as well as to the preservation of the dignity of human life. He accepted as communicants those who adhered to the faith of Nicaea and who by extension refused to describe the Holy Spirit as a creature. All theological formulations that leant towards Nicaea were considered as orthodox by the communion of the church since they had a direct impact on a person's salvation. Theological formulations that did not align with a Nicene confession of faith, Basil asserted, "the catholic and apostolic church anathematises" (ἀναθεματίζει ἡ καθολικὴ καὶ ἀποστολικὴ Ἐκκλησία).³⁴ This is because these formulas were interpreted as a threat to the communion of the church in that they disrupted the equality of the persons "of the divine and saving Trinity" (τῆς θείας καὶ σωτηρίου Τριάδος)³⁵ and therefore their communion.

Communion in the life of the Trinity was founded upon an equality of divinity amongst all three persons. Basil held that if the persons of the Trinity were not all divine, then they could not all be equal and in full communion with each other. In promoting pro-Nicene faith and doctrinal harmony in the church, his letters

---

30   *Ep.* 159.1: Courtonne, II, 86.
31   *Ep.* 92.3: Courtonne, I, 202.
32   *Ep.* 159.1: Courtonne, II, 86.
33   *Ep.* 92.3: Courtonne, I, 202.
34   *Ep.* 125.2: Courtonne, II, 33.
35   *Ep.* 90.2: Courtonne, I, 196.

were advocating a theology of communion amongst believers that had a direct impact on a believer's way of life. A non-Nicene faith position, for Basil, had repercussions on one's spiritual well-being. It deprived people from communion with people of like faith (ὁμοδοξούντων κοινωνία). For those people belonging to the correct confession of faith, Basil's pastoral canons became the guiding principles for achieving and maintaining communion.

6. Episcopal

The human instrument responsible for manifesting, conveying and safeguarding communion for the local eucharistic community is the canonical bishop. The head of every eucharistic community is Christ; however, in each eucharistic community, Christ is represented through the ministry of a presiding bishop. The bishop had the responsibility of maintaining the "communion of the good" (τῆς τοῦ ἀγαθοῦ κοινωνίας)[36] for the faithful entrusted to his care. As a chosen instrument by God, the bishop "in conjunction with the Spirit" (συνεργείᾳ τοῦ πνεύματος)[37] was required to attend to the care (ἐπιμέλεια) and pastoral solicitude (φροντίς) of Christ's flock.[38] As God's vessel, the bishop was used to impart divine grace amongst the communion of believers in the life of the church. He was entrusted to proclaim "with complete boldness" (πάσῃ παρρησίᾳ) the correct teachings contained in the conscience of the church and to "refute those who do not walk uprightly according to the Gospel" (ἔλεγχε τοὺς μὴ ὀρθοποδοῦντας πρὸς τὴν ἀλήθειαν τοῦ Εὐαγγελίου).[39]

In a liturgical setting, the bishop offered the Eucharist to God in the name of the local church, and thus brought before God the communion of believers, the body of Christ. For Basil and his fel-

---

36 *Ep.* 199.24: Courtonne, II, 159.
37 *Ep.* 227: Courtonne, III, 30.
38 See *Ep.* 197.
39 *Ep.* 250: Deferrari, IV, 7. Courtonne, III, 89.

low bishops, the unity of the church in the Eucharist became synonymous with the unity of the church in the bishop. The presence of the bishop personified the Eucharist and the communion of the church, and was regarded as the place in which the fullness of the church dwelt. Consequently, where there was no communion with the local bishop, so too was there no communion with all other bishops, which meant that one "cut themselves off from the whole church" (πάσης ἑαυτῶν τῆς Ἐκκλησίας ἀπορρηγνύς).[40] When bishops wrote a letter to a local church, they would address this letter to its "God-beloved bishop" (θεοφιλέστατον ἐπίσκοπον) with the understanding that it was the bishop who represented the communion of the local church.

A bishop is canonical by virtue of his being "in strict agreement and unity" (ἐν ἀκριβεῖ συμφωνίᾳ καὶ ἑνότητι)[41] with all other bishops and in this way is accepted by them (ἐπισκόπων παραδοχῆς),[42] through "a canonical synodical letter" (συνοδικῷ γράμματι κανονικῶς),[43] as espousing the same pro-Nicene faith. It was not uncommon for letters to be drawn up for the sole purpose of being "signed by all those in communion" (ὑπογραφῆναι δὲ πάντων τῶν κοινωνικῶν).[44] These letters, if needed, acted like licenses which validated a bishop's canonicity and bore witness to his communion with the church. Basil's letters present the bishop as the essential ecclesial reality through which communion exists and functions, both within a bishop's own diocese as well as throughout the whole "catholic church" (καθολικὴν Ἐκκλησίαν).[45] The church's mission for communion rested on the theological consensus (τὴν πίστιν συμφωνίας)[46] and collegiality of its bishops, who subsequently governed their churches "in harmony and

---

40 *Ep.* 204.7: Courtonne, II, 180.
41 *Ep.* 91: Courtonne, I, 197.
42 *Ep.* 188.1: Courtonne, II, 124.
43 *Ep.* 92.3: Courtonne, I, 203.
44 *Ep.* 120: Courtonne, II, 25.
45 *Ep.* 188.1: Courtonne, II, 121.
46 *Ep.* 191: Courtonne, II, 144.

accord with all the churches of God" (ταῖς τοῦ Θεοῦ ἐκκλησίαις συνῳδά ἐστι καὶ σύφωνα).[47]

7. Ascetical

Asceticism in Basil's letters was incorporated into every aspect of church life and encapsulated the attitude of spiritual life that was applicable to all Christians whether they were monastics or not. All members of the communion of the church were considered by Basil as being on a spiritual journey "leading to the Lord" (πρὸς τὸν Κύριον ἄγουσαν)[48] that had ethical conduct, charity and doctrinal harmony as its enchiridion. The level of asceticism was different for each individual believer and was based on his or her ability to respond to the commandments found in Scripture. When practised from within the communion of the church, asceticism was regarded as a genuine expression of a person's desire to love God and to be in communion with God. Asceticism in Basil's letters aimed to address moral and doctrinal errors, which, he argued, were intrinsically linked.

When Basil emphasised the ascetic ideal in the life of his diocese, he was in principle responding to the lack of unity and cooperation that existed in the churches of his diocese, as well as the lack of ascetic fervour amongst Christian leaders. At a spiritual level, he believed that sin leading to moral failure was the ultimate reason for the spread of heresy in the East. He said that a soul "that is darkened by the passions" (ἐπισκοτουμένην πάθεσι) cannot "receive the rays of the Holy Spirit" (ὑποδέξασθαι τοῦ Ἁγίου Πνεύματος τὰς ἐλλάμψεις).[49] Basil expected his clergy to exercise their ecclesiastical leadership with monastic values in that asceticism was considered essential for effective church ministry and for

---

47 *Ep.* 208.3: Courtonne, II, 186.
48 *Ep.* 150.2: Courtonne, II, 73.
49 *Ep.* 210.6: Courtonne, II, 196.

combatting "heretical impiety" (αἱρετικῆς δυσσεβείας).⁵⁰ Monastic principles of self-renunciation and charity underpinned successful pastoral care, and were considered indispensable for the formation of social morality within the church's broader community. A lack of spiritual life amongst the clergy had negative consequences on the laity whom they served. "Whatever the rulers are", states Basil, "such for the most part are the characters of those governed accustomed to become".⁵¹ When he raised the quality of spiritual life amongst his clergy (καθηγούμενοι), he saw it as only natural for the laity to follow "in accord" (μετὰ συμπνοίας).⁵²

Basil presented spiritual life as having purpose only when it was aligned with a Nicene confession of faith. He always advocated that "both should go together" (δεῖ ἀμφότερα συνεῖναι)⁵³ since it was Nicene faith that made communion with the divine accessible. The usefulness of asceticism as a necessary expression of a person's desire for communion with God was manifested in its ability to restore and preserve communion both for the individual believer and the diocesan bishop. Asceticism brought moral uprightness and enhanced the cooperation of the churches within a diocese. Ascetic fervour and Nicene faith amongst church leaders were essential hallmarks of their spiritual life that fostered communion.

8. Institutional

Communion, while being both an interpersonal and a spiritual reality, was essentially an institutional reality as well, which had to take into account the political landscape and other demographics pertaining to its functioning in any given location. The socio-po-

---

50   *Ep.* 243.4: Courtonne, III, 72.
51   *Ep.* 190.1: Deferrari, III, 71. Ὅτι ὁποῖοι δ᾽ ἄν ὦσιν οἱ προεστῶτες, τοιαῦτα, ὡς ἐπὶ τὸ πολύ, καὶ τὰ ἤθη τῶν ἀρχομένων γίνεσθαι εἴωθεν. Courtonne, II, 141.
52   *Ep.* 222: Courtonne, III, 7. See *Ep.* 150.4.
53   *Ep.* 295: Courtonne, III, 170.

litical environment in which communion functioned created the impetus to manifest Christ's love and to act in ways that lead to the "edification of the churches of Christ" (οἰκοδομὴν τῶν Ἐκκλησιῶν τοῦ Χριστοῦ).[54] A bishop's social interactions were very much considered to be an extension of his prayer life and contributed to his respective see's regional importance. Creating a network of social interactions allowed Basil to provide a context in which he could establish meaningful relationships so as to harness communion. His homes for the poor, his schools, hostels and hospitals, his church edifices and monastic centres, the organisation of the clergy in his diocese, and his official correspondence as a bishop, all expressed his desire to build communion institutionally.

For Basil, promoting the communion of the church necessarily took into account the existing social order in that he sought to co-operate as best as he could with the leading people of the state. It involved the common good of the empire and the general welfare of the empire's citizens. Government subsidies and an enhanced financial position gave church leaders greater leverage to request aid from their civil counterparts for their various welfare and building projects. The church needed significant financial investment for its institutions to remain active. In Basil's view, the more the state provided to the church, the greater beneficiary it was of the church's prayer and affection. His relationship with those in civil leadership allowed him to appropriate the authority and structure of the state in a way that he saw as beneficial to his immediate pastoral environment and to fulfilling his ecclesiological vision for establishing communion.

9. Identifying with the Poor

Communion is social in nature and calls a person to empathise with other people through acts of social justice. Personal holiness

---

54 *Ep.* 203.4: Courtonne, II, 171–172.

only exists when one relates to the needs of the other and considers them as "equal in honour" (ὁμοτιμίας ἰσότης)[55] to himself or herself. From this perspective, empathising with the other and having regard for them is instrumental for spiritual progress and serves as a powerful indication of one's participation in the communion of the church. In Basil's view, to identify with the poor and afflicted (συμπαθείας τῶν θλιβομένων)[56] required the sensitivity to see their need as one's very own need. Outside this sensitivity towards social responsibility, Basil held that a person was not true to himself or herself and consequently was inhibited from relating to the other.

In Basil's letters, Christian life required being in communion with one's neighbours through "works of righteousness" (ἔργων τῆς δικαιοσύνης)[57] in response to their need. According to Basil, this involved: "Visits to the sick, the consolation of those who grieve, the assisting of those who are in distress, succour of all kinds".[58] For Basil, love, charity and good works can only be realised when a person's life is lived in continuous communion with others. The use of the word κοινός in his writings highlighted that all things are to be used for the common benefit of all. In this way, material possessions and spiritual gifts were considered to be not the private property of an individual but rather the common property of all. As such, a κοινωνικὸς ἄνθρωπος is a person who is aware of his or her common bond with all human beings. Its opposite, ἀκοινώνικος ἄνθρωπος, is a person who keeps exclusively for himself or herself what in essence is for common use.

The monastic attitudes promoted in Basil's letters nurtured communion with God in the church through encouraging a life of

---

55 *Ep.* 262.1: Courtonne, III, 119.
56 *Ep.* 31: Courtonne, I, 73.
57 *On the Holy Spirit*, 8.18: SC 17. 310.
58 *Ep.* 243.4: Deferrari, III, 447. Ἐπισκέψεις τῶν ἀσθενούντων, παράκλησις τῶν λυπουμένων, βοήθεια τῶν καταπονουμένων, ἀντιλήψεις παντοδαπαί. Courtonne, III, 72–73.

shared resources and unconditional charity. The success behind Basil's *Basiliad* (as discussed in Chapter Three) was the implementation of his social vision of a shared community life. Basil believed that no individual Christian or Christian community can be spiritually healthy if they are ignoring the interests and needs of others. Heavenly blessings are incommunicable without the distribution of charity below.

10. Catholic

In Basil's letters, communion affects all people in the whole life of the church, and for this reason was regarded by him as being catholic. According to Basil, there was no place for an individual monad in the communal existence of the church, but "all should be fellow-citizens and neighbours to all" (πάντας πᾶσι πολίτας καὶ οἰκείους εἶναι).[59] Christian life in its fullness demanded the ability to be in communion with God and one's neighbours. Communion with others was regarded by Basil as a fundamental constituent of human existence that sustained daily life. The person, therefore, as a created communal being, becomes displaced when communion with the *other* is broken. Basil explains: "For whenever I look upon these very limbs of ours and see that no one of them is sufficient in itself to produce action, how can I reason that I of myself suffice to cope with the difficulties of life?"[60] If one member of the church suffers, whether through moral failure, humanitarian need or theological error, all suffer. Reconciliation was not only directed towards God but also towards the communion of the believers that make up the church.

In his ministry Basil wants the life of the Christians, both clergy and laity, to be equal in their devotion to Christian living

---

59 *Ep.* 203.3: Courtonne, II, 171.
60 *Ep.* 97: Deferrari, II, 163. Ὅταν γὰρ πρὸς αὐτὰ ταῦτα ἀπίδω τὰ μέλη ἡμῶν, ὅτι ἓν οὐδὲν ἑαυτῷ πρὸς ἐνέργειαν αὔταρκες, πῶς ἐμαυτὸν λογίσομαι ἐξαρκεῖν ἑαυτῷ πρὸς τὰ τοῦ βίου πράγματα; Courtonne, I, 210.

and for them to be united in indivisible kinship through "communion in prayer" (προσευχαῖς κοινωνίαν).[61] To live "the way that is according to Christ's polity" (τῆς ὁδοῦ τῆς κατὰ Χριστὸν πολιτείας),[62] as "ecclesiastical members" (ἐκκλησιαστικῶν μελῶν)[63] of the body of Christ, implied communion between God and the person that was without division but at the same time without confusion. In one of the many different analogies that Basil makes with respect to the human body, he presents his point in a most tangible way: "For the hands need each other, and the feet steady each other, and it is through their working in concert (συμφωνίᾳ) that the eyes possess their clearness of perception".[64]

Basil's letters accept that communion exists to include all (μίαν ἕνωσιν),[65] and that a person's exclusion from communion is simultaneously an invitation that offers every possibility to enter into communion. Basil asked those people who were not in communion with the Nicene church, to abandon their non-Nicene faith. Those people who were cut off from the communion of the church as a result of their continuous wilful desire to sin, Basil asked to repent. In Basil's world-view, there was no justification for Christians to remain outside of the communion of the church. There was no such thing as a non-communal Christian. Although Christians may co-operate with error, he insisted that they were created to be in communion with God and with each other. He fervently believed that Christians have the necessity of communion as a constituent of their existence, "for we all need each other in the communion of our members" (χρῄζομεν γὰρ ἀλλήλων πάντες

---

61   Ep. 150.2: Courtonne, II, 73.
62   Ep. 150.1: Courtonne, II, 71.
63   Ep. 203.3: Courtonne, II, 170.
64   Ep. 203.3: Deferrari, III, 149. Εἴτε καὶ ἐν ἄλλῃ τάξει τῶν ἐκκλησιαστικῶν μελῶν ἑαυτοὺς τάσσετε, οὐ δύνασθε λέγειν τοῖς ἐν τῷ αὐτῷ σώματι κατατεταγμένοις ἡμῖν τό· χρείαν ὑμῶν οὐκ ἔχομεν. Αἵ τε γὰρ χεῖρες ἀλλήλων δέονται καὶ οἱ πόδες ἀλλήλους στηρίζουσι καὶ οἱ ὀφθαλμοὶ ἐν τῇ συμφωνίᾳ τὸ ἐναργὲς τῆς καταλήψεως ἔχουσιν. Courtonne, II, 170. See Epp. 29, 97, 263.2.
65   Ep. 133: Courtonne, II, 47.

κατὰ τῶν μελῶν κοινωνίαν).⁶⁶

11. Accessible and Safeguarded

Basil's letters reveal that communion needed to be as accessible as possible while at the same time safeguarded from the "wicked action" (κακούργημα) of people that was "unacceptable to the church" (ἀπροσδέκτους ποιήσωσι τῇ Ἐκκλησίᾳ).⁶⁷ Basil believed that where heresy was present, communion remained unguarded (ἀφυλάκτου κοινωνίας)⁶⁸ and threatened anywhere the church existed.

Leniency and severity used in the interpretation of canons came with pastoral overtones in that they sought to bring about reconciliation and "to restore communion into the body of Christ" (ἀποκαταστήσονται εἰς τὴν κοινωνίαν τοῦ σώματος τοῦ Χριστοῦ).⁶⁹ Pastoral canons aimed to "show indulgence to the weaker" (συμπεριενεχθῆναι τοῖς ἀσθενεστέροις), but did so "without causing harm to souls" (μηδὲν βλάπτομεν τὰς ψυχάς)⁷⁰ which was caused by receiving people "prematurely into communion" (προσληφθῆναί [...] εἰς κοινωνίαν).⁷¹ Within his own ministry, Basil refrained from applying the strictness of the rule (δουλεύειν ἀκριβείᾳ κανόνων) "for the sake of the pastoral dispensation of the many" (οἰκονομίας ἕνεκα τῶν πολλῶν)⁷² and out of fear of "standing in the way of those being saved" (ἐμποδίσωμεν τοῖς σωζομένοις).⁷³

Under the correct circumstances, reconciliation into the communion of the church was instant and all errors, whether in conduct or doctrinal affiliation, were forgiven. As Basil would say:

66   *Ep.* 266.2: Courtonne, III, 135.
67   *Ep.* 188.1: Courtonne, II, 123.
68   *Ep.* 263.2: Courtonne, III, 122.
69   Canon 82 in *Ep.* 217.82: Courtonne, II, 216.
70   *Ep.* 113: Courtonne, II, 17.
71   *Ep.* 240.3: Courtonne, III, 64.
72   *Ep.* 188.1: Courtonne, II, 123.
73   Canon 1 in *Ep.* 118.1: Courtonne, II, 123.

"We do not consider the past, if only the present be sound".[74] Essentially Basil was trying to reconcile, in the easiest possible way, people back into the communion of the church. He considered it his pastoral duty to keep within the communion of the church as many people as possible. Basil's letters invite the believer to participate in the church's communion through the recognition of Nicene Christianity which he saw as protecting that communion, and at the same time through his or her keeping away from "the faction of those not in communion" (οἱ τῆς μερίδος τῶν ἀκοινωνήτων).[75] Within the "right confession of faith" (ὀρθὴ ὁμολογία) and the practice of "good works" (ἀγαθῶν ἔργων)[76] through the "withdrawal from sin" (ἁμαρτίας ἀναχώρησις),[77] lay the perfection of the Christian person (ἄρτιος ᾖ ὁ τοῦ Θεοῦ ἄνθρωπος).[78] It is a combination of orthodoxy and orthopraxy that, according to Basil, ensured that the communion of the church remained "pure, having no weed mixed with it" (καθαρὰ [...] μηδὲν ζιζάνιον ἑαυτῇ περαμεμιγμένον ἔχουσα).[79]

12. Mutually Responsible

Basil's letters testify that communion is the responsibility of every Christian and that it is to be desired at all times, in all places and for all people. The Christian becomes affected when communion in any of its forms ceases to exist. Every person has the need to be in communion (ἀναγκαῖον τῆς κοινωνίας)[80] and the ability to contribute towards it where it does not exist. Each Christian is responsible for all and the care of the churches is a mutual respon-

---

74 *Ep.* 210.4: Deferrari, III, 207. Οὐ σκοποῦμεν τὰ παρελθόντα, τὰ παρόντα μόνον ὑγιαινέτωσαν. Courtonne, II, 194.
75 *Ep.* 250: Courtonne, III, 88.
76 *Ep.* 295: Courtonne, III, 170.
77 Canon 3 in *Ep.* 188.3: Courtonne, II, 125.
78 *Ep.* 295: Courtonne, III, 170.
79 *Ep.* 114: Courtonne, II, 19.
80 *Ep.* 97: Courtonne, I, 210.

sibility bestowed upon all Christians. In the spirit of "ecclesiastical law" (ἐκκλησιαστικὸν θεσμόν)[81] that is founded upon love (ἀγάπην),[82] Basil maintained that every Christian must not only aspire towards communion for his or her own edification, but that they must also desire and facilitate its manifestation wherever and for whomever it does not exist. To those who were not in κοινωνία, Basil exhorted that every effort should be made, in fulfilment of "the laws of love" (θεσμοὺς τῆς ἀγάπης), to be "united [...] in communion" (προσκαλεῖσθαι [...] εἰς συνάφειαν).[83] He said: "Nothing is so proper to our nature as to share our lives with each other, and to need each other, and to love our own kind".[84]

Bishops, in particular, had to do everything within their means to safeguard and uphold the communion of the church, especially wherever they saw that the church's communion was being compromised or threatened. Basil depended on his fellow bishops to "to bring back the churches into union" (τὸ ἐπαναγαγεῖν πρὸς ἕνωσιν τὰς Ἐκκλησίας).[85] He asked that bishops "not let schisms loose among the churches", and that they should "by every means urge into unity (ἕνωσις) those who hold identical doctrines" to Nicaea.[86] Basil considered communion to be "the greatest of all blessings" (τὸ μέγιστον τῶν ἀγαθῶν)[87] in the life of the church and for this reason only natural to human existence.

13. Doing God's Will

---

81 *Ep.* 126: Courtonne, II, 35.
82 *Ep.* 65: Courtonne, I, 156.
83 *Ep.* 128: Courtonne, II, 39.
84 *Saint Basil the Great: On the Human Condition*, Harrison, 117. Οὐδὲν γὰρ οὕτως ἴδιον τῆς φύσεως ἡμῶν, ὡς τὸ κοινωνεῖν ἀλλήλοις, καὶ χρῄζειν ἀλλήλων, καὶ ἀγαπᾶν τὸ ὁμόφυλον. PG 31. 917A.
85 *Ep.* 114: Courtonne, II, 18.
86 *Ep.* 69.2: Deferrari, II, 47. Μὴ ἐναφῶσι ταῖς Ἐκκλησίαις τὰ σχίσματα, ἀλλὰ τοὺς τὰ αὐτὰ φρονοῦντας παντὶ τρόπῳ εἰς ἕνωσιν συνελάσωσι. Courtonne, I, 164.
87 *Ep.* 156.1: Courtonne, II, 82.

Basil sees κοινωνία as a fundamental component of human life, and as a natural consequence of living out the will of God. He insists that the person is a κοινωνικὸν ζῷον: "a being that is communal by nature",[88] and so, for Basil, the most intimate relationship with God involves a communion with persons as well. Communion in his letters, however, apart from its ethical dimension of bringing about an ordered life, was also identified as doing God's will (βούλησιν Θεοῦ)[89] for the survival of the church. In fact, communion was a distinguishing sign of the existence of the church and it was considered by Basil to be the church's "most fervent prayer" (εὐχῆς τῆς ἀνωτάτω).[90] Through God's grace, communion kept people "bound by the unity of love in the body of Christ" (διὰ τῆς ἀγάπης ἑνώσει [...] ἐν σώματι Χριστοῦ δεδέσθαι).[91] Without communion, Basil argued that it was not possible to "see the providence of God" (ἰδεῖν τὰς οἰκονομίας τὰς τοῦ Θεοῦ).[92] Because communion was in accordance to God's will, it brought "peace among the churches" (εἰρήνην τῶν ἐκκλησιῶν)[93] and ensured the continuation of the church's mission.

14. Beneficial

Communion in Basil's letters exists only to be beneficial to the church and to each of its members "so that the body of Christ may be made perfect" (ἵνα ἄρτιον γένηται τὸ σῶμα τοῦ Χριστοῦ).[94] Basil considered a break in communion to be damaging (ζημίαν φέρειν τὸν διασπασμὸν τῆς ὁμονοίας)[95] to the functioning of the local and universal church. For this reason, repeatedly in his letters,

---

88   See the third rule of Basil's *Longer Rules*. PG 32. 181A-C.
89   *Ep.* 227: Courtonne, III, 32.
90   *Ep.* 244.9: Courtonne, III, 83.
91   *Ep.* 70: Courtonne, I, 164-165.
92   *Ep.* 313: Courtonne, III, 187.
93   *Ep.* 28.3: Courtonne, I, 70.
94   *Ep.* 92.3: Courtonne, I, 203.
95   *Ep.* 203.3: Courtonne, II, 171.

he insisted that "communion in prayer" (προσευχαῖς κοινωνίαν) can only bring about "great gain" (πολὺ κέρδος).[96] The establishment of harmony among the churches (τῇ κοινῇ καταστάσει τῶν Ἐκκλησιῶν),[97] as an imperative condition for communion, was a definitive mark of Basil's episcopal ministry. With this in mind, it is most fitting to end this summary of his characteristics of communion with the words of Basil himself: "It is beneficial to unite what has been formerly divided". (Εὐεργεσία δέ ἐστιν ἑνωθῆναι τὰ τέως διεσπασμένα.)[98]

The letters of Basil reveal that his fundamental understanding of the church is one of a communion that is founded upon and realised in Christ. In Basil's theology, κοινωνία refers not only to the church's intimate unity, but also to the church's participation by grace in the life of the Godhead. Basil makes it clear that where there is no communion with God, there too is there no real communion with people, and therefore the church ceases to exist. Through Basil's use of the term κοινωνία and its associated metaphors, his ecclesiology of communion is conveyed to his readers in a way where they are either included in it and are encouraged, or else are invited to participate in it through a confession of faith that is deeply connected to their way of life. As "instruments of communion", Basil's letters fulfilled their purpose: they allowed the bishop of Caesarea to restore, maintain, express and promote communion both for the individual believer and the universal church.

This book, as a single volume, has made no claim to exhaust all that there is to say about Basil's letters. The following final comments will explain some of the reasoning behind this important admission. To begin with, there are many more things that could be said about how Basil used his letters, both specifically and generally, as "instruments of communion". In fact, each letter could be

96 *Ep.* 150.2: Courtonne, II, 73.
97 *Ep.* 99.1: Courtonne, I, 214.
98 *Ep.* 113: Courtonne, II, 17.

a thesis topic in itself, such is the depth of theology and the richness of meaning contained in Basil's letters. Many more volumes could be written, even if they were limited to simply studying the notion of communion in Basil's letters. The identified examples in this book of how Basil used his letters as "instruments of communion" should not, therefore, be taken to be exhaustive, rather they are to be indicative. It remains the task of students of Basil to verify this claim and compliment the work that has been undertaken in this book.

There is also much more that can be said about the notion of communion, and what this actually meant both for Basil in particular, and the Nicene communion of churches generally. This book has gone to great lengths to present Basil's understanding of communion as aligning with that of the Nicene communion of churches and vice versa. More could be said as to why this is so and how this is so. Basil's priority was that of eucharistic communion for the individual believer, the local church and the universal church. More could be said on the inter-connectedness and the inter-dependence of these three levels of communion.

Characteristically, all non-Nicene confessions of faith are generally grouped together in this book. Especially in terms of being incompatible with the communion of faith upheld in the Nicene church. Admittedly, the question needs to be asked, are all such non-Nicene statements of faith unworthy to bring about a communion of faith with the Nicene church? It is the purposeful contention of this book that all non-Nicene statements of faith lead to a break in communion with the Nicene church. Beyond the explanations already given, more could be said not only in response to what degree this is so for each non-Nicene confession, but also as to whether there are any possibilities available to foster communion through modifying non-Nicene statements of faith.

According to Basil, along with non-Nicene confessions of faith, personal sin has also been emphasised as bringing about a hindrance to eucharistic communion. However, to what extent can this be the case, given that at all moments of life no one can escape from being influenced by the consequences of sin. All sin separates a person from being in communion with God and leads to destruction. Basil's canonical letters have much to say in this area. As yet, no Basilian scholar has taken the opportunity to address the issue of sin and repentance and how these are reconciled to bring about communion. Additionally, this book, through tracing Basil's thinking, has presented a connection between sin and heresy where, in certain circumstances, sin and heresy are indicative of each other. This difficult truth, especially for today, needs to be further developed and explained if it is to be readily accepted.

Lastly, and perhaps most importantly, is a break of communion in the church incompatible with God's love, God's mercy, a person's love, and a person's salvation? For Basil, the answer is absolutely no. If then this is so, is communion even necessary? For Basil, the answer here is absolutely yes. Both the unequivocal answers to these two questions raised have been taken for granted in this book. In today's time, where communion is prayed for in every Christian expression of faith, these presented truisms of Basil need to be spelt out. It is the hope of the author of this book that a future writing can flesh out these two questions on the basis of two necessary premises. Firstly, that communion is an inherent Christian vocation, and therefore a precious gift and a fundamental necessity, that is accessible in freedom by all, and secondly, that communion is the greatest participation, in all ways, of a life in Christ.

Bibliography

Primary Sources and Translations:
Aristotle: *The Politics*. Translated by Carnes Lord. Chicago: University of Chicago, 1984.
Ἀθανάσιος Ἀλεξανδρείας: Τὰ Εὑρισκομένα Πάντα. Patrologia Graeca vol. 25, no. 1, edited by Jacques Paul Migne. Paris: Imprimérie Catholique, 1857.
_____. Τὰ Εὑρισκομένα Πάντα. Patrologia Graeca vol. 26, no. 2, edited by Jacques Paul Migne. Paris: Imprimérie Catholique, 1857.
_____. Τὰ Εὑρισκομένα Πάντα. Patrologia Graeca vol. 27, no. 3, edited by Jacques Paul Migne. Paris: Imprimérie Catholique, 1857.
_____. Τὰ Εὑρισκομένα Πάντα. Patrologia Graeca vol. 28, no. 4, edited by Jacques Paul Migne. Paris: Imprimérie Catholique, 1857.
Athanasius: *Contra Gentes and De Incarnatione*. Edited and translated by Robert W. Thomson. Oxford Early Christian Texts. Oxford: Clarendon, 1971.
_____. *On the Incarnation*. Edited and translated by A Religious of C.S.M.V. New York: St. Vladimir's Seminary, 1953.
_____. *Select Works and Letters*. Translated by Archibald Robertson, A Select Library of Nicene and Post-Nicene Fathers of the Christian Church, volume 4. Second Series, edited by Philip Schaff and Henry Wace. Edinburgh: T&T Clark, 1989.
_____. *The Life of Antony and the Letter to Marcellinus*. Translated by Robert C. Gregg. New York: Paulist, 1980.
Basile: *Aux jeunes gens*. Edited and translated by Fernand Boulenger. Paris: Les Belles Lettres, 2002.
_____. *Lettres*, 3 vols. Edited and translated by Yves Courtonne. Paris: Les Belles Lettres, 1957–1966.
Basile de Césarée: *Contre Eunome I*. Sources Chrétiennes no. 299, edited by Bernard Sesboüé. Paris: Cerf, 1982.
_____. *Contre Eunome II*. Sources Chrétiennes no. 305, edited by Bernard Sesboüé. Paris: Cerf, 1983.
_____. *Homélies de L'Hexaéméron*. Sources Chrétiennes no. 26, edited by Stanislas Giet. Paris: Cerf, 1968.
_____. *Sur le baptême*. Sources Chrétiennes no. 357, edited by U. Neri. Paris: Cerf, 1989.
_____. *Sur le Saint-Esprit*. Sources Chrétiennes no. 17, edited by Benoît Pruche. Paris: Cerf, 2002.

_____. *Sur l'origine de l'homme: Homélies X–XI de l'Hexaéméron*. Sources Chrétiennes no. 160, edited by Alexis Smets and Michel van Esbroeck, Paris: Cerf, 1970.

Βασίλειος Ο Μέγας. Έλληνες Πατέρες της Εκκλησίας: Τόμος Δέκατος. Edited by Παναγιώτη Κ. Χρήστου & Στεργιός Ν. Σάκκος. Θεσσαλονίκη: Πατερικαί Εκδόσεις «Γρηγόριος Ο Παλαμάς», 1974.

_____. Βιβλιοθήκη Ελλήνων Πατέρων και Εκκλησιαστικών Συγγραφέων: Τόμος Πεντηκοστός Δεύτερος. Edited by Κωνσταντίνου Γ. Μπόνη, Αθήνα: Αποστολικής Διακονίας της Εκκλησίας της Ελλάδος, 1998.

Βασιλείου: Τὰ Εὑρισκομένα Πάντα. Patrologia Graeca vol. 29, no. 1, edited by Jacques Paul Migne. Paris: Imprimérie Catholique, 1857.

_____. Τὰ Εὑρισκομένα Πάντα. Patrologia Graeca vol. 30, no. 2, edited by Jacques Paul Migne. Paris: Imprimérie Catholique, 1857.

_____. Τὰ Εὑρισκομένα Πάντα. Patrologia Graeca vol. 31, no. 3, edited by Jacques Paul Migne. Paris: Imprimérie Catholique, 1857.

_____. Τὰ Εὑρισκομένα Πάντα. Patrologia Graeca vol. 32, no. 4, edited by Jacques Paul Migne. Paris: Imprimérie Catholique, 1857.

Basil: *A Homily on the Martyr Gordius*. Translated by Pauline Allen. London: Routledge, 2003.

_____. *Address to Youth*. Edited by Dimitri Kepreotes. Sydney: St. Andrew's Orthodox Press, 2011.

_____. *Against Eunomius*. Translated by Mark Delcogliano and Andrew Radde-Gallwitz, The Fathers of the Church, volume 122. Washington, DC: Catholic University of America, 2011.

_____. *Ascetical Works*. Translated by M. Monica Wagner, The Fathers of the Church, volume 9. Washington, DC: Catholic University of America, 1962.

_____. *Exegetical Homilies*. Translated by Agnes C. Way, The Fathers of the Church, volume 46. Washington, DC: Catholic University of America, 1963.

_____. *Letters and Selected Works*. Translated by Blomfield Jackson, A Select Library of Nicene and Post-Nicene Fathers of the Christian Church, volume 8. Second Series, edited by Philip Schaff and Henry Wace. Peabody: Hendrickson, 1994.

_____. *On the Holy Spirit*. Translated by David Anderson, edited by John Behr. New York: St. Vladimir's Seminary, 1980.

_____. *The Letters*, Four Volumes. Translated by Roy J. Deferrari. Edited by Edward Capps, Thomas E. Page and William H.D. Rouse. Loeb Classical Library. London: William Heinemann, 1926.

Basil the Great: *Gateway to Paradise*. Translated by Tim Witherow, edited by Oliver Davies. New York: New City, 1991.

———. *On Christian Doctrine and Practice*. Translated by Mark DelCogliano. New York: St. Vladimir's Seminary, 2012.

———. *On Christian Ethics*. Translated by Jacob N. Van Sickle. New York: St. Vladimir's Seminary, 2014.

———. *On Fasting and Feasts*. Translated by Susan R. Holman and Mark DelCogliano. New York: St. Vladimir's Seminary, 2013.

———. *On Social Justice*. Translated by C. Paul Schroeder. New York: St. Vladimir's Seminary, 2011.

———. *On the Holy Spirit*. Translated by Stephen Hildebrand. New York: St. Vladimir's Seminary, 2002.

———. *On The Human Condition*. Translated by Nonna V. Harrison. New York: St. Vladimir's Seminary, 2005.

Bauer, Walter. *A Greek-English Lexicon of the New Testament and Other Early Christian Literature*. Translated by William Arndt and F. Wilbur Gingrich, 2nd ed. Chicago: University of Chicago, 1979.

Bibliothek der Symbole und Glaubensregeln der Alten Kirche. Edited by August Hahn. Breslau: E. Morgenstern, 1897.

Bousset, Wilhelm. *Apophthegmata*, Tübingen: Mohr, 1923.

Cyprien de Carthage: L'Unité de l'Église. Sources Chrétiennes no. 500, edited by Jean Daniélou, Henri de Lubac and Claude Mondésert. Paris: Cerf, 2006.

Cyprian: Treatises. Translated by Roy J. Deferrari et al., The Fathers of the Church, volume 36. Washington, DC: Catholic University of America, 1958.

Decrees of the Ecumenical Councils: Nicaea I – Lateran V, ed. Norman P. Tanner Washington, DC: Georgetown University, 1989.

Eunomius: The Extant Works. Translated by Richard P. Vaggione. Oxford: Clarendon, 1987.

Eusèbe de Césarée: Histoire Ecclésiastique. Sources Chrétiennes no. 55, edited by Gustave Bardy. Paris: Cerf, 1958.

Εὐσεβίου τοῦ Παμφίλου: Τὰ Εὑρισκομένα Πάντα. Patrologia Graeca vol. 19, no. 1, edited by Jacques Paul Migne. Paris: Imprimérie Catholique, 1857.

———. Τὰ Εὑρισκομένα Πάντα. Patrologia Graeca vol. 20, no. 2, edited by Jacques Paul Migne. Paris: Imprimérie Catholique, 1857.

———. Τὰ Εὑρισκομένα Πάντα. Patrologia Graeca vol. 21, no. 3, edited by Jacques Paul Migne. Paris: Imprimérie Catholique, 1857.

———. Τὰ Εὑρισκομένα Πάντα. Patrologia Graeca vol. 22, no. 4, edited by Jacques Paul Migne. Paris: Imprimérie Catholique, 1857.

———. Τὰ Εὑρισκομένα Πάντα. Patrologia Graeca vol. 23, no. 5, edited by Jacques Paul Migne. Paris: Imprimérie Catholique, 1857.

Eusebius: Church History, Life of Constantine the Great, Oration in Praise of Constantine. Translated by Arthur C. McGiffert, A Select Library of Nicene and Post-Nicene Fathers of the Christian Church, volume 1. Second Series, edited by Philip Schaff and Henry Wace. Peabody: Hendrickson, 1994.

Eusebius of Caesarea: The History of the Church. Translated by Geoffrey A. Williamson. London: Penguin Books, 1989.

———. *The Life of Constantine*. Translated by Averil Cameron and Stuart G. Hall. Oxford: Clarendon, 1999.

Eusebius Werke, Band II. Die Griechischen Christlichen Schriftsteller der Ersten Drei Jahrhunderte, edited by Eduard Schwartz. Leipzig: J.C. Hinrichs'sche Buchhandlung, 1908.

Funeral Orations by St. Gregory Nazianzen and St. Ambrose. Translated by Leo P. McCauley et al., The Fathers of the Church, volume 22. Washington, DC: Catholic University of America, 1953.

Geerard, Mauritius. *Clavis Patrum Graecorum. Volumen II: Ab Athanasio ad Chrysostomum*. Turnhout: Brepols, 1974.

———. *Clavis Patrum Graecorum. Volumen III: A Cyrillo Alexandrino ad Iohannem Damascenum*. Turnhout: Brepols, 2003.

Grégoire de Nazianze: Discours 1–3. Sources Chrétiennes no. 247, edited by Jean Bernardi. Paris: Cerf, 1978.

———. *Discours 20–23*. Sources Chrétiennes no. 270, edited by Justin Mossay. Paris: Cerf, 1980.

———. *Discours 42–43*. Sources Chrétiennes no. 384, edited by Jean Bernardi. Paris: Cerf, 1992.

Γρηγορίου τοῦ Θεολόγου: Τὰ Εὑρισκομένα Πάντα. Patrologia Graeca vol. 35, no. 1, edited by Jacques Paul Migne. Paris: Imprimérie Catholique, 1862.

———. Τὰ Εὑρισκομένα Πάντα. Patrologia Graeca vol. 36, no. 2, edited by Jacques Paul Migne. Paris: Imprimérie Catholique, 1862.

———. Τὰ Εὑρισκομένα Πάντα. Patrologia Graeca vol. 37, no. 3, edited by Jacques Paul Migne. Paris: Imprimérie Catholique, 1862. All translations are based on this text.

———. Τὰ Εὑρισκομένα Πάντα. Patrologia Graeca vol. 38, no. 4, edited by Jacques Paul Migne. Paris: Imprimérie Catholique, 1862.

Gregory of Nazianzus: On God and Christ – The Five Theological Orations and Two Letters to Cledonius. Translated by Federick Williams. New York: St. Vladimir's Seminary, 2002.

———. *Oration 43*. Sources Chrétiennes no. 384, edited by J. Bernardi, Paris, 1992.

———. *Select Orations*. Translated by Charles G. Browne and James E. Swallow, A Select Library of Nicene and Post-Nicene Fathers of the Christian Church, volume 7. Second Series, edited by Philip Schaff and Henry Wace. Peabody: Hendrickson, 1994.

Grégoire de Nysse: Contre Eunome. Sources Chrétiennes no. 521, edited by Raymond Winling. Paris: Cerf, 2008.

———. *Vie de Sainte Macrine*. Sources Chrétiennes no. 178, edited by Pierre Maraval. Paris: Cerf, 1971.

Gregory of Nyssa: Ascetical Works. Translated by Virginia W. Callahan, The Fathers of the Church, volume 58. Washington, DC: Catholic University of America, 1967.

———. *Dogmatic Treatises*. Translated by William Moore and Henry Austin, A Select Library of Nicene and Post-Nicene Fathers of the Christian Church, volume 5. Second Series, edited by Philip Schaff. New York: Cosimo, 2007.

———. *Encomium of Saint Gregory, Bishop of Nyssa, on His Brother Saint Basil, Archbishop of Cappadocian Caesarea*. Translated by James A. Stein. Patristic Studies, volume 17. Washington, DC: Catholic University of America, 1928.

———. *The Letters*. Translated by Anna M. Silvas. Leiden: Brill, 2007.

Sancti Eusebii Hieronymi: Cursus Completus. Patrologia Latina vol. 23, edited by Jacques Paul Migne. Paris: Imprimérie Catholique, 1845.

———. Cursus Completus. Patrologia Latina vol. 27, edited by Jacques Paul Migne. Paris: Imprimérie Catholique, 1866.

Ignace d'Antioche, Polycarpe de Smyrne: Lettres, Martyre de Polycarpe. Sources Chrétiennes no. 10, edited by Pierre T. Camelot. Paris: Cerf, 1998.

Jerome: Letters and Selected Works. Translated by William H. Fremantle, A Select Library of Nicene and Post-Nicene Fathers of the Christian Church, volume 6. Second Series, edited by Philip Schaff and Henry Wace. Edinburgh: T&T Clark, 2007.

Lampe, Geoffrey W.H. (ed.) *A Patristic Greek Lexicon*, Oxford: Oxford University, 1961.

Les manuscrits des lettres de Saint Grégoire de Nazianze. Translated and edited by Paul Gallay, Collection d'études anciennes, volume 12. Paris: Belles lettres, 1957.

Libanius: Autobiography and Selected Letters. Edited and translated by Albert F. Norman. Loeb Classical Library. Cambridge: Harvard University, 1992.

Liddell, Henry G. and Robert Scott. *A Greek-English Lexicon*. Ninth Edition. Revised by Sir Henry Stuart Jones, London: Clarendon, 1966.

Μηναῖον τοῦ Ἰανουαρίου. Ἐν Ἀθήναις: Ἀποστολικὴ Διακονία, 1991.

Patrology, Volume Three. Edited by Johannes Quasten. Antwerp: Spectrum, 1960.

Πηδάλιον τῆς νοητῆς νηὸς τῆς Μιᾶς Ἁγίας Καθολικῆς καὶ Ἀποστολικῆς τῶν Ὀρθοδόξων Ἐκκλησίας, ἤτοι ἅπαντες οἱ ἱεροὶ καὶ θεῖοι κανόνες. Edited by Σεργίου Χ. Ραφτάνη. Ἀθῆναι: Ἐκδοτικὸς οἶκος «Ἀστήρ», 1990.

Saint Basil on the Value of Greek Literature. Edited by Nigel G. Wilson. London: Duckworth, 1975.

Sallust: The War with Catiline 6. Translated by John C. Rolfe. Loeb Classical Library. Cambridge: Harvard University, 1985.

Socrate de Constantinople: Histoire Ecclésiastique, Livre I. Sources Chrétiennes no. 477, edited by Pierre Maraval. Paris: Cerf, 2004.

_____. *Histoire Ecclésiastique, Livres II–III*. Sources Chrétiennes no. 493, edited by Günther C. Hansen. Paris: Cerf, 2005.

Socrates, Sozomenus: Church Histories. Translated by Chester D. Hartranft, A Select Library of Nicene and Post-Nicene Fathers of the Christian Church, volume 2. Second Series, edited by Philip Schaff and Henry Wace et al. Grand Rapids: William B. Eerdmans Publishing Company, 1976.

Σωκράτους Σχολαστικοῦ, Ἑρμείου Σωζομένου: Ἐκκλησιαστιή Ἱστορία. Patrologia Graeca vol. 67, edited by Jacques Paul Migne. Paris: Imprimérie Catholique, 1864.

Sozomène: Histoire Ecclésiastique, Livres V–VI. Sources Chrétiennes no. 495, edited by Joseph Bidez and Günther C. Hansen. Paris: Cerf, 2005.

Synésios de Cyrène: Correspondance II–III, Edited by Antonio Garzya, translated by Denis Roques. Paris: Les Belles Lettres, 2003.

The Apostolic Fathers: Greek Texts and English Translations, Third Edition. Edited and Translated by Michael W. Holmes. Grand Rapids: Baker Academic, 2007.

The Apostolic Fathers. Translated by Francis X. Glimm et al., The Fathers of the Church, volume 1. Washington, DC: Catholic University of America, 1947.

The Ascetical Homilies of Saint Isaac the Syrian. Translated by Holy Transfiguration Monastery. Brookline: Holy Transfiguration Monastery, 1984.

The Church History of Rufinus of Aquileia Books 10 and 11. Translated by Philip R. Amidon. Oxford: Oxford University, 1997.

The Divine Liturgy of Our Father among the Saints John Chrysostom. Translated by John A.L. Lee. Sydney: Greek Orthodox Archdiocese of Australia, 1999.

Théodoret de Cyr: Correspondance III. Sources Chrétiennes no. 111, edited by Yvan Azéma. Paris: Cerf, 1965.

_____. *Histoire Ecclésiastique, Livres I–II*. Sources Chrétiennes no. 501, edited by Jean Bouffartigue. Paris: Cerf, 2006.

_____. *Histoire Ecclésiastique, Livres III–V*. Sources Chrétiennes no. 530, edited by Günther C. Hansen. Paris: Cerf, 2009.

Theodoret, Jerome, Gennadius, Rufinus: Historical Writings. Translated by Blomfeld Jackson, A Select Library of Nicene and Post-Nicene Fathers of the Christian Church, volume 3. Second Series, edited by Philip Schaff and Henry Wace et al. New York: Cosimo Classics, 2007.

The Later Christian Fathers: A Selection from the Writings of the Fathers from St. Cyril of Jerusalem to St. Leo the Great. Translated and edited by Henry Bettenson. New York: Oxford University, 1970.

The New Greek – English Interlinear New Testament. Edited by James D. Douglas. Illinois: Tyndale House, 1993.

The Seven Ecumenical Councils. Translated by Henry R. Percival, A Select Library of Nicene and Post-Nicene Fathers of the Christian Church, volume 14. Second Series, edited by Philip Schaff and Henry Wace. Peabody: Hendrickson, 1994.

Secondary Sources:
Aghiorgoussis, Maximos. "Applications of the Theme 'Eikon Theo' (Image of God) according to Saint Basil the Great". *Greek Orthodox Theological Review*, vol. 21, no. 3 (1976): 265–288.
Allen, Pauline. "Prolegomena to a Study of the Letter-Bearer in Christian Antiquity". *Studia Patristica* 62 (Leuven: Peeters, 2013): 481–491.
_____. "The Festal Letters of the Patriarchs of Alexandria: Evidence for Social History in the Fourth and Fifth Centuries". *Phronema*, vol. 27, no. 1 (2014): 1–19.
Allen, Pauline, Bronwen Neil and Wendy Mayer. *Preaching Poverty in Late Antiquity: Perceptions and Realities.* Leipzig: Evangelische Verlagsanstalt, 2009.
Amand de Mendieta, Emmanuel. "The Official Attitude of Basil of Caesarea as a Christian Bishop towards Greek Philosophy and Science". In *The Orthodox Churches and the West: Papers Read at the Fourteenth Summer Meeting and the Fifteenth Winter Meeting of the Ecclesiastical History Society.* Ed. Derek Baker (Oxford: Blackwell, 1976): 25–49.
Ayres, Lewis. *Nicaea and Its Legacy.* New York: Oxford University, 2004.
Ayres, Lewis and Andrew Radde-Gallwitz. "Basil of Caesarea". In *The Cambridge History of Philosophy in Late Antiquity.* Ed. Lloyd Gerson (Cambridge: Cambridge University, 2010): 1:459–470.
Baghos, Mario. "Apology of Athanasius: The Traditional Portrait of the Saint According to Rufinus and the Byzantine Historians". *Phronema*, vol. 28, no. 2 (2013): 55–88.
Barnes, Timothy D. *Athanasius and Constantius: Theology and Politics in the Constantinian Empire.* Cambridge: Harvard University, 1993.
_____. "Christians and Pagans under Constantius". *L'église et l'Empire au IVe siècle*, vol. 34 (Geneva: Fondation Hardt, 1989): 301–338.
_____. *Constantine and Eusebius.* Cambridge: Harvard University, 1981.
_____. *Early Christianity and the Roman Empire.* London: Variorum Reprints, 1984.
_____. "Emperor and Bishops, A.D. 324–344: Some Problems". *American Journal of Ancient History*, vol. 3, no. 1 (1978): 53–75.
_____. "Himerius and the Fourth Century". *Classical Philology*, vol. 82, no. 3 (1987): 206–225.
_____. "Statistics and the Conversion of the Roman Aristocracy". *Journal of Roman Studies*, vol. 85 (1995): 135–147.

_____. "The Career of Athanasius". *Studia Patristica* 21 (Leuven: Peeters, 1989): 390–405.

_____. *The New Empire of Diocletian and Constantine*. Cambridge: Harvard University, 1982.

Barrois, Georges. (ed. and trans.) *The Fathers Speak: Saint Basil the Great, Saint Gregory Nazianzus, Saint Gregory of Nyssa*. New York: St. Vladimir's Seminary, 1986.

Bauer, Walter. *Orthodoxy and Heresy in Earliest Christianity*. Philadelphia: Fortress, 1971, reprint Singler, 1996.

Baynes, Norman H. *Byzantine Studies and Other Essays*. London: The Athlone, 1955.

Beeley, Christopher. "The Holy Spirit in the Cappadocians: Past and Present". *Modern Theology*, vol. 26, no. 1 (2010): 90–119.

Behr, John. *Formation of Christian Theology: The Nicene Faith*, Volumes One and Two. New York: St. Vladimir's Seminary, 2004.

Blowers, Paul. "Envy's Narrative Scripts: Cyprian, Basil, and the Monastic Sages on the Anatomy and Cure of the Invidious Emotions". *Modern Theology*, vol. 25, no. 1 (2009): 21–43.

Bobrinskoy, Boris. "The Indwelling of the Spirit in Christ: Pneumatic Christology in the Cappadocian Fathers". *St. Vladimir's Theological Quarterly*, vol. 28, no. 1 (1984): 49–65.

_____. *The Mystery of the Trinity*. New York: St. Vladimir's Seminary, 1999.

Bonis, Constantine G. "The Problem concerning Faith and Knowledge as Expressed in the Letters of Saint Basil the Great to Amphilochius of Iconium". *Greek Orthodox Theological Review*, vol. 5, no. 2 (1959): 27–44.

Bowersock, Glen W. "From Emperor to Bishop: The Self-Conscious Transformation of Political Power in the Fourth Century A.D". *Classical Philology*, vol. 81, no. 4 (1986): 298–307.

_____. *Hellenism in Late Antiquity*. Ann Arbor: University of Michigan, 1990.

_____. *Julian the Apostate*. Cambridge: Harvard University, 1978.

Breck, John. *Spirit of Truth: The Origins of Johannine Pneumatology*. New York: St. Vladimir's Seminary, 1991.

Bright, William. *The Orations of St. Athanasius Against the Arians According to the Benedictine Text: With an Account of His Life*. Eugene OR: Wipf and Stock, 2005.

Brown, Peter. *Poverty and Leadership in the Later Roman Empire*. Hanover: University of New England, 2002.

_____. *Power and Persuasion in Late Antiquity: Towards a Christian Empire*. Madison: University of Wisconsin, 1992.

_____. *Religion and Society in the Age of Saint Augustine*. London: Faber & Faber, 1971.

_____. *Society and the Holy in Late Antiquity.* Berkeley: University of California, 1982.

_____. *The Body and Society.* New York: Columbia University, 1988.

_____. *The Rise of Western Christendom: Triumph and Diversity, A.D. 200–2000.* Oxford: Wiley-Blackwell, 1996.

_____. *The World of Late Antiquity AD 150–750.* London: W.W. Norton & Company, 1971.

Brown, Raymond E. *The Churches The Apostles Left Behind.* New York: Paulist, 1984.

Brown, Schuyler. "Koinonia as the Basis of New Testament Ecclesiology". *One in Christ*, vol. 12, no. 1 (1976): 157–167.

Browning, Robert. *The Emperor Julian.* London: Weidenfeld and Nicholson, 1975.

Burgess, Stanley M. *The Holy Spirit: Ancient Christian Traditions.* Peabody: Hendrickson, 1984.

Burns, J. Patout and Gerald M. Fagin. *The Holy Spirit: Message of the Fathers of the Church.* Delaware: Michael Glazier, 1984.

Calligiorgis, Jeremiah. "The Bishop is in the Church and the Church is in the Bishop". *The Jurist*, vol. 66, no. 1 (2006): 47–53.

Cameron, Averil. *Christianity and the Rhetoric of Empire: The Development of Christian Discourse.* Sather Classical Lectures 55. Berkeley: University of California, 1991.

_____. *The Later Roman Empire AD 284–430.* Cambridge: Cambridge University, 1993.

Campenhausen, Hans von. *Ecclesiastical Authority and Spiritual Power in the Church of the First Three Centuries.* Peabody: Hendrickson, 1997.

_____. *The Fathers of the Greek Church.* Translated by Stanley Godman. New York: Pantheon, 1959.

Casiday, Augustine and Frederick W. Norris (eds.) *The Cambridge History of Christianity: Volume Two, Constantine to c. 600.* Cambridge: Cambridge University, 2008.

Cavallin, Anders. *Studien zu den Briefen des hl. Basilius.* Lund: Gleerupska Universitetsbokhandeln, 1944.

Chadwick, Henry. "Bishops and Monks". *Studia Patristica* 24 (Leuven: Peeters, 1993): 45–61.

_____. *Heresy and Orthodoxy in the Early Church.* Collected Studies 342. Aldershot: Variorum, 1982.

_____. *History and Thought of the Early Church.* Collected Studies 164. London: Variorum, 1991.

_____. "New Letters of St. Augustine". *Journal of Theological Studies.* ns, vol. 34, pt. 2 (1983): 425–452.

———. *The Early Church*. London: Penguin Books, 1993.
Charry, Ellen T. "The Case for Concern: Athanasian Christology in Pastoral Perspective". *Modern Theology*, vol. 9, no. 3 (1993): 265–283.
Chrestou, Panagiotes K. *Greek Orthodox Patrology: An Introduction to the Study of the Church Fathers*. New Hampshire: Orthodox Research Institute, 2005.
Chryssavgis, John. *The Way of the Fathers: Exploring the Patristic Mind*. Thessalonika: Patriarchal Institute for Patristic Studies, 1988.
Clare, S.M. (ed.) *Word and Spirit: A Monastic Review*. Still River: St. Bedes's Publications, 1979.
Clark, Elizabeth A. *Reading Renunciation: Asceticism and Scripture in Early Christianity*. Princeton, NJ: Princeton University, 1999.
Clarke, W.K. Lowther. *St Basil the Great: A Study in Monasticism*. Cambridge: Cambridge University, 1913.
Clover, Frank M. and R. Stephen Humphreys (eds.) *Tradition and Innovation in Late Antiquity*. Madison, Wis.: University of Wisconsin, 1989.
Coakley, Sarah. "'Persons' in the 'Social' Doctrine of the Trinity: A Critique of Current Analytic Discussion". In *The Trinity: An Interdisciplinary Symposium on the Trinity*. Eds. Stephen D. Davis, Daniel Kendall and Gerald O'Collins (Oxford: Oxford University, 1999): 123–144.
Congar, Yves. *I Believe in the Holy Spirit*. Translated by David Smith. New York: Crossroad, 1997. Originally published as *Je crois en l'Esprit Saint*. Paris: Cerf, 1979–1980.
Constantelos, Demetrios J. *Byzantine Philanthropy and Social Welfare*. New Brunswick: Rutgers University, 1968.
Cooper, J. Eric and Michael J. Decker. *Life and Society in Byzantine Cappadocia*. New York: Palgrave Macmillan, 2012.
Corcoran, Simon. *The Empire of the Tetrarchs: Imperial Pronouncements and Government, AD 284–324*. Oxford: Clarendon, 2000.
Costache, Doru. "Christian Worldview: Understandings from St. Basil the Great". *Phronema*, vol. 25 (2010): 21–56.
Croke, Brian and Alanna Emmett (eds.) *History and Historians in Late Antiquity*. Sydney: Pergamon, 1983.
Cunningham, Mary B. and Elizabeth Theokritoff (eds.) *The Cambridge Companion to Orthodox Christian Theology*. Cambridge: Cambridge University, 2008.
Daley, Brian E. "Building a New City: The Cappadocian Fathers and the Rhetoric of Philanthropy". *Journal of Early Christian Studies*, vol. 7, no. 3 (1999): 431–461.
Davidson, Ivor J. *A Public Faith: From Constantine to the Medieval World, AD 312–600*, The Monarch History of the Church Series, vol. 2. Edited by Tim Dowley, Grand Rapids: Monarch Books, 2005.
Δημόπουλος, Γεώργιος. Ο Φωστὴρ τῆς Καισαρείας (Ο Μέγας Βασίλειος). Ἀθῆναι: Ἀδελφότης Θεολόγων «Ο Σωτήρ», 1964.

DelCogliano, Mark. *Basil of Caesarea's Anti-Eunomian Theory of Names: Christian Theology and Philosophy in the Fourth Century Trinitarian Controversy.* Leiden: Brill, 2010.

Delisle, Jean and Judith Woodsworth. *Translators through History.* Amsterdam/Philadelphia: John Benjamin, 1995.

Doyle, Dennis. *Communion Ecclesiology*, Maryknoll, NY: Orbis books, 2000.

Drake, Harold A. *Constantine and the Bishops: The Politics of Intolerance.* Baltimore: The Johns Hopkins University, 2000.

———. "The Impact of Constantine on Christianity". In *The Cambridge Companion to the Age of Constantine.* Ed. Noel Lenski (Cambridge: Cambridge University, 2006): 111–136.

Drecoll, Volker H. *Die Entwicklung der Trinitätslehre des Basilius von Cäsarea: Sein Weg vom Homöusianer zum Neonizäner.* Göttingen: Vandenhoeck & Ruprecht, 1996.

Drobner, Hubertus R. *The Fathers of the Church: A Comprehensive Introduction.* Translated by Siegfried S. Schatzmann. Peabody: Hendrickson, 2007.

Ebbeler, Jennifer. "Tradition, Innovation, and Epistolary Mores". In *A Companion to Late Antiquity.* Ed. Philip Rousseau, Blackwell Companions to the Ancient World (Chichester, 2009): 270–284.

Edwards, Denis. *Breath of Life: A Theology of the Creator Spirit.* Maryknoll, NY: Orbis Books, 2004.

Elert, Werner. *Eucharist and Church Fellowship in the First Four Centuries.* Translated by Norman E. Nagel. Saint Louis: Concordia Publishing House, 1966.

Elm, Susanna. *'Virgins of God': The Making of Asceticism in Late Antiquity.* Oxford: Clarendon, 1994.

Elton, Hugh. *Warfare in Roman Europe AD 350–425.* Oxford: Clarendon, 1996.

Farely, Lawrence R. *The Empty Throne: Reflections on the History and Future of the Orthodox Episcopacy.* Chesterton IN: Ancient Faith Publishing, 2016.

Farrell, Joseph P. *Saint Photios: The Mystagogy of the Holy Spirit.* Brooklyn: Holy Cross Orthodox Press, 1987.

Fedwick, Paul J. (ed.) *Basil of Caesarea: Christian, Humanist, Ascetic (Parts One and Two).* Toronto: Pontifical Institute of Mediaeval Studies, 1981.

———. (ed.) *Bibliotheca Basiliana Vniveralis,* volumes 1–5. Turnhout: Brepols, 1996–2004.

———. *The Church and the Charisma of Leadership in Basil of Caesarea.* Eugene OR: Wipf and Stock, 1979.

Ferguson, Everett. *Encyclopaedia of Early Christianity.* New York: Garland Publishing, 1990.

Finn, Richard. *Almsgiving in the Later Roman Empire: Christian Promotion and Practice 313–450.* Oxford: Oxford University, 2006.

Florovsky, Georges. *Bible, Church, Tradition: An Eastern Orthodox View*. Belmont: Nordland Publishing Company, 1972.

———. *The Eastern Fathers of the Fourth Century*. Belmont: Buchervertriebsanstalt, 1987.

———. "The Function of Tradition in the Ancient Church". *Greek Orthodox Theological Review*, vol. 9, no. 2 (1963): 181–200.

Fowden, Garth. "Bishops and Temples in the Eastern Roman Empire, A.D. 320–435". *Journal of Theological Studies*. ns, vol. 29, pt. 1 (1978): 53–78.

Fox, Patricia. *God as Communion*. Collegeville: Liturgical Press, 2001.

Frazee, Charles A. "Anatolian Asceticism in the Fourth Century: Eustathius of Sebasteia and Basil of Caesarea". *Catholic Historical Review*, vol. 66, no. 1 (1981): 16–33.

Gain, Benoît. *L'Église de Cappadoce au IVe siècle d'après la correspondance de Basile de Césarée*. Orientalia Christiana Analecta 225, Rome: Pontificium institutum Orientale, 1985.

Geanakopoulos, Deno J. "St. Basil, 'Christian Humanist' of the 'Three Hierarchs' and Patron Saint of Greek Letters". *Greek Orthodox Theological Review*, vol. 25, no. 1 (1980): 94–102.

Gibson, Roy. "On the Nature of Ancient Letter Collections". *Journal of Roman Studies*, vol. 102 (2012): 56–78.

Gillard, Frank D. "Senatorial Bishops in the Fourth Century". *The Harvard Theological Review*, vol. 77, no. 2 (1984): 153–175.

Gillett, Andrew. "Communication in Late Antiquity: Use and Reuse". In *Oxford Handbook of Late Antiquity*. Ed. Scott F. Johnson, Oxford Handbooks in Classics and Ancient History (Oxford, 2012): 815–846.

Gillmann, F. *Das Institut der Chorbischöfe im Orient: Historisch-kanonistische Studie*. Munich: 1903.

Gribomont, Jean. "Christ and the Primitive Monastic Ideal". *Word and Spirit*, no. 5 (1983): 96–116.

Gwynn, David M. "*Hoi peri Eusebion*: The Polemic of Athanasius". *Studia Patristica* 21 (Leuven: Peters, 2006): 53–57.

———. *The Eusebians: The Polemic of Athanasius of Alexandria and the Construction of the 'Arian Controversy'*. Oxford: Oxford University, 2007.

Hainz, Joseph. "Koinonia, Koinoneo, Koinonos". In *Exegetical Dictionary of the New Testament*. Eds. Horst Balz and Gerhard M. Schneider (Grand Rapids: William B. Eerdmans Publishing Company, 1991): 2:303–305.

Hanson, Richard P.C. "Basil's Doctrine of Tradition in Relation to the Holy Spirit". *Vigiliae Christianae*, vol. 22, no. 4 (1968): 241–255.

———. *The Search for the Christian Doctrine of God*. Edinburgh: T&T Clark, 1988.

———. "The Achievement of Orthodoxy in the Fourth Century A.D". In *The Making of Orthodoxy: Essays in honour of Henry Chadwick*. Ed. Rowan Williams (Cambridge: Cambridge University, 1989): 142–156.

———. *Tradition in the Early Church*. Eugene OR: Wipf and Stock, 2009.

Harkianakis, Stylianos. *The Infallibility of the Church in Orthodox Theology*. Translated by Philip Kariatlis. Adelaide/Sydney: ATF /St Andrew's Orthodox Press, 2008.

Hauk, Friedrich. "Koinos, Koinonos, Koinoneo, Koinonia, Sygkoinonos, Synkoinoneo, Koinonikos, Koinoo". In *Theological Dictionary of the New Testament*. Ed. Gerhard Kittel (Grand Rapids: William B. Eerdmans Publishing Company, 1981): 3:789–809.

Haykin, Michael A.G. "And Who is the Spirit? Basil of Caesarea's Letters to the Church at Tarsus". *Vigiliae Christianae*, vol. 41, no. 4 (1987): 377–385.

———. "A Sense of Awe in the Presence of the Ineffable: 1 Cor. 2:11–12 in the Pneumatomachian Controversy of the Fourth Century". *Scottish Journal of Theology*, vol. 41, no. 3 (1988): 341–357.

———. "Defending the Holy Spirit's Deity: Basil of Caesarea, Gregory of Nyssa, and the Pneumatomachian Controversy of the 4th Century". *Southern Baptist Journal of Theology*, vol. 7, no. 3 (2003): 74–79.

———. *The Spirit of God: The Exegesis of 1 and 2 Corinthians in the Pneumatomachian Controversy of the Fourth Century*. Leiden: Brill, 1994.

Hazlett, Ian (ed.) *Early Christianity: Origins and Evolution to A.D. 600, In Honour of W.H.C. Frend*. Oxford: S.P.C.K. University, 1990.

Hefele, Karl J. and Henri Leclercq, *Histoire des Conciles*, vol. 2. Paris: Letouzey et Ané, 1908.

Hildebrand, Stephen M. "A Reconstruction of the Development of Basil's Trinitarian Theology: The Dating of Ep. 9 and Contra Eunomium". *Vigiliae Christianae*, vol. 58, no. 4 (2004): 393–406.

———. *The Trinitarian Theology of Basil of Caesarea: A Synthesis of Greek Thought and Biblical Truth*. Washington, DC: Catholic University of America, 2007.

Holder, Arthur G. "Saint Basil the Great on Secular Education and Christian Virtue". *Religious Education*, vol. 87, no. 3 (1992): 380–395.

Holman, Susan R. "The Entitled Poor: Human Rights Language in the Cappadocians". *Pro Ecclesia*, vol. 9, no. 4 (2000): 466–489.

———. *The Hungry are Dying: Beggars and Bishops in Roman Cappadocia*. Oxford: Oxford University, 2001.

———. "The Hungry Body: Famine, Poverty and Basil's Homily 8". *Journal of Early Christian Studies*, vol. 7, no. 3 (1999): 337–363.

_____. "You Speculate on the Misery of the Poor: Usury as a Civic Injustice in Basil of Caesarea's Second Homily on Psalm 14". In *Organised Crime in Antiquity*. Ed. Keith Hopwood (London: Duckworth/Classical of Wales, 1999): 207-228.

Holmes, Augustine. *A Life Pleasing to God: The Spirituality of the Rules of St. Basil*. Kalamazoo, MI: Cistercian Publications, 2000.

Hopkins, Keith. "Christian Number and its Implications". *Journal of Early Christian Studies*, vol. 6, no. 2 (1998): 184-226.

Hopko, Thomas. "On Ecclesial Conciliarity". In *The Legacy of St. Vladimir*. Eds. John Breck, John Meyendorff and Eleana Silk (New York: St. Vladimir's Seminary, 1990): 209-225.

Hunt, Anne. "The Trinity and the Church: Explorations in Ecclesiology from a Trinitarian Perspective". *Irish Theological Quarterly*, vol. 70, no. 9 (2005): 215-35.

Hunt, David. "The Church as a Public Institution". In *The Cambridge Ancient History*. Eds. Averil Cameron and Peter Garnsey, vol. 13 (1998): 238-276.

Jones, Arnold H.M. *The Cities of the Eastern Roman Provinces*. Second Edition. Oxford: Clarendon, 1971.

_____. *The Later Roman Empire 284-602: A Social, Economic and Administrative Survey*, Volumes One and Two. Norman: University of Oklahoma, 1964.

Jones, Christopher P. *Between Pagan and Christian*. Cambridge: Harvard University, 2014.

Kane, Michael A. "St. Basil's *On the Holy Spirit:* A Secret Tradition on the Rule of Faith". *Diakonia*, vol. 35, no. 1 (2002): 23-37.

Καρμίρης, Ιωάννης Ν. Η Εκκλησιολογία τοῦ Μεγάλου Βασιλείου. Ἀθῆναι: ΕΕΘΣΠΑ, 1958.

_____. "The Ecclesiology of the Three Hierarchs". *Greek Orthodox Theological Review*, vol. 6, no. 2 (1960-1961): 111-124.

Kariatlis, Phillip. "Affirming Koinonia Ecclesiology: An Orthodox Perspective". *Phronema*, vol. 27, no. 1 (2012): 51-65.

_____. *Church as Communion: The Gift and Goal of Koinonia*. Sydney: St. Andrew's Orthodox Press, 2011.

_____. "St. Basil's Contribution to the Trinitarian Doctrine: A Synthesis of Greek Paideia and the Scriptural Worldview". *Phronema*, vol. 25 (2010): 57-83.

Kasper, Walter. *Sacrament and Unity: The Eucharist and the Church*. Translated by Brian McNeil. New York: Crossroad Publishing Company, 2004.

_____. *Theology and Church*. Translated by Margaret Kohl. New York: Crossroad Crossroad Publishing Company, 1989.

Kazhdan, Alexander P. (ed.) *The Oxford Dictionary of Byzantium*. New York: Oxford University, 1991.

Keidel, Anne. "*Hesychia*, Prayer and Transformation in Basil of Caesarea", *Studia Patristica* 21 (Leuven: Peeters, 2001): 110-120.

Kelly, John N.D. *Early Christian Doctrines*. London: A & C Black, 1989.

Kelly, Louis G. *The True Interpreter: A History of Translation Theory and Practice in the West*. Oxford: St Martin's, 1979.

Khodr, Georges. "Basil the Great: Bishop and Pastor". *St. Vladimir's Theological Quarterly*, vol. 29, no. 1 (1985): 5-27.

Kilby, Karen. "Perichoresis and Projection: Problems with Social Doctrines of the Trinity". *New Blackfriars*, vol. 81, no. 956 (2000): 432-445.

Kopecek, Thomas A. "The Cappadocian Fathers and Civic Patriotism". *Church History*, vol. 43, no. 3 (1974): 293-303.

_____. "The Social Class of the Cappadocian Fathers". *Church History*, vol. 42, no. 4 (1973): 453-466.

Kurt, Aland. "The Relation between Church and State in Early Times: A Re-interpretation". *Journal of Theological Studies*. ns, vol. 19, pt. 1 (1968): 115-127.

Lane Fox, Robin. *Pagans and Christians: In the Mediterranean World from the Second Century A.D. to the Conversion of Constantine*. Harmondsworth and New York: Penguin Books, 1986.

Larson, Mark. "A Re-examination of De Spiritu Sancto: Saint Basil's Bold Defence of the Spirit's Deity". *Scottish Bulletin of Evangelical Theology*, vol. 19, no. 1 (2001): 65-84.

LaVerdiere, Eugene. *The Eucharist in the New Testament and the Early Church*. Minnesota: Liturgical Press, 1996.

Lee, John A.L. "Why Didn't St. Basil Write in New Testament Greek?" *Phronema*, vol. 25 (2010): 3-20.

Leftow, Brian. "Anti Social Trinitarianism". In *The Trinity: An Interdisciplinary Symposium on the Trinity*. Eds. Stephen D. Davis, Daniel Kendall and Gerald O'Collins (Oxford: Oxford University, 1999): 203-250.

Lennan, Richard. "Communion Ecclesiology: Foundations, Critiques and Affirmations". *Pacifica*, vol. 20, no. 1 (2007): 24-39.

Lenski, Noel. *Failure of Empire: Valens and the Roman State in the Fourth Century A.D.* Berkeley: University of California, 2002.

Liebeschuetz, John H.W.G. *Barbarians and Bishops*. Oxford: Clarendon, 1990.

Lienhard, Joseph T. "Basil of Caesarea, Marcellus of Ancyra, and 'Sabellius'." *Church History*, vol. 58, no. 2 (1989): 157-167.

_____. *Contra Marcellum: Marcellus of Ancyra and Fourth Century Theology*. Washington, DC: Catholic University of America, 1999.

_____. "The 'Arian' Controversy: Some Categories Reconsidered". *Theological Studies*, vol. 48, no. 3 (1987): 415-437.

Limouris, Gennadios (ed.) *Come Holy Spirit Renew the Whole Creation*. Boston: Holy Cross Orthodox Press, 1990.

Lizzi, Rita. "Vir Venerabilis: The Bishop, Fiscal Privileges and Status Definition in Late Antiquity", *Studia Patristica* 34 (Leuven: Peeters, 2001): 125–144.

Lossky, Vladimir. *In the Image and Likeness of God*. New York: St. Vladimir's Seminary, 1976.

_____. *Orthodox Theology: An Introduction*. New York: St. Vladimir's Seminary, 1989.

_____. *The Mystical Theology of the Eastern Church*. New York: St. Vladimir's Seminary, 1976.

MacMullen, Ramsay. *Christianity and Paganism in the Fourth to Eighth Centuries*. New Haven: Yale University, 1997.

_____. *Christianizing the Roman Empire (A.D. 100–400)*. New Haven: Yale University, 1984.

_____. "The Roman Emperor's Army Costs". *Latomus*, vol. 43 (1984): 571–580.

MacMurray, John. *Persons in Relation*. New York: Humanity Books, 1961.

_____. *The Conditions of Freedom*. London: Faber & Faber, 1950.

Malherbe, Abraham J. *Ancient Epistolary Theorists*. Society of Biblical Literature, Sources of Biblical Study no. 19, Atlanta: Scholars, 1988.

Marzheuser, Richard. "The Holy Spirit and the Church: a Truly Catholic Communio". *New Theology Review*, vol. 11, no. 3 (1998): 60–66.

Matthews, John. *Political Life and Culture in Late Roman Society*. Collected Studies 217. London: Variorum, 1985.

Mayer, Annemarie C. "Ecclesial Communion: The Letters of St Basil the Great Revisited". *International Journal for the Study of the Christian Church*, vol. 5, no. 3 (2005): 226–241.

_____. "Κοινωνία on Purpose? Ecclesiology of Communion in the Letters of St. Basil the Great". *Studia Patristica* 41 (Leuven: Peeters, 2006): 375–381.

McGinn, Bernard. John Meyendorff and Jean Leclercq (eds.) *Christian Spirituality: Origins to the Twelfth Century*. New York: St. Vladimir's Seminary, 1985.

McGuckin, John A. *St. Gregory of Nazianzus: An Intellectual Biography*. New York: St. Vladimir's Seminary, 2001.

_____. *The Ascent of Christian Law: Patristic and Byzantine Formulations of a New Civilization*. New York: St. Vladimir's Seminary, 2012.

Meredith, Anthony. "Asceticism: Christian and Greek". *Journal of Theological Studies*. ns, vol. 27, pt. 2 (1976): 312–332.

_____. "Orthodoxy, Heresy and Philosophy in the Latter Half of the Fourth Century". *The Heythrop Journal*, vol. 16, no. 1 (1975): 5–21.

_____. *The Cappadocians*. New York: St. Vladimir's Seminary, 2000.

Meyendorff, John. *Catholicity and the Church*. New York: St. Vladimir's Seminary, 1997.

_____. *Imperial Unity and Christian Division: The Church 450–680 A.D.* The Church in History Series, Volume Two. New York: St. Vladimir's Seminary, 2011.

———. *Living Tradition: Orthodox Witness in the Contemporary World*. New York: St. Vladimir's Seminary, 1997.

———. "Saint Basil, Messalianism and Byzantine Christianity". *St. Vladimir's Theological Quarterly*, vol. 24, no. 4 (1980): 211–224.

———. *The Byzantine Legacy in the Orthodox Church*. New York: St. Vladimir's Seminary, 2000.

Mitchell, Jane F. "Consolatory Letters in Basil and Gregory Nazianzen". *Hermes*, vol. 96, no. 3 (1968): 299–318.

Mitchell, Stephen. *A History of the Roman Empire AD 284–641*. Malden: Blackwell Publishing, 2007.

Momigliano, Arnaldo (ed.) *The Conflict between Paganism and Christianity in the Fourth Century*. Oxford: Clarendon, 1963.

Monge, Rico G. "Submission to the One Head: Basil of Caesarea on Order and Authority in the Church". *St Vladimir's Theological Quarterly*, vol. 54, no. 2 (2010): 219–243.

Morison, Ernest F. *St. Basil and His Rule: A Study in Early Monasticism*. London: Frowde, 1912.

Murphy, Margaret G. *St. Basil and Monasticism*. Catholic University of America Patristic Studies 25, Washington, DC: Catholic University of America, 1930.

Neil, Bronwen and Pauline Allen (eds.) *Collecting Early Christian Letters: From the Apostle Paul to Late Antiquity*. Cambridge: Cambridge University, 2015.

Norton, Peter. *Episcopal Elections, 250–600: Hierarchy and Popular Will in Late Antiquity*. Oxford: Oxford University, 2007.

Padelford, Frederick M. "Essays on the Study and Use of Poetry by Plutarch and Basil the Great". *Yale Studies in English*, vol. 15 (1902): 33–43.

Panikulum, George. *Koinonia in the New Testament: A Dynamic Expression of Christian Life*. Rome: Biblical Institute, 1979.

Papanikolaou, Aristotle. *Being with God: Trinity, Apophaticism, and Divine-Human Communion*. Indiana: University of Notre Dame, 2006.

Patsavos, Lewis J. *A Noble Task: Entry into the Clergy in the First Five Centuries*. Brookline: Holy Cross Orthodox Press, 2007.

———. "The Image of the Priest According to the Three Hierarchs". *The Greek Orthodox Theological Review*, vol. 21, no. 1 (1976): 55–70.

Pelikan, Jaroslav. *The Christian Tradition Volume One: The Emergence of the Catholic Tradition (100–600)*. London: University of Chicago, 1975.

Pelzel, Morris. *Ecclesiology: The Church as Communion and Mission*. Chicago: Layola, 2002.

Petterson, Alvyn. *Athanasius*. London: Geoffrey Chapman, 1995.

Phan, Peter C. *Grace and the Human Condition*. Michael Glazier: Wilmington, 1993.

_____. (ed.) *The Cambridge Companion to the Trinity*. Cambridge: Cambridge University, 2011.
Prestige, George L. *Fathers and Heretics: Six Studies in Dogmatic Faith with Prologue and Epilogue*. Bampton Lectures for 1940. Oxford: S.P.C.K. University, 1940.
_____. *St. Basil the Great and Apollinaris of Laodicea*. Edited by Henry Chadwick. Oxford: S.P.C.K. University, 1956.
Radde-Gallwitz, Andrew. *Basil of Caesarea: A Guide to His Life and Doctrine*. Eugene OR: Cascade Books, 2012.
_____. *Basil of Caesarea, Gregory of Nyssa, and the Transformation of Divine Simplicity*. New York: Oxford University, 2009.
Ramsay, William M. *The Historical Geography of Asia Minor*. Boston: Adamant Media Corporation, 2002.
Rapp, Claudia. *Holy Bishops in Late Antiquity: The Nature of Christian Leadership in an Age of Transition*. Berkeley: University of California, 2005.
_____. "The Elite Status of Bishops in Late Antiquity in the Ecclesiastical, Spiritual and Social Context". *Arethusa*, vol. 33, no. 3 (2000): 379–399.
Rener, Frederick M. *Interpretation: Language and Translation from Cicero to Tytler*. Amsterdam: Rodopi, 1989.
Robertson, David G. "Basil of Caesarea on the Meaning of Prepositions and Conjunctions". *The Classical Quarterly*, vol. 53, no. 1 (2003): 167–174.
Rodopoulos, Panteleimon. *An Overview of Orthodox Canon Law*. Rollinsford: Orthodox Research Institute, 2007.
Rousseau, Philip. *Ascetics, Authority, and the Church in the Age of Jerome and Cassian*. Oxford: Oxford University, 1978.
_____. *Basil of Caesarea*. London: University of California, 1994.
_____. "Basil of Caesarea: Choosing a Past". In *Reading the Past in Late Antiquity*. Ed. Graeme W. Clarke et al., (Rushcutters Bay: Australian University and Pergamon, 1990): 37–58.
_____. "Basil of Caesarea, *Contra Eunomium:* The Main Preoccupations". In *The Idea of Salvation*. Eds. David W. Dockrill and Ronald G. Tanner (Auckland: Prudentia, 1988): 77–94.
_____. "Christian Asceticism and the Early Monks". In *Early Christianity: Origins and Evolution to A.D. 600, In Honour of W.H.C. Frend*. Ed. Ian Hazlett (Oxford: S.P.C.K. University, 1990): 112–122.
_____. "Human Nature and its Material Setting in Basil of Caesarea's Sermons on the Creation". *The Heythrop Journal*, vol. 49, no. 2 (2008): 222–239.
_____. "The Spiritual Authority of the 'Monk-Bishop': Eastern Elements in Some Western Hagiography of the Fourth and Fifth Centuries". *Journal of Theological Studies*. ns, vol. 22, pt. 2 (1971): 380–419.
Russell, Norman. *Fellow Workers with God: Orthodox Thinking on Theosis*. New York: St. Vladimir's Seminary, 2009.

Ryder, Andrew. "Led by the Spirit: St. Basil the Great". *A Journal of Catholic Spirituality*, vol. 64, no. 3 (2005): 301–315.

Salzman, Michele R. *The Making of a Christian Aristocracy: Social and Religious Change in the Western Roman Empire*. Cambridge: Harvard University, 2002.

Schanz, John P. *A Theology of Community*. Washington, DC: University of America, 1977.

Schmidt, Karl M. "Ecclesia". In *Theological Dictionary of the New Testament*. Ed. Gerhard Kittel (Grand Rapids: William B. Eerdmans Publishing Company, 1981): 3: 501–536.

Schor, Adam M. *Theodoret's People: Social Networks and Religious Conflict in Late Roman Syria*. Berkeley: University of California, 2011.

Schwobel, Christopher (ed.) *Trinitarian Theology Today: Essays on Being and Act*, Edinburgh: T&T Clark, 1995.

Scouteris, Christopher B. *Ecclesial Being*. South Canaan: Mount Thabor Publishing, 2006.

Sheather, Mary. "Pronouncements of the Cappadocians on Issues of Poverty and Wealth". In *Prayer and Spirituality in the Early Church*. Eds. Pauline Allen, Raymond Canning and Lawrence Cross, vol. 1 (1998): 375–392.

Silvas, Anna M. *Macrina the Younger, Philosopher of God*. Turnhout: Brepols, 2008.

———. "St. Basil: Passages of Spiritual Growth". In *Prayer and Spirituality in the Early Church*. Eds. Pauline Allen, Raymond Canning and Lawrence Cross, vol. 1 (1998): 353–366.

———. *The Asketikon of St. Basil the Great*. New York: Oxford University, 2005.

———. "The Emergence of Basil's Social Doctrine: A Chronological Enquiry". In *Prayer and Spirituality in the Early Church*. Eds. Geoffrey D. Dunn, David Luckensmeyer and Lawrence Cross, vol. 5 (2009): 133–176.

———. "The Letters of Basil of Caesarea and the Role of Letter-Collections in their Transmission". In *Collecting Early Christian Letters. From the Apostle Paul to Late Antiquity*. Eds. Bronwen Neil and Pauline Allen (Cambridge: Cambridge University, 2015): 113–128.

Simonopetritis, Aimilianos. *The Church at Prayer: The Mystical Liturgy of the Heart*. Athens: Indiktos Publishing Company, 2005.

Smith, Richard T. *Saint Basil the Great*. New York: Pott, Young, and Co., 1879.

Snee, Rochelle. "Valens' Recall of the Nicene Exiles and Anti-Arian Propaganda". *Greek, Roman and Byzantine Studies*, vol. 26, no. 4 (1985): 395–419.

Staniloae, Dumitru. *Theology and the Church*. Translated by Robert Barringer. New York: St. Vladimir's Seminary, 1980.

Steiner, George. *After Babel: Aspects of Language and Translation*. Oxford: Oxford University, 1975.

Steinhauser, Kenneth B. "Basil the Great on Education". *Living Light*, vol. 30, no. 4 (1994): 41–48.

Sterk, Andrea. "On Basil, Moses, and the Model Bishop: The Cappadocian Legacy of Leadership". *Church History*, vol. 67, no. 2 (1988): 227–253.

———. *Renouncing the World Yet Leading the Church: The Monk-Bishop in Late Antiquity*. Cambridge: Harvard University, 2004.

Stevenson, James and William H.C. Frend (eds.) *Creeds, Councils, and Controversies: Documents Illustrative of the History of the Church to A.D. 337*. Grand Rapids: Baker Academic, 2012.

Stewart, Alistair C. *The Original Bishops: Office and Order in the First Christian Communities*. Grand Rapids: Baker Academic, 2014.

Stramara, Daniel F. "Double Monasticism in the Greek East, Fourth through Eighth Centuries". *Journal of Early Christian Studies*, vol. 6, no. 2 (1998): 269–312.

Sullivan, Francis. *From Apostles to Bishops: The Development of the Episcopacy in the Early Church*. New York: The Newman, 2001.

Swain, Simon and Mark J. Edwards (eds.) *Approaching Late Antiquity: The Transformation from Early to Late Empire*. Oxford: Oxford University, 2004.

Taylor, Justin. "St. Basil the Great and Pope St. Damasus I". *Downside Review*, vol. 91, no. 304 (1973): 186–203, 262–274.

Tibbs, Clint. "The Spirit (World) and the (Holy) Spirits among the Earliest Christians: 1 Corinthians 12 and 14 as a Test Case". *Catholic Biblical Quarterly*, vol. 70, no. 2 (2008): 313–330.

Torrance, Thomas F. (ed.) *Theological Dialogue Between Orthodox and Reformed Churches*, Volume Two. Edinburgh: Scottish Academy, 1993.

Trombley, Frank. *Hellenic Religion and Christianization c. 370–529*. Leiden: E.J. Brill, 1994.

Turcescu, Lucian. "Prosopon and Hypostasis in Basil of Caesarea's Against Eunomius and the Epistles". *Vigiliae Christianae*, vol. 51, no. 4 (1997): 374–395.

Vaggione, Richard P. *Eunomius of Cyzicus and the Nicene Revolution*. Oxford: Oxford University, 2000.

Van Dam, Raymond. *Becoming a Christian: The Conversion of Roman Cappadocia*. Philadelphia: The University of Pennsylvania, 2003.

———. "Bishops and Society". In *The Cambridge History of Christianity*. Eds. Augustine Casiday and Frederick W. Norris (Cambridge: Cambridge University, 2008): 2:343–366.

———. "Emperor, Bishops, and Friends in Late Antique Cappadocia". *Journal of Theological Studies*. ns, vol. 37, pt. 1 (1986): 53–76.

———. *Families and Friends in Late Roman Cappadocia*. Philadelphia: University of Pennsylvania, 2003.

———. *Kingdom of Snow: Roman Rule and Greek Culture in Cappadocia*. Philadelphia: University of Pennsylvania, 2003.

Ware, Kallistos. "Patterns of Episcopacy in the Early Church and Today: An Orthodox View". In *Bishops, But What Kind? Reflections on Episcopacy*. Ed. Peter Moore (London: SPCK, 1982): 1–24.
_____. *The Orthodox Way*. New York: St. Vladimir's Seminary, 1995.
Webb, Joseph M. and Robert Kysar. *Greek for Preachers*. Missouri: Chalice, 2002.
Whittaker, John. "Christianity and Morality in the Roman Empire". *Vigiliae Christianae*, vol. 33, no. 3 (1979): 209–225.
Whittow, Mark. "Ruling the Late Roman and Early Byzantine City: A Continuous History". *Past and Present*, vol. 129, no. 1 (1990): 3–29.
Wilken, Robert L. "The Spirit of Holiness: Basil of Caesarea and Early Christian Spirituality". *Worship*, vol. 42, no. 2 (1968): 77–87.
Williams, Rowan. *Arius: History and Tradition*. Grand Rapids: William B. Eerdmans Publishing Company, 2002.
_____. (ed.) *The Making of Orthodoxy: Essays in honour of Henry Chadwick*. Cambridge: Cambridge University, 1989.
Yamamura, Kei. "The Development of the Doctrine of the Holy Spirit in Patristic Philosophy: St. Basil and St. Gregory of Nyssa". *St. Vladimir's Theological Quarterly*, vol. 18, no. 1 (1974): 3–21.
Young, Frances M. *From Nicaea to Chalcedon: A Guide to the Literature and Its Background*. Second Edition. Grand Rapids: Baker Academic, 2010.
Young, Frances M, Lewis Ayres and Andrew Louth (eds.) *The Cambridge History of Early Christian Literature*. Cambridge: Cambridge University, 2007.
Zizioulas, John D. *Being as Communion: Studies in Personhood and the Church*. New York: St. Vladimir's Seminary, 1985.
_____. *Communion and Otherness: Further Studies in Personhood and the Church*. New York: T&T Clark, 2006.
_____. *Eucharist, Bishop, Church: The Unity of the Church in the Divine Eucharist and the Bishop During the First Three Centuries*. Brookline: Translated by Elizabeth Theokritoff. Holy Cross Orthodox Press, 2001.
_____. *Lectures in Christian Dogmatics*. London: T&T Clark, 2008.
_____. "The Doctrine of the Holy Trinity: The Significance of the Cappadocian Contribution". In *Trinitarian Theology Today: Essays on Divine Being and Act*. Ed. Christoph Schwoebel (Edinburgh: T&T Clark, 1995): 44–60.
_____. "The Early Christian Community". In *Christian Spirituality: Origins to the Twelfth Century*. Eds. Bernard McGinn, John Meyendorff and Jean Leclerq (London: Routledge and Kegan Paul, 1986): 23–43.
_____. "The Eucharistic Community and the Catholicity of the Church". *One in Christ*, vol. 6, no. 3 (1976): 314–337.

Glossary of Terms

Anomeans A theological position held by Eunomius and his followers characterised by taking on an extreme form of Arianism that denied the divinity of the Son. *See Arius, Eunomius.*

Arius A priest of the Alexandrian church (c. 250–336) who taught that the divine Logos (the Word), was subordinate to God the Father. Arius claimed that the Son had a beginning and was neither eternal nor part of the essence of God. The thrust of Arius' argument lay in establishing the primacy and therefore superiority of the Father to the Son, with the created Son being the product of the will of the creator Father. At c. 318 Bishop Alexander of Alexandria deposed Arius accusing him of heresy. Arius' teachings were formally rejected at the Council of Nicaea in 325.

Asceticism The enduring attitude towards spiritual life invoked from God's love, where self-discipline, sobriety and moral uprightness, become a genuine expression of a person's desire to love God. Through asceticism, consisting of a life of prayer, fasting and self-denial, the believer fights temptation to sin and thereby grows in spiritual strength.

Baptism The sacramental rite involving a triple immersion (βαπτίζω – to be immersed) conducted in the name of the Father, the Son, and the Holy Spirit, where a person becomes a Christian and is joined to the communion of the church.

Bishop A spiritual leader (ἐπίσκοπος, overseer) of a local community of Christians. The size of the local community can range from an individual congregation to a group of congregations within a geographical area that consists of assistant bishops and priests. A bishop is the third and highest rank of the three orders of the ordained ministry in the church: bishop, priest and deacon. A priest, occupying the second degree of ordination, serves in the name of a bishop but cannot conduct ordinations. A deacon, occupying the first degree of ordination, assists the bishop and priest, but cannot preside over the Eucharist or participate in any other liturgical service without the presence of a bishop or priest.

Canon A Greek work for "rule", "standard", or "measure". The term was first used to signify the canon of Scripture, that is, the list of books making up the Old and New Testaments that were regarded as inspired. From the fourth century "canon" also referred to the rules and decrees of church law that were either issued or subsequently ratified by early church councils. "Canonical" implies corresponding to the ecclesiastical laws of the Nicene communion of churches. In a pastoral setting "canons" refer to the implementation of penances for disciplinary matters with the intention of reforming the penitent.

Catechumen A candidate to baptism who undertakes instruction (κατήχησις – catechesis).

Church The assembly of the faithful united to Christ and to each other, who profess Nicene statements of faith. In Greek ἐκκλησία has a root meaning which implies "to be call out", which was the rendering of the Hebrew *kahal*. The church is thus the in-gathering of God's elect people.

Communion The highest form of union in the church between Christians and God that is especially realised in the Eucharist.

Council *See Synod*

Count (Latin *comes*) Literally "companion", implying the companion of the emperor or the delegate of the emperor. In the Eastern empire, Count denoted the high rank of a provincial official, either military or administrative. In the Western empire, Count was a generic term indicating a military commander but had no reference to specific rank. The "Count of the East" (*comes Orientis*) was the title of the emperor's representative and came to designate one of the highest government officials in the Eastern empire.

Doxology The act of giving glory (δόξα) to God especially in worship. Doxology is viewed as the most accurate form of expressing theological truth, especially when confronted with the transcendence of God.

Deacon *See Bishop*

Diocese The administrative jurisdiction of a local church that was defined by reference to its bishop. Ecclesiastical dioceses corresponded to the civil provinces and sub-provinces with the bishop of the capital city of each province becoming the metropolitan bishop, his civil counterpart being the prefect/governor.

Economia Literally meaning "law of the house", referred to a way in which canons (rules) were applied by bishops in the pastoral ministry of the church, generally in a more lenient and flexible way so as to be more conducive to a penitent's correction and growth. Its opposite was ἀκρίβεια (precision, exactness), which was considered to be a rigid and strict application of a canon. *Economia* allowed for a flexibility or dispensation of the canon in question in response to human weakness and had as its primary purpose the facilitating of God's plan (*economia*) for a person's salvation.

Essence The nature of God. "Essence" (οὐσία) designates what is common in God. God the Father, the Son, and the Holy Spirit are "of one essence". The "essence" is never alone in the sense of being without a *hypostasis* or being without a mode of existence (τρόπος ὑπάρξεως). Thus the Father is the divine "essence" plus unbegotteness, the Son is divine "essence" plus begotteness, and the Holy Spirit is divine "essence" plus procession. God's essence will always transcend humanity's understanding; a person will never be able to know exactly and definitely what or who God is. To know God in his essence would be equivalent to becoming God by nature. God is known by his activities (ἐνεργειῶν), by means of one reflecting (κατ' ἐπίνοια) on his presence in the world.

Eucharist Taken from the Greek word meaning "thanksgiving". The Eucharist designates the central sacramental act of Christian worship, Holy Communion, whereby through the elements of bread and wine the faithful partake of the body and blood of Jesus Christ. Participation in the Eucharist is exclusively only for baptised members of the church.

Eunomius The disciple of the non-Nicene Aetius, who held the position that the Son was essentially "unlike" (ἀνόμοιος) the Father. Eunomius claimed that the essence of the Father was "unbegotten" and therefore ontologically superior to the "begotten" essence of the Son. He died c. 393.

Excommunication The self-willed exclusion from the Nicene communion of churches. It excludes a person form the sacramental life of the church. An excommunication is administered for the salvation of the person being cut off from communion, with the view that the excommunication will ultimately facilitate the lapsed Christian to repentance and therefore lead him or her back into the communion of the church.

Heresy A particular teaching or theory that is strongly at variance with the accepted beliefs and established doctrines of the church. Heresy was seen as a discrepancy on vital issues of faith and therefore brought about the negation of the unity of the church. Heresiarch is the title given to the founder or leader of a heretical movement, while individuals who espouse heresy or commit heresy are known as heretics.

Homoiousios The theological teaching advocating that the Son is of like/similar essence to the Father as opposed to being of the same essence with the Father. *See Homoousios.*

Homoousios (Latin: *consubstantialis* – consubstantial) The theological term affirming the divinity of the Son and the Holy Spirit. *Homoousios* (of one essence/of the same essence) establishes that "being" is the same in the Father as it is in the Son and in the Holy Spirit.

Hypostasis A technical theological term for "person" that is used to describe the three persons of the Holy Trinity: God the Father, Son and Holy Spirit. *Hypostasis* is used to describe what is three in God. The existence of God manifests itself as an event of inseparable communion where the "one" *hypostasis* of the Father eternally requires "the other two" in order to exist. God is one and three simultaneously as opposed to being first one and then three. The *hypostasis* of the Father, Son and Holy Spirit is both particular and relational. Father, Son and Holy Spirit are all names indicating relationship. No divine person can be different unless the divine person is related.

Julian Emperor in the East from 361–363 committed to bringing about a revival of paganism. Under Julian, Christian clergy no longer had tax exemptions or were the beneficiaries of land holdings and grain distributions, but rather were required to fulfil their fiscal and civil obligations to their cities. One of Julian's most publicised measures saw him forbid Christians from serving as rhetoricians and teachers within the cities of the empire. The attempt to replace the Christianity that began with the imperial mission of Constantine with the old divine order was also strategic to Julian's military advances and successes into the territories of the Persian Empire. Julian's untimely death at thirty two years of age in 363 saw him replaced by the pro-Christian Jovian.

Jurisdiction The sole responsibility of a bishop within the canonical territorial boundaries of his diocese. No other bishop could interfere, whether pastorally or administratively, with the episcopal ministry of a bishop who is acting within the ecclesiastical boundaries of his diocese.

Ordination The sacramental act administered by the laying on of hands of a bishop which appoints a man for the ministry of the church.

Parasynagogue A para-ecclesial group (παρασυναγωγή, parasynagogue) or rival congregation set up by those in schism. This led to a breach of ecclesiastical unity and therefore resulted in an exclusion from eucharistic communion. *See Schism*

Perichoresis A term first appearing in the writings of St Maximus the Confessor that refers to the interpenetrating communion of love existing amongst the three persons of the Holy Trinity. Father, Son and Holy Spirit, with their distinct personal attributes, exist in unceasing interpersonal communion through reciprocating a movement of love. Perichoretic love, as lived out in communion, is central to the very being of God.

Pneumatomachians The Pneumatomachians (Spirit-fighters) first emerged in the 360s in Constantinople, and were commonly referred to as "Macedonians" after their founder Macedonius (d. 360s), a semi-Arian bishop. The Pneumatomachians were united in their denial of the divinity of the Holy Spirit and its consubstantiality with the Father and the Son. They claimed that the Spirit of God was simply another creature, similar to an angel, that was created to serve God. It was from the use of prepositions that Pneumatomachians were accustomed to argue against the divinity of the Holy Spirit. They appealed to ancient philosophy, most notably Aristotelian, for an understanding of prepositions and relationships. In their doxological glorification of the Holy Trinity, the Pneumatomachians preferred to use "in" the Spirit, because to them "in" implied space and therefore justified their reasoning that since the Holy Spirit is contained in space, it must be a creature.

Prefect   The appointed leader of an imperial administrative area who is also called a governor. Along with ensuring that a city met its tax obligation to the empire, prefects held executive powers over public buildings and services, and administered proceedings for local courts of justice. Praetorian prefects, the highest administrative officials, presided over each of the four general prefectures of the empire, these being the East, Illyricum, Italy and Gaul.

Province   An administrative area of control within the Roman Empire, also called a prefecture. By the early fourth century, the empire had over one hundred provinces that were each administered by a provincial governor (prefect) who in turn was supported by a substantial staff of lawyers and other advisors.

Priest   *See Bishop*

Sabellius   Sabellius, who flourished in c. 215, refused to accept in the Trinitarian God three distinct persons. Instead he maintained that God was essentially an impersonal monad who at any given time took on one of three appearances: that of the Father, or the Son, or the Holy Spirit. Sabellius was excommunicated by Pope Callistus in 220. In the Sabellian view, Father, Son and Holy Spirit are three ways or modes in which humanity perceives God. Sabellianism denied the eternal distinction among the three persons of the Holy Trinity in order to avoid any perceived identification with pagan polytheism. As such, its proponents claimed that Father, Son and Holy Spirit were not full persons in an ontological sense but "roles" assumed by the one God.

Schism   Bishops of the fourth century tended to view schism (σχίσμα) as a disagreement (διαφορά) between church members concerning ecclesiastical questions capable of mutual solution. Often these disagreements were not of such a serious nature so as to warrant a lasting division among members of church communities. Consequently, unlike the heretics who in some circumstances needed both repentance and baptism to be brought into the communion of the church, those from schismatic (σχίσματα) or para-ecclesial groups (παρασυναγωγάς, parasynagogues) only needed to repent so as to be restored into the communion of the church. The ordained orders of those coming over from schisms and parasynagogues, however, if they were to be accepted, needed to have been originally bestowed by a church in communion with Nicaea. *See Parasynagogue*

Synaxis   From the Greek word "assembly". "Synaxis" is the word used for the ancient Greek Senate. From the fourth century it referred to a gathering of bishops and other clergy for fellowship, the discussion of pastoral concerns and administrative issues, and culminated in the celebration of the Eucharist.

Synod A council of the church, whether local or general, attended by clergy and convened to decide doctrinal, pastoral, moral, liturgical and administrative issues. The word "synod" comes from the Greek σύνοδος meaning "assembly" or "meeting". In Latin the word for synod is *concilium* from which we get "council". The decisions decided at general synods become part of church life when they are received by the entire church.

Tradition Literally that which is handed down, passed on. Tradition is the life of the church in the Holy Spirit. The Scriptures are central to tradition but not exhaustive of it. Tradition manifests the existence of the church under the inspiration of the Holy Spirit.

Trinity A reference to God the Father, God the Son, and God the Holy Spirit: one God, three persons; one in essence and inseparable.

Word of God (Λόγος) The second person of the Trinity, the Son of God, who from the mystery of his eternal birth is called the Word of the Father.

Index

References to Basil occur in every page of this book and therefore are not included in this list.

A
Aetius, 83, 302, 373
Alexandria 23, 25, 28, 40, 41, 51, 55, 100, 127, 128, 132, 160, 183, 189, 200, 201, 274, 303, 310, 319
Almsgiving, 24, 135, 136, 138, 157, 159, 163, 167, 173
Ambrose, bishop of Milan, 25, 47, 184, 232, 272
Amphilochius, bishop of Iconium, 16, 25, 64, 92, 93, 185, 213, 228, 232, 245, 248, 249, 250, 251, 253, 255, 260, 261, 271, 295, 308
Annisa, 24, 55, 56, 57, 58, 68, 69, 74, 82
Anomeans, 95, 211, 371
Anthimus, bishop of Tyana, 150, 206
Antioch, 23, 26, 28, 42, 45, 118, 127, 128, 132, 191, 192, 193, 194, 195, 196, 197, 199, 200, 206, 267, 275, 285, 302
Apollinarius, 63, 98, 203, 204, 205, 211, 265, 302, 307
Apostasy, 188, 253, 255
Apostolic succession, 309
Arianism, 6, 39, 40, 42, 95, 199, 371
Aristotle, 50, 79, 173
Arius, 6, 40, 41, 42, 83, 84, 86, 98, 105, 118, 125, 131, 132, 199, 200, 211, 265, 266, 302, 310, 371
Armenia, 147, 148, 155, 156, 190, 193, 206, 234, 274, 276, 280, 298, 299, 323
Asceticism, 54, 55, 62, 68, 74, 91, 168, 172, 227, 228, 337, 338, 371
Assembly, 58, 203, 265, 297, 299, 300
Assistant bishop, 33, 137, 141, 146, 247, 283, 284, 285, 287, 288, 289, 291, 371
Athanasius, 16, 25, 42, 47, 98, 99, 100, 107, 160, 183, 189, 190, 191, 192, 193, 194, 195, 196, 198, 199, 200, 201, 207, 240, 245, 274, 277, 303, 310, 319
Athens, 49, 50, 51, 53, 55, 142
Augustine, bishop of Hippo, 23, 33, 47, 114

B
Baptism, 11, 57, 62, 67, 90, 94, 110, 111, 113, 117, 219, 223, 242, 243, 247, 248, 249, 250, 251, 252, 253, 262, 263, 276, 290, 321, 371
Basiliad, 11, 165, 166, 167, 168, 169, 170, 171, 172, 178, 341

C

Caesarea, 5, 6, 8, 11, 18, 20, 21, 22, 23, 25, 34, 45, 46, 49, 50, 52, 54, 56, 63, 67, 68, 69, 70, 71, 72, 73, 84, 93, 94, 98, 107, 108, 122, 124, 126, 146, 147, 150, 151, 152, 153, 154, 162, 163, 166, 167, 168, 179, 185, 205, 220, 224, 232, 279, 280, 287, 294, 323, 347

Cappadocia, 9, 46, 57, 68, 69, 72, 73, 107, 108, 109, 114, 138, 146, 147, 150, 151, 152, 163, 165, 190, 240, 274, 275, 279, 281, 323

Christianity, 11, 17, 43, 45, 62, 69, 70, 77, 79, 108, 124, 125, 126, 127, 129, 130, 139, 140, 143, 159, 171, 183, 188, 192, 197, 203, 224, 225, 226, 231, 232, 262, 265, 275, 283, 309, 310, 318, 319, 321, 334, 344

Church, 5, 6, 7, 8, 9, 10, 11, 12, 16, 17, 18, 25, 26, 27, 35, 39, 40, 41, 42, 43, 44, 47, 52, 54, 56, 57, 58, 59, 61, 63, 64, 66, 67, 68, 69, 70, 71, 72, 74, 76, 77, 78, 81, 82, 83, 84, 91, 93, 94, 109, 118, 119, 121, 124, 125, 126, 127, 128, 129, 130, 131, 132, 133, 134, 135, 137, 139, 140, 142, 144, 145, 146, 147, 154, 155, 156, 158, 165, 166, 167, 169, 171, 172, 174, 178, 183, 188, 189, 190, 192, 193, 194, 195, 196, 197, 198, 200, 201, 202, 203, 204, 205, 206, 207, 208, 209, 210, 211, 212, 213, 214, 215, 216, 217, 218, 219, 220, 221, 222, 223, 224, 225, 226, 227, 228, 229, 230, 231, 233, 234, 235, 236, 238, 240, 241, 244, 245, 246, 247, 248, 249, 250, 251, 252, 253, 254, 256, 258, 259, 260, 261, 262, 263, 264, 265, 266, 267, 268, 269, 270, 271, 272, 273, 275, 276, 277, 278, 279, 280, 281, 282, 283, 284, 286, 287, 288, 289, 290, 291, 292, 293, 294, 296, 297, 298, 299, 300, 301, 302, 303, 304, 305, 306, 307, 308, 309, 310, 311, 312, 313, 314, 315, 316, 317, 318, 319, 320, 321, 322, 323, 324, 325, 326, 327, 328, 329, 330, 331, 332, 333, 334, 335, 336, 337, 338, 339, 340, 341, 342, 343, 344, 345, 346, 347, 348, 349

Cicero, 13

Communion, 5, 6, 7, 8, 9, 10, 11, 12, 35, 39, 40, 47, 60, 70, 72, 74, 75, 76, 82, 85, 88, 92, 94, 98, 110, 111, 114, 120, 121, 123, 124, 125, 130, 133, 142, 149, 170, 173, 174, 177, 178, 183, 184, 187, 190, 191, 195, 196, 197, 200, 201, 202, 203, 204, 205, 206, 207, 208, 209, 210, 211, 212, 213, 214, 215, 216, 217, 218, 219, 220, 223, 225, 230, 231, 232, 233, 234, 235, 236, 237, 238, 239, 240, 243, 244, 245, 246, 247, 249, 250, 251, 252, 253, 255, 257, 258, 259, 260, 261, 262, 263, 264, 265, 266, 267, 269, 270, 272, 278, 279, 280, 281, 282, 283, 284, 289, 290, 291, 292, 293, 294, 295, 297, 298, 299, 300, 301, 302, 303, 304, 305, 306, 307, 308, 309, 310, 311, 312, 313, 314, 315, 316, 317, 318, 319, 320, 321, 322, 323, 324, 325, 326, 327, 328, 329, 330, 331, 332, 333, 334, 335, 336, 337, 338, 339, 340, 341, 342, 343, 344, 345, 346, 347, 348, 349

Constantine, 6, 41, 42, 69, 70, 125, 126, 127, 128, 130, 132, 135, 136, 140, 143, 144.

Constantinople, 40, 44, 47, 49, 71, 83, 105, 122, 128, 146, 152, 154

Constantius, 69, 129, 130, 131, 143, 199

Consubstantial. See Homoousios.

Council, 6, 41, 42, 47, 71, 83, 115, 119, 122, 128, 129, 131, 132, 136, 137, 147, 149, 154, 166, 249, 250, 251, 255, 263, 265, 285, 296, 297, 334

Cyprian, bishop of Carthage, 267

D

Damasus, bishop of Rome, 47, 193, 275, 310, 312, 314
Dianius, bishop of Caesarea, 67, 83, 84, 164
Doctrine, 6, 8, 17, 40, 46, 47, 48, 59, 61, 78, 86, 90, 97, 104, 107, 109, 113, 115, 118, 119, 120, 137, 187, 205, 212, 220, 223, 227, 234, 235, 251, 252, 274, 275, 295, 296, 302, 313, 315, 323, 326, 345

E

Ecclesiology, 7, 11, 12, 93, 183, 244, 269, 318, 329, 330, 347
Economia, 254, 372
Education, Basil's, 11, 35, 39, 48, 49, 54, 68, 74, 189
Episcopacy, Basil's, 20, 26, 27, 68, 70, 72, 73, 75, 91, 124, 148, 150, 220, 285, 286
Essence, 22, 31, 40, 44, 48, 76, 81, 83, 85, 86, 87, 88, 89, 94, 96, 97, 98, 102, 105, 107, 108, 109, 112, 113, 114, 116, 123, 175, 176, 199, 239, 240, 330, 340
Eucharist, 8, 12, 133, 145, 219, 235, 236, 245, 247, 254, 255, 256, 257, 258, 259, 261, 265, 266, 267, 269, 270, 283, 284, 290, 293, 294, 297, 299, 300, 307, 308, 316, 320, 321, 322, 325, 326, 327, 328, 335, 336, 348
Eunomianism, 95, 96
Eunomius, 11, 70, 81, 82, 83, 84, 85, 86, 87, 92, 95, 96, 97, 102, 105, 106, 109, 114, 115, 123, 165, 211, 238, 239, 240, 302
Eupsychius, martyr in Caesarea, 63, 294, 295, 325
Eusebius, bishop of Caesarea, 68, 69, 71, 98, 107, 126
Eusebius, bishop of Samosata, 23, 26, 41, 45, 163, 166, 177, 186, 206, 275, 278, 295
Eustathius, bishop of Sebasteia, 25, 51, 52, 55, 74, 82, 98, 157, 192, 203, 207, 210, 211, 212, 227, 262

F

Famine, 163, 165, 166, 171, 175, 176, 177, 179
Fasting, 64, 141, 162, 163
Fedwick, Paul, 8, 18, 22, 23, 26, 27, 29, 30, 45, 58, 60, 62, 69, 77, 82, 89, 127, 150, 155, 171,173, 174, 197, 204, 228, 229, 241, 271, 294, 296

G

Gain, Benoit, 8, 23, 25, 26, 33, 148, 150, 151, 159, 160, 186, 188, 225, 255, 275, 277, 296
Grace, 29, 32, 43, 49, 89, 93, 176, 177, 186, 198, 213, 236, 244, 263, 266, 271, 272, 273, 276, 282, 288, 290, 293, 300, 321, 327, 335, 346, 347
Gregory of Nazianzus, 13, 16, 17, 18, 27, 47, 49, 50, 51, 52, 55, 61, 62, 68, 70, 73, 74, 93, 114, 122, 140, 159, 160, 161, 163, 164, 166, 169, 172, 188, 193, 234, 278, 281
Gregory of Nyssa, 22, 23, 24, 34, 46, 47, 53, 54, 57, 82, 96, 165, 167, 170, 193, 281, 288

H

Heresy, 7, 79, 84, 118, 189, 190, 191, 196, 197, 199, 203, 207, 211, 215, 217, 218, 220, 227, 230, 233, 250, 261, 287, 292, 296, 301, 302, 303, 304, 306, 307, 310, 311, 312, 313, 314, 315, 316, 317, 322, 323, 324, 337, 343, 349

Heretics, 7, 131, 192, 198, 223, 231, 261, 262, 263, 297, 301, 324

Holy Spirit, 6, 11, 46, 47, 49, 61, 71, 74, 76, 80, 82, 84, 85, 88, 89, 90, 91, 92, 93, 94, 95, 97, 98, 99, 100, 101, 102, 103, 104, 105, 106, 110, 111, 112, 113, 114, 115, 116, 117, 118, 119, 120, 121, 122, 123, 124, 174, 176, 177, 183, 186, 189, 201, 206, 211, 226, 232, 237, 238, 239, 240, 241, 242, 243, 244, 245, 249, 263, 269, 271, 273, 276, 283, 299, 300, 309, 319, 320, 321, 328, 329, 330, 331, 334, 337, 340

Homoiousios, 109

Homoousios, 103, 109, 276

Homotomia, 123

Hypostasis, 22, 48, 88, 98, 99, 101, 103, 108, 109, 110, 112, 123, 238, 240

J

Jerome, 84, 132

Jovian, 70, 144

Julian, 63, 69, 70, 136, 144, 159

L

Late antiquity, 9, 11, 13, 14, 16, 20, 23, 24, 34, 50, 124, 125, 126, 127, 128, 132, 134, 135, 137, 138, 139, 140, 142, 148, 150, 158, 163, 166, 172, 178, 183, 228, 229

Letter collections, 9, 14, 20, 21, 23, 26, 34

Letter-carrier, 10, 28, 30, 31, 32, 33, 34, 35

Letter-writing, 8, 10, 13, 14, 18, 28, 34, 39, 100, 183, 184

Libanius, 13, 14, 15, 33, 49

M

Macedonians, 92, 105, 115, 302

Macedonius, 105

Macrina, 24, 48, 53, 54, 56, 57, 58

Marcellus, bishop of Ancyra, 100, 193, 199, 200, 211, 302, 303

Meletius, bishop of Antioch, 45, 192, 193, 194, 195, 196, 198, 199, 206, 275

Modestos, 145, 148

Monarchia, 110, 114, 115, 123, 330

Monasticism, 8, 35, 39, 52, 53, 54, 55, 56, 58, 59, 61, 62, 74, 75, 173, 178, 227

N

Neocaesarea, 18, 49, 55, 94, 155, 205, 209, 232, 282, 285, 313, 315

New Testament, 46, 49, 65, 100, 128, 191, 201, 203, 331, 332

Nicaea, 6, 41, 42, 44, 47, 70, 71, 83, 96, 98, 99, 102, 107, 108, 109, 115, 116, 117,

118, 119, 128, 131, 132, 133, 148, 166, 193, 199, 200, 206, 207, 208, 212, 227, 239, 250, 251, 255, 262, 265, 274, 275, 280, 297, 309, 333, 334, 345
Nicene Creed, 42, 116, 117, 122

O

Ousia, 97, 99, 101, 102, 108, 208, 322

P

Pagan, 49, 52, 53, 54, 63, 69, 70, 78, 79, 100, 125, 129, 131, 132, 139, 143, 144, 159, 166, 187
Parasynagogue, 260, 261, 262, 264
Pastoral care, 10, 138, 164, 173, 253, 263, 273, 338
Paulinus, bishop of Antioch, 191, 192, 193, 194, 196, 199, 275
Perichoresis, 235, 237
Philanthropy, 64, 144, 145, 160, 161, 166
Philosophy, 49, 50, 53, 77, 78, 88
Pneumatomachianism, 95, 104, 120
Pneumatomachians, 88, 89, 95, 104, 105, 119, 211, 302
Poverty, 61, 158, 160, 161, 168, 172, 174, 177
Prayer, 7, 28, 44, 51, 56, 57, 58, 59, 62, 64, 66, 91, 138, 141, 145, 154, 169, 170, 217, 222, 223, 238, 257, 265, 266, 269, 271, 281, 289, 294, 332, 339, 342, 346, 347
Primacy, 41, 112, 132, 313

R

Repentance, 59, 62, 207, 219, 247, 252, 253, 254, 255, 257, 262, 263, 290, 321, 349
Rhetoric, 49, 50, 52, 69, 74, 77, 79, 80, 104, 138, 177, 184, 198, 313
Rome, 43, 47, 127, 128, 132, 135, 153, 199, 275, 296, 312, 313, 316, 324
Rousseau, Philip, 6, 8, 21, 24, 27, 31, 44, 45, 46, 52, 55, 58, 59, 63, 64, 67, 68, 71, 74, 77, 78, 80, 81, 82, 86, 91, 92, 93, 138, 146, 147, 148, 155, 162, 163, 166, 168, 172, 188, 197, 203, 227, 230, 249, 254
Rufinus, 44, 129, 130

S

Sabellianism, 95, 98, 99, 100, 199, 211, 315
Sabellius, 95, 99, 100, 103, 302
Salvation, 17, 39, 44, 75, 76, 111, 116, 160, 165, 217, 234, 254, 269, 274, 276, 301, 318, 328, 334, 349
Sasima, 281
Schism, 6, 71, 130, 131, 155, 190, 191, 192, 194, 195, 200, 215, 216, 226, 250, 251, 260, 261, 262, 263, 275, 298, 300, 301, 307, 308, 345

Scripture, 11, 30, 39, 48, 56, 57, 62, 63, 64, 65, 75, 76, 77, 78, 80, 81, 82, 88, 89, 100, 104, 122, 165, 176, 189, 203, 253, 256, 290, 332, 337
Severus, bishop of Antioch, 23, 26
Social justice, 11, 24, 124, 157, 160, 161, 162, 164, 166, 171, 175, 177, 179, 331, 339
Socrates, church historian, 40, 44, 129
Sozomen, church historian, 44, 63, 69, 159
Synaxis, 269, 295, 316
Synesius, 15
Synod, 63, 84, 99, 129, 136, 137, 199, 204, 212, 251, 252, 280, 285, 292, 295, 296, 297, 312, 313, 333, 336

T
Theodoret, bishop of Cyrrhus, 26, 30, 44
Theodosius, 24, 46, 155
Theodotus, bishop of Nicopolis, 18, 155, 156, 227, 280
Tradition, 11, 14, 22, 42, 49, 57, 74, 75, 76, 77, 78, 79, 107, 118, 121, 203, 220, 224, 249, 250, 251, 263, 273, 276, 289, 306, 332, 333
Trinity, 5, 6, 46, 47, 76, 81, 88, 89, 90, 94, 95, 97, 98, 99, 100, 101, 104, 106, 107, 108, 109, 110, 111, 112, 113, 114, 115, 116, 119, 121, 123, 183, 199, 208, 235, 236, 237, 238, 239, 240, 244, 320, 322, 329, 330, 331, 334
Tyana, 150, 151, 152, 206, 279

V
Valens, 45, 71, 73, 124, 130, 131, 147, 148, 150, 151, 152, 154, 155, 169, 194, 221, 265, 318
Valentinian, 197, 302

W
Word [of God], 40, 93, 100, 146, 199, 200, 256
Worship, 56, 57, 58, 59, 66, 76, 77, 88, 89, 90, 91, 106, 113, 122, 123, 125, 126, 129, 170, 241, 242, 255, 256, 257, 265, 293, 320, 321, 326, 327, 330, 332

www.ingramcontent.com/pod-product-compliance
Lightning Source LLC
Chambersburg PA
CBHW071329080526
44587CB00017B/2781